ENTRADA

ENTRADA

THE LEGACY OF SPAIN AND MEXICO IN THE UNITED STATES

Bernard L. Fontana

Southwest Parks and Monuments Association
Tucson
The University of New Mexico Press
Albuquerque

Library of Congress Number 92-0621235
Paperbound edition: Southwest Parks and Monuments Association, Tucson, Arizona. ISBN 1-877856-24-X

Clothbound edition: The University of New Mexico Press, Albuquerque, New Mexico. ISBN 0-8263-1544-5

SPMA Production Management: T.J. Priehs
Edited by Ronald J. Foreman
Editorial Assistance by Gregory McNamee
Maps by Donald Bufkin
Designed by Kimura/Bingham Design, Tucson, Arizona
Printed in the United States of America by BookCrafters, Inc.

This book is printed on acid-free paper, with a minimum fifty percent recycled fiber including ten percent post-consumer fiber.

Cover, counterclockwise from top left: "Portrait of a Man Called Christopher Columbus" by Sebastiano de Piombo (courtesy The Metropolitan Museum of Art, New York, gift of J. Pierpont Morgan, 1900); Detail of map published by Abraham Ortelius in *Theatrum Orbis Terrarum*, 1582 (courtesy University of Arizona Library Special Collections, Tucson); seventeenth-century Spanish cavalryman (courtesy Archivo de Indias, Seville, Spain); 1805 Narbona expedition pictograph, Canyon de Chelly National Monument, Arizona (George H. H. Huey); bell tower at Mission San Juan Capistrano, San Antonio Missions National Historical Park, San Antonio, Texas (George H. H. Huey).

For J.P.S.,
for whose friendship I am everlastingly grateful

and for L.C.P.,
whose voyage through life has been one of never-ending discovery
and a steady source of inspiration

Contents

ILLUSTRATIONS

page

This book was commissioned by Southwest Parks and Monuments Association executive director T. J. Priehs. Inspired by the quincentennial year of the arrival of Christopher Columbus in the Western Hemisphere, he and the association wanted a book that would help remind American citizens and other visitors to units of our National Park system of the ever-present but largely overlooked imprint left on the United States by Spain and, after 1821, by Mexico.

Not surprisingly, United States history has traditionally been taught from the point of view of its creators and their descendants. These have been for the most part Anglo Americans or, at least, teachers whose forebears arrived in America from the British Isles, whether English, Irish, Scots, Cornish, or Welsh. Ultimately they were the victors over Native Americans and over other European contenders for the land. And it was principally they who fashioned a Declaration of Independence and the Constitution of the United States. So has it been their Captain John Smith and the 1607 Jamestown colonists, rather than the Spanish Captain General Pedro Menéndez de Avilés and the 1565 settlers of San Augustín, Florida, who have become imprinted on the minds of generations of students. The *Mayflower* and the Pilgrims are part of our national lore. But what of Menéndez's flagship *San Pelayo* and the six hundred men and women who laid the foundations for what was to become the first permanent European settlement in today's continental United States? Other than a handful of scholars and students of the history of Florida and the Southeast, who has ever heard of them?

History, whether spoken or written, needs to be distinguished from the past itself. What we call "history" is a recitation of events selected from the past, which in its most literal sense is all that has preceded the present: a rock that fell, a dog that barked, an infant who cried, a woman who coughed, a prince who was enthroned king. All historians—and on occasion each of us is a historian—select from this infinity of events those we deem worth telling. The basis of that selection provides the built-in bias of history. History, more than being a debate about the past, is an argument about the present and future. It often tells us less about what was and more about who we are. It is a tool used by all of us either to justify or to condemn the status quo. It is a statement of the world either as we now perceive it to be or as we think it ought to be. The past is immutable, but history, a battleground for the public mind, is ever changing.

This book is written with the conscious realization that in today's United States calls grow louder for recognition and acceptance of cultural diversity. Since the early sixteenth century our country has known the continuing presence of persons of Iberian background, including Castilians, Catalans, and Basques. Thanks in part to our proximity to Mexico, to Spanish-speaking countries of the Caribbean, and to Spanish-speaking Central America, there has been continued immigration and growth in the population of this segment of our society. Persons of Latino or Hispanic heritage, like members of other minority groups in the United States, are beginning to assert their own histories and thereby to make their own arguments about their present and future roles in American society.

This book is limited in its scope in two important ways. First, it is preeminently about the cultural legacy of Spain and of the Mexican empire and early republican Mexico in the United States. It is not centered on Native Americans, nor is it about the other European contenders for hegemony in North America, although the interrelationships among these groups are necessarily considered. We are living today with the still-evolving outcome of those interrelationships.

Second, this book is meant to direct visitors to those units of our National Park system where the story of Spain and Mexico in the United States can be better understood. Equally, it is intended to enable visitors to those sites—be they parks, monuments, recreation areas, seashores, preserves, historic sites, or memorials administered by the National Park Service—to extend their educational experience beyond the units' boundaries. There is no pretense that this is a detailed chronicle of the history of Spain and Mexico in the United States. It is a park-related volume, one that can be taken home to be read during leisure hours. I hope, too, that it will encourage its readers to read more widely and deeply on this neglected subject.

With books of this kind, authors become indebted to others for their help. *Entrada* is no exception, and I wish to acknowledge with thanks the innumerable men and women of the National Park Service who gave so unselfishly of their time during my too brief visits to some of the units I had not seen before; who made available unpublished manuscripts from their files; and who read all or parts of this manuscript and who made helpful corrections and suggestions. I alone, however, accept full responsibility for whatever sins of omission and commission may occur.

I also wish to thank the directors and members of the Southwestern Mission Research Center, Inc. for having allowed me for a quarter of a century to edit their *SMRC Newsletter*, a publication that has become a quarterly newsletter of annotated bibliography and news concerning studies in the so-called Spanish Borderlands. That experience more than any other has provided me with the credentials, such as they may be, to write this book.

Finally, without the vision, enthusiasm, and gentle prodding of executive director T. J. Priehs of the Southwest Parks and Monuments Association, to say nothing of the association's financial commitment, this volume would never have become reality. ✠

Coat of arms of Christopher Columbus, whose epochal voyage in 1492 altered the course of human history, unleashing profound ecological, economic, and cultural changes worldwide. (Reprinted with the permission of Macmillan Publishing Company from Columbus, *written and illustrated by Bjorn Landstrom. Copyright 1966 by Bjorn Landstrom.)*

In its issue for July 8, 1991, *Time* magazine posed the question on its cover, "Who Are We?" The cover stories that followed were headed, "Whose America? A growing emphasis on the nation's 'multicultural' heritage exalts racial and ethnic pride at the expense of social cohesion."

Critics of this new emphasis on multiculturalism are concerned that moving in directions away from the assimilationist "melting pot" notion of the United States is leading the country toward a new kind of tribalism, a body politic splintered among groups of differing racial and ethnic origins, each demanding its proportionate piece of the political and economic pie.

That all of this should have become a matter of national concern on the eve of the five-hundredth anniversary of the discovery of America by Christopher Columbus is not without irony. It was he who led the vanguard of those who shattered whatever may have been the cultural and ecological situation—whether "balanced" or not—that existed among the many hundreds (thousands?) of linguistically and culturally disparate groups who peopled the Americas before A.D. 1492, some of whose ancestors had been living in the Western Hemisphere for thousands of years. The rich cultural stew to be found in the Americas in 1491 was to be reflavored by the addition as well as elimination of many ingredients—racial, social, and technological—over the next five centuries.

That most Native Americans died and that many individual cultures became wholly extinct is a tragedy, a holocaust, defying description. That some small fraction of these people managed to survive both individually and culturally, however altered in character, is a miracle of human biology and a triumph of the spirit of independence or, some would say, a symptom of segregation and prejudice. But survive they have. Five hundred years after their initial encounter with Europeans, their descendants constitute an essential element in the compound that is the American character. Native Americans are never far from the national consciousness nor conscience. Their stubborn unwillingness—others would argue "inability"—to lose their identity in that of the dominant culture, to become the Vanishing American, is one reason the idea of a melting pot has been called into question.

The image of Christopher Columbus and the icon he represents in our society has changed drastically over time. In the hands of early nineteenth-century writer Washington Irving, his first serious American biographer, Columbus was cast as a visionary, a person in whom were "combined the practical and poetical." His was a "daring but irregular genius" that "bore him to conclusions far beyond the intellectual vision of his contemporaries." Charges leveled against Columbus "that his stipulations with the Spanish court were selfish and avaricious" are dismissed by Irving as "inconsiderate and unjust. He aimed at dignity and wealth in the same lofty spirit in which he sought renown; they were to be part and parcel of his achievement, and palpable evidence of his success. . . . Thus his ambition was truly noble and lofty;

Christopher Columbus inadvertently became the vanguard of Spain's rush to establish dominion in the "New World" of the Americas. ("Portrait of a Man Called Christopher Columbus" by Sebastiano del Piombo, courtesy The Metropolitan Museum of Art, New York, gift of J. Pierpont Morgan, 1900.)

1

instinct with high thought and prone to generous deed."[1]

The conduct of Irving's Columbus

> was characterized by the grandeur of his views and the magnanimity of his spirit. Instead of scouring the newly-found countries, like a grasping adventurer eager only for immediate gain, as was too generally the case with contemporary discoverers, he sought to ascertain their soil and production, their rivers and harbors; he was desirous of colonizing and cultivating them; of conciliating and civilizing the natives; of building cities; introducing the useful arts; subjecting everything to the control of law, order, and religion; and thus of founding regular and prosperous empires. In this glorious plan he was constantly defeated by the dissolute rabble which it was his misfortune to command; with whom all law was tyranny, and all other restraint. They interrupted all useful works by their seditions; provoked the peaceful Indians to hostility; and after they had thus brought down warfare and misery on their own heads, and overwhelmed Columbus with the ruins of the edifice he was building, they charged him with being the cause of the confusion.[2]

Columbus continued to ride high in the waters of national acclaim throughout the nineteenth century, especially after the first edition of Irving's four-volume biography appeared in 1828, followed by no fewer than ninety editions and printings in the United States, Latin America, England, and elsewhere in Europe. In 1869 the United States commemorated his October 1492 landing on a fifteen-cent postage stamp. To celebrate the quatercentennial of his epic 1492 voyage, Chicago staged the World Columbian Exposition in 1893. That same year the United States released the Columbian Exposition issue of sixteen postage stamps in denominations ranging from a penny to five dollars, each stamp engraved with a different illustration depicting people, ships, or events relevant to the Columbus saga.

Admiring biographies of Columbus written in English continued well into the present century, the most notable among them being the two-volume work by Samuel Eliot Morison, *Admiral of the Ocean Sea*, published during the 450th anniversary of Columbus's first sea voyage to a west unknown to Europe.[3]

But what a difference fifty years can make! As scholars have come less to depend on what Columbus and his contemporary allies, including his son, said and wrote about him and have examined in greater detail other contemporary sources, the man who was a hero a half century ago has been invested with blame for many of the ills plaguing modern American society. The Columbian discovery of the Americas has been reinterpreted as an unmitigated disaster, if not for the entire world, then certainly for the Western Hemisphere. And Columbus himself has been depicted as a ruthless, none-too-bright, barely competent sea captain who was even more incompetent as an administrator on land. He was, principally via the introduction of diseases to which Native Americans had no immunity, the first in a procession of villainous Europeans who rained death and destruction on millions of innocent and unsuspecting men, women, and children who had preceded him here. He was also an unconscionable despoiler of the natural environment, one to whom we can ultimately trace depletion of the ozone layer; contaminated streams, rivers, seas and groundwater; toxic wastes; deforestation; extirpation of plant and animal species; and, in general, an exploitative attitude that may ultimately spell doom for the human species.[4]

The onslaught of criticism directed at Columbus seems to have grown from the period of the U.S. war in Vietnam. It was a time of national agony and upheaval. Old values thought to be rock solid, like unquestioning patriotism and belief in the unfailing basic goodness of the American psyche, were challenged by realities shown daily on American television screens. Young people, especially, called into question virtually all beliefs which until then had been held sacrosanct in the temple of idealized American culture. American blacks rallied in Washington; American Indians raided the Washington offices of the Bureau of Indian Affairs and occupied an abandoned Alcatraz Island as Indian Country. Heroes of American history were found to have feet of clay and, one after the other, they were felled from their lofty perches in Americans' minds.

Columbus was among the victims.

A formidable early blow was struck two decades before the quincentennial with the publication by historian Alfred W. Crosby, Jr. of *The Columbian Exchange: Biological and Cultural Consequences of 1492.*[5] The exchanges between Old World and New World, especially those involving diseases and foodstuffs, we now perceive to have been wrought with horrendous consequences. Crosby ended his book on a less than optimistic note: "The Columbian exchange has left us with not a richer but a more impoverished genetic pool. We, all of the life on this planet, are the less for Columbus, and the impoverishment will increase" (p. 219).

The *Columbian Exchange* was followed by books with titles even more directly to the point: *Their Number Become Thinned: Native American Population Dynamics in Eastern North America;*[6] *American Indian Holocaust and Survival;*[7] *The Missions of California: A Legacy of Genocide;*[8] *Vectors of Death: The Archaeology of European Contact;*[9] and *Disease, Depopulation, and Culture Change in Northwestern New Spain, 1518-1764.*[10] Nor are these likely to be the last.

What books like these, as well as innumerable articles in both popular and professional journals, tell us is that

> smallpox, measles, diphtheria, trachoma, whooping cough, chicken pox, scarlet fever, amoebic dysentery, influenza, malaria, and certain varieties of tuberculosis and venereal disease [had an impact] on Amerindians . . . *at least* equal to that of cold steel and gunpowder. Just about every successful invasion of the Americas was accompanied by or preceded by an epidemic.
>
> Humans born into industrial societies are inclined to exaggerate their powers. It is true that people culturally like us "conquered" the New World. But the full

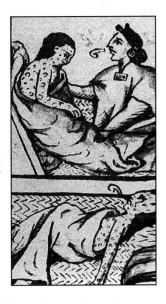

Fray Bernardino de Sahagún's General History of the Things of New Spain *depicts the scourge of smallpox introduced among the Aztecs during the 1519 invasion of México by Hernán Cortés. (Courtesy Smithsonian Institution.)*

3

truth is that humans discovered the Americas many thousands of years before Columbus was born, and the post-1492 "conquest" was not accomplished by one or two varieties of *Homo sapiens*, but by a number of species. The smallpox virus, for instance, was much more important than George Armstrong Custer in breaking Amerindian military resistance, and, unlike him, was invariably successful.[11]

Introduced diseases may have reduced populations of the New World by 66 to 95 percent! Natives not killed by epidemics, we are informed by some authors, were eliminated by direct military action. So was their resistance even to indigenous pathogens lowered as a result of depression and malaise occasioned by culture changes forced upon them, including forced labor and enslavement.

With such reassessments as these of the Columbian encounter before us, the nation cannot be characterized as being celebratory with regard to the Columbian Quincentenary. "Reflective" or "contentious" are two words that come more readily to mind.

While there is no harm in reflection, there can be harm in contentiousness. American Indians and legions of non-Indians who share their point of view organized counter-celebrations and offered such pronouncements as "Columbus makes Hitler look like a juvenile delinquent."[12] The National Council of Churches formally declared that "for the descendants of the survivors of the subsequent invasion, genocide, slavery, 'ecocide' and exploitation of the wealth of the land, a celebration is not an appropriate observance of this anniversary."[13]

For more than a few people, it is as if the old *Leyenda Negra*, the "Black Legend," has been resurrected. Persons in the United States who are of Hispanic descent, especially those who are Roman Catholic—and whose numbers are increasing both absolutely and in proportion to the rest of the population—may bear the brunt of newly inflamed prejudice. Indeed, the shrill anti-Columbus sentiments (as if Columbus could any longer care) could be an expression, whether conscious or unconscious, of prejudice toward Hispanics buried at shallow depths beneath the surface of the North American world view.

Writing two decades before the Columbian Quincentenary, historian Philip Wayne Powell put the matter succinctly: "Our national habit of condescension and oversimplification of virtually all phenomena of the Hispanic world is a habit that stretches from our elementary schools to universities to the White House, and it grows out of ancestral antagonisms that have come to constitute a perennial prejudice as unjustifiable as it can be dangerous."[14] These "ancestral antagonisms" can be traced to the Black Legend, "an atmosphere created by the fantastic accounts of Spain which have been published in almost all countries; the grotesque descriptions which are forever being made of the character of Spaniards individually and collectively."[15]

As Powell explains,

The basic premise of the Black Legend is that Spaniards have shown themselves,

This Pre-Columbian male effigy figure found in a burial cave in Nayarit, Mexico, dates from A.D. 200-800 and is covered with lesions characteristic of either syphilis or yaws, diseases endemic to the Americas. (Courtesy Dr. William Kaiser.)

4

historically, to be *uniquely* cruel, bigoted, tyrannical, obscurantist, lazy, fanatical, greedy, and treacherous; that is, that they differ so much from other peoples in these traits that Spaniards and Spanish history must be viewed and understood in terms not ordinarily used in describing and interpreting other peoples. Thus, Spaniards who came to the New World seeking opportunities beyond the prospects of their European environment, are contemptuously called cruel and greedy "goldseekers," or other opprobrious epithets virtually synonymous with "Devils"; but Englishmen who sought New World opportunities are more respectfully called "colonists," or "homebuilders," or "seekers after liberty."[16]

In Anglo America many of these same attitudes have persisted on the part of a non-Hispanic majority, although the target of this prejudice is no longer so much the people of modern Spain as it is the New World descendants of an earlier Spain, most of whom are the inheritors of cultural elements—as well as genes—of both Spaniards and Indians. And in the United States, the history of Spain's involvement with our own past remains a subject of continuing neglect.

The origins of the Black Legend are not difficult to trace. In the early sixteenth century, Spain was the most powerful nation in Europe. A Catholic country, her people were hated and feared universally by Dutch, French, German, and English Protestants. Spain's many detractors, in addition to fighting her on the ground and at sea, after 1560 waged a war of pamphleteering, propagandists characterizing Spaniards as bloodthirsty, tyrannical monsters. Spaniards were accused in widely circulated print of being braggarts who were shadows without substance; of being mongrels and barbarians, unclean and filthy swine, and thieves. Spaniards were said to be "the most loathsome, infected, and slavish people that ever lived on earth."[17]

It did not help, as essayist David Duncan has pointed out, that

> the propagandists had a great deal of raw truth to draw on. The Spanish, trying to hold together an unwieldy empire, behaved ruthlessly in a ruthless age. In the Americas they showed all the brutal expediency one might expect during the largest and most remote gold rush in history. What the propagandists didn't say, however, is that Spanish behavior in Europe and in the Americas was hardly unique. German, Dutch, and English conquerors shared the Spaniards' taste for gold, slaves, and territory, and seldom shied away from brutalizing European enemies or, when the time came, Indian and African populations.[18]

What propagandists, then as now, have also failed to emphasize is that among sixteenth-century Spaniards themselves there were powerful reformers who decried the most inhumane aspects of the Spanish conquest of America. Chief among them was a Dominican priest, Bartolomé de las Casas, who in 1540 submitted a report to Charles I of Spain, "A Brief Account of the Destruction of the Indies." In his zeal to effect reform in behalf of America's aboriginal population, he ignored whatever was positive that may have developed in interrelationships between Spaniards and Indians and emphasized exclusively the many atrocities committed by Spaniards

5

against natives. Las Casas and his fellow reformers were able to bring about the so-called New Laws, a Spanish legal code intended to overcome the most blatant aspects of ill treatment of Indians. But so did Las Casas' efforts supply Spain's enemies with ammunition for a later barrage of pamphleteering propaganda. Indeed, Fray Bartolomé's 1540 observations were being published in the United States as recently as 1898 as a means of drumming up support for the Spanish American War.[19]

Attitudes born of the Black Legend have persisted in the American character. Historian Joseph Sánchez writes that "cowardly, untrustworthy Mexicans" have survived as stereotypes in such Texas folk songs as "The Ballad of Ben Milam," who in legend only was the first Texas hero and who in the song, but not in fact, died in the Battle of the Alamo. The anti-Mexican sentiment is apparent in the words of this nineteenth-century song:

> They're the spawn of hell
>
> We heard him tell
>
> They will knife and lie and cheat.
>
> At the board of none
>
> Of that swarthy horde
>
> Would I deign to sit and meet.
>
> They held it not
>
> That I bled and fought
>
> When Spain was their ruthless foe.
>
> O, who will follow Old Ben Milam
>
> To San Antonio?[20]

A lesson that may ultimately emerge from a deeper examination of the meanings of the Columbian encounter and of the history of Spain in the United States is that of our common humanity as well as of our common inhumanity. Historian Charles Polzer wisely observed, "the 'New' World was not just another world, but the whole world newly revealed."[21] As human beings, and regardless of cultural affiliation, in each of us there is the capacity for heroism and cowardice, savagery and kindness, hatred and love.

We may also come to understand, as Thoreau reminded us long ago, that our ancestors had no other future than our present.[22] What wrongs may have happened in the past are no longer ours to set aright. They are the wrongs of the present we must address. We are now "the conqueror and the conquered, the Indian and the *encomendero*, the slave owner and the slave . . . fused in the hereditary spirit."[23] So are we at once the oppressor and oppressed, victim and victimizer, dominator and dominated. And while only present and future belong to us, the past remains ours to plumb for a more hopeful—and objective—definition of our collective selves.

In this woodcut first published in Guiliano Dati's edition of Columbus's 1493 letter, Columbus meets the Taíno on Hispaniola. King Ferdinand appears on his throne in the left foreground. The engraver used information in the letter to depict the natives' dress. (Courtesy New York Public Library Rare Books and Manuscripts Division.)

In its simplest form, the Spanish word *entrada* is an entrance or an entering. In America, however, *entrada* has also come to mean an attack, an assault, or even a "goring,"[1] a telling evolution of meaning from the sixteenth century, when Spaniards used the term more benignly to refer to a formal entry into a new land.[2]

In a very real sense, the Columbian voyages were themselves *entradas*, having been formally sanctioned by the Spanish Crown. And while there were the inevitable freebooters who tried their private hands at exploration, conquest, and exploitation of people and resources, most sixteenth- and seventeenth-century Spanish efforts in these same directions were authorized under Spanish law and were, therefore, entradas.

What were the forces that in the late fifteenth century headed the *Niña*, *Pinta*, and *Santa María* toward the west? Some would say "opportunity"; others would say "greed."[3] But while economic motivations were surely critical, so were Utopian ideals. Such Greek and Latin writers as Hesiod, Virgil, Lucretius, and Ovid had written about a lost Golden Age, an earthly paradise where there was no death and where people lived "as gods, with the soul without sorrows, away from pain and tiredness."[4] At least since the time of Plato and Homer people had imagined such an earthly paradise. In time, however, to the idea of the Golden Age was added that of the Golden Fleece: an El Dorado, a Quivira, a Cíbola.[5]

Writer Mary Austin added another dimension:

> Put it that Spain had swarmed, as a little later the English. Whatever the urge that compels great populations to sow themselves to all four quarters of the earth, the desire to spread the blessings of Christianity was, in the sixteenth century, a popular way of rationalizing it.[6]

To "God, Gold, and Glory" must be included a more straightforward incentive for exploration and conquest: land. Even ordinary Spaniards were potentially recipients of land grants in the Indies, a powerful inducement for those with visions of becoming wealthy farmers or ranchers.[7]

When Columbus set sail, Spain and Spaniards were inspired by these motivations and more.

CHRISTOPHER COLUMBUS

Before he died in 1506, Christopher Columbus, or Cristóbal Colón, made four round-trip voyages between Spain and the Americas, most notably to islands in the Caribbean. Most of us do not normally associate Columbus as having had an immediate connection, in a physical sense, with today's United States. But during his

ENTRADA

A crucifix and religious medal stamped with the image of Our Lady of Guadalupe and the inscription "N.S. DE GVADALVPE DE MEXICO A[NO] 1798" signify one of Spain's major motives for embracing the New World. (George H. H. Huey from the Enrique E. Guerra collection.)

9

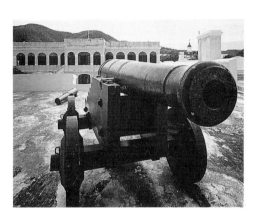

Fort Christiansvaern at Christiansted National Historic Site, St. Croix, Virgin Islands. It was near here, at Salt River Bay, that some of Columbus's men landed on November 14, 1493. (Larry Ulrich.)

second voyage, outfitted with at least seventeen ships and between 1,200 and 1,500 colonists and lasting from September 1493 to June 1496, he dropped anchor off the island of St. Croix in the U.S. Virgin Islands as well as off the west coast of Puerto Rico.

The U.S. territory of the Virgin Islands—principally comprising the islands of St. John, St. Thomas, and St. Croix—were named Las Once Mil Virgenes by Columbus for St. Ursula and her "11,000 seagoing virgins from Cornwall who, according to legend, were martyred by the Huns at Cologne after a long and pleasant yachting cruise."8 Some of these islands were purchased by the United States from Denmark in 1917. It was November 14, 1493, when some of Columbus's men—but not Columbus himself—landed on Santa Cruz (i.e., St. Croix), probably on its north shore at Salt River Bay and not far to the east of where Christiansted National Historic Site is now located. In February 1992, by way of commemorating the Columbian quincentenary, President George Bush signed legislation to create a 912-acre national park at Salt River Bay, 312 acres on land and 600 on water. It is officially the Salt River Bay National Historical Park and Ecological Preserve.9

Washington Irving has offered an extended account in English of Columbus's landing here:

> A boat well-manned was sent ashore to get water and to procure information. They found a village deserted by the men, but secured a few women and boys, most of them captives from other islands. They soon had an instance of Carib courage and ferocity. While at the village they beheld a canoe from a distant part of the island come from round a point of land and arrive in view of the ships. The Indians in the canoe, two of whom were females, remained gazing in mute amazement at the ships, and were so entranced that the boat stole close upon them before they perceived it. Seizing their paddles they attempted to escape, but the boat being between them and the land, cut off their retreat. They now caught up their bows and arrows and plied them with amazing vigor and rapidity. The Spaniards covered themselves with their bucklers [shields], but two of them were quickly wounded. The women fought as fiercely as the men, and one of them sent an arrow with such force that it passed through and through a buckler.
>
> The Spaniards now ran their boat against the canoe and overturned it; some of the savages got upon the sunken rocks, others discharged their arrows while swimming, as dexterously as though they had been upon firm land. It was with the utmost difficulty they could be overcome and taken. One of them, who had been transfixed with a lance, died soon after being brought aboard the ships. One of the women, from the obedience and deference paid her, appeared to be their queen. . . . The hair of these savages was long and coarse. Their eyes were encircled with paint, so as to give them a hideous expression; and bands of cotton were bound firmly above and below the muscular parts of the arms and legs, so as to cause them to swell to a disproportionate size; a custom prevalent among various

10

tribes of the New World. Though captive in chains, and in the power of their enemies, they still retained a frowning brow and an air of defiance. Peter Martyr, who often went to see them in Spain, declares, from his own experience, and that of others who accompanied him, that it was impossible to look at them without a sensation of horror, so menacing and terrible was their aspect. This sensation was doubtless caused in great measure by the idea of their being cannibals. In this skirmish, according to the same writer, the Indians used poisoned arrows; and one of the Spaniards died within a few days, of a wound received from one of the females.[10]

Although Irving followed the lead of others in referring to these Indians as "Caribs," as have nearly all historians since, Kirkpatrick Sale tells us it is unlikely that Caribs ever settled nearer than two hundred miles from St. Croix and that the Virgin Islands' native inhabitants were probably eastern Tainos, a people also known as Arawaks. Columbus, Sale's reasoning goes, early acquired the habit of calling any natives who opposed him "Caribs," while others who were peaceful he called "Tainos." He remarks, "The idea of fierce and hostile Caribs, in short, was never more than a bogey, born of Colón's own paranoia or stubborn ferocity and spread to his comrades, to the chroniclers of Europe, and to history." Neither, Sale adds, is there any good evidence that Caribs ever practiced cannibalism.[11]

Whether Caribs, Tainos, or other natives whose name for themselves is now lost to history, those in the violent encounter of November 14, 1493, were in the first pitched battle and the first to die in armed conflict between Indians and Europeans within what today are the territorial limits of the United States.

By November 19 Columbus's fleet had reached the south coast of a large island that the natives called Boriquén or Borinquen and Columbus named San Juan Bautista. We know it today as Puerto Rico, a commonwealth of the United States whose residents, like those of the U.S. Virgin Islands, are U.S. citizens. The fleet anchored on November 20 on the west coast, probably at Añasco Bay. There was a landing during which Spaniards filled their casks with fresh water and visited a deserted Taino village. But the group sailed soon for Hispaniola (the island divided today into Haiti and the Dominican Republic) where Columbus had been on his first voyage and where his capital was established. Except that Columbus is believed to have landed on Mona Island, a part of modern Puerto Rico, during his third journey (1498-1500), St. Croix and Puerto Rico quickly passed out of Columbian history.

In the continental United States, the National Park Service has as one of its responsibilities the maintenance of the Columbus Memorial Fountain in front of Union Station in the District of Columbia in National Capital Parks—Central. It was here on October 12-14, 1991, that a festival of multicultural entertainment was held as a "Columbus Quincentennial Kick-Off."

Juan Ponce de León was granted a royal charter in 1512 to locate and settle "the island of Bininy." León instead made landfall on the North American peninsula he named La Florida. (Engraving from Historia general de los hechos de los castellanos *courtesy Florida Museum of Natural History, Gainesville.)*

JUAN PONCE DE LEÓN

Juan Ponce de León, at age nineteen, had been one of Columbus's shipmates during the second voyage. He was destined to return to Puerto Rico in 1508.[12] In the late fifteenth century he had participated with other Spaniards in what contemporary and later Spanish critics characterized as the ruthless conquest of the island of Española (Hispaniola). He was still living in Española when Ponce was told by a native of Boriquén (Puerto Rico), who showed him a nugget to back his assertion, that his island had plenty of gold. Governor Nicolás de Ovando of Hispaniola, Columbus's successor, gave Ponce permission to sail to Boriquén with a hundred soldiers to capture it if he could. The Tainos were no match for the invaders, and before the year was out the ambitious Spaniard had established a capital at a place known as Caparra but which he named Villa de San Germán. In 1509, by way of confirming his successful conquest, the Spanish crown named Ponce governor of Puerto Rico.

There was, in fact, gold on the island, and its first European governor prospered mightily for the next three years. Fray Bartolomé de las Casas flatly charged that he grew rich "on the labors, blood and sufferings his subjects,"[13] the hapless Tainos.

In 1512, Don Diego Colón, Cristóbal's son, successfully asserted his hereditary right to appoint the governors for Puerto Rico, a place whose gold placers and native population were by then falling into sharp decline. Ponce, no longer a governor, petitioned the crown for a right to search for still more lands to conquer, possibly hoping to capture Indians whom he could sell as slaves. The contract was issued in 1512. His expedition, to be outfitted at his own cost, was supposed to locate and settle "the island of Bininy [Bimini]" and to apportion its natives in *repartimiento*, the formal means whereby Indian workers were distributed or allotted to Spanish employers—a form of slavery.[14] He was, moreover,

> to have the ownership of all the houses and estates that he would establish with his own funds. He was to assume the executive and judicial functions in the new territory, but the construction and direction of forts was to be a royal prerogative and responsibility. He would receive a share of all the revenues and profits except from royal properties. Gold and other precious metals were to be the property of Ponce and his men except the share reserved for the crown. . . . Finally, Ponce was to receive the title of adelantado and governor of Bimini and other lands.[15]

No mention was ever made in any contractual documents of the fabled "Fountain of Youth" for which Ponce allegedly searched in what was to become La Florida. But it makes a good story, as all fables do, one perpetuated to the present day. The sixteenth-century historian Gonzalo Fernández de Oviedo, we are told by twentieth-century historian Samuel Eliot Morison, "makes it clear that Ponce wanted a cure for *el enflaquecimiento del sexo*, the debility of sex. At the age of thirty-nine he could hardly have needed this cure himself; but plenty of older conquistadors, lacking in the New World the traditional aphrodisiacs such as unicorns' horns, could well profit by it."[16]

Morison goes on to tell us there were both Old World and New World versions of the Fountain of Youth myth. The Spanish humanist Peter Martyr, writing in 1511, said that on an island north of Cuba named Boiuca or Bimini there was a spring flowing with the rejuvenating waters, a story Ponce himself may have heard. "As a well-educated Spanish nobleman he must also have heard the parallel Eurasian myth, a familiar feature in Renaissance painting. There, the Fountain of Youth is always connected with profane, gallant, and erotic love."[17] As good as the story is, a more realistic appraisal is offered by geographer Carl Sauer: "Ponce, in vigorous middle age, was not spending his wealth in search of a fountain of youth, nor did his conduct in Florida support the romantic story that is still told in school books."[18]

Ponce set sail with his three-ship fleet from Puerto Rico on his quest for Bimini on March 4, 1513. The vessels included the flagship *Santiago*, the *San Cristóbal*, and the *Santa María de la Consolación*. Many historians have tried to reconstruct the precise route and landings of his seven-month journey, but no two are the same in details.[19] What seems to be generally agreed, though, is that after leaving the region of the Bahamas and continuing to sail westward, Ponce struck the mainland of La Florida on its east coast somewhere between places later known as Cabo Cañaveral (Cape Canaveral) and San Agustín (St. Augustine). It was Ponce who gave the place the name that has survived, from *Pascua Florida*, the Floral Passover, or Easter season. The date was April 2, 1513, just six days following Easter Sunday and still within the time of the Christian Easter festival. His men went ashore on April 3. Ponce believed then and until he died he had found an island.

Morison writes that he finds no evidence to suggest that Ponce

ever visited the site of St. Augustine. No prudent sailor wanting to return to Puerto Rico would have done so, on account of the force of the Gulf Stream. That extraordinary current's full force—five to six knots—Ponce first felt the next week [Historian Antonio de] Herrera [writing in 1601] says that on 8 April the fleet 'sailed again the same way,' i.e., north, but meeting a counter-current along the edge of the land, Ponce turned south, where he met a head current so strong that it drove them back, although they had a 'fair wind.' This was the Gulf Stream, which always runs south to north.[20]

Morison places the site of this first landing by a Spaniard in what more than two centuries later was to become the continental United States of America at "a little inlet near Daytona Beach, fifty miles south of St. Augustine, which has been named for Ponce de León." Historian Robert Weddle agrees, but observes that on modern maps

John White's sixteenth-century drawings of La Florida natives were most likely based on drawings from life by the Frenchman Jacques le Moyne. (Courtesy University of Arizona Library Special Collections, Tucson.)

the inlet is just to the north and closer to New Smyrna Beach than to the more northerly Daytona Beach.[21]

In any event, the landfall was adjacent to today's Canaveral National Seashore. A visitor to this relatively undisturbed stretch of beach can get at least some impression of how the landscape may have appeared to Juan Ponce de León in April 1513. It also gives pause for thought that where a European first touched land within today's continental United States is but a stone's throw from Cape Canaveral and the John F. Kennedy Space Center, from which Americans first left the earth to visit the moon.

There is no record that Ponce and his men saw any human beings at their first landing on the east Florida beach on April 3. But seventeen days later, on April 20, the seaman spotted natives' huts next to the sea. "Ponce went ashore in his longboat, which an Indian welcoming committee tried to seize; Ponce scuffled with them, reserving his fire power until one Christian had been stunned by a blow on the head; then he let go, but little damage was suffered by the natives. Next day they sailed to a river where they took on wood and water. . . ."[22]

The Native Americans who so rudely greeted these first European mainland visitors were probably members of the Timucuan-speaking Agua Dulce, or Fresh Water, chiefdom.[23] It may be that Ponce and his crew provoked the hostilities or it may be that the Indians had had previous unpleasant encounters with Europeans, either on Caribbean islands or—a more intriguing possibility—with Europeans who had earlier been in their territory but of whose visit or visits no records are yet known. In any event, Ponce's tiny fleet headed slowly southward down the east Florida coast, staying close to the shore in an effort to take advantage of the counter current of the powerful north-flowing Gulf Stream. Their course took them past "the sites of [a future] Palm Beach, Ft. Lauderdale, and Miami," and they went "ashore wherever they saw signs of a native village."[24]

In the first half of May, the Spaniards stopped at a Tequesta (or Tekesta) village, Abaiós, on the Miami River just beyond the north end of Biscayne National Park. The natives, like the neighboring Timucuans to the north, were hostile and they killed a Spaniard. Not wanting a fight, Ponce's men filled their water casks, cut firewood, and got back on their ships. They continued southward, sailing past a string of island reefs within which there was a bay, almost certainly Biscayne Bay. Here, on May 13, they landed on an island they called Santa Pola to get more water.[25]

Two days later, Ponce and his mariners found the Florida Keys and Marquesas Keys at La Florida's south tip, presumably moving around them on the outside and staying away from the mainland. However, rounding the tip of La Florida beyond the keys, they sailed northward up the west coast of La Florida. How far north they got is a subject of debate among scholars, but Robert Weddle, at least, suggests a possibility of a landing between Cape Romano and Cape Sable, the latter the southwesternmost point within Everglades National Park.[26]

14

This time the Spaniards' encounter was with Calusas, and, as in nearly all of their earlier meetings with the natives, there were violence and death. Historian Weddle elaborates:

> When the voyagers reached these islands [between capes Sable and Romano?], they found a passage between them and the mainland. The ships entered the channel to take on wood and water and anchored until June 3. . . . At first the Indians, among them one who spoke Spanish, crossed the inlet in canoes to barter pelts and *guanín*, a low-grade gold. Then they turned hostile, seizing the anchor cables and trying to board the ships. The Spaniards captured four Indian women. . . . Before the voyagers could get away . . . the ships were assaulted from twenty canoes. A number of Indians and one Spaniard were killed, and Ponce's men took four more captives.[27]

The next day the Calusas showed up in eighty canoes and carried on what amounted to a day-long sham battle, one in which Indian warriors fired arrows harmlessly beyond reach of Spanish guns and crossbows. After remaining in the vicinity another nine days, the fleet headed toward the southeast or south-southeast, encountering islands Ponce named Las Tortugas, "The Turtles," today's Dry Tortugas National Park and the site of Fort Jefferson. In one night his men caught 160 giant sea turtles, each "as big as a war shield"; fourteen *lobos marinos* (seals or manatees); and seven thousand pelicans, gannets, and other sea birds.[28]

With little to show for his efforts, Ponce returned to Puerto Rico before sailing to Spain, where he obtained a royal grant to colonize the "island" he believed he had discovered. In 1521 he returned to the west coast of La Florida, this time with "several" vessels, two hundred men, fifty horses, missionary priests, and a good stock of seeds, roots, ratoons, and all kinds of domestic livestock.[29] There are even fewer surviving records of this expedition than of the 1513 voyage, and no one knows precisely where on La Florida's west coast Ponce tried to plant his colony. Weddle believes it may have been at the northwest edge of the Florida Everglades, near today's Everglades City.[30] But whether here or elsewhere, once more it ended in failure for the Spaniards. The Calusas did all in their power to resist Spanish efforts to build a town on their shores, and Ponce was severely wounded by the Indians in a fight. He sailed to the nearest port in Cuba, but in spite of all efforts to save him he died in July 1521. His name is forever fixed in fountain of youth legend as well as in United States history as the first European leader known to have spent time on its continental soil.

The hostilities initiated between Ponce de León and Native Americans in Florida were not formally to end until 1886 when Geronimo, after his final surrender, was brought to Fort Bowie, today's Fort Bowie National Historic Site in Arizona. Before he was finally exiled to Fort Sill, Oklahoma, where he died in 1909, Geronimo and some of his fellow Chiricahua Apaches were sent briefly as prisoners of war to Fort Pickens in present-day Gulf Islands National Seashore next to Pensacola while other Apaches were imprisoned in the fort at Castillo de San Marcos National Monument in St. Augustine. It probably never occurred to them, nor to anyone else at the time, that armed hostilities within today's continental United States that had begun between Native Americans and non-Indians in Florida in 1513 were sealed in the jailing of Native Americans, also in Florida, 373 years later.

HERNÁNDEZ DE CÓRDOBA

Although his impact on United States history as well as on the native population appears to have been close to nil, Hernández de Córdoba deserves at least some mention as an early Spanish visitor to peninsular Florida. By 1516 Hernández had become a wealthy Cuban planter who was also reputed to be "very able at kidnaping and killing Indians." In February 1517 he set out on a voyage of discovery that took him and his fellow expedition members to the Yucatán peninsula. There the venturers encountered Mayans who succeeded in driving them back to their boats and the sea.

Finding themselves in desperate straits, the decision was made to sail for La Florida. One of their number, Anton de Alaminos, had sailed with Ponce de León in 1513 and knew the Gulf's currents. On April 18, 1517, their three ships anchored in a bay on the southwest coast of La Florida. Some of the men, including twenty soldiers, went ashore where they dug wells and filled their casks with good water:

> Then came the alarm from one of the sentries: Indians were approaching both on foot and in canoes, large men dressed in deerskins, carrying long bows and lances. "They came straight toward us shooting arrows," making to seize the Spaniards' boat. The soldiers, wading in waist-deep water, fought back with swords and crossbows. When the fight was over, they had half a dozen wounded, including Alaminos. A sentry . . . was taken alive by the Indians, thirty-two of whom lay dead along the shore and in the shallows.[31]

ALONSO ALVAREZ DE PINEDA

One of the more shadowy characters in the Spanish-period history of the United States is Alonso Alvarez de Pineda, captain-general of a fleet of four ships dispatched in 1519 by Governor Francisco de Garay of Jamaica to explore the shoreline of the northern Gulf of Mexico in regions yet uncharted either by Ponce de León or by Spaniards who had already sailed to the southwestern rim of the Gulf to land on the east coast of Mexico. Garay hoped to claim the lands "discovered" by his captain-general.

Alvarez de Pineda's journey took him from Jamaica to within site of La Florida's western mainland coast and, no doubt, islands of today's Gulf Islands National Seashore. Continuing eastward and failing to find a channel around the north end of the presumed island, he sailed down the west side of the La Florida peninsula. Adverse winds and currents forced his ships to turn around. This time they moved along the east and north Gulf Coast in a counterclockwise direction. Although no first-person account of the voyage survives, Garay petitioned the crown for the right to settle the newly discovered region, submitting a *relación*, or report, in the process. The royal *cédula* (order) issued in response summarizes Garay's report, and it is from that summary, as well as from a map compiled by Alvarez de Pineda, the first map of the Gulf of Mexico, that we learn a few details concerning his historic journey.

Robert Weddle writes that on June 2, 1519, the tiny fleet noted the mighty discharge from the Mississippi, a great river to which Alvarez gave the name Río del Espíritu Santo. "All along the coast Alvarez de Pineda discovered," continues Weddle,

The first map to chart the entire Gulf of Mexico, derived from information gained during the 1519 voyage of Alonso Alvarez de Pineda. This tracing of the original in the Archivo General de Indias in Seville, Spain, has been enhanced for greater legibility. (Courtesy Institute of Texan Cultures, San Antonio.)

he found land, ports, and rivers pleasing to the eye. This "very good land" was peaceful and healthful, offering a variety of fruits and other means of sustenance. The rivers yielded "fine gold," as evidenced by the specimens the Indians displayed and by the gold jewelry they wore "in their nostrils, on their ear lobes, and on other parts of the body." The people were affectionate by nature, indicating "much success could be attained in their conversion and indoctrination to our Holy Catholic Faith." Some of the people, we are told in a somewhat doubtful passage, were giants more than seven feet tall, while others were dwarfs growing to no more than four feet.[32]

The lands sighted during this 1519 journey were

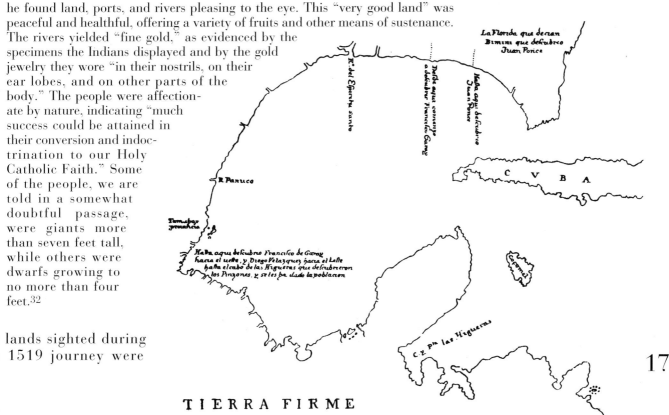

TIERRA FIRME

17

named Amichel by the Spaniards. They include northwestern Florida, Alabama, Mississippi, Louisiana, Texas, and northeastern Mexico. Although details are vague on Alvarez's map, the likelihood is that he and his men were the first Spaniards to view much of the southern coast of the United States, including lands within Florida's De Soto National Memorial, Gulf Islands National Seashore in Florida and Mississippi, and Padre Island National Seashore in Texas. Did he land at any of these places? The record stands mute.

The Otter Cliffs of Mount Desert Island, Acadia National Park, Maine, have changed little since the region was visited by Esteban Gómez in 1524. (Carr Clifton.)

ESTEBAN GÓMEZ AND HIS PREDECESSORS

Although hardly a household name along the Atlantic coast of the northeastern United States, and often going without mention in U.S. histories, Esteban Gómez was among the very early Europeans to visit what eventually was to become the New England coast. He had been preceded in the region of the north Atlantic coast of America by nearly five centuries by Norsemen. In A.D. 1001 Leif Ericson sailed along the Labrador coast before landing, according to some authorities, on the north coast of Newfoundland, where he and his men built houses at the site later named L'Anse aux Meadows and spent the winter.

By the late fifteenth century, and possibly before 1492, Bristol sailors and fishermen—and perhaps Portuguese and Basques as well—had tried their hands in the waters of the North Atlantic off the east coast of today's Canada. And in 1497 John Cabot, who was possibly like Columbus a Genoese, sailed under British auspices and landed somewhere either on the north coast of New England or, possibly, on the east coast of Newfoundland during his unsuccessful search for a water passage to the Orient. Wherever he landed, Cabot claimed the land for Henry VII of England.[33]

Between 1524 and 1528 the Italian Giovanni da Verrazzano, sailing in the service of France, discerned the outlines of much of the eastern seaboard of today's United States. If Samuel Morison is correct, in March 1524 he made his first landfall, after leaving the Portuguese-owned Madeiras Islands, at Cape Fear in North Carolina. He then headed northward along the coast to Cape Breton Island, anchoring en route in the narrows between Staten Island and Long Island in New York Harbor, possibly the first European to do so. The bridge that today spans the narrows between these two islands bears his name, as does the narrows itself.

Verrazzano made his way back to France, having managed to link La Florida to Canada. Later, in 1528, he set out on a journey which took him to some unknown

18

point on the coast of La Florida, to the Bahamas, and the Lesser Antilles, where he was killed by the natives.[34]

If England and France could show some interest in finding an east-west strait through North America, so could Spain. Thus it was that in March 1523 Esteban Gómez received from Carlos V of Spain his royal commission as a captain with a license to locate the elusive passage to the Orient. He set sail from Corunna, Spain, possibly in September 1524, going first to the east coast of Nova Scotia before going south possibly as far as the northern coast of Florida.[35] He returned to Spain in August 1525, his ship filled with Indians he had captured as slaves, possibly natives from the vicinity of Newport, Rhode Island.

Gómez, like Verrazzano before him, sailed past or, perhaps, into Lower New York Bay within view of today's Gateway National Recreation Area and Fire Island National Seashore. He may also have seen Liberty Island, the site of the Statue of Liberty National Monument, and Ellis Island, site of the United States immigration station now operated as a unit of the Statue of Liberty National Monument. His voyage further took him past Cape Cod, Massachusetts, within sight of Cape Cod National Seashore. And his route lay "close to the beautiful island of Mount Desert that Verrazzano had just named after one of the daughters of Navarre [i.e., Catherine], believed it to be a promontory, and named its fjord-like and mountain-bordered Somes Sound *Río de Montañas.*"[36] Maine's Mount Desert Island and nearby Isle Au Haut are the setting for today's Acadia National Park.

Information supplied by Gómez found its way onto early sixteenth-century maps that had a profound effect on cartography and explorations of the day.[37]

ÁLVAR NUÑEZ CABEZA DE VACA

If there is a story of Homeric proportions in the history of North America, it is the odyssey of Spanish soldier Álvar Núñez Cabeza de Vaca (Núñez "Cow's Head"). Born in Spain about 1490, he was perhaps thirty-eight years old when he landed on the west coast of peninsular Florida in 1528 as treasurer of what became the ill-fated effort of Pánfilo de Narváez to become governor, captain-general, and *adelantado* (founder) of whatever territory in La Florida he could conquer. Had the expedition succeeded, Narváez's discoveries were to be his to govern, independent from the viceroyalty of Nueva España (New Spain).

Narváez's attempt had been preceded two years earlier, in 1526, by that of Spanish lawyer Lucas Vásquez de Ayllón. Vásquez de Ayllón had actually tried to plant a colony on the Atlantic coast of North America by setting out from Santo Domingo with six ships and five hundred men, women, children, priests, and the first black slaves to reach North America. Vásquez de Ayllón's was the initial European settlement in today's contiguous United States, founded in Guale Indian country somewhere north

Title page of Álvar Nuñez Cabeza de Vaca's 1542 account of the ill-fated Narváez expedition and the survivors' eight-year trek through the uncharted interior of North America. (Courtesy Florida Museum of Natural History, Gainesville.)

19

of St. Catherine's Island on either the north Georgia or southern South Carolina coastline. He named it San Miguel de Gualdape. Before the year was out, Indian attacks, disease, the death of its leader, and mutiny among the colonists resulted in the venture's total failure. Only 150 survivors made it back to their Caribbean island home.[38]

The Narváez expedition consisted of five vessels, eighty horses, 390 men, and ten women, the wives of some of those taking part. The ships' west-peninsular La Florida landfall was on the shores of Bahía de la Cruz in what may have been Timucuan territory. Precisely which bay this was is unknown, but Sarasota Bay and Tampa Bay are two good possibilities.[39] Either way, the site was very near that of De Soto National Memorial, which lies south of Tampa Bay and close to the north entrance to Sarasota Bay.

Narváez split his expedition into one by land and another by sea. Those who went by land were never to connect with the seafarers again. Three hundred men, forty of them mounted on horses and the rest on foot, headed northward into Apalachee country looking for gold and other riches. They included Narváez; Núñez Cabeza de Vaca; infantry captain Andrés Dorantes de Carranza; his slave, a possibly black Moroccan native named Estebanico (or Esteban); and Captain Alonso del Castillo Maldonado. All but Narváez were about to walk their way into the annals of North American history.

The march of the expeditionary forces was through hostile country. Trees fallen from a hurricane and swollen rivers blocked their route. Apalachees raided at will, killing Spaniards and their horses one at a time. Disease took its toll. With no gold discoveries to boost morale and their situation becoming desperate, the Spaniards still alive made their way southward to the Gulf where, using improvised tools, they built five barges and set sail toward the west, hoping to reach Mexico. Food and water supplies ran low, and men died of starvation. More died of disease and still more in sporadic Indian attacks. Others died from drinking brackish water. More Spaniards drowned. Survivors sought shelter in Pensacola Bay behind Florida's present-day Gulf Islands National Seashore, but the Panzacola Indians killed three of them and wounded all fifty soldiers covering the withdrawal.

At long last, on November 6, 1528, the makeshift boat carrying Núñez Cabeza de Vaca and some forty-odd castaways was beached on the east Texas coast, possibly on Galveston Island or, as Robert Weddle believes is more likely, on the more westerly Follet Island (now connected to the mainland). One other boat with an additional forty or so castaways, including Andrés Dorantes and Alonso del Castillo, landed on the same island. By April 1529 all but fourteen survivors of the Narváez expedition had either died on the island during the winter or had wandered off to an unknown fate.

Eventually, there were only four survivors: Núñez Cabeza de Vaca, Dorantes, Castillo, and Esteban. They walked all the way across Texas and northern Mexico to Culiacán on Mexico's west coast, arriving there in 1536—eight incredible years after they had landed near Tampa Bay. Their overland route remains the subject of much speculation, but there seems to be agreement that they touched the Río Grande in the vicinity of modern-day El Paso, Texas. If so, they were within reach of today's Chamizal National Memorial,[40] the first in a long progression of Spaniards destined to cross the Río Grande at this pass of northern Nueva España.

FRAY MARCOS DE NIZA

The 1536 arrival in Mexico City of the four overland survivors of the Narváez expedition caused a sensation. Their journey appeared as heroic then as it seems to us today. And in 1536 it carried added weight in official circles: the Spaniards and the slave had seen people and lands until then unknown to Spain, and they brought with them stories of the possibility of yet untapped riches lying to the north. They had been told, they said, about settled peoples who lived in villages in structures four and five stories high, who practiced horticulture, and who traded in emeralds, turquoises, and buffalo robes. A new viceroy, Antonio de Mendoza, had assumed his lofty post only the previous year and was anxious to add to the size of his dominion of Nueva España and secure his position against such potential contenders as Hernando de Soto, governor of Cuba and adelantado of La Florida, who was himself about to embark on an expedition of conquest on the mainland to the north.

Viceroy Mendoza tried unsuccessfully to enlist one of the three Spanish survivors to make an entrada northward into unknown lands. As an alternative he bought Esteban from Dorantes to serve as guide for what was intended as little more than a kind of scouting trip for a full-scale expedition planned for the next year, to be led by Francisco Vásquez de Coronado.

The reconnaissance party set off to the north in March 1539 from Culiacán. Its leader was a Franciscan friar, Marcos de Niza, a seasoned traveler who had seen six years of service in Santo Domingo, Guatemala, and Peru before arriving in Mexico City in 1537. His fellow explorers, in addition to the guide Esteban, included a Franciscan brother named Onorato and Mexican Indians, including some from the area beyond Culiacán where the group was headed. By the time they reached the Río Sinaloa on the northwest coast of Nueva España, Brother Onorato had become so ill he had to be carried back to Culiacán on a litter.

Historian Herbert E. Bolton describes the retinue:

> Apparently everyone went on foot, unaided by horse, mule, or burro, although two greyhounds belonging to the Negro Stephen trotted along with the party. In contrast to black Stephen, from whose arms and ankles bells jingled merrily, Fray Marcos, at the request of Coronado, was clad in a sober habit of gray Zaragoza cloth, and in his pack he carried samples of pearls, gold, and precious stones to

21

show the Indians met along the way, as a means of ascertaining what treasures of this sort were known to them. Stephen's baggage, carried by Indian servants, included dishes of various colors, and a gourd rattle decorated with strings of little bells and two feathers, one white and one red. The rattle was one he had acquired while among the Indians of western Texas.[41]

Esteban (Stephen), the guide, went ahead of the rest of the party as it moved north. He was accompanied by Indian couriers who were to send back to Fray Marcos a white cross, the size of the cross symbolizing the degree of importance of whatever it was Esteban was encountering. In time, a man-sized cross returned with word that Esteban had found the fabled Seven Cities of Cíbola. After that, there were no more crosses. Esteban had found the Zuni Indian villages on what was later to become the western border of central New Mexico, and the Zunis—for whatever reason—had killed him.

As with virtually all early Spanish entradas, precisely where Marcos de Niza went and the routes he used to get there and back remain the subject of scholarly debate. We know with certainty that the friar hurried back to Nueva España once he received word of the untimely demise of Esteban. On his return he penned a report that geographer Carl Sauer called, justifiably or not, "a strange tissue of hearsay, fantasy, fact and fraud."[42]

How far north the Franciscan got or which river valleys he followed in doing so remain in the realm of conjecture. What seems within the realm of possibility, however, if not within the surer realm of probability, is that if he entered today's United States (and Esteban indisputably seems to have done so), it was in southern Arizona moving northward up the San Pedro River Valley.[43]

Fray Marcos's journey was a prelude to more dramatic events to unfold in what today is regarded as the heartland of the American Southwest.

HERNANDO DE SOTO

Taking up where Narváez had left off, and hoping to succeed where his predecessors, including Ponce de León, had failed, Spanish conquistador Hernando Méndez de Soto y Gutiérrez Cardeñosa offered to become the conqueror of La Florida. And at his own expense.

De Soto, born in Spain about 1500, had gone at age fourteen to Central America, where he became involved with Pedrarias Dávila in the conquest of Darién (eastern Panama), Nicaragua, and Castillo del Oro (Panama) before joining Francisco Pizarro and Diego Almagro in Peru in 1532 in their conquest of the Inca empire. De Soto, it was said, was "much given to the sport of slaying Indians."[44]

In 1537 the Spanish Crown awarded de Soto the governorship of Cuba and the right to conquer La Florida. Should he succeed, he would be given generous grants of

Born in Spain about 1500, Hernándo de Soto went to Central America in 1514 and promptly became involved in a series of expeditions there and in Peru. In 1537 he was awarded the right to conquer La Florida. (Courtesy Florida Museum of Natural History, Gainsville.)

land, both shoreline and inland, with a lifetime title of adelantado. He could also keep much of whatever he could take by way of precious metals or other valuable commodities. It was partially the threat of having another Spanish government adjacent to Nueva España that had spurred Viceroy Mendoza into authorizing the Coronado expedition and sending Fray Marcos de Niza on his way, although the viceroy assured de Soto the paths of the two expeditions would not cross.[45]

Preliminary to his landing in La Florida, de Soto dispatched Juan de Añasco and two ships to reconnoiter the west Florida coast for a landing spot. Añasco, who sailed in the winter of 1538-39, not only found a secure and inhabited harbor but also returned to the Havana debarkation point with four Indians who might serve as interpreters. By May 18, 1539, when de Soto's expedition set sail, these La Florida natives had already acquired a working knowledge of Spanish.[46]

The expedition that reached La Florida on May 25, 1539, some two and a half months after Fray Marcos de Niza had begun his northward walk from Culiacán, was no small one. There were 237 horses and 513 soldiers in addition to nearly two hundred sailors and servants and a few women, all loaded into five ships, two caravels, and a pair of brigantines. De Soto's flagship was the *San Cristóbal;* that of the captain destined for eventual fame as the leader of survivors, Luis de Moscoso de Alvarado, was *La Concepción.*[47]

As with sites of earlier landings, so is the precise location of de Soto's landing in dispute. "[A]ll we can really say," writes archeologist Jeffrey Brain,

This romantic depiction of de Soto's landing at Tampa Bay in 1539 belies the atrocious conduct and legacy of his entrada. (From Ballou's Pictorial Drawing Room Companion, 1855, courtesy Florida Museum of Natural History, Gainesville.)

> is that De Soto probably landed in the Central Gulf Coast region among peoples of the late prehistoric-protohistoric Safety Harbor culture. But . . . ultimately it will be possible to confirm the general venue of landing, if not the exact point of debarkation. It is important to do so because much of what has been written about the southern Timucua and Calusa has been predicated on De Soto's landing in one location rather than in another.[48]

Brain and other investigators leave unresolved the question of the linguistic and cultural affinity of peoples of the archeologically labeled Safety Harbor culture, a group also known as Tocobaga Indians, whom de Soto and Narváez first encountered. Ethnohistorian Henry Dobyns, however, identifies them as a Timucuan chiefdom.[49]

The Central Gulf Coast region of western peninsular Florida where de Soto landed may well have been at or very near the site of the unit of our National Park System

Spanish rapiers like this one made in Toledo, Spain, in 1604, were used by common soldiers throughout Spain's possessions in the Americas into the early eighteenth century. (George H. H. Huey from the Enrique E. Guerra collection.)

created to recall that fateful event, De Soto National Memorial. With its visitor center, monument, informational signs, and Camp Ucita demonstration area, named for the Indian village where de Soto's men made their first encampment and where each December through April members of the park staff provide living history demonstrations, the memorial is an excellent place to visit to deepen one's understanding of the saga of Spain in the United States.

Where de Soto made his landing, "a treasure trove in human shape was acquired," a Spaniard named Juan Ortiz. Ortiz had arrived in La Florida in 1528 as a young man of eighteen on the crew of a ship looking for members of the ill-fated Narváez expedition. He and three other sailors went ashore, only to be captured by natives. Their ship left, and three of the sailors were killed. Ortiz was "saved by the intercession of the cacique's [headman's] wife and no fewer than three daughters, a whole family of Pocahontases. He joined de Soto and proved most valuable as interpreter, but did not survive the long journey."[50] That journey lasted until September 10, 1543, when 311 survivors, after having sailed down the Mississippi and across the Gulf of Mexico in makeshift brigantines constructed at the mouth of the Arkansas River, arrived at the Río Pánuco (Tampico) in Nueva España. De Soto had died on May 21, 1542, and Luis Moscoso had taken his place as commander of the expedition. He led the survivors to eventual safety.[51]

The locations of routes taken by members of the de Soto expedition during their lengthy odyssey have long been a matter of speculation and academic debate. It is possible, however, that the village of Ichisi or Ochisi, which is described in accounts of the journey, is the protohistoric-period archeological site now known as the Lamar Mounds and Village, a 45-acre detached unit of Ocmulgee National Monument near Macon, Georgia. It was here or near here that the expedition crossed the Ocmulgee River.[52]

The de Soto expedition is perhaps most remembered in United States history as the first by Europeans to discover the Mississippi River and to sail on its waters. But the men of this entrada were also the first Europeans to visit vast tracts of land in Florida, central Georgia, western South Carolina, eastern Tennessee, central Alabama, and great parts of Mississippi, Arkansas, Louisiana, and eastern Texas—places their four-year journey had taken them. Even so, it would have to be characterized as a disaster by almost any measure. Not only did de Soto fail to find the riches he was seeking, but his ruthless ways had also earned him the well-deserved enmity of the native populations, and he had met armed resistance throughout the region.

Morison writes,

> Although one cannot but admire De Soto's organizing ability, stubborn pride and ruthless courage which more than once saved his force from annihilation, one must admit that his Greater Florida expedition was wasted effort. The amount of

gold that he extorted was not enough to tempt a second expedition. . . . De Soto's expedition led to no colonizing effort, much less to a viceroyalty like those of Mexico and Peru. Final honors go to the red men who fought valiantly for their hearths and homes against these cruel invaders. They at least gained a respite of centuries before white men seized their lands and removed the survivors to Oklahoma.[53]

But the pain inflicted on the "red men" was greater than Morison surmised. In 1559-61, some of the Native American settlements that had been visited by de Soto in Alabama, Georgia, and Tennessee were revisited by members of the Tristán de Luna expedition. Similarly, Juan Pardo revisited villages in South Carolina and Tennessee in 1566—68 that de Soto had seen two decades earlier. Comparing accounts of these entradas with de Soto's, it becomes tragically clear that the numbers of Indians had become drastically lowered in the intervening years. While a small part of this reduction might be attributed to de Soto's military actions, it appears far more likely to have been caused by de Soto's having "blazed a trail through the immune systems of thousands of people during their four-year reconnaissance."[54] The paramount destroyers were European pathogens against which native American populations had not developed immunities, diseases such as smallpox, measles, typhus, and typhoid.[55]

As one scholar has written, "There can be no question of the significance of the social, demographic, ecological, and ideological consequences of the de Soto entrada. It quite literally marked the end of native hegemony in the Southeast and the beginning of European dominance, for better or worse."[56]

As a footnote, the de Soto expedition has been credited with the introduction of the "agile, long-snouted razorback hog of the South" into the region, where it has since flourished.[57]

FRANCISCO VÁSQUEZ DE CORONADO

On February 22, 1540, about a month before de Soto left his winter encampment at the site of modern Tallahassee, Florida, Francisco Vásquez de Coronado mustered his huge expeditionary force gathered in Compostela, Nueva España. It was then the capital of Nueva Galicia; today it is a town in the southernmost part of the state of Nayarit near the Pacific Ocean and the northern border of Jalisco.

Assembled at this remarkable rendezvous were 225 mounted troops and 62 foot soldiers; three women, two who were wives and one who became the expedition's nurse; about 700 Indian "allies," who were servants, wranglers, and herdsmen responsible for the sheep and cattle intended as a walking commissary; and five Franciscan friars, including the expedition's principal guide, Marcos de Niza. At least 48 additional persons joined the retinue after it headed north from Compostela, a

Vásquez de Coronado searched in vain for fabled wealth in the North American interior, 1540-42. The expedition traveled as far as the plains of Kansas before turning back. (Portrait by Bill Ahrendt courtesy W. E. Hinkley.)

25

number that does not include the crews of three ships commanded by Hernando de Alarcón who sailed up the Sea of Cortez (Gulf of California) believing he was going to help supply the overland expedition.[58] The viceroy himself was in Compostela to see them off. Included in the party after he caught up with it in southern Sinaloa was the *alcalde mayor* (district governor) of Compostela, Melchior Díaz. Díaz knew the territory and served as guide immediately north of Culiacán.

Besides the Spaniards and Indians, there were at least two blacks, five Portuguese enlistees, two Italians, a Frenchman, a Scotsman, and a German bugler. There were also more than a thousand horses (only two of them mares) and one mule to carry people, provisions, munitions, arms, and baggage. Coronado himself was adorned in "gilded suit and helmet with crested plume." He also had twenty-three horses and four suits of horse armor. Coats and breeches of mail, buckskin jackets, chin-pieces, and arms such as arquebuses, crossbows, two-handed swords, ordinary swords, cuirasses, and lances were common among the men. So were Native American weapons, probably such items as bows and arrows, clubs, spears, and slings. Coronado's army presented a colorful, even formidable, sight.[59]

About three months after they had set out from Compostela, in late May 1540, Coronado led a part of his expedition into what today is southern Arizona. Majority opinion among both scholars and popularizers brings the expedition, like that of Marcos de Niza the preceding year, into the United States along the San Pedro River near the tiny settlement of Palominos at the base of the eastern flank of the Huachuca Mountains. Overlooking the region from the southeastern side of the mountains is Coronado National Memorial. Its fine visitor center with museum displays and good hiking trails allow visitors to enjoy spectacular views toward the south, east, and west overlooking for many, many miles what in 1540 was northern Nueva España. Few modern developments mar the scene, one that Coronado himself might recognize were he still alive.

This advance army continued northward in search of the fabled cities of Cíbola. In July they arrived at the Zuni Indian villages in what today is central eastern New Mexico. The Zuni towns, devoid of gold, were Cíbola, but not the Cíbola the conquistadors had been hoping for. Coronado dispatched Captain Pedro de Tovar at the head of a scouting party of some twenty men to the northwest in search of another rumored seven cities, those of the province of Tusayán. These turned out to be the whole group of Hopi Indian towns and as devoid of gold as Zuni. While here, Tovar heard of a great river to the west, possibly the very river the viceroy had sent Hernando de Alarcón to explore. The news was enough to cause Coronado to dispatch yet another exploring party from Cíbola to check out the possibilities. This time, on August 25, 1540, twenty-five horsemen led by a young nobleman, don García López de Cárdenas, went searching for the substance of a rumor. Cárdenas rode to Tusayán where he obtained Hopi guides who then took him to the south rim

Toroweap Point, Grand Canyon National Park, Arizona. The Grand Canyon and Colorado River, first seen by members of the Vásquez de Coronado expedition in 1540, proved to be an impassable barrier to Spanish exploration. (George H. H. Huey.)

26

of the Grand Canyon inside of today's Grand Canyon National Park, probably in the vicinity of Grandview Point. In October or November 1540 Cárdenas and his fellow scouts became the first Europeans to view the mightiest chasm in today's United States. Pedro de Castañeda, who became the chief chronicler of the Coronado expedition, and historian Herbert Bolton tell what happened:

"They spent three days trying to find a way down to the river, which from above appeared to be only a fathom wide, although, according to what the Indians said, it must be a half a league across." They apparently meant it was that far from precipice to precipice. "The descent was found to be impossible, for at the end of these three days Captain Melgosa, with Juan Galeras and another companion, they being the lightest and most agile, undertook to clamber down at a place that appeared to them the least difficult. They kept descending in sight of the men left above until they were lost to view. . . . At four o'clock on the afternoon they returned, without having been able to reach the bottom because of the great obstacles they encountered, for what from above had appeared to be easy, proved to be, on the contrary, rough and difficult. They said they had been only a third of the way down, but from the place they reached, the river looked very large; indeed, judging from what they saw, it must be as wide as the Indians had said.

The men who remained above estimated that some small rocks jutting out from the wall of the canyon must be about as high as a man; but those who went down swore that when they reached them they were found to be taller than the highest tower of Seville." Now, to observers standing on the brink of the "divine abyss," a group of modern houses less than half way down the Bright Angel Trail appear to be about the size of beehives.[60]

The Grand Canyon became a barrier to travel and exploration for the remainder of Spain's time in the United States, and no Spanish settlements, including missions, were ever established on its north side. The Coronado expedition, however, left its mark inside Grand Canyon National Park. The park's El Tovar Hotel in Grand Canyon Village; Cárdenas Butte on the south rim near the park's eastern boundary; and the south rim's prehistoric Tusayán ruins and museum are small reminders of the Coronado venture.

Having gone with Coronado all the way to the Zuni settlements, Melchior Díaz, soon after their arrival there in July 1540, was sent by Coronado back to the south. He was to order Captain Tristán de Luna y Arellano to move the main force, still waiting in the Sonora River Valley, to Cíbola. He was further instructed to organize a small group of soldiers into a supply depot that could serve the expedition in the north. Finally, he was to travel to the west over unexplored desert to find the supply ships of Hernando de Alarcón, which had sailed northward up the Mar Vermejo, today's Sea of Cortez, or Gulf of California.[61]

Díaz followed Coronado's instructions. He left to look for Alarcón in December

27

1540. His route to the lower Colorado River near its mouth at the head of the Gulf of California cannot be given with certainty. Majority opinion, however, takes him to the oasis settlement of Sonoyta in what today is northwestern Sonora on the border with the United States and immediately opposite Lukeville, Arizona. He may then have gone westward across the famed Camino del Diablo, the "Devil's Highway." If so, he doubtless paused at the permanent springs at Quitobaquito, a reliable desert watering place within present-day Organ Pipe Cactus National Monument.

From here he went to the Colorado, where he found a message left two months earlier by the since-departed Alarcón. Alarcón had reached the upper gulf with his three ships by August 26, precisely the time Coronado had sent Cárdenas on a westward errand to find the Colorado River. It was still August 26 when he managed to sail his three ships to anchorage at the mouth of the river he named Buena Guía, "Unfailing Guide," but which is now known as the Colorado. Taking two launches, he continued upstream; how far is uncertain. He seems, though, to have reached the junction of the Gila and Colorado rivers. He and some of his men also stepped ashore on the west side of the Colorado, thereby becoming the first Europeans to set foot on the soil of today's California.

Unable to make contact with members of the Coronado expedition, he turned back in October, but not before leaving letters buried at the base of a tree next to the river on which he had carved

ALARCÓN CAME THIS FAR. THERE ARE LETTERS AT THE FOOT OF THIS TREE.

Díaz found both tree and letters, the latter reporting that California was a peninsula rather than an island and giving details of Alarcón's adventures on the lower Colorado.

Díaz and his men became the second group of Spaniards to set foot in California when they crossed the Colorado to its west bank. While they were west of the river, possibly in northern Baja California, Díaz threw his lance at a dog that was harassing the sheep his little party had brought with them as an assured source of meat. The lance stuck diagonally in the ground, and, unable to turn his horse, Díaz was pierced in the groin by the blunt end of the handle. He remained alive, and his soldiers carried him southeastward on a litter for twenty days—trying at least to get him to a priest—before he died somewhere in the Sonoran Desert in January 1541. The likelihood is again strong that they passed along the southern reaches of Organ Pipe Cactus National Monument, with Díaz but a few days from death.[62]

Late in August 1540, while Alarcón was vainly trying to make contact with the land expedition and Cárdenas was on his way to the Grand Canyon, Coronado dispatched another of his trusted lieutenants, twenty-three-year-old Hernando de

The 1540 overland route of Melchior Díaz to the lower Colorado River passed within site of the Ajo Mountains of today's Organ Pipe Cactus National Monument. (George H. H. Huey.)

28

Alvarado, on a scouting expedition to visit Indian villages east of Zuni. Two Towa-speaking natives, having heard of Coronado's presence at Zuni, had walked there some three hundred miles from their village of Cicuye. Their pueblo, also known as Pecos, was one of the largest in Nuevo México in 1540. Its ruins are today preserved as Pecos National Historical Park.

The two Puebloan emissaries, nicknamed Cacique (Governor) and Bigotes (Whiskers) by the Spaniards, led Alvarado and his reconnaissance party east from Zuni to Ácoma Pueblo, possibly pausing along the way to water men and horses at the natural water catchment beneath Inscription Rock in the heart of the twentieth-century El Morro National Monument. If so, they resisted the temptation to do as Native Americans had done before and as Native Americans, Spaniards, Mexicans, and Anglo Americans have done since: to engrave pictures, names, and initials on the face of the sandstone cliff above and near the pool.

From Ácoma, Alvarado, his men, and Indian guides continued eastward to the valley of the Río Grande. By October they had reached the northern settlement of Taos Pueblo. Soon afterward, Alvarado retraced his steps to the south before turning northeastward on a route that took him through the Galisteo Valley and over Glorieta Pass to Pecos Pueblo, the place known in Spanish documents as Cicuye. He and his men were the first Europeans ever to visit this great settlement, one whose ruins and museum/visitor center can now be richly experienced at Pecos National Historical Park.[63]

Pecos had been occupied for at least 140 years by the time Alvarado reached it. Monumental construction had begun nearly a century earlier, about 1450, its people building a defensible single-unit, multistoried apartment building in the shape of a large rectangle around a central plaza. In 1540 the two thousand inhabitants lived in what was the easternmost of the pueblo city-states. Their community lay at the gateway to the Great Plains, and Plains Indians were in regular trading relationships with the Pecos puebloans. So were there slaves from the plains in the pueblo.

The fall 1540 reception given these foreigners by the people of Pecos and the actions of the strangers in response are described by historian John Kessel:

> They all came out to gawk and to receive the Spaniards. "With drums and flageolets similar to fifes, of which they have many," they escorted their visitors into the pueblo. The mood was one of guarded festivity. As an offering, the Indians laid before Alvarado and his men quantities of native dry goods—cotton cloth, feather robes, and animal skins. As intently as any fortune seeker, Fray [Juan de] Padilla studied these natives for just one ornament of gold, for some indication of trade with the rich Seven Cities he sought so passionately.
>
> But they wore none. Their beads and pendants were of turquoise, shell, and non-precious stones. They prized eagle claws and grizzly bear teeth. Flageolets, whistles, and rasps they fashioned from bone, and singles from shell. . . .

Remnants of the Tiwa pueblo at Pecos National Historical Park, New Mexico. (George H. H. Huey.)

29

At some point during the festivities, Alvarado was obliged to explain to assembled Cicuye what it meant to be vassals of the Spanish crown. Almost certainly he had the *requerimiento* read to them. . . . This remarkable manifesto, which had accompanied all Spanish conquerors in America since 1514, related how God the creator and lord of mankind had delegated His authority on earth to the Pope, "as if to say Admirable Great Father and Governor of men," and the Pope in turn had donated the Americas to Their Catholic Majesties, the kings of Spain. Therefore, Cicuye must acknowledge the sovereignty of "the Church as the ruler and superior of the whole world," the Pope, and in his name, Charles, king of Spain. They must also consent to have the Holy Catholic Faith preached to them. They would not be compelled to turn Christian unless they themselves, "when informed of the truth, should wish to be converted." If they did, there would be privileges, exemptions, and other benefits.

But should they refuse, the requerimiento continued, "we shall forcefully enter your country and shall make war against you in all ways and manners that we can, and shall subject you to the yoke and obedience of the Church and of their highnesses." Their wives and children would be sold into slavery, their goods confiscated, and their disobedience punished with all the damage the Spaniards could inflict. "And we protest that the deaths and losses which shall accrue from this are your fault, and not that of your highnesses, or ours, or of these soldiers who come with us."

If they understood any of it, which is unlikely, the people of Cicuye did not object, at least not initially.[64]

Coronado left Zuni in November to spend winter among the Southern Tiwa Indians on the Río Grande. He was followed there in December by Tristán de Luna y Arellano who had managed to bring the main force of the army there from the Sonora River Valley in spite of winter snow storms in the mountains of central Arizona and western New Mexico. Both may have passed by the site of El Morro in reaching the Río Grande.

The winter of 1540-41 is one likely never to be forgotten in the oral traditions of Puebloan Indians. Resisting demands put upon them by the Spaniards for food and clothing, as well as reacting to individual outrages perpetrated upon them by Spanish soldiers, the Puebloans rebelled in what has been called the Tiguex War. Those in the Río Grande settlements of Arenal and Moho openly challenged the invaders to fight. With horses and superior weapons on their side, the Spaniards made an example of the villages and their inhabitants, one sure to strike terror into the hearts of natives of other communities.

At Arenal the pueblo walls were breached with the aid of battering rams and the natives were smoked out by suffocating smudge fires ignited on the ground floors of the multistoried structures. Those who emerged were either cut down with swords or taken captive and tied to stakes where they were burned alive. At Moho the Spaniards laid siege to the village, eventually killing many of its inhabitants and taking the rest as slaves.[65]

In late April or early May 1541 Coronado led his entire force through Pecos en route to the Great Plains. Still searching for gold, this time for "Quivira" rather than for "Cíbola," they journeyed through northeastern Texas, the Oklahoma Panhandle, and into central Kansas before they accepted defeat at the hands of reality. Coronado's gold—like that of conquistadors in La Florida before him—had been shadow rather than substance. By October he and his men were back in the Río Grande, once more having passed through Pecos.

"The army that had set out gaily two years before to gain wealth and renown," writes geographer Sauer, "dragged back to Mexico in the fall of 1542, destitute and dispirited. The viceroy, Coronado and his wife, and a lot of gentry had lost fortunes to find that the fables of northern riches were only fables."[66]

JUAN RODRÍGUEZ CABRILLO

Cabrillo's biographer, Harry Kelsey, argues he was Spanish-born.[67] Others, however, stubbornly cling to an older scholarly opinion, that his real name was João Rodrigues Cabrilho and that he had been born in Portugal.[68] Either way, he was sailing in the service of Spain when he left the port of Navidad on the west coast of Mexico and headed northward to the Pacific Ocean off the west coast of peninsular California. It was June 27, 1542, just three days after Coronado, since returned to Nueva España, had set out from Culiacán headed for Compostela and, ultimately, Mexico City, and some two months after the body of the deceased de Soto had been secretly sunk by his men in the Mississippi River to prevent Native Americans from finding it.

Cabrillo's journey, like that of Coronado, was commissioned by Viceroy Mendoza. Word had reached the viceroy that the Portuguese may have found an open-water passage in the north linking Atlantic and Pacific, the fabled Straits of Anian. A sea voyage of exploration, which might incidentally bring better news of the elusive Quivira, appeared to be in order.

Explorer Cabrillo's flagship was the sizable *San Salvador*. Another ship was the smaller brigantine or frigate *Victoria*. The name of a third vessel is unknown. His flag pilot was an Italian Levantine named Bartolomé Ferrer (or Ferrelo). In early July, Cabrillo and his two ships rounded the southern tip of Baja California and headed northward up the west coast. On September 27, 1542, he crossed the imaginary line now separating Mexico's territorial waters from those of the United States and sailed into a "closed and very good harbor" he named San Miguel. We now know it as San Diego Bay. Cabrillo stepped ashore on September 28 and interacted peaceably with the Yuman-speaking Ipai or Tipai (formerly known as the Kamia and Diegueño, and whose modern descendants

Viceroy Antonio de Mendoza commissioned both Vásquez de Coronado's 1540-42 expedition and Juan Rodríguez Cabrillo's 1542 voyage up the California coast. (From Manuel Rivera Cambas, Los gobernantes de México [Mexico, 1872-73]. Courtesy DeGolyer Library, Southern Methodist University, Dallas.)

31

Juan Rodríguez Cabrillo may have been the first Spanish explorer to see Santa Rosa Island, now part of Channel Islands National Park, when he sailed along the California coast in 1542. (Larry Ulrich.)

call themselves the Kumeyaay). These "comely and large" people, who wore animal skins, indicated to Cabrillo by making signs they were aware of other bearded men whose weapons were swords and crossbows, no doubt a sign of lingering knowledge of the Coronado expedition as represented by Alarcón and Díaz nearly two years earlier.

Because his was the first European contact with coastal California, he and the moment have been commemorated in Cabrillo National Monument, situated adjacent to Point Loma guarding the entrance to San Diego Bay from a western arm reaching down from the north. The visitor center has exhibits and literature concerning Cabrillo's expedition, and programs are offered daily in the auditorium. A bayside trail leads those who care to walk on a tour through the region's natural setting. One can also visit tidepools and, in late December through February, the whale overlook for sightings of gray whales during their annual migration to Scammon's Lagoon in Baja California.

After waiting out a storm, on October 3 the men of Cabrillo's three ships continued northward, in the process becoming the first Europeans known to have seen the islands of Santa Catalina and San Clemente and the first to sail into the Bahía de los Humos, the "Bay of Smoky Haze," today's Santa Monica Bay next to Los Angeles. (A few things, like the haze, have not changed in more than four and a half centuries.) Visitors to the adjacent Santa Monica Mountains National Recreation Area can avail themselves of an overlook of the coastline along which the *San Salvador* and *Victoria* sailed. There is even a possibility that Cabrillo went ashore at Mugu Lagoon in early October. If so, he was within the boundaries of the recreation area.

From October 9 to early November the doughty explorers visited the native Chumash in their settlements along the coast from Point Mugu to Point Concepción at the north end of the Santa Barbara Channel. Spaniards and natives got along well, some of the Chumash being so friendly as voluntarily to spend the night on board the Spanish ships. During their northward journey, from October 19 to 25, they visited some of what they called the islands of San Lucas, today's Channel Islands and the site of Channel Islands National Park. One of these they named Isla de Posesión. While they were on Posesión Cabrillo fell and broke his arm near the shoulder, a painful calamity. Notwithstanding, Cabrillo continued his northward voyage, sailing past the Golden Gate without either seeing it or realizing what a splendid bay lay behind it. He anchored instead on November 16 in another bay he called Los Pinos, "The Pines," and which some historians have tentatively identified as what has since been named Drake's Bay. Others have suggested the more southerly Monterey Bay. If the former identification is correct, Cabrillo preceded Englishman Sir Francis Drake to the same anchorage by nearly thirty-seven years. It was not until June 17, 1579, that the English buccaneer put into the bay harbor, one whose shoreline, like that of the adjacent Pacific Ocean shore to the west, is protected today as Point Reyes National Seashore. Thanks to the National Park Service, the vistas from the bay remain today much as they were in 1542 and again in 1579.

33

A monument commemorating Juan Rodriguez Cabrillo's 1542 expedition stands on the bluff overlooking Cuyler Harbor on San Miguel Island, part of Channel Islands National Park. Cabrillo died on the return voyage and is believed to be buried on one of the islands in the chain. (Ralph Clevenger.)

Because the sea was high, Cabrillo did not go ashore at Los Pinos. Even so, he took care to claim the bay and adjacent lands for Spain. Drake, who later claimed what may have been the same lands for England, spent five weeks here. He visited with—and provided accounts of—the resident Coast Miwok peoples in the process.

Cabrillo's ships continued northward up the coast, but stormy weather soon turned them back. How far north they got is a matter of pure conjecture. Going south, they once again missed the Golden Gate. On November 23 they came to winter on the Channel Island they had earlier named Isla de Posesión, probably San Miguel Island. San Miguel is the northernmost of five major islands within the confines of the park, and in 1937 a stone-carved monument with a pedestal topped by a cross was set in place here to commemorate Cabrillo's northern sea voyage. It stands on a hill overlooking Cuyler Harbor, where the Spanish ships are believed to have anchored.

On January 3, 1542, Cabrillo died from the effects of the fall he had taken in October. Before he died, he appointed Bartolomé Ferrer as his successor as commander of the expedition, ordering him to complete the exploration of the Alta California coastline. Ferrer carried out Cabrillo's command and set out again for the north. Once more, on February 23, 1543, he reached Cabo Pinos and what may be today's Point Reyes.

By the end of the month he and his fellow sailors reached their northernmost point, a place possibly as far north as Cape Mendocino in Northern California. A frightening storm turned them around, and by March 5 they were back on Posesión, by then renamed Isla Juan Rodríguez for their departed captain. From there they took the sea journey which led them back to San Diego, where they spent March 11-15 before sailing to the port of Navidad on the west coast of Nueva España, from which their journey had begun. They sailed into port on April 14, 1543.[69]

As with all such sixteenth-century accounts of Spanish entradas, there is disagreement among the experts concerning sea routes, landfalls, and areas of inland exploration. The Cabrillo voyage is no exception, and even the island on which he died—although certainly within Channel Islands National Park—remains in dispute. His grave has never been located nor has any archeological evidence of the few weeks' stay of the sailors on Isla de Posesión. What has been found, however, is an enigmatic 13-inch-long slab of sandstone that has incised on one of its flat surfaces the monogrammed initials JR (possibly, even, JRC), a small cross, and a headless stick figure of a human being. The stone was picked up in 1901 by archeologist Philip Mills Jones on a surface-collecting trip on Santa Rosa Island, one of the Channel Islands. Archeologist Robert Heizer, who reexamined the evidence in 1972, believed there was a good possibility that the stone, bearing his initials, had been the grave marker of Juan Rodríguez Cabrillo. If so, the likelihood is that the expedition's Posesión was Santa Rosa Island rather than San Miguel Island where the Cabrillo monument is located. As matters stand, the secret of Cabrillo's final resting place may never be known.[70]

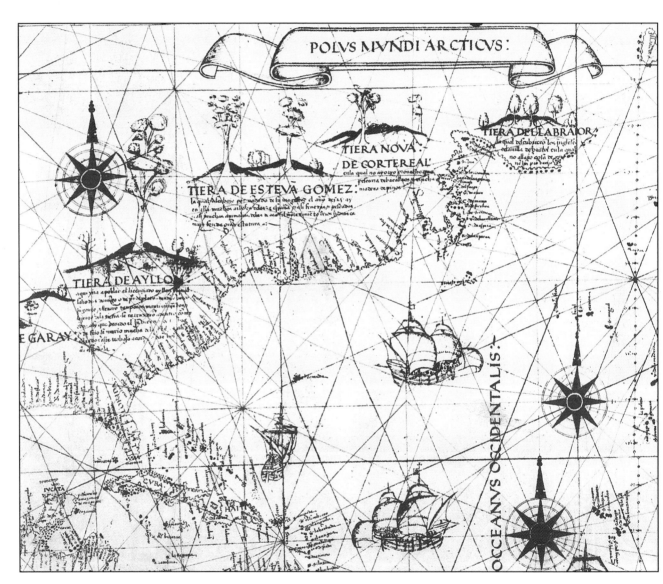

Diego Ribero's manuscript map of the world, 1529, contains both accurate and speculative information about the Caribbean and North American mainland. (Courtesy Newberry Library, Chicago.)

By the middle of the 1500s the period of initial Spanish exploration and efforts at conquest of lands north of Hispaniola and Nueva España had drawn to a close. There remained vast areas of *tierra incógnita*, unknown lands, in the north, but the crude outlines, at least, had been delineated both on maps and in the experience of navigators and would-be conquerors of the inland. By then it had also become painfully clear to the Spaniards that the lands they coveted were already inhabited by people who were loath to relinquish them, as well as themselves, to control by the Spanish crown.

Beginning in the mid-sixteenth century, the Spanish program for the north, if it can be called that, began gradually to shift away from one of naked military conquest to one of attempted assimilation by religious persuasion and to colonization by immigrant men, women, and children who were Spaniards, *criollos* (Spaniards born in America), *mestizos* (people of Spanish and Indian descent), Christianized Indians, blacks (both slaves and free), mulattos, and Spanish subjects of other racial mixtures.

A retablo, ca. 1795-1820, from Pecos National Historical Park, New Mexico, depicting the Virgin Mary as Nuestra Señora de Guadalupe, the patroness of Mexico. (George H. H. Huey.)

The Spanish mission program was rooted in *patronato*, a legally regulated grant of the Roman Catholic church, in this case a grant to the crown of Spain. The principles of *patronato real*, or royal patronage, were outlined in 1508 in a bull issued by Pope Julian II. Basically, the notion was that the crown would oversee the spread of Christianity and maintenance of the Roman Catholic church, paying for the enterprise from its royal coffers. In return, the church would support the crown and allow royal intervention in ecclesiastical affairs.

Patronato real was the crown's license to exercise control over missionaries in viceregal Nueva España. Missionaries, preferably Spaniards, coming to Spanish America had to sail from Spanish ports with what amounted to Spanish passports. The king was de facto head of the church in America, and missionaries were essentially a branch of the civil service. "These missionaries," wrote historian Herbert Bolton, "became a veritable corps of Indian agents, serving both Church and State. . . . [T]he rulers of Spain . . . made use of the religious and humanitarian zeal of the missionaries, choosing them to be to the Indians not only preachers, but also teachers and disciplinarians."[1]

It was, in short, the job of the missionaries not only to make Roman Catholic Christians out of the Indians, but also to bring Indians to the vassalage of the crown, to make European-clothes-wearing, Spanish-speaking, surplus-food-producing, and tax-paying subjects out of them. Indians, under the direction of missionaries, were to become Spaniards.[2]

As for colonization, Lucas Vásquez de Ayllón had tried unsuccessfully in 1526-27, with the help of Dominican friars, to implant a five-hundred-person colony at San Miguel de Gualdape on the Atlantic Coast in La Florida. It was to be another three decades before a similar attempt would be made. In time, however, the Spanish toehold became a foothold until, before the end of the sixteenth century, the whole Spanish body was permanently ashore, affixed there through judicious use of both cross and sword.

FRAY LUIS CÁNCER DE BARBASTRO

The first Dominican friars arrived in the New World at Santo Domingo in 1510. The best known of all Dominicans in the Americas, Bartolomé de las Casas, had come to Hispaniola in 1502. He took his holy orders afterward and celebrated his first Mass in 1510.

Dominicans, having accompanied Ayllón's ill-fated colonists during their 1526-27 venture in the northern reaches of La Florida, had early experienced contact with natives on the northern mainland. In 1545 it was a Dominican friar, Luis Cáncer de Barbastro, who volunteered to go to La Florida to right the wrongs done there by "the four tyrants (Ponce de León, Ayllón, Narváez, and de Soto) who went to Florida and did no good service, but only evil." [3]

Father Cáncer had enjoyed notable success in proselytizing among the indigenes in Guatemala while working without military support. He believed he could succeed in La Florida where others had failed, although he was warned by de las Casas not to land where Spaniards had preceded him. In May 1549, whether intentionally or inadvertently, the Dominican's pilot, Juan de Arano, sailed to the shores of Tampa Bay where Narváez and de Soto had earlier earned the Tocobaga's enmity. There were no initial problems with the Indians, but Cáncer soon learned that of the four men who had been left at the initial landing site, the Dominican priest and a lay brother had been killed; the sailor had been enslaved; and the female Indian interpreter, Magdalena, had defected. As if anticipating martyrdom, Father Cáncer wrote his reports and got his affairs in order before wading toward the shore on June 26 to inform himself of the situation at first hand. The natives, whose hostility seemed apparent, clubbed him to death in a thicket of trees just on shore. The peaceful mission approach to assimilation was off to a bad start. [4]

SHIPWRECKED DOMINICANS

By the mid-sixteenth century the sea lanes tying the provinces of Nueva España to Havana and to the mother country had become well established and well used. A thriving trade had developed between viceroyalty and crown. Ships laden with the raw materials of the Americas, including gold and silver, made their regular way to Spanish ports even as ships from Spain brought finished products and more people to her Western Hemisphere possessions. Although most of these ships made their voyages unmolested, there was ever-present danger, not only from pirates and from ships of unfriendly countries, but also from the hurricanes and other storms that routinely savaged the shores surrounding the Gulf of Mexico and the lands of the eastern seaboard and Florida Keys.

In April 1554 four ships, the *Santa María de Yciar*, the *San Esteban*, the *Espíritu Santo*, and the flagship *San Andrés*, set out from Veracruz en route for Spain via Havana. In the holds were barrels of cochineal, the rich red dye extracted from tiny insects that nest on the green pads of prickly pear cacti. So were there gold, silver, and bales of cowhides.

Among the passengers and crew, some four hundred of them, were five Dominican friars. One, Father Juan Ferrer, is said to have prophesied before the ships left port that they would never reach their destination, that many people would die, and that there would be great suffering. And true enough, twenty days after it had set sail, the little fleet was struck by a hurricane just off the coast of Padre Island, Texas, at the southern end of Padre Island National Seashore.

All but the flagship, the *San Andrés*, went to the bottom in shallow water. A few persons on board the *San Esteban*, probably sailing in one of their ship's boats, managed to make their way to safety either in Pánuco or Veracruz. The others, perhaps as many as 250 people, became castaways on Padre Island. All of them, including the two eventual survivors, underwent almost unimaginable hardships.[5]

Although friendly at first, the island's resident Karankawas soon attacked those who were wrecked on their shores, indiscriminately killing men, women, and children. Fleeing in terror toward the south, those Spaniards who could, some of them shoeless, their feet burned by the hot sands, walked and ran nearly the length of Padre Island while leaving to their fate those who could not keep up. Francisco Vásquez, going it alone, doubled back to the site of the wrecks where he hid in the dunes and subsisted on food salvaged from the sunken ships—and thereby saved his life.[6] The others, poorly clothed and with little food, elected to continue the southerly march to Pánuco. Robert Weddle tells what happened then:

> Constantly stalked by Indians, they crossed the Río Grande (Río Bravo, as it is known in Mexico) on a raft of driftwood, losing their crossbows in the river. The natives on the other side, perceiving they were unarmed, pressed more closely, occasionally taking a captive whom they stripped of his clothing. Believing that clothing was the Indians' objective, the marchers cast off their garments and went naked.
>
> The women and children walked ahead to lessen their shame. Suffering severe thirst, this strange vanguard reached the Río de las Palmas (present-day Soto la Marina) ahead of the men and fell down to drink. The Indians attacked; when the men arrived, not a woman or a child remained alive.

39

At "the last big river before the Pánuco," the surviving men saw a canoe full of Indians coming toward them and attempted to hide in the tall grass, only to be attacked by swarms of vicious ants. Throwing themselves into the river to escape the insects, they were assaulted by the natives and many of them were killed. Fray Marcos de Mena, a [Dominican] lay brother, had seven arrow wounds and was left for dead in the river's shallows. His blood brother, Fray Juan de Mena, died a short distance from the stream, an arrow in his back. Fray Marcos roused himself, plucked the arrows from his body, and went after his companions. They carried him across the river, but he had no strength to continue. Believing that he had but a short time to live, they buried him in the sand with his face exposed to allow him to breathe. The warm sand soothed his pain. As he slept, strength came back into his body. Throwing off his covering of sand, he arose and crept through the darkness. After walking only a short distance, he came upon the bodies of the last of his companions.

Finally reaching the Pánuco River, Fray Marcos was taken in an Indian canoe to the village of Tampico. . . . After recuperating at the more populous village of Pánuco, he went on to Mexico.[7]

By the time Fray Marcos reached Tampico, those who had made their way back by boat from the sunken *San Esteban* had already alerted authorities concerning the calamity. By mid-June, the *alcalde mayor* of Pánuco had conducted salvage operations and had recovered gold and silver valued at some 32,000 pesos from the *San Esteban*, the largest and most visible of the three wrecks off Padre Island's shore. A second salvage operation was carried out between July 23 and September 12 by García de Escalante Alvarado and Ángel de Villafañe. They managed to locate less than half the gold and silver listed as having been on the ships. And because he had arrived at the site on July 22, the feast day of Mary Magdalene, Escalante contributed the name still on the maps, the Médanos de Magdalena, Magdalene's Dunes, on the adjacent Padre Island shore.[8]

TRISTÁN DE LUNA Y ARELLANO AND ÁNGEL DE VILLAFAÑE

One of many astounding aspects of the story of Spaniards in North America concerns the almost superhuman stamina of some of the dramatis personae. Names of key players that appear in Texas or in northwestern Nueva España appear later in settings as far away as Paraguay and Brazil, as in the case of Alvar Núñez Cabeza de Vaca, or as distant as La Florida, as in the case of Don Tristán de Luna y Arellano. And all of this took place in an age when the only means of travel were by foot, horse, or ship.

In 1557 La Florida, which with the death of de Soto had become a "vacant" province, became formally attached to Nueva España. That same year, Doctor Pedro de Santander, royal overseer at Veracruz, sent a proposal to the crown for the occupation of La Florida. It may have been his proposal that prompted newly enthroned Philip II in 1558 to launch a three-vessel exploring expedition under command of Guido de Lavazares to reconnoiter the region for a possible colony site. Lavazares set out in September and soon afterward arrived at a point just west of Mobile Bay, Alabama. From Mobile Bay he continued eastward to Choctawhatchee Bay, Florida, passing the length of today's Gulf Islands National Seashore in Mississippi and Florida en route. He turned back at Choctawhatchee Bay, which he named Ancón de Velasco and where he made a formal claim of possession. Foul weather had prevented his entering Pensacola Bay. He returned to Mexico in December.[9]

Lavazares's reconnaissance was followed immediately by yet another, this one conducted by a single ship captained by Juan de Rentería. Its purpose, like that of the Lavazares voyage, was to discover La Florida ports in advance of the proposed colonizing expedition. The journey, which seems to have taken place beginning in late 1558 or early in 1559, "discovered the port of Polonza [the name given to Pensacola Bay], the port of Filipina [Mobile Bay], the coast of Apalache, and the coast of Médanos [the Médanos de Magdalena of Padre Island] in the land of La Florida and the coast of Nueva España."[10]

The voyage, which moved in a counterclockwise direction around the Gulf of Mexico, took Rentería and his fellow sailors to the region of Gulf Islands National Seashore as well as to that of Padre Island National Seashore in Texas. Historian Weddle believes that this trip, rather than that of Lavazares, determined the site chosen for the Florida landing of the colonizing expedition.[11]

The reconnoitering done, it was time to act. Tristán de Luna y Arellano, who had once been an associate of Hernando de Soto, had also been a captain in Coronado's army in 1540-42. When Lope de Samaniego, who had been deputy commander of the Coronado expedition, was killed by Indians near Chiametla in 1540, don Tristán assumed his post. It was he who managed to bring the main army of the Coronado expedition from the Sonora River Valley over Arizona's mountains to the Zuni villages in the dead of winter.

De Luna, having successfully fought against rebellious Indians in Oaxaca after his experiences during the Coronado entrada, had been named governor of La Florida in November 1558, a month before Lavazares's return. The new viceroy of Nueva España, Luis de Velasco, placed de Luna in charge of the Florida-colonizing expedition. It consisted of some three hundred infantrymen, two hundred cavalrymen, a thousand civilians, two hundred and forty horses, and enough food, seeds, breeding stock, and tools, including weapons, to get the colony off to a good beginning. They were to land in northeastern La Florida and to march overland to the site of the proposed permanent colony of Santa Elena near the South Carolina coast.

Among the colonists were survivors of the de Soto expedition who had gotten back to Nueva España. So were there Tlaxcalan Indians from the plateau of Nueva España—men, women, and children who were expected to become the agricultural backbone of the colony. These Indians were Christians and free Spanish subjects, members of a tribe whose people had befriended Hernán Cortés in his struggles against the Aztecs nearly four decades earlier. There were also blacks, mulattos, mestizos, various artisans, and wives and families of soldiers.

The de Luna expedition, loaded onto eleven ships, set sail from San Juan de Ulúa on the east coast of Nueva España on June 11, 1559. In mid-July, the ships put into harbor at Mobile Bay. By mid-August, they had sailed to what they believed to be their proper landing place, Pensacola Bay. To get there, they sailed through the entrance lying between Santa Rosa Island and Perdido Key in Florida's Gulf Islands National Seashore. De Luna chose a townsite as his base of operations "on an eminence sloping toward the anchorage." It has yet to be located.[12]

De Luna dispatched one of his ships to Mexico to inform the viceroy that the colonists had arrived safely—although many of their horses had died—in La Florida. And in September, a hurricane destroyed seven of the remaining ten vessels still at anchor in Pensacola Bay, killing many sailors and colonists still on board and destroying most of the provisions. From this point forward, the colonization effort headed toward disaster. The Spaniards were unable to get enough food supplies from the natives' villages, the largest of which had earlier been decimated by the de Soto expedition, and relief supplies from two ships from Havana were too little and too late.[13]

Historian Charlton Tebeau summarizes what happened next:

A classic example of Spanish defensive architecture can be seen at El Castillo del Morro, San Juan National Historic Site, Puerto Rico. (Doris Brookes.)

> By February, 1560, a council called by de Luna decided to move inland to Nanicapana on the Alabama River, where the largest amount of Indian food had been found. . . . Nanicapana proved to be another disaster. Beset with ill health and dissension, and with his leadership seriously questioned, de Luna led the famished colonists back to Pensacola Bay, where he found not reinforcements but a royal order to occupy Santa Elena [on the South Carolina coast] at once. Accordingly, on August 10, 1560, the governor dispatched two frigates and a small bark with men to claim and occupy the site. They never reached their destination. Stripped and damaged in a storm, the small ships made their way to Mexico. The settlement at Santa Elena had to await new pressures to occupy that coast. Travelers from Pensacola went to Cuba and to Mexico to complain of de Luna's leadership. By September of 1560 he had lost control of his unhappy charges, who refused to follow his order to go inland to the fabled [Indian town of] Coosa. In April 1561, Angel de Villafañe, who had been appointed on January 31 to replace de Luna, arrived at Pensacola. The frustrated and defeated de Luna returned to Spain by way of Havana to defend his regime in Florida.[14]

42

Villafañe could do little better. He left some fifty men at Pensacola while he personally led the evacuation of more than two hundred others to Cuba. Most of them deserted altogether. Villafañe sailed from Cuba with some sixty soldiers in addition to servants and sailors in another effort to found a settlement at Santa Elena. The four ships, failing to find a suitable colony site and being struck by a squall and by a hurricane, gave up the effort and returned to Havana. His final task in the enterprise was to rescue the people he had left behind at Pensacola. "Thus," writes Robert Weddle, "ended another attempt to occupy Florida without apparent benefit to God or king."[15]

And so were Pensacola and the lands within Gulf Islands National Seashore—silent witnesses to most of these events—to be forgotten by Europeans for the next 125 years.

THE SETTLEMENT THAT STAYED

The story of today's St. Augustine, Florida, the oldest continually inhabited non-Indian city in today's continental United States, cannot be told without reference to the sixteenth century French incursion into the Southeast. Neither can it be fully appreciated without visits to Florida's Canaveral National Seashore, Castillo de San Marcos National Monument, Fort Matanzas National Monument, Fort Caroline National Memorial and Timucuan Ecological and Historic Preserve, and Cumberland Island National Seashore.

Older than St. Augustine is San Juan, capital of the Commonwealth of Puerto Rico. The capital of Puerto Rico was moved here in 1521 from the now-abandoned site of Caparra, the first capital, established by Juan Ponce de León in 1508. Much of old San Juan is preserved and interpreted today by the National Park Service as the San Juan National Historic Site, including El Castillo de San Felipe del Morro, the fortified headlands on which construction began in 1598; El Castillo de San Cristóbal, an eighteenth-century fortress; and El Cañuelo or Fortín de San Juan de la Cruz, a small seventeenth-century fort.[16] It was Spanish San Agustín, however, that was to become the first successful European settlement in what eventually became the continental United States.[17]

As early as 1521 French corsairs had captured a Spanish treasure ship dispatched by Hernán Cortés from Nueva España to Spain. Throughout the sixteenth and seventeenth centuries there was little love lost between France and Spain, and they contended for power both in Europe and in America. A Jean Ribault-led French incursion into La Florida in 1562 hurried the Spaniards into authorizing another abortive effort, this one led by Ángel de Villafañe, to found a colony in South Carolina at Santa Elena. Ribault (or Ribaut), a staunch anti-Catholic Huguenot (a French Protestant), sailed from France with two small ships to Florida, where on May 1 they landed at the mouth of the St. Johns River near today's Jacksonville. They erected a stone marker at the site and claimed the surrounding land for France.

Castillo de San Marcos National Monument is a symbol of Spanish continuity and the permanence of St. Augustine, Florida, the oldest European settlement in the continental United States. (Joseph L. Fontenot.)

43

Ribault continued his reconnaissance by sailing north past the St. Marys River, the dividing line between modern Florida and Georgia, until he came to a harbor at Port Royal Sound on the South Carolina coast. Ribault liked what he saw. He raised another stone monument, claimed this land for France as well, and built a small fortified post, Charlesfort, at Parris Island. He asked for volunteers to hold the fort until he could return with supplies and reinforcements.

Unfortunately for the French colonists, when Ribault got back to France, a civil and religious war was underway, and Ribault was unable to keep his promise to return within six months. Those who had volunteered to stay behind, faced with starvation and uncertainty, quarreled among themselves and mutinied against their leader, killing him. Others went off to live with the Indians. And some managed to build a small boat in which they tried to sail to France, a disastrous effort in which survivors were reduced to cannibalism after they had eaten their shoes and leather jerkins. The few still alive were rescued by a passing English ship.[18]

Having learned of this French incursion into La Florida, in May 1564 the Spaniards sent twenty-five Spanish soldiers under Hernando de Manrique de Rojas to rid the country of Frenchmen. Manrique found one French survivor, a boy of sixteen, who led him to the abandoned Charlesfort. The Spanish commander burned everything not already burned in a previous fire and sailed off to Havana, taking the boy as a prisoner.

An even more serious French incursion culminated in a permanent Spanish settlement in North America. This time it consisted of a large Huguenot expedition led by René de Laudonnière, a lieutenant on Ribault's first expedition. Three ships with three hundred men and four women sailed from France in April 1564, reaching the La Florida coast two months later. They first looked at the area around St. Augustine before deciding that a site near the mouth of the St. Johns River would make a more suitable location for their fort.

The building of Fort Caroline, today recalled in a reconstruction at Fort Caroline National Memorial and Timucuan Ecological and Historic Preserve, began in July 1564. Relationships between the Frenchmen and Timucuans, friendly at first, deteriorated into warfare by 1565. The situation became so bad that Laudonnière was about to abandon the enterprise when Ribault arrived from France with seven large ships carrying five hundred soldiers and artisans and seventy women. He also carried orders putting him in command in place of Laudonnière.[19]

By the time Ribault arrived at Fort Caroline, King Philip II of Spain had already licensed Pedro Menéndez de Avilés as adelantado by giving him a conquest contract for the settlement of La Florida. Menéndez de Avilés joined his financial resources with those of the crown in putting together an armada to eliminate France's threat to Spanish hegemony in the region.[20]

Ribault landed at the beleaguered Fort Caroline on August 28, 1565. Within a week, on September 4, Menéndez' fleet—which had first made landfall at Cabo

Cañaveral at today's Canaveral National Seashore—found the Huguenot ships. The Spaniards pursued the French vessels without initial success, and Menéndez elected to solidify his position on land. Three of his ships had already chosen an anchorage at an inlet next to the mouths of the Matanzas and Tolomato rivers, and some of his troops with their ammunition were safe on shore. The adelantado sent his own men ashore where they dug ditches, made an earthen breastworks, fortified a large Timucuan dwelling, and built houses.[21]

A succession of nine wooden forts was constructed by the Spaniards at San Agustín between 1565 and 1675. Poor construction, the humid climate, fire, and in one case an attack in 1586 by the English pirate Sir Francis Drake spelled doom for each of them. Finally, in 1672 ground was broken for a stone fortress that today is preserved and interpreted by the National Park Service for the public as Castillo de San Marcos National Monument. In 1763 Florida was ceded by Spain to England, and Castillo de San Marcos became Fort St. Mark. In 1784 Florida again became a part of Spain and remained so until 1821, when it was turned over to the United States through a treaty of cession. Castillo de San Marcos became Fort Marion in 1825, but in 1942 Congress restored the original Spanish name to what in 1924 had become a national monument.[22]

The foothold at San Agustín established, Menéndez set out by land with five hundred soldiers to attack the French at Fort Caroline. On a September night in 1565 the Spaniards caught the French by surprise and in less than an hour Spanish flags flew above the post. Of some 240 French living at Fort Caroline—renamed San Mateo by the Spaniards—132 were killed. Fifty women and children and six drummers and a trumpeter were taken prisoner. Laudonnière and fifty or sixty others, including the artist Jacques Le Moyne, whose depictions were to become the earliest drawn or painted by Europeans in North America, escaped by fleeing into the woods. Later, they sailed away in two boats, one returning to France, the other swept to Swansea Bay in South Wales.[23]

Jean Ribault and a second group of Huguenots were not in the battle because they had earlier sailed southward in four large ships and eight small pinnaces in a vain effort to attack San Agustín. The French vessels were wrecked in a storm and the survivors found themselves in dire straits on the seacoast south of San Agustín. Natives reported their presence to the Spaniards. Menéndez and his troops at once headed by boat and on foot down the beach, where they encountered two large contingents ten days apart. Before it was over, most of the Frenchmen had surrendered to the adelantado. Menéndez, deeming them to be heretics, bound the prisoners' hands and, with the exception of twenty-six drummers, fifers, trumpeters, and Catholics, put them to the knife. The Spaniards massacred some 230 men, Jean Ribault among them.[24]

The struggle for control of La Florida took a bloody turn when Menéndez de Avilés massacred 230 shipwrecked French Huguenot "heretics" near the site of today's Fort Matanzas National Monument. (From Retratos de los españole un epítome de sus vidas *[Madrid, 1791], courtesy St. Augustine Historical Society, Florida.)*

45

This French coin, dated 1552, and other artifacts recovered from the Armstrong site at Canaveral National Seashore strongly suggest that this was the place to which twenty Frenchman fled from Spanish forces in 1565, evading capture for more than forty years. (Courtesy National Park Service Southwest Archeology Center, Tallahassee, Florida.)

The place a few miles south of San Agustín where the massacre occurred came to be known as Matanzas, a Spanish word for "slaughters" or "place of slaughters." A Spanish fort was eventually built here in 1740, and today the structure and immediately surrounding area are protected and interpreted as Fort Matanzas National Monument.[25]

Not all of Ribault's men surrendered to Menéndez. Some 170 of them managed to make their way southward once again to Cabo Cañaveral, where the French ship *Trinité* had been beached by the storm. Hearing that they were trying to use the ship's timbers and supplies to construct a fort and to build another boat, Menéndez went on the search one more time. He caught up with his adversaries in November 1565. He offered them safe passage to Europe as prisoners if they agreed to surrender—a promise he kept. Twenty of the Frenchmen, however, chose instead to flee. What became of the twenty is not known with certainty, but there is a report that in 1608 a boatload of elderly Frenchmen was taken aboard a Spanish ship off the Florida coast. Even more intriguing, however, is the fact that in the early 1970s relic hunters using metal detectors began turning up numerous artifacts at a site on the edge of Mosquito Lagoon in what since has become Canaveral National Seashore. Many of these objects, including Spanish and French coins dating from the mid-sixteenth century, as well as other archeological remains excavated as recently as 1990 at what has been named the Armstrong Site, suggest the possibility that this may be the place where the twenty Huguenots chose to take their chances among the Indians rather than with the Spaniards.[26]

The contest at Fort Caroline ended on a violent note of French revenge. In 1567, after Menéndez had effectively if brutally snuffed out for the time being the threat of further French claims to the region, Dominique de Gourgues, a Gascon nobleman and corsair, took matters into his own hands. In 1556 he had been captured by the Spaniards and had been condemned to row as a galley slave for the Spanish crown. Further angered by the insult Menéndez had inflicted on his nation by killing his countrymen, de Gourgues set sail for La Florida as a private avenger.

In April 1568 the small French fleet arrived in the vicinity of Fort San Mateo. After the Spaniards had captured Fort Caroline and renamed it, fearing Timucuan Indian hostilities, they had further strengthened their position by building a pair of blockhouses, San Gabriel and San Esteban—both within the boundaries of the Timucuan Ecological and Historic Preserve—as well as a watchtower on the banks of the St. Johns River well below the fort. De Gourgues was able quickly to renew former French alliances with leaders of local groups of Eastern Timucuans. He and his men and native allies easily overran both blockhouses and fort, burning them and hanging ten Spanish defenders in the process. His mission of vengeance accomplished, the Gascon nobleman returned to France.[27]

Fort San Mateo was rebuilt after its burning by de Gourgues, but its days were numbered. In 1569 the Spaniards established Fort San Pedro de Tacatacuru on

Cumberland Island off the south Georgia coast on what today is Cumberland Island National Seashore, and Fort San Mateo was phased out. It may, in fact, have been abandoned by the time Fort San Pedro was constructed. A large number of Spanish colonists had arrived at Santa Elena on Parris Island in late 1568, and the coastal waterway, rather than the peninsular channel, became the principal route of connection between Santa Elena and San Agustín. This lessened the importance of a place such as San Mateo, and the Spaniards gave it up.[28]

A final sixteenth-century La Florida battle between Frenchmen and Spaniards occurred in 1580 when Spaniards got wind of the landing of a French ship and forty men at the mouth of the St. Johns River. The Spanish attack ended in the loss of a Spanish ship, the death of eighteen Spaniards, and the demise of all forty Frenchmen, who very probably were there simply to trade with the natives and acquire wood and water.[29]

It would be the eighteenth century before Frenchman and Spaniard would clash once again near where Fort Caroline had once stood. By then few would recall that France had instigated Spain to found what was to be her, and Europe's, first lasting settlement in North America.

Map of La Florida, published by Abraham Ortelius in Theatrum Orbis Terrarum, *1570. (Courtesy University of Arizona Library Special Collections, Tucson.)*

THE MISSIONS OF LA FLORIDA

Both secular priests and Catholic missionaries of the regular clergy had accompanied Juan Ponce de León during his abortive 1521 effort to colonize La Florida. In doing so, they became— so far as is known—the first Catholic priests to set foot on the soil of today's mainland United States. Subsequent sixteenth-century Spanish expeditions to La Florida had missionaries with them as well, including seculars, Dominicans, and Franciscans. Not until 1565 and the arrival of Pedro de Menéndez in La Florida did Spanish efforts to convert La Florida's native population to Christianity and make Spanish subjects of them become sustained. The words of Menéndez to Philip II echoed those of conquistadores who had preceded him and presaged those of Spanish men of power who would follow him in North America:

Your Majesty may be assured that if I had a million [ducats] more or less, I would spend it all on this undertaking, because it is of such great service to God Our Lord, for the increase of our Holy Catholic Faith, and for the service of Your Majesty. And therefore, I have offered to Our Lord all that He may give me in this world, all that I may acquire and possess, in order to plant the Gospel in this land for the enlightenment of its natives; and in like manner I pledge myself to Your Majesty.[30]

By 1763, when Spaniards abandoned La Florida to the British under terms of the Treaty of Paris, all Timucuan-speaking peoples were virtually extinct and the Calusa nearly so. Death, largely induced by European diseases, had taken its terrible toll.[31]

Although Menéndez had brought both Franciscan and secular clergy with him to La Florida, as early as October 1565 he petitioned the Society of Jesus (Jesuits) in Spain to send missionaries to work among the native population. The petition was granted. But the adelantado was anxious to get started before their arrival, so he dispatched lay Spaniards whose credentials were simply their professions of religious zeal to administer missions out of military posts. By 1567 such posts extended from the north at Parris Island on the Atlantic all the way around the peninsula to the Gulf Coast. When the Jesuits arrived in La Florida beginning in September 1566, they found at least the rudiments of a mission system awaiting them.[32]

Jesuit efforts in La Florida were far from productive, unless crowns of martyrdom can be taken as measures of success. Before they abandoned their La Florida efforts in 1572 nine Jesuits—three priests, three novices, and three lay brothers—had been killed by Indians. The first of the nine Jesuits to fall at the hands of the Indians, Timucuans in this case, was Father Pedro Martínez. In 1566 he was clubbed to death on the shores of Tacatacuru, possibly today's Cumberland Island. Jesuits returned briefly to La Florida in 1743 when a pair of priest-explorers engaged in a short-lived attempt to work among natives in the Florida Keys.[33]

Nine Jesuit missionaries were martyred in Florida before the Order abandoned its efforts there in 1572. This engraving, from Societas Iesu Militans *by Mathias Tanner S. J. (Prague, 1675) depicts the murder of Father Segura and three companions. (Courtesy Bridwell Library Special Collections, Perkins School of Theology, Southern Methodist University, Dallas.)*

Foreshadowing events nearly two centuries later in the Sonoran Desert of the American Southwest, La Florida's Jesuits were succeeded in 1573 by members of the Order of Friars Minor (Franciscans). For more than two decades Franciscan efforts proceeded only tentatively. Prospects seemed to brighten in 1595 with the arrival of a dozen new missionaries, but a 1597 revolt of Guale Indians in Georgia resulted in the martyrdom of five Franciscan friars. It was 1606 before Spaniards regained the territory.

By the second half of the seventeenth century, Franciscan missions, at least thirty of them throughout La Florida, had spread as far westward as Pensacola. In the early eighteenth century, with the steady advance of the English in the Carolinas and Georgia and with the precipitous drop in numbers of Indians, missions fell into a steady decline until their disappearance in 1763 with the British takeover of Florida.[34]

Other than as archeological sites, there are no remaining physical reminders of Spain's missionary presence in the southeastern United States. And of the archeological sites, only those within the boundaries of Cumberland Island National Seashore and the Timucuan Ecological and Historic Preserve are under the jurisdiction of the National Park Service. Within the latter, on Fort George Island near Fort Caroline National Memorial, are the buried ruins of the 1587-founded Mission San Juan del Puerto, home much of the time for Fray Francisco Pareja from 1595 until his death sometime after 1626. Father Pareja became the authority on Timucuan and published at least four works on the language before he died, studies now heavily relied upon by modern linguists with an interest in this extinct tongue.[35]

Both secular and regular clergy carried out their duties at San Agustín throughout Spain's control of the region, a fact of which there are many reminders in the modern St. Augustine, Florida. The city's modern Cathedral of St. Augustine is the home of the United States' oldest Christian parish in North America. St. Augustine also boasts a replica of the chapel of the church founded in 1602 at Nombre de Dios, which houses the shrine of Nuestra Señora de la Leche.

The Spanish mission history of Cumberland Island, some 85 percent of which today is encompassed by Cumberland Island National Seashore, is a dramatic one. After Jesuit missionary Pedro Martínez was clubbed to death, possibly on Cumberland Island, in 1566, and after 1573 when the fort built on the island in 1569 appears to have been abandoned, Franciscans established the Mission of San Pedro. The job of converting the island's Timucuan population was begun in 1587 by Fray Baltasar López. In June 1588 a Spanish visitor reported that Father López already had many baptized Christians in his care.[36]

In 1592, the hundredth anniversary of Columbus's discovery of a New World, there were only three Franciscan priests and two lay brothers in the whole of La Florida. In 1588 England had sent half the Spanish Armada to the bottom of the sea and Spain's imperial power was in decline.[37]

In 1595 La Florida's missionary program got a boost with the arrival of a fresh group of Franciscans, including a new and energetic superior. Domingo Martínez de Avendaño, who had become governor of La Florida the preceding year, personally accompanied newly arrived friars to their mission stations. He delivered Fray Pedro Fernández de Chozas to the Timucuan village of Puturibato on Cumberland Island where the mission was christened San Pedro y San Pablo de Puturibato. And while the record is ambiguous, it appears that Baltasar López simultaneously continued to serve a separate community at Mission San Pedro de Mocamo.[38]

In 1597 the Guale Indians, whose territory lay immediately to the north of Cumberland Island, revolted against the Spaniards and martyred five Franciscans in the process. Before the rebellion died down Guales attacked the Spanish missionaries and their Timucuan allies on the island, but they were successfully repelled. When

49

the attack occurred fathers Pareja and Fernández de Chozas were on the island, the former filling in for López at Mocamo and the latter being at his regular post at Puturibato. Father López happened to be away on a trip toward the west. Shortly after the revolt, all three men were assigned to other stations to make up for the shortage of priests the Guale rebellion had brought about.[39]

In 1602 Father López returned to Cumberland Island, and at the beginning of 1603, Governor Gonzalo Méndez de Canzo embarked on a plan to rebuild the dilapidated church at San Pedro de Mocamo. He hoped that the mission would become a model for Timucuan and Guale Indians alike. San Pedro, home of the loyal Timucuan Christian cacique whom the Spaniards had christened Don Juan, provided a Spanish success story. As historian John Tate Lanning explains,

> the Indians of Cumberland Island observed the *Semana Santa* [Holy Week] as they do in Seville. . . . The inhabitants of all the villages in the vicarage of San Pedro, numbering one hundred and ninety-two Christian Indians, and those of Timucua converged on San Pedro during Christmas, Holy Week, saints' days, or principal fiestas, said Mass, heard a sermon, listened to the reading of official communications, and conducted their processions. Through their crude streets in . . . San Pedro during the Holy Week they carried their *cofradias de sangre*, images of Christ and the Virgin, and on Holy Thursday they gave themselves completely to religious celebration, spending the whole night in religious revelry.[40]

Governor Méndez de Canzo sent word to Father López to have the necessary building materials for the new church at San Pedro assembled in time for his arrival on Cumberland Island with skilled builders. But the friar gathered only enough logs and nails for the completion of two of the main walls, and matters were delayed while the governor sent for more nails in San Agustín and while his men went into the woods for more timber. Finally, however, the job was done. On March 10, 1603, the new building was dedicated with great ceremony. While there is no description of it, in 1608 La Florida's new Spanish governor, Pedro de Ybarra, said it was as large as the church at San Agustín and was valued at two thousand ducats.[41]

The seventeenth century marked the end of Spanish missionary activity on Cumberland Island. By 1674, when the island was visited by the Bishop of Santiago de Cuba, Gabriel Díaz Vara Calderón, both San Pedros had disappeared from the historical record and been replaced by a San Felipe de Athuluteca. The British were moving down from the north toward lands claimed by Spain, and in 1683 Englishmen temporarily took possession of the island. Although it later reverted to Spanish ownership before again becoming a part of Great Britain in the eighteenth century, the island's mission or missions were abandoned by 1699, as were all others north of the St. Marys River, by that time the unofficial boundary between La Florida and Georgia.[42]

EL NUEVO MÉXICO

Just as Spaniards were busy securing their hold in the Southeast, so were they looking to a region that one day would become the Southwest. Although the two-year-long expedition of Vásquez de Coronado in 1540-42 had yielded nothing in the way of riches for its members, the Spanish frontier pushed relentlessly northward until by the 1570s its boundaries had extended in Mexico beyond the rich silver mines discovered in 1548 at Zacatecas. The Spaniards' reach stretched beyond Nueva Galicia to a newly established province, Nueva Vizcaya. Francisco de Ibarra was appointed its governor in 1562, and the next year he founded the town of Durango as its capital. From here it was a short move into what today is southern Chihuahua and to the settling of Santa Bárbara, once an important mining town and commercial center on the headwaters of one of the tributaries of the Río Conchos.[43]

A captive Indian from the north was brought to Santa Bárbara in 1579. He regaled his captors with wonderful stories of his homeland, speaking of "very large settlements of Indians who had cotton and who made blankets for clothing, and who used maize, turkeys, beans, squash, and buffalo meat for food."[44] The Indian's words fell on the ears of Fray Agustín Rodríguez, a zealous Franciscan lay brother and native of Spain who lived in nearby San Bartolomé and who was anxious to carry the message of the Holy Gospel northward from Santa Bárbara. It was not long before he obtained the necessary viceregal permission to carry out his plan, taking with him additional friars and as many as twenty men as an escort. In short order he persuaded confreres Fray Francisco López and Fray Juan de Santa María to join in the mission, the former as superior. For an escort he recruited frontiersmen Captain Francisco Sánchez Chamuscado, Pedro de Bustamente, Hernán Gallegos, and six additional men. Nineteen Native American servants accompanied them as they set out from Santa Bárbara in the dust and heat of early June 1581. They had with them six hundred head of stock, ninety horses, provisions, and trade goods.[45]

With Fray Agustín as leader, the little party followed the Río Conchos to a village near its junction with the Río Grande, La Junta, and in the vicinity of today's Ojinaga, Chihuahua, and Presidio, Texas. En route and elsewhere they impressed the natives whom they met by firing their arquebuses, erecting crosses, and giving away cheap trade goods.[46]

The expedition turned northwestward and followed the Río Grande upstream past today's El Paso and the location of Chamizal National Memorial. From here it continued along the stream northward until August 21 when it arrived at an inhabited pueblo—probably one of Piro peoples—about thirty miles south of today's Socorro,

"Shaggy cow," bison illustration from the 1554 Historia *of Francisco López de Gómara. (Courtesy Museum of New Mexico, Santa Fe.)*

51

New Mexico. For the next five months the men continued to visit Pueblo Indians throughout this northern land. Reminded as they were by the Puebloans of the native lifestyles of Indians in the heartland of Nueva España, they referred to this land as "el nuevo México," a label destined to survive to the present.[47]

During their exploratory trips the Spaniards visited dozens of Pueblo communities. Among them was one they called Nueva Tlaxcala after the capital of the Tlaxcalan Indians of Mexico. It was described later by chronicler Gallegos as having had "five hundred houses of from two to six and even seven stories." Historians George Hammond, Agapito Rey, and John Kessell believe it was the "Cicuye" visited by Vásquez de Coronado four decades earlier. If so, it was the Towa Indian settlement known in more recent times as Pecos Pueblo, a great abandoned ruin now preserved and interpreted by the National Park Service within the confines of Pecos National Historical Park.[48]

Soon after the men visited Nueva Tlaxcala, they went their separate ways. Fray Juan de Santa María parted with two Indian servants to report the insubordination of their military escort—Chamuscado and the others having long since foregone the pretense of following Fray Rodríguez—and to bring back more Franciscan missionaries. Indians killed Fray Juan in September 1581 on the east side of the Manzano Mountains. The other two friars elected to remain with their Indian servants in Nuevo México to continue their efforts to bring the Puebloans to vassalage and God. Thus it was that the soldiers under Chamuscado's command returned to Santa Bárbara alone. A sickly Chamuscado, bled by his companions with a horseshoe nail in an effort to save him, died in camp within thirty leagues of their destination.[49]

The Conde de Coruña, then the viceroy of Nueva España, was interested in what Hernán Gallegos and the other survivors had to report about their expedition. And when Franciscan superiors learned that three of their number had been abandoned in these northern lands, it was agreed a relief party should be organized. Fray Bernardino Beltrán of Durango agreed to get "the authorization and permission of his superior" to accept an offer proffered by Antonio de Espejo to outfit the expedition. A wealthy cattle rancher and buyer, Espejo was then living in the Nueva Vizcaya frontier to avoid his sentence, a sizeable fine, as a convicted accomplice in a murder. As a lay officer of the Inquisition, he was looked upon as a pious individual, criminal conviction notwithstanding. With Fray Beltrán's recommendation, he was able to get the required permit from the alcalde mayor of Cuatro Ciénegas.[50]

Official permission having been granted for the entrada, whose avowed purpose was to bring relief to the three friars who had preceded them to Nuevo México, the party—a dozen or fourteen soldiers, the wife and three small children of one of the soldiers, and Father Beltrán—set out from San Bartolomé in the Santa Bárbara district on November 10, 1582. By this time they had received word that fathers Santa María and López were already dead, but the hope that Brother Rodríguez might yet be alive still provided them with a legal reason for the journey.[51]

The route taken by Espejo to Nuevo México followed roughly in the footsteps of the Rodríguez-Sánchez Chamuscado expedition: down the Conchos to the Río Grande and up the Río Grande through El Paso and the site of the modern Chamizal National Memorial into Pueblo Indian country where they encountered the first Puebloans on February 1, 1583. In mid-February Espejo, two soldiers, and some Indian servants took a brief trip away from the river to the east, going to the Manzano Mountains in the vicinity of Chililí and Quarai, where Father Juan de Santa María had been killed by Indians in 1581 and where in the next century Franciscans were to mount a major missionary effort. Quarai is now a part of Salinas Pueblo Missions National Monument.

Espejo soon rejoined the rest of his party on the Río Grande, and by February's end he and the others had visited and "taken possession of" several pueblos of Piros, Tompiros, Southern Tiwas, and Keresans. He had also learned with certainty that Brother Agustín Rodríguez had been killed, as had the other two friars. This was enough for Father Beltrán to call for an end to the expedition and a return to Nueva Vizcaya. But don Antonio, over the objections of the Franciscan, decided to look for still more pueblos as well as for mines.[52]

Espejo's wanderings, more in the nature of prospecting, took him and his men, Father Beltrán included, to the pueblo of Zuni, where they found four Mexican Indians who had been left there by Coronado in 1540. Leaving the others behind, the opportunistic Spaniard rode with nine soldiers to the Hopi villages—the first Europeans since Coronado to explore lands in today's Arizona. From the Hopi country he and four of his men continued for some hundred miles to the southwest, still looking for mines. The adventurers apparently reached the copper deposits in the vicinity of Jerome, Arizona, where they were disappointed in finding no silver. En route they may have seen—and were certainly close to—the prehistoric ruins today protected and interpreted by the National Park Service as Tuzigoot National Monument and Montezuma Castle National Monument. Both places had been abandoned before the arrival of Columbus in America, but both would have been impressive ruins in 1583, even as they are today.[53]

Everyone in the Espejo expedition reassembled at Zuni in May 1583, by which time the pro- and anti-Espejo forces among them had come to irreconcilable differences. A brief mutiny against Espejo failed, but the mutineers, who included Father Beltrán, were allowed to return to Santa Bárbara unmolested. With eight loyal soldiers, Espejo set out on a troublemaking journey among the pueblos, killing people who resisted them in any way and in one instance putting a village to the torch. Other Puebloans simply fled from the nine murderous Spaniards or acquiesced to them out of fear.[54]

In early July the Spaniards arrived at Pecos. One of the soldiers was later to describe it as "the best and largest of all the towns discovered by Francisco Vásquez de Coronado. It is set down on rocks, a large part of it congregated between two

Remains of the prehistoric Sinagua settlement of Tuzigoot in Arizona's Verde Valley lie in a region prospected by Antonio de Espejo in 1583. (George H. H. Huey.)

53

arroyos. The houses, of from three to four stories, are whitewashed and painted [inside?] with very bright colors and paints [or paintings]. Its fine appearance can be seen from far off."[55]

Before Espejo departed from Pecos, he took with him as captives two of its Towa-speaking inhabitants. One managed to escape, but the other was forced to accompany the little expedition on its southward journey. This time their route lay down the Pecos River. They met Indians who guided them to the Río Grande, possibly via the modern locations of Toyahvale, Fort Davis, and Marfa, Texas. Fort Davis, in addition to being a Texas town, was an important United States military post begun in 1854 and rebuilt after the Civil War in 1867. It is now preserved and administered by the National Park Service as Fort Davis National Historic Site.[56]

Hoping to receive the royal charter for the conquest and colonization of Nuevo México, Espejo, after returning home to San Bartolomé on September 10, 1583, issued glowing reports on the lands of the Pueblo Indians. He also sent his Indian captive from Pecos to Mexico City, where he was placed under the tutelage of Fray Pedro Oroz, the commissary general, the highest ranking Franciscan official, for Nueva España. In 1584, Father Oroz wrote:

> In this city of Mexico there is an Indian whom they brought from that land, and he is a man of great intelligence, very friendly and conversant with everyone, and he is learning doctrine so that he may be baptized, and together with it he learns the Mexican tongue. Four Indians from here are learning the language of this Indian of the new Mexico [la nueva México] (for thus they call the new country), so that after they have learned it they may go with the first religious who should enter that country for its conversion.[57]

When he was baptized the Pecos native took the name Pedro Oroz. Although he died before the next approved colonization expedition was launched, one of the Mexican Indians to whom he taught his Towa language, Juan de Dios, later entered Pecos Pueblo in 1598, where he was able to preach the Holy Gospel to its residents in their native tongue—which surely must have surprised them.[58]

The penultimate colonizing expedition to Nuevo México was promulgated by "a man of much courage, energy, and aggressiveness," the first alcalde mayor of the city that was later to become Monterrey, Mexico, and lieutenant governor of the province of Nuevo León, Gaspar Castaño de Sosa.

Unbridled ambition comes to mind when trying to explain why Castaño elected to chance everything by undertaking an unauthorized and blatantly illegal expedition in an effort to colonize Nuevo México. New laws had been effected by Spain in 1573 to protect the rights of Indians, and permission for expeditions into new lands were strictly controlled by the crown. Castaño, however, presumably believed that should he succeed he would be made adelantado after the fact, awarded great estates as well as the right to grant lands and Indian tribute. He may not have known that in 1590 Viceroy Marqués de Villamanrique warned his successor to beware of Castaño and his followers, whom he characterized as "outlaws, criminals, and murderers—who practice neither justice nor piety and are raising a rebellion in defiance of God and king. These men [in defiance of Spain's laws] invade the interior, seize peaceable Indians, and sell them in Mazapil, Saltillo, Sombrerete, and indeed everywhere in the region."[59]

As if in affirmation of the viceroy's words, on July 27, 1590, Castaño set out for the presumed riches of Nuevo México with the entire population of Almadén (today's Monclova, Coahuila) in tow, nearly two hundred men, women, and children—but no priest, a fact unprecedented in such undertakings. He even had a train of wagons in addition to the usual supplies and equipment.[60]

While the stingy documentary record rules out certainty, historians Hammond and Rey surmise that from Almadén the slavers and would-be colonists went directly northward, striking the Río Grande just downriver from the site of modern Del Río, Texas. If so, they were at the Río Grande at or near the site of the modern Amistad Dam and Amistad National Recreation Area. From here, historians speculate, they moved upstream to what today is the western end of Amistad Reservoir and to the Pecos River. According to Hammond and Rey, they followed the Pecos rather than the Río Grande northward into Nuevo México.[61]

Running low on food and moving rather slowly because of the wagons, Castaño ordered a dozen men to go ahead of them and capture native guides who could lead them to settlements. Two days before Christmas 1590 the advance party returned on foot, leading their exhausted horses. They had discovered a major settlement, a pueblo with sixteen kivas (underground ceremonial chambers), five plazas, and as many house blocks with the houses in them four and five stories tall. While their initial reception had been warm, after the Spaniards tried to help themselves to some of the Puebloans' winter supply of corn, the welcome became hot. The soldiers were driven from the village, forced to leave half their guns, saddles, and other equipment behind. Like Vásquez de Coronado, Chamuscado and Rodríguez, and Espejo before them, they had found Cicuye.

Learning of the calamity, Castaño pushed forward with twenty handpicked men until he came within sight of the pueblo on December 31. Aided and abetted by European guile and superior weapons, including two bronze cannons, he was able to capture Pecos in spite of the determined resistance of its inhabitants. "Suddenly the battle was over," writes historian John Kessell.

> Like Cortés, Gaspar Castaño de Sosa, utilizing horses, fire power, and steel had humbled a foe that greatly outnumbered him. He had suffered a very few wounded and no dead. "As a sign of rejoicing and victory" he sent his ensign and

55

> the buglers to the top of the strongest block house to blow their trumpets. "Now, as the lieutenant governor [of Nuevo León] walked through the pueblo with some of his men, no Indian threw a stone or shot an arrow. On the contrary, all tried by signs to show that they wanted our friendship, making the sign of the cross with their hands and saying 'Amigos, Amigos, Amigos."[62]

A triumphant Castaño and his soldiers left Pecos on the Feast of Epiphany, January 6, 1591. But his victory was a empty one. At the end of March, after having reunited with his main party on the Pecos River, visited pueblos throughout the region, and revisited Pecos formally to seal his victory there, he was met at the Keresan Indian Santo Domingo Pueblo by a party of Spaniards led by Juan Morlete, who had been sent by the viceroy to arrest him for having embarked on an illegal expedition. The colonizers were led from Nuevo México to Nueva España in disgrace, Castaño in irons. He spent 1592 in Mexico City, probably without reflecting on the meaning of what Columbus had wrought a century earlier. In 1593 he was sentenced to exile in the military service in the Philippines. By the time word arrived that he had been acquitted of all charges based on an appeal sent to the Council of the Indies in Spain, mutinous Chinese galley slaves had killed him on a ship headed for the Moluccas. In faraway Nuevo México, he had left a legacy of dread among the people of Pecos. But so did he leave posterity a lengthy and invaluable description, authored possibly either by himself or by his secretary, Andrés Pérez de Verlanga, of this greatest of all sixteenth-century Nuevo México settlements. It was his final "Memoria."[63]

Captain Juan Morlete probably followed Castaño's route from the province of Nuevo León to the Río Grande. If he did, he too passed through the region of today's Amistad National Recreation Area in Texas. Hammond and Rey believe he bypassed the Pecos River and traveled into Nuevo México up the Río Grande, a route that would have taken him through El Paso and the neighborhood of Chamizal National Memorial. But unlike his many Spanish predecessors in Nuevo México he seems to have gone no farther north than Santo Domingo Pueblo, and he failed to visit Pecos. With Castaño and the others as his prisoners, he seems to have returned to Mexico via the same route by which he had come.[64]

Details of an unauthorized and illegal 1593 expedition to Nuevo México are scanty. But enough of the historical record has survived to make it clear that in that year a Nueva Vizcayan soldier, Captain Francisco Leyva de Bonilla, and an even more shadowy figure, Antonio Gutiérrez de Humaña, recruited some other soldiers as well as Indian servants to invade Nuevo México to seek their fortunes. They headquartered at the Tewa pueblo of San Ildefonso and, before the year was out, made a northeastward exploration into the buffalo country of the Great Plains. They were possibly searching for the fabled Quivira.

Their route to Kansas took them through Pecos Pueblo. Somewhere on the Plains, Leyva de Bonilla and Gutiérrez de Humaña had a quarrel and Gutiérrez killed the expedition's leader. Plains Indians subsequently killed Gutiérrez and others of their party. Five Mexican Indians managed to escape.

Little of this would ever have been known were it not for the 1598 testimony offered by one of the Mexican Indians, Jusepe Gutiérrez, a native of the village of Culhuacán north of Mexico City who had accompanied the expedition as a servant. After the melee in Kansas, Jusepe was taken prisoner by Apaches. He heard in 1598 that Spaniards had come again to Nuevo México, and he made his way to the Tewa pueblo of San Juan where he was able to tell his story.[65]

With the final illegal Spanish expedition out of the way, Nuevo México was at last on the threshold of becoming, in Spain's eyes if not necessarily in those of its native population, a legitimate part of the Spanish Empire.[66]

A Permanent Nuevo México

"The last conquistador," New Mexico historian Marc Simmons has labeled him.[67] He was don Juan de Oñate y Salazar, who came to be to Nuevo México, and to what eventually became much of the American Southwest, what Pedro Menéndez de Avilés had a little more than three decades earlier been to La Florida, the southeastern United States. Just as Menéndez had laid the foundations for the edifice of a prolonged Spanish Florida, Oñate, at last, successfully contracted to do the same for Nuevo México.

Don Juan de Oñate was among those "attended by swarms of family, servants, and hangers-on," one of

Coat of arms of Don Juan de Oñate, first governor of Nuevo México. (Courtesy Museum of New Mexico, Santa Fe.)

> the rich and powerful moguls of New Spain's northern marches [who] held court in their fortified adobe castles, dispensed justice like patriarchs, and welcomed travelers with prodigal hospitality. Because these *hombres ricos y poderosos* colonized, governed, and sustained vast reaches of the silver-rich north at their own expense, the king granted them notable, almost feudal independence. Not that he ever intended it to last. Always royal lawyers hovered about, eager to retract the privileges of an adelantado who defaulted. For their part, the frontier ricos kept agents at court, married their daughters to royal judges, and applied bribes and favors where they would do the most good.[68]

Oñate won out in the conquest among the northern frontier's wealthy opportunists for the right to colonize Nuevo México in the wake of all previous failures. He was born in Zacatecas of a family that had made its fortune in silver. He married the daughter of a family that had done likewise. Her name was Isabel de Tolosa Cortés Moctezuma, and she was the granddaughter of Hernán Cortés, the Spanish conqueror of Nueva España, and Isabel Moctezuma, the daughter of the late Aztec emperor.[69]

57

In September 1595 don Juan Oñate, some forty-three years of age, entered into a contract with Viceroy Luis de Velasco in which Oñate agreed at his personal expense to equip, arm, and feed two hundred men as soldier-colonists on a venture to Nuevo México. He also agreed to take with them blacksmithing tools, mining equipment, medicines, sowing wheat, plows, other farming equipment, a thousand head of cattle, a thousand sheep for wool and another thousand for mutton, a thousand goats, a hundred head of black cattle, a hundred and fifty mares, corn, jerked beef, and Indian trade goods. In return, he was to be governor and adelantado as well as captain-general with the right to exercise all criminal and civil jurisdiction in Nuevo México. These titles were to be his for life and could be inherited by his immediate heirs.

As if these inducements were not enough, he was to be paid six thousand ducats per year as governor and given a loan of three artillery pieces from the royal arsenal. He could make land grants to settlers as well as grants of Indian tribute; he could establish a royal treasury, construct presidios (forts), name officials, exploit mines, and establish governmental districts. At the crown's expense, he could take with him five priests and a lay brother. After five years' residence in Nuevo México, Oñate's male colonists would be awarded the title of *hidalgo*, the lowest rank of nobleman. And finally, he would report directly to the Council of the Indies in Spain rather than to the viceroyalty in Nueva España, thus relieving him of a huge layer of bureaucracy.[70]

Making good on his part of the contract, at least in part, on October 21, 1595, Velasco appointed don Juan "governor, captain general, caudillo, discoverer, and pacifier," the latter a euphemism replacing the earlier and now-objectionable "conqueror." But Velasco was transferred to Peru, and his successor, don Gaspar de Zúñiga y Acevedo, Conde de Monterrey, took a dim view of the contract provision allowing Oñate to deal directly with the Council of the Indies. He demurred and forced the would-be conquistador to agree to accept viceregal authority over the proposed venture.[71]

After what were to Oñate aggravating setbacks and delays, the party of colonists—much smaller than that of Vásquez de Coronado, which had preceded them in 1540—set out for Nuevo México in late January 1598, two years after the time originally planned. The motley group of some five hundred people included eight Franciscan priests, two Franciscan lay brothers, and 129 soldiers who ranged in age from their mid-teens into their sixties. So were there an unknown number of wives and children of soldiers as well as personal servants, packers, herders, and drivers of various ethnic backgrounds: mestizos, mulattos, and Indians, among the latter a few slaves owned by Oñate. As larder on the hoof and as work or riding animals there were perhaps seven thousand head of stock—sheep, cattle, oxen, horses, and mules. The men carried their supplies in 83 wagons.[72]

Oñate's route to Nuevo México out of Nueva Vizcaya was more direct than those that had preceded it. When they crossed the Río Conchos after leaving Santa

Bárbara, the settlers, rather than follow the Conchos to its junction with the Río Grande, opened a new *camino real* by heading more or less directly northward to arrive on the south side of the Río Grande a mere twenty-five miles or so downstream from El Paso. Here, next to an abundance of fish and surrounded by easily bagged wild waterfowl, they rested for a week. While looking for a place to ford the river, a few of Oñate's men met some local natives whom they dubbed Mansos ("Tame Ones"), the name by which they became known throughout history. After the Mansos were given clothing and gifts, they returned with more of their people, bringing the Spaniards "great quantities of fish" in response to Spanish hospitality. This event today is regarded by citizens of El Paso, Texas—somewhat to the chagrin of residents of Plymouth, Massachusetts—as the first Thanksgiving celebration in today's United States.[73]

If a later account by eyewitness Gaspar Pérez de Villagrá can be credited, the celebration was a grand one:

> The governor then ordered a large chapel built under a grove of shady trees. Here the priests celebrated a solemn high Mass, after which the learned commissary preached an excellent sermon. Then some of the soldiers enacted a drama written by Captain Farfán [de los Godos]. This drama depicted the advent of the friars to Nuevo México. We saw the priests coming to this land, kindly received by the simple natives, who reverently approached on bended knee and asked to be received into the faith, being baptized in great numbers.
>
> After this was over the entire army began celebrating with great joy and mirth. The horsemen gathered in their most gala attire and splendid accoutrements and glistening arms. . . .
>
> The entire army was drawn up in formation, and in the presence of the multitude the governor solemnly took possession of the newly discovered land.[74]

Oñate's formal declaration asserted King Philip II's claim to Nuevo México as well as Oñate's various privileges, titles, and rights to virtually everything and everyone in these new lands. What Oñate claimed, unbeknownst to Nuevo México's Puebloan and other Indians, was

> tenancy and possession, real and actual, civil and natural . . . without excepting anything and without limitations, including the mountains, rivers, valleys, meadows, pastures, and waters. In [the king's] name I also take possession of all the other lands, pueblos, cities, towns, castles, fortified and unfortified houses which are now established in the kingdoms and provinces of Nuevo México, those neighboring and adjacent thereto, and those which may be established in the future, together with their mountains, rivers, fisheries, waters, pastures, valleys, meadows,

59

springs, and ores of gold, silver, copper, mercury, tin, iron, precious stones, salt, *morales*, alum, and all the lodes of whatever sort, quality, or condition they may be, together with the native Indians in each and every one of the provinces, with civil and criminal jurisdiction, power of life and death, over high and low, from the leaves of the trees in the forest to the stones and sands of the river, and from the stones and sands of the river to the leaves in the forest.[75]

This pronouncement, like the *requerimiento* doubtless read to the natives of Pecos Pueblo by Hernando de Alvarado nearly six decades earlier, represented the fulfillment of Spain's legal requirement in the taking of new possessions. Divine Right sanctioned the taking. Three centuries later, in an Anglo-American setting, it would be somewhat less divine Manifest Destiny.

The settlers headed north up the Río Grande. Oñate paused at Pueblo settlements along the way, with a particularly long pause at Santo Domingo Pueblo, where he convened a gathering of Indian leaders from every direction and explained to them both the sacred and secular reasons for the Spaniards' coming. He insisted upon vassalage and obedience to Philip II and to himself, a request at least outwardly granted by the assembled Puebloans.

The colonists' next major stop, on July 11, 1598, was at the Tewa pueblo of San Juan Bautista del Okhe. It was here that Oñate elected to erect his first capital. It remained on the site until about 1600, when it was moved across the Río Grande about a quarter mile away, facing the pueblo of San Gabriel del Yunge. San Gabriel was destined to serve the Spaniards as their headquarters until in 1610 Oñate's successor, don Pedro de Peralta, formally established the capital in Santa Fe, where it has remained to the present. Some of Oñate's colonists had begun a settlement here as early as 1608. San Gabriel is now an archeological ruin. San Juan Pueblo, however, like Santa Fe, continues to thrive.[76]

A cross marker commemorates the site of San Gabriel del Yunge, founded in 1599 or 1600 by Juan de Oñate as the second capital of Nuevo México. (Courtesy Museum of New Mexico, Santa Fe.)

On the way to San Juan, Oñate had dispatched the brothers (and his nephews) Juan and Vicente de Zaldívar on a side trip through Abó Pass to make a hasty reconnaissance of some pueblo settlements said to exist at the edge of a great plain. These so-called Salinas Pueblos, named for salt deposits in the region, included the settlements of Abó, Quarai, and Las Humanas (Gran Quivira), the ruins of which are now protected as Salinas Pueblo Missions National Monument. Somewhat later, in October, Oñate himself would pay a visit to these pueblos. The Zaldívars and the adelantado had been preceded here by Antonio de Espejo, and there were Puebloans living in this region who had killed Father Juan de Santa María in 1581.[77]

Two weeks after arriving at San Juan and deciding to establish his capital there, on July 25 Oñate arrived with sixty armed and mounted men at Pecos Pueblo, where they had ridden to receive homage from this greatest of all of Nuevo México's settlements. With him was Juan de Dios, the Mexican Indian who had learned the Towa tongue spoken at Pecos from Pedro Oroz, the Indian who had been taken captive to Mexico City by Antonio de Espejo. How the people of Pecos reacted to this foreign Indian, a complete stranger, who could speak their language is not recorded. However, as historian John Kessell notes, "This day the Pecos chose not to fight. Apparently they permitted the Spaniards the usual ritual acts—the harangues and planting of the cross and volleys. In honor of the day [July 25], the friars assigned Santiago as patron saint of Pecos. The governor and his party left the next day."[78]

In September, and using his authority as "governor, captain general, and adelantado of the kingdoms and provinces of Nuevo México and those adjacent and bordering their pacifier and colonizer for the king our lord," don Juan de Oñate conceded the provinces, pueblos, and Indian doctrinas of Nuevo México to the Franciscans, giving the friars "full faculty and license to build in each of them the churches and conventos they deem necessary for their residence and the better administration of Christian doctrine." Pecos was included, as were the Salinas Pueblos.[79]

The first minister to the "province of the Pecos," as the Spaniards labeled it, was Fray Francisco de San Miguel. In mid-September 1598 he and Juan de Dios began their ministry in Pecos Pueblo, destined to last no longer than three months. In that short time they may have been responsible for construction of a simple, hall-shaped adobe church measuring some twenty-five by eighty feet and situated a little more than three hundred yards north-northeast of the main Pecos house block. Whether this structure, later uncovered by archeologists, was the Franciscan's church or not, he and his Indian interpreter left Pecos in a hurry on orders from Nuevo México's leading Franciscan, Father Commissary Alonso Martínez.

The cause for concern was the fact that the Keresan people of Ácoma Pueblo had killed Oñate's nephew Juan de Zaldívar and a dozen of his soldiers on December 4. It became immediately obvious that Spaniards were not safe in Pueblo settlements. After Father Francisco's departure from Pecos, the people there appear to have torn down the church and to have used some of its beams and adobes in constructing a kiva. It would be in the next century before another church would appear among them, eventually more ruins to be uncovered by archeologists within today's Pecos National Historical Park.[80]

Before the Ácomas' killing of Zaldívar and his men, while he was visiting the Salinas Pueblos, Nuevo México's first governor decided to make a journey toward the west where he hoped to find the South Sea, which is to say the Pacific Ocean. In October he and his men headed directly westward, going all the way to Ácoma Pueblo, where he visited in peace, although he later learned the residents had intended to kill him by treachery and to force a war with the Spaniards. From Ácoma the troops and their commander continued westward for Zuni Pueblo, stopping along the way at Agua de la Peña to fill their water bags. They became the first Spaniards known with certainty to have visited this famed water hole, later known as El Morro.

61

A few weeks later they would return to the site, and in another seven years the adelantado would leave his name on the face of the sandstone cliff by the pool of water.[8]

From Zuni, Oñate and his troops proceeded farther westward to the Hopi villages in today's northern Arizona, where the governor, recalling the accounts of Antonio de Espejo, inquired about metallic ores. As with Espejo, the Hopis pointed southwestward in the direction of the Verde Valley, so Oñate dispatched the reliable Captain Farfán de los Godos to see what he could learn. In 1598 Farfán, as may have Espejo before him, could have seen prehistoric ruins in central Arizona now reserved within the confines of Montezuma Castle National Monument and Tuzigoot National Monument. Whether he did or not, he found pieces of ore filled with virgin silver, and he later reported to his commander that the claims he had staked "appeared to be the richest in Nueva España."[82]

In mid-January 1599 Oñate sent Vicente de Zaldívar, brother of the slain Spanish commander, to exact revenge and bring the pueblo of Ácoma to heel. Vicente and his well-armed soldiers succeeded in their bloody mission, killing several hundred Ácomas and accepting the surrender of the five hundred survivors, mostly women and children. There was only one Spanish casualty. As if such victory were not sweet enough, in its wake Oñate decreed either mutilation, such as the severing of hands or feet, or servitude for the surrendered captives. Sixty of the small girls were shipped off to Mexico City, never to see their homeland again.[83]

The Nuevo México colony somehow managed to survive in the face of thinly veiled Puebloan hostility and of burgeoning dissatisfaction and disaffection among the colonists themselves. The governor had found no riches, mineral or otherwise; the natives were intractable and not given to submitting to Spanish demands on their labor; and, indeed, it had become a struggle for the settlers merely to subsist.

In spite of all the problems, or perhaps because of them, don Juan set out on another of the many expeditions that characterized his tenure in Nuevo México. This time it

"Paso por aqui el adelantado don Ju de oñate del descubrymiento de la mar del sur a 16 de abril de 1605." This message was inscribed on Inscription Rock by Juan de Oñate on his return journey from the mouth of the Colorado River and Gulf of California. The historic sandstone bluff is preserved at El Morro National Monument, New Mexico. (George Grant photo courtesy National Park Service Western Archeological and Conservation Center, Tucson, Arizona.)

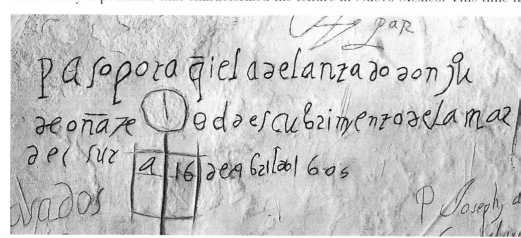

was a journey to the west once again to search for the South Sea and its possible pearl fisheries as well as a good harbor where ships might anchor to supply his needy colonists.

Oñate left some fifty people in the capital of San Gabriel, taking a relatively small band of explorers with him on an extraordinary trip. They departed San Gabriel on October 7, 1604, and went westward to Zuni and Hopi, once again pausing at El Morro for water. From Hopi they climbed down from the Colorado Plateau to the Verde Valley, then on to the Bill Williams River, which they followed to its mouth on the Río Colorado. They headed south down the Colorado until at last, in late January 1605, they reached the "South Sea," the salt water at the head of the Gulf of California. Their return trip was by the same route. This time, when they reached the watering place at El Morro, the doughty Spaniard left his mark—seemingly the first European to do so—on the walls of Inscription Rock: *Paso por aqui el adelantado don juo de oñate del descubrymiento de la mar del sur a 16 de abril de 1605* [Passed by here the Adelantado don Juan de Oñate from the discovery of the South Sea on the sixteenth of April 1605]. It remains there for all to see, a direct link to this extraordinary man and to Nuevo México's epic history.[84]

Oñate's days in Nuevo México were numbered. Complaints concerning his rule as governor had reached Mexico City as well as Spain, and in 1606 Philip III ordered the new viceroy, don Luis Velasco, who had just returned from Peru and who had authorized Oñate's expedition in the first place, to recall don Juan from the Río Grande. Before that happened, however, in August 1607 the governor tendered his resignation. The viceroy appointed don Pedro de Peralta as his successor, and in 1610, with Santa Fe about to become the capital, the "last conquistador" traveled south to Mexico City. His venture had been a personal failure, but so had it bequeathed to Spain a territorial legacy to last her until the success of the Mexican War of Independence in 1821.[85]

Manila Galleons and the California Coast

The failure of Columbus to find a western route to the Indies became even more of an issue among competing crowns of Europe when in 1497, by sailing eastward around southern Africa's Cape of Good Hope, Portuguese sailor Vasco da Gama reached India and returned to Lisbon in 1499 with a cargo of pepper, cloves, nutmeg, cinnamon, and precious stones—a far greater haul than that so far made by Spaniards in America.[86]

Taking note of his countryman's success, and believing strongly that a western sea route to the Indies was possible, Fernão da Magalhães—whom we know in English as Ferdinand Magellan—offered his services to the Portuguese crown. Like Columbus before him, he was rejected and turned instead to Spain. Between September 1519

63

and March 1521 Magellan and his men were able to sail the length of the southern half of the east coast of South America; to locate a passage around the southern tip of South America through what became known as the Straits of Magellan; and to reach Pacific islands later called the Philippines in honor of an infant prince who would one day be Philip II of Spain. Although Magellan was killed by Filipino natives, his men were able to complete the westward journey around India and Africa to Spain, proving once and for all that the world was indeed a globe.[87]

The success of Magellan's voyage led eventually to a thriving trade among China, the Philippines, Nueva España, and Spain. As early as 1508 Spanish navigators began to try their hands at round-trip voyages between the Philippines and Nueva España. Their efforts to find an easy return route from the Pacific islands to Nueva España's mainland, however, were frustrated until finally, in 1564, a Basque, General Miguel López de Legazpi, sailed to the Philippines to conquer these islands for Spain. In 1565 two of López's ships discovered that by going far enough to the north one could avoid the east-to-north trade winds, picking up westerlies instead. And better yet, one could ride the west-to-east Kuroshio and North Pacific currents to the coast of northern California. From there, in the region between Cape Mendocino and Monterey Bay, it was a relatively sure journey down the Pacific Coast past the southern tip of Baja California to the port of Acapulco. The sailors and navigators credited with this important discovery were Esteban Rodríguez, Fray Andrés de Urdaneta, Alonso de Arellano, and Lope Martín.[88]

In 1566 Spanish cargo ships began making a yearly voyage between Acapulco and Manila, usually leaving Nueva España in March and arriving in the Philippines in late May or early June. The longer return trips left early in July and arrived in Acapulco in late January or early February of the following year. The stakes were raised in 1572 when Spanish trade was extended to include goods from China, including silks, porcelains, and other exotic items. They were raised again in 1579 when the English privateer, Sir Francis Drake—who in 1586 was to sack and burn San Agustín in La Florida—surprised Spain by raiding Spanish ships along the Pacific Coast, sailing as far north as Cape Mendocino in northern California and putting in for repairs, presumably in or near Drake's Bay in today's Point Reyes National Seashore. He was able to return unmolested to England via the Pacific and Indian Ocean and up the west coast of Africa.[89]

Many Spanish ships, including Manila galleons, sailed along parts of the west coast of California during the second half of the sixteenth century, although California was not their destination. They were variously en route from Manila to Acapulco; in search of the mythical Strait of Anian (also known as the Northwest Passage), supposed to offer a northern sea route linking the Atlantic to the Pacific; or attempting to make accurate charts of the region and locate a suitable port. Among the more

A 1486 woodcut by Edward Revwich of a carrack, a type of galleon or merchant ship used from the fourteenth through the sixteenth centuries. (From Bernard Von Breydenbach's The Crusades to Jerusalem. *)*

noteworthy of these California coastal visits were those of Francisco Gali (1584), Pedro de Unamunu (1587), Sebastián Rodríguez Cermeño (1595), and Sebastián Vizcaíno (1602).

Francisco Gali was "a soldier, a prudent man, an excellent pilot and a noted cosmographer, and he had served the Spanish King all his life." In 1585 he was chosen by Archbishop Pedro Moya, the viceroy of Nueva España, to seek a midway anchorage between Manila and Acapulco; to look for the Strait of Anian; and, motivated by a report written earlier by Nuevo Mexicano prospector Antonio de Espejo, to find a port from which Nuevo México could be supplied by sea.[90]

Little of Gali and his accomplishments would be known were it not for the fact that he kept a diary of an earlier 1583-84 journey from Acapulco to Manila to Macao to California and back to Acapulco. Published in Dutch translation in 1595, his diary indicates that on this easterly trip from Macao on board the *San Juan Bautista* he made landfall at 37° 30' North latitude off the California coast. "It is a high land, covered with trees and without snow," he wrote. "At a distance of 4 leagues from land I found great bunches of roots and leaves and canes and a number of seals, which made me believe that there must be many good harbours on the whole of this coast as far as the Port of Acapulco." If Gali's estimate was correct, his landfall was in the vicinity of Half Moon Bay south of San Francisco Bay.[91]

Gali returned to Manila and would have made the eastward voyage mandated by the viceroy had he not died early in 1586. The man chosen as his replacement was Pedro de Unamunu (or Unamuno). With Fray Martín Ignacio de Loyola, a Franciscan; two Portuguese Franciscans and a young Japanese boy who were Fray Martín's companions; pilot Alonso Gómez; a few soldiers and a few natives of Luzon, he set out from the Philippines on July 12, 1587.[92]

Following orders, he searched fruitlessly for an island that would provide a midway anchorage between the Philippines and Nueva España. Continuing eastward, on October 17, he sighted the California coast at 35.5°, about equidistant from San Francisco and Los Angeles. He anchored in what he called Puerto San Lucas, a place identified by historian Henry Wagner as Morro Bay and by Michael Mathes, who gives the landfall at 37° 30', as Santa Cruz.[93]

Either way, the incident is noteworthy because Unamunu went ashore with Father Martín, a dozen soldiers and the guns, and "some Luzon Indians with their swords and shields." They spent a day trying unsuccessfully to make contact with some Indians—who may have been either Chumash or Salinan—they had seen from their ship. Failing in this, they tried again a second day, this time with Father Francisco de Noguera, twelve armed soldiers, and eight sword-and-shield-carrying Filipinos. The party camped on land, and on the third day, as they were returning to their ship, they were attacked by the local natives. Five of Unamunu's men were wounded, two of

65

them mortally. The decision was made to abandon this part of California, and the ship, with its international crew and passengers, continued southward to Acapulco, arriving there November 22.[94]

Because of the many difficulties facing ships returning to Nueva España via the California coast—not the least of which were attacks by British privateers off the tip of Baja California—voyages by cargo ships for mapping and exploration in these waters were suspended after 1588. Galleons returned to the more strenuous, but safer, southerly route, thus avoiding California altogether. But this was about to change in the person of a Portuguese-born navigator.[95]

Little is known about Rodríguez Cermeño beyond the fact that he was another of many Portuguese who found service under auspices of the Spanish crown. It is also known that he arrived on the stage of California history when don Luis de Velasco, the viceroy of Nueva España who was Juan de Oñate's personal friend, was especially concerned with the Philippine trade. Velasco was anxious to learn more about possible ports along the California coast, which led in 1594 to Rodríguez's assignment to combine a trading trip to the Philippines with a Pacific coastal reconnaissance. In doing so he was to follow the usual southerly Acapulco to Manila route and return with a loaded galleon via California, looking for potential harbors along the way.[96]

Rodríguez made the Acapulco-to-Manila voyage as scheduled, and in July 1595 he set sail from the Philippines in the *San Agustín* headed in the more northerly return direction. The nearly eighty men on board included the commander, ship's pilot, Spanish soldiers, seven Negro slaves, seven Indian ship boys (whether Mexican Indians or Filipinos is unclear), and a Franciscan friar. In early November the galleon reached the California coast at what Rodríguez called Cabo Mendocino, which historian Wagner thinks more likely was the more northerly Rocky Point. If Wagner is correct, the sailor's California landfall was immediately south of the modern Redwood National Park.[97]

Continuing southward in bad weather, the *San Agustín* sailed past Cape Mendocino and continued to hug the coast until arriving on November 6 at Drake's Bay. Here the commander decided to disembark to build a smaller vessel for coastal exploration while leaving the galleon anchored in deeper and presumably safer waters offshore. But on the last day of November, a tremendous storm drove the *San Agustín* aground, damaging it beyond repair. This meant the much smaller launch being constructed would have to take all seventy to eighty men to Acapulco.[98]

Rodríguez Cermeño's stay at Drake's Bay was eventful. Almost as soon as the galleon anchored, one of the local natives, a Coast Miwok, paddled out to the *San Agustín*, where he was given some cotton and silk cloth and a red cap. The next day four more men paddled out to the ship and were equally rewarded for their efforts. Then Rodríguez went ashore in the ship's boat with twenty-two men, seventeen of them carrying the arquebuses. The Spaniards visited the Miwok village and, with

Returning from the Philippines in 1595 with orders to reconnoiter the California coast for a suitable site to establish a port, Rodríguez Cermeño made landfall at Drake's Bay, now part of Point Reyes National Seashore. (Carr Clifton.)

66

Franciscan Fray Francisco de la Concepción doing the honors, formally christened the bay La Baya de San Francisco, although Drake's Bay is how it eventually came to be known.[99]

The Miwoks initially treated the Spaniards kindly, giving them food. But when a few of Rodríguez's men tried to retrieve some timbers from the *San Agustín* the natives had taken, possibly for firewood, the Indians resisted and wounded one of the Spaniards with an arrow. Matters were soon smoothed over, and the foreigners sailed away on December 8 without further incident in the newly built launch, the *San Buenaventura*.[100]

Scattered artifacts left behind from the wreck of the *San Agustín* have been of considerable interest to archeologists, as has the location of the wreck of the *San Agustín* itself. Archeologists of the National Park Service continue to hope that their underwater surveys within the boundaries of Point Reyes National Seashore will eventually lead them to the site and that they will be able to record and study the galleon's remains.[101]

Leaving Drake's Bay, the crowded *San Buenaventura* "passed close to the islands on the mainland side about a league away," the unpopulated Farallon Islands where Sir Francis Drake landed briefly in 1579, now administered by the National Oceanic and Atmospheric Administration as a part of the Farallones National Marine Sanctuary. They missed San Francisco Bay and continued to run the coast southward with occasional stops where they met Indians and restocked their meager supplies of food. On December 14 "two islands were discovered," San Miguel and Santa Rosa, and the next day, without realizing it was a different island, they discovered Santa Cruz. All are within the present Channel Islands National Park.[102]

Several hours later the little ship with its sick and hungry crew and passengers sailed past Santa Monica Bay, parts of which today are within the Santa Monica Mountains National Recreation Area. "It was not reached during daylight, and as the night was good and no port was found in which to anchor," wrote the expedition's chronicler, "[Captain Rodríguez] went running along the coast near land until morning," passing Point Loma and missing the splendid harbor of San Diego Bay along the way.[103]

The Rodríguez Cermeño odyssey came to a less than glorious conclusion on the west coast of Nueva España. Finally,

> the Captain came to land in the launch on the coast of Compostela, a league from the Puerto de Chacala, where from a ranch some corn and sun-dried beef was brought to aid them, and with which the men relieved their hunger. This was on the 7th of January of this year [1596]. Here the Captain disembarked and the sick who came on board remained there. He dispatched the launch from there to Acapulco.[104]

Although Rodríguez Cermeño asserted that he had made a careful inspection of the California coastline, it was apparent to Spanish officialdom that the sorry condition of his homemade ship and of his men had made it imperative that they hurry their return to Acapulco. It is now clear, as was suspected and as evidenced by his failure to note San Francisco and San Diego bays, that he merely skirted the coast and skipped by bays from point to point. His failure made it equally obvious that if the coast were to be charted, it should be done by an expedition intended solely for that purpose rather than by a loaded galleon returning from Manila.[105]

The person on whose shoulders the task fell was the Spaniard Sebastián Vizcaíno. Born in 1548, probably in Extremadura, in 1580 he served in the Spanish invasion of Portugal, his horses and retainers being paid for by his hidalgo father, a member of Spain's minor nobility. He came to Nueva España in 1583 and three years later went to Manila, where he became a merchant and served in the port guard. In 1589 he returned to Mexico to live the life of an investor and merchant, but one perpetually interested in adventure, navigation, and speculation.[106]

In 1596-97 Vizcaíno explored and attempted to trade in Baja California, establishing a short-lived settlement at La Paz. In spite of the total failure of this particular venture, Viceroy Gaspar Zúñiga y Acevedo, Conde de Monterrey, commissioned him as general of an expedition intended precisely to explore the western coast of North America, taking soundings of ports and noting their landmarks, making maps and measurements of latitude and longitude, looking for pearls in the ports, and, as later asserted by the official chronicler, keeping a sharp eye out for Gran Quivira and the Strait of Anian.[107]

With three vessels—the flagship *San Diego* and the *Santo Tomás*, and a frigate, the *Tres Reyes*—the expedition left Acapulco May 5, 1602. On board the three ships were Vizcaíno; his son Juan; three Carmelite friars, including cosmographer and chronicler Father Antonio de la Ascensión; seven officers; and 126 crew members, both soldiers and sailors.[108]

On November 10, 1602, the expedition reached the splendid bay and harbor that Rodríguez Cabrillo had visited six decades earlier and named San Miguel. On November 12, the feast day of St. James of Alcalá, or San Diego, a Mass was celebrated and the bay and harbor were renamed in the saint's honor. While ashore, Vizcaíno, his son, Fray Antonio, and fifteen armed men encountered some Ipai (Diegueños) who received them well and gave the strangers gifts of net bags, small fishing nets, and some animal pelts. And for the first time, the bay was carefully charted by cosmographer Gerónimo Martín Palacios. His original charts were later turned over to printer, cartographer, and engineer Enrico Martínez, whose contemporary copies, unlike the originals, have survived in the archives. All the activities of Vizcaíno's men at San Diego were in view of today's Cabrillo National Monument where the story is interpreted for the public.[109]

68

Vizcaíno's little fleet left San Diego on November 20 and sailed to Catalina Island, giving it the name by which it is known today. On the first or second of December they proceeded northward through the Santa Barbara Channel, stopping at an island they called Santa Barbara, which historian Wagner believes was Anacapa.[110] In either event, Vizcaíno's was the first expedition to leave behind a chart, however crude, of the islands within today's Channel Islands National Park.

By December 16 they had made their way to a port they named Monterey in honor of the Conde de Monterrey, viceroy of Nueva España. On December 29 Vizcaíno sent the *Santo Tomás* back to Acapulco carrying forty sick crew members, a report of what the expedition had accomplished to date, and a request for supplies for an exploration of the Gulf of California upon their return from Cape Mendocino. The rest remained until January 4, 1603.[111]

The two remaining vessels, the *San Diego* and the *Tres Reyes*, sailed up the coast to Cermeño's San Francisco Bay (Drake's Bay). The "real" San Francisco Bay continued to conceal the secret of its majestic presence behind the narrow opening of the Golden Gate. The expedition made a chart of Point Reyes and the two vessels went all the way to Cape Mendocino. The flagship and frigate became separated, and the *Tres Reyes*, piloted by Antonio Flores, sailed beyond to Cabo Sebastián and Cabo Blanco, presumably the modern capes Sebastian and Blanco on the southern coast of Oregon. It appears certain in any case that the frigate of Vizcaíno's fleet sailed along the shores of California's Redwood National Park.[112]

As with previous Spanish expeditions to this region, the homeward journey, with crew and passengers sick and dying of scurvy, was marked with haste. Those who had survived the journey on board the *San Diego*, Vizcaíno included, arrived in Acapulco on March 21, 1603. The *Tres Reyes* had preceded them to the west coast, landing at the port of Navidad on February 29.[113]

He had found neither Gran Quivira nor the Strait of Anian, but Vizcaíno had charted much of the coast and had come home with a strong conviction that Monterey was the ideal location for a major Spanish settlement. But it was not to be, at least for now. Although it was 1811 before the last Manila galleon sailed to Acapulco, the route in the preceding two centuries had reverted to the more southerly course. And immediately after Vizcaíno's voyage, politics and a new viceroy had intervened. In the words of historian Charles Chapman, "Alta California was saved for a hundred and fifty years in the blissful obscurity it needed if [descendants of] the English colonists who were just making their first successful settlements along the Atlantic coast were ever to have their opportunity to acquire the golden area on the Pacific."[114]

A frigate from Sebastián Vizcaíno's expedition of 1603-4 was among the first to skirt the coast of northern California and its primeval forest now preserved in Redwood National Park. (Larry Ulrich.)

69

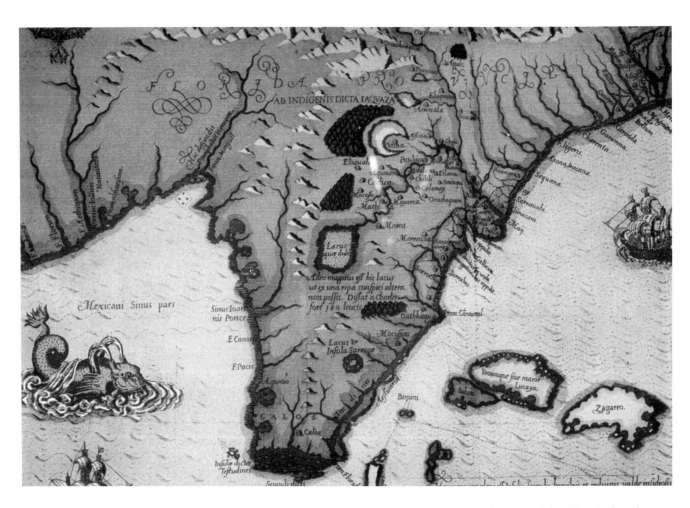

Jacques le Moyne, a refugee from the ill-fated French colony at Fort Caroline destroyed by Menéndez de Avilés in 1565, provided the original map on which this more elaborate and fanciful one is based. (From le Moyne's Brevis narratio, *1591. Courtesy Florida Museum of Natural History, Gainsville.)*

Although the seventeenth century brought further expansion of Spain into North America, with movement into the Southeast, Texas, and what today is Arizona, it was chiefly a century of securing what already been acquired, fending off both Indian resistance and increasing competition from other European powers. With the defeat of the Spanish Armada in the English Channel in 1588, the English, especially, became a potential threat to Spain's hold on her New World possessions.

LA FLORIDA

Georgia and the area northward along the Atlantic Coast still belonged to Spain throughout the seventeenth century, but possession was more a matter of paper than of reality. While there continued to be a handful of Spanish missions in Georgia, the removal of the capital from Santa Elena in South Carolina to San Agustín in 1587 signaled a willingness on the part of the Spaniards to relinquish these more northerly lands, even as it indicated their determination to cling to La Florida proper.

La Florida, even more than lands encompassed by what were to become Georgia and the Carolinas, was of strategic importance. Her long arm lay on the major shipping lane between Nueva España and Spain, and the country—or pirates of whatever nationality—controlling her anchorages governed the free flow of nearby ocean traffic. It was essential for Nueva España, if not for Spain herself, to remain firmly in control of this peninsula of land and, later, its western extension along the Gulf of Mexico.

The Franciscan missionary push toward the west from San Agustín began in 1614. At the time of a visitation in 1674-75 by Gabriel Díaz Vara Calderón, Bishop of Santiago de Cuba, there were thirty-four Franciscan missions in La Florida, including San Felipe de Athuluteca within the Cumberland Island National Seashore and San Juan del Puerto on Fort George Island in the Timucuan Ecological and Historic Preserve. Founded no later than 1587, the latter survived until its invasion by English Governor James Moore of Carolina in 1702 and was among the most long-lived of La Florida missions. Its population and that of its nine *visitas*, or visiting stations, numbered five hundred in 1602. In 1606 Juan de las Cabezas de Altamirano, Bishop of Santiago de Cuba, confirmed 482 Indians there as well as six chiefs and five chieftainesses from five visitas. Only thirty people were enumerated here in 1675, but by 1689 the number had risen to about 125. The year before its 1702 invasion, fewer than two hundred people were reported in residence.[1]

At the northern edge of St. Augustine, a short distance from Castillo de San Marcos National Monument, is the site of the first Christian mission to the North American Indian, Nombre de Dios (Name of God). It was established by Pedro de Menéndez, possibly as early as 1566. It was the longest-enduring La Florida mission and the only one to survive beyond 1706 more or less in its original location. Its archeological remains lie beneath the earth inside the city's Fountain of Youth Park.[2]

Cruciform stirrups like this one were used by sixteenth-century Spanish soldiers on the frontier of Spain's North American possessions. (George H. H. Huey from the Enrique E. Guerra collection.)

71

While 1675 may, as historian Michael Gannon asserts, have "marked the finest hour in the missionary movement in Florida," the story is one that "came to an unbelievably tragic end." What at least partly contributed to the succeeding period of "decline and ruin" was the period of English expansion heralded by the founding of Jamestown in 1607. By 1674 the British were entrenched as far south as Charleston in today's South Carolina. "Drawn on by a profitable trade in skins, the English moved out from Charleston into the Yamassee and Creek country of central and western Georgia, where, with their cheaper and more abundant supply of manufactured goods (and firearms, which Spaniards had never provided the Indians), they easily won the trade and friendship of the interior tribes. With the tribes in tow, they then moved east to the coast and south toward the Gulf."[3]

Even were it not for the British, the future of Franciscan endeavors in Florida would have been less than bright. The natives, the raison d'être for missions, were being reduced in number at an alarming rate. What was possibly bubonic plague struck between 1613 and 1617, cutting at least by half the Christianized Indian population. Yellow fever struck in 1649; smallpox in 1653; and measles in 1659 and again in 1672. And even during the "finest hour," 1675, Captain Juan Fernández de Florencia reported that among the Apalachee, "I have not taken a census and they die daily," possibly from the effects of a smallpox epidemic.[4]

What amounted to the coup de grâce to the Spanish mission system in northern Florida was applied during the 1702-04 War of the Spanish Succession (Queen Anne's War) when "South Carolina militia burned some settlements, captured thousands of Timucuans, and marched them off to slavery in South Carolina." A 1703 raid by Colonel James Moore—the former Carolina governor—leading a thousand Creek Indians in assaults on Spanish-founded Apalachee mission settlements was at least partially in response to a 1695 attack by Spaniards and Apalachee Indians on several towns along the Ocmulgee River. Burned in the Spanish attack was the town of Ocmulgee itself, the site of which is preserved at today's Ocmulgee National Monument. Finally, there appears to have been another serious outbreak of illness among surviving Indians in northern La Florida in 1716.[5]

Mission San Juan del Puerto, the site of which is within today's Timucuan Ecological and Historic Preserve, was destroyed by Governor Moore in 1702, although Spaniards may have tried briefly to revive it in 1715. As for Nombre de Dios, a "cannon shot" from Castillo de San Marcos, its hermitage of Nuestra Señora de la Leche was also destroyed in 1702, but it was rebuilt from coquina rock, a conglomerate of sea shells. By the 1720s its Christian Indians were chiefly Yamassees from Carolina who had once been English allies but now occasionally raided their former friends. In March 1728 they were themselves attacked in their La Florida settlement by a combined force of Indians and Englishmen under Colonel John Palmer.

Thirty defenders were wounded and many more were hauled away in captivity, leaving behind a burned out hermitage chapel, and, in a very real sense, the ruins of the Spanish mission system in La Florida.[6]

From its beginnings in 1565 until 1675, San Agustín, ever the anchor in Spain's La Florida enterprise, was poorly protected by a succession of nine wooden forts. When pirate Sir Francis Drake descended on the little colony in 1586, for example, he had no trouble in overpowering the town's Fort San Juan de Pinos and carting away its bronze artillery and two thousand pounds sterling.[7]

Because Spaniards based in Florida helped protect ships headed from Nueva España to Spain from roving corsairs, the crown believed—and decreed—that the expenses of the colonists, including salaries for soldiers as well as food and clothing, should come from Nueva España. The predictable result was that residents of San Agustín, who had not taken vows of poverty as had the Franciscans, were poverty-stricken nonetheless. By 1668 eight years' payments, more than 400,000 pesos, were owed La Florida by the viceroy's treasury.[8]

The laxity in payments, if not outright penuriousness, extended even to the military. The succession of failed forts, built of wood from local trees, signified cheap construction. As early as 1586, soon after the discovery that locally available coquina, or shell stone, could be shaped into strong building blocks, requests were made for money with which to buy slaves and to hire engineers to build a stone fort. But time and again, funds either were not forthcoming or had to be spent for food simply to keep the settlers alive.[9]

Events of the 1660s were destined to change San Agustín's future. In 1665 the British crown granted some of its subjects a patent for occupation of lands on the Atlantic coast of North America extending from the James River in Virginia south through the Carolinas and Georgia all the way into northern Florida, including San Agustín. Englishmen were encouraged by their government to take what they could get, and if Spaniards had to be removed, so be it. Moreover, the British had attacked Santo Domingo and had captured Jamaica, both ominous portents for Hispania.[10]

Matters finally came to a head on May 28, 1668, in a ploy reminiscent of the Trojan horse and a Hollywood swashbuckler movie. On that day a large vessel arrived off San Agustín harbor professing to be from Veracruz in Nueva España and carrying needed flour for the colony. A Spanish launch went out to greet the ship and to put the harbor pilot aboard to check its credentials. The launch crew shouted questions to those on board, and the right answers came back. Before the harbor pilot boarded the ship, the signal was given from the launch that all was well, and the soldiers in San Agustín put their weapons away while the town rejoiced.

But it was not what it seemed. Once on the deck, the harbor pilot found himself a prisoner of English pirates from Jamaica. He was held captive and in silence until

73

Construction on Castillo de San Marcos in St. Augustine, Florida, began in 1672 in response to threats from British raiders. (Bill Keogh.)

before dawn the next morning, when four longboats loaded with a hundred corsairs rowed quickly to the unsuspecting town. Although a fisherman shouted a warning, it was too late.

Before the melee was over, eleven pirates were dead and nineteen wounded. Also killed were five Spanish soldiers defending the wooden fort. Two more pirate ships arrived during the day, and while the men were unable to take the fort, the town itself was easy prey. The British sacked it. They killed sixty people, carried off everything of value, and took seventy men, women, and children hostage. These, except for natives to be taken to Jamaica as slaves, were ransomed for water, meat, and firewood. On June 5 the raiders sailed away. San Agustín had not been burned to the ground because the pirates intended to capture it later as a base of operations. Before they left, they took soundings in the inlet, noted landmarks, and carefully measured the latitude.[11]

Just as the French threat had given birth to San Agustín, the English threat gave birth to Castillo de San Marcos. The pirates' 1668 audacity loosened strings on the Spanish purse: the colony's frigate was given new masts and rigging to assure its regular ability to contact supply bases; the 1669 payroll was released, as were extra funds for repairs, weapons, gunpowder, and lead for bullets; and the fort was allowed to keep an eighteen-pounder bronze cannon salvaged from a shipwreck. And in 1670 fifty-one new recruits arrived from Nueva España, chiefly mulattos, mestizos, and men exiled from criminal court. Beggars such as the colonists, especially those decimated by pirates, could not be choosy.[12]

In 1669 Mariana, Queen Regent of Spain, ordered her viceroy to support construction of a new fort at San Agustín strong enough to withstand serious assault. Charleston, an English settlement planted a year later on Spanish soil in La Florida in what the British called Carolina, was too close for comfort. And while a treaty between Spain and England allowed this "established" town to remain, the need for heavy-duty fortifications at San Agustín became more obvious than ever.[13]

Finally, in October 1672 ground was broken for Castillo de San Marcos. It was to be a citadel built of coquina. Those involved in its construction would include quarrymen; Timucuan, Guale, and Apalachee laborers; convict laborers, including blacks, mulattos, and Spaniards; black slaves; carpenters; blacksmiths; masons; lime burners; stonecutters; engineers; soldiers; and, at one point, even the governor of La Florida himself. By 1695 the basic fortress was complete, its massive curtain walls, bastions, and living quarters in place. A fitting memorial to the Columbian bicentenary, San Agustín was secure at last.

The castillo was the most imposing presidio in all of North America, and while there would be later additions and modifications, it was the seventeenth century which gave it form. All of it is preserved today at Castillo de San Marcos, and there is nothing else like it in the continental United States.[14]

FRANCE, THE MISSISSIPPI, TEJAS, AND LA FLORIDA

With the security of San Agustín in the face of a British threat assured for the moment, Spanish attention again turned toward the far west and the entire Gulf Coast. As had been the case in La Florida in the 1560s, the concern this time was with the French.[15]

During much of the seventeenth century the French relentlessly extended their interests up the Saint Lawrence River, westward across the Great Lakes, and southward down the Mississippi. In mid-1673, French explorer Louis Jolliet and Jesuit missionary Jacques Marquette with five men in two canoes paddled the Mississippi as far south as the mouth of the Arkansas River. This was not far from a site where in 1683 a trading post was established by the French among the Quapaw Indians, one eventually to be known and interpreted by the National Park Service as the Arkansas Post National Memorial. Hernando de Soto had died near here in 1542.[16]

In 1682 another Frenchman, René Robert Cavelier, Sieur de la Salle, completed the journey down the Mississippi to its mouth. Standing in view of the Gulf of Mexico, he erected the "arms of the King," claimed the entire valley in the name of his sovereign, Louis XIV, and named the territory Louisiana in the king's honor. On his return voyage up the Mississippi he awarded one of his men, Henri de Tonti, a large tract of land at the mouth of the Arkansas River. La Salle envisioned a valuable trade being promoted among the friendly Quapaw. Little did he or the unsuspecting natives know that by 1698 their numbers would be decimated. In that year a French missionary described the tragic consequences of a smallpox epidemic:

> We were deeply afflicted by finding this nation of the Arkansas, formerly so numerous, entirely destroyed by disease. Not a month has elapsed since they had rid themselves of smallpox, which had carried off most of them. In the villages are now nothing but graves, in which they were buried two together, and we estimated that not a hundred men were left. All of the children had died, and a great many women.[17]

The European invasion of the continent continued to take its toll on descendants of its first inhabitants.

Word of La Salle's achievement may not have fallen immediately on Spanish ears. But earlier, in 1678, royal nerves had been set on edge when rumors reached the Spanish court that a renegade Spaniard Diego Dionisio de Peñalosa, who from 1661 to 1664 had been governor of Nuevo México, had tried to interest both England and France in conquering certain provinces of northern Nueva España.[18] If the crown thought the Gulf Coast lands it had once called Amichel were threatened, it had even more cause for alarm when in 1684 La Salle sailed from France in four ships carrying four hundred soldiers, artisans, and would-be colonists for the lower Mississippi

In 1682 René Robert Cavelier, Sieur de la Salle, led an expedition that extended French claims along the Mississippi from its confluence with the Arkansas River south to the Gulf of Mexico. He named the territory Louisiana, after French King Louis XIV. (Painting by G. P. A. Healy courtesy Chicago Historical Society.)

75

In the late seventeenth century, partially to counter presumed French and Indian threats in the Río Grande region, Spanish forces began to venture north along the river, where they encountered landscapes like Upper Grew Gulch in the Chisos Mountains of today's Big Bend National Park, Texas. (George H. H. Huey.)

Valley. One of the vessels was captured en route by Spanish corsairs and the others missed the Mississippi. In January 1685 the passengers, La Salle included, were unloaded at Matagorda Bay, Texas, on soil clearly claimed by Spain. Two of the ships were wrecked almost at once; the third sailed back to France before the error in landing location—if it was that—was discovered.

The French venture proved to be a fiasco. The colonists faced nothing but hardships, and in 1687 La Salle was murdered by one of his own men. The small numbers of French adventurers who did not die from disease or at the hands of hostile Indians either found refuge in Caddo villages or made their overland way to Illinois settlements where their countrymen were told of the disaster. A few even ended up in Santa Fe in 1694 accompanying Spanish colonists to that northern province.[19] "Word of these events," wrote one historian, "sent Spanish officialdom into a panic."[20]

After the wreck of the 1554 Spanish flotilla off the coast of Padre Island, Spain's attention had been diverted away from this stretch of her lands on the west Gulf Coast for more than a century. It was only after Spaniards got word of the French colony in the region of Matagorda Bay that Spanish interest in the region truly came alive. An expedition from Nuevo León in 1686 led by Alonso de León to locate the French fort got as far north as the mouth of the Río Grande. A second expedition, also led by León, tried again in 1687, this time going along the coast next to Padre Island as far as Baffin Bay. Finally, in 1688 León and his men succeeded in locating the abandoned French post at the head of what today is Lavaca Bay, once again passing along the mainland just to the west of Padre Island, this time for its entire length.[21]

Spanish panic further showed itself when the governor of Nueva Vizcaya sent one of his ablest soldiers, Juan Fernández de Retaña, and ninety Spaniards and Indian allies also to investigate the French incursion. In 1688 Fernández set out from the presidio of San Francisco de los Conchos (south of the modern Chihuahua City, Mexico) and traveled eastward, possibly all the way to the bay of Espíritu Santo behind Matagorda Island in the Gulf of Mexico. Whether he got that far or only to the Pecos River near the Río Grande, before he turned back in March 1689 he learned from an Indian of the death of La Salle and of some of his followers. The likelihood is excellent that his 1689 journey put him in or very near the area included within today's Amistad National Recreation Area.[22]

Fernández was back at his post for only a few years when in 1693 he was ordered again to the north, this time to pacify Chisos Indians in the Big Bend area who had been hostile to Spaniards. He crossed the Río Grande at La Junta before heading east beyond the Chisos Mountains of Big Bend National Park. When he caught up with the Chisos, they surrendered and returned to La Junta, where they had been living for a long period of time. They even asked that missionaries be sent among them.[23]

Among the expeditions sent to counter the French threat in the east was one led overland to Tejas in 1690 by Alonso de León, governor of Coahuila, and Fray Damián Massanet. Father Massanet, a Franciscan, founded Mission San Francisco de los Tejas that same year. The next year Fray Massanet returned to Tejas with the new governor of Coahuila, Domingo Terán, in an effort to found another seven missions. San Francisco de los Tejas was abandoned in 1693; reestablished on a different site in 1716; abandoned again in 1719; reestablished in 1721; and finally moved to San Antonio in 1731 where it became Mission San Francisco de la Espada, one of the units now protected within the confines of San Antonio Missions National Historical Park.[24]

In 1691 the governor of Coahuila, Domingo Terán de los Ríos, escorted twenty-one friars to eastern Tejas to help them establish more missions there, in the process exploring a sizeable portion of the Tejas interior. It is possible that one of his camping places during his 1691-92 journey, a site called Yanaguana, may have been in the precise location where in 1731 the friars established Mission San Juan Capistrano, now one of the missions within San Antonio Missions National Historical Park.[25]

Just as the Spaniards were inspired to move on Tejas in the face of a perceived French threat, so were they anxious to secure the Gulf Coast in western La Florida. Not since the abortive efforts of Don Tristán de Luna to establish a colony at the site of Pensacola between 1559 and 1561 had anyone made another effort to do the same. But more than a century later, in 1686, a move in that direction was made by seaman Juan Jordán de Reina, who sailed into the inlet protected by today's Gulf Islands National Seashore where he "saw a bay, the best I have ever seen in my life. . . . The Indians call this bay Panzacola."[26]

In 1693 Nueva España's well-known mathematician and geographer Dr. Carlos de Sigüenza y Góngora accompanied Admiral Andrés de Pez on an expedition to Pensacola Bay, naming it Bahía de Santa María de Galve for the viceroy of Nueva España, Conde de Galve, who had sent them there. After anchoring, their first landing in a small boat loaded with surveying instruments was on Santa Rosa Island, no doubt in an area within the modern Gulf Islands National Seashore. For their mapping calculations they took as a fixed point on the opposite shore "what appeared to be a bluff of dark-colored clay," the place inside the national seashore where Fort Barrancas would later be built.[27]

With Sigüenza's having charted Pensacola Bay, the way was set for its colonization by Spaniards in 1698 and the beginnings of its permanent occupation by a succession of subjects of Spain, France, Britain, and citizens of the United States. The original colonizing force of "three hundred forced soldiers, convicts, beggars, and other flotsam and jetsam of the population" of Nueva España made the voyage from

Mission San Francisco de la Espada was founded on the San Antonio River in 1731. It is now a part of San Antonio Missions National Historical Park, Texas. (JC Leacock.)

77

Veracruz in a "dreary little fleet" of three vessels commanded by don Andrés de Arriola. They began their settlement somewhere within view of the present Gulf Islands National Seashore, even as all of Pensacola is today. And just in time; not far behind them was a French colonizing force under Pierre Le Moyne d'Iberville. Arriola refused them permission to enter the bay, so they sailed westward, first past the Gulf Islands to Biloxi Bay, Mississippi, and later, in 1702, into Mobile Bay and up the Mobile River where they founded Mobile in today's Alabama.[28]

To help insure protection of the Pensacola settlement, Arriola ordered Jaime Franck, his Austrian military engineer, to build a wooden fortification on the red cliffs, the *barrancas coloradas*, opposite the west end of Santa Rosa Island, which guarded the bay. Finished in 1698 and christened San Carlos de Austria, its location was within the Pensacola Forts area of today's Gulf Islands National Seashore. Also built here was the village, or *población*, of Santa María de Galve. Such communities housed those troops and their families who could not be accommodated within the restricted confines of the fort, and they were invariably adjacent to Spanish military installations of the period.[29]

> Fires were a constant hazard because the huts were thatched with palmetto leaves which rapidly dried out. Franck wrote of one fire which took place in January, 1699. It began "through the carelessness of gamblers. Some soldiers' barracks, the chapel, Jordan's [an officer's] quarters . . . and the provision magazine were consumed by fire in less than a quarter hour. Nothing of mine was burned, but I was robbed a plenty." Little wonder that Franck concluded one of his letters be referring to San Carlos de Austria as a "disagreeable wilderness" and saying that he had never been "in such a sorry job."
>
> Added to these difficulties was the fact that the garrison was never at full troop strength, and the caliber of the troops left much to be desired. Many of them were criminals "whereby the jails and junk shops of Mexico . . . [were] cleaned out." Life at the fort was hard. The men and officers lived in primitive barracks and huts, and their pay was small and erratic. Auxiliary buildings, such as warehouses, a chapel, guard house and hospital, were built either within or close by the stockade. A cemetery was established to the west of the compound. With so little to offer, it was difficult to recruit soldiers and laborers.[30]

The ever-contested lines separating Spain from France had been drawn, extending northward from the Gulf of Mexico. By the end of the seventeenth century La Florida proper remained in Spanish hands and Texas lay within her purview. But Carolina and Georgia were effectively in English control, and France had challenged Spain by laying claim to Louisiana and parts of what were to become Arkansas, Alabama, and Mississippi. The contest for supremacy in North America would occupy all three nations, as well as a new United States, in the century to follow.

NUEVO MÉXICO

The year 1610 marked an early turning point in the history of Nuevo México. Don Juan de Oñate departed from the colony he had successfully, however precariously, founded. With the arrival on the scene of his successor, don Pedro de Peralta, Spanish control of Nuevo México entered into what one historian has described "as essentially a holding measure." In addition to the motive of effecting religious conversion among the region's native populace, he writes,

> Spain's support of its "white elephant" in Nuevo México was influenced by another factor. This was the fact that as long as there was a Spanish force in the area, Madrid retained a claim to the vast country lying to the north, as France, England, and even the Netherlands had already challenged Spain's exclusive control in the Western World. . . . No attempt was made to define the limits of the province of Nuevo México, and in general it included most of what is now the western United States.[31]

In 1607 or 1608 some of Oñate's settlers—with the governor's approval—had moved from San Gabriel to the south. One result was a fledgling community given the name of "Holy Faith," Santa Fe. Governor Peralta elevated its status in 1610 to that of capital, a lofty position it has enjoyed ever since. It is, in fact, the oldest capital city among those of the fifty United States.[32]

The Spaniards' grip on Nuevo México in 1610 was tenuous at best. With this remote northern province in mind, the viceroy of Nueva España grumped to his sovereign in 1608, "No one comes to America to plow and sow, but only to eat and loaf."[33] It is doubtful, however, that many Nuevo Mexicano settlers were loafing and eating well. Even those who toiled diligently found themselves in a struggle for mere survival.

For the seven decades between the 1610 establishment of Santa Fe as the capital and the 1680 rebellion of the province's Puebloan peoples, those who worked hardest to ensure that Spain's flag would continue to fly over these lands so distant from Mexico City were confreres of the Order of Friars Minor, blue-robed Franciscan priests and brothers. At least 250 friars worked in the Pueblos during this great missionary era, with the crown spending more than a million pesos on missionaries' salaries, supplies, and construction of monumental churches and mission complexes. These concerted efforts to bring about the religious, economic, and political assimilation of Native Americans extended from Pecos, at the edge of the plains, to Hopi villages on plateaus to the west, south to the Tano pueblos in the Galisteo Basin and to the Salinas pueblos of the Tompiros, and farther south to the Piro pueblos of the lower Río Grande.[34]

Like Spaniards who had preceded them, the friars found in seventeenth-century Nuevo México thousands of men, women, and children who lived in compact and

79

solidly constructed towns, often of two- and three-story structures, built around central plazas. A few of these communities, *pueblos* in Spanish, may have had nearly two thousand residents. Most were home for fewer than four hundred people. Well-developed systems of agriculture provided crops of corn, squash, beans, and cotton; hunting game and gathering wild plants supplemented subsistence. So were there extensive networks of trade over vast expanses of territory.

These Puebloans spoke dialects of at least nine mutually unintelligible languages: Hopi, Zuni, Tewa, Tiwa, Towa, Keres, Tano, Piro, and Tompiro. With the exception of the last three all continue to be spoken today among the residents of the Hopi villages in northern Arizona and of nineteen pueblo reservations in New Mexico. There are also "Tigua" settlements at Tortugas, New Mexico, and El Paso, Texas, in the suburb of Ysleta del Sur. These are inhabited by descendants of various Pueblo peoples who fled or who were taken to the lower Río Grande in the wake of the 1680 Pueblo Revolt. The Tigua reservation at El Paso, whose residents—like those of Tortugas—speak only Spanish and English, is not far from Chamizal National Memorial.

Although missionary efforts of the Spaniards were directed primarily at Puebloan peoples, the presence of Spaniards in Nuevo México had inevitable consequences for other regional Native Americans as well. There were Athapaskan-speaking natives whose modern descendants are to be found among the Navajo, Jicarilla, Chiricahua, and Mescalero. So were there Utes and Comanches whose lives as well as those of generations of their progeny were forever changed by the arrival of permanent European dwellers within and next to their aboriginal lands.

The consequences of the contact between American cultures in Nuevo México—as elsewhere—were often immediate, multitudinous, and unanticipated by both donors and recipients. Spaniards poured new sources of potentially consumable energy into the region's arid environment in the form of domestic animals: cattle, sheep, goats, pigs, and domestic fowl. New crops such as melons and fruit trees, but most notably wheat—which unlike corn, squash, and beans can be grown in the winter—greatly expanded the range of food sources. Horses, mules, and burros added to human efficiency by allowing one person to increase his or her workload.

Also introduced were such new agricultural technologies as the plow; a new language, Spanish; the new arts of reading and writing; a new religion with its

Introduction of the Spanish plow and beasts of burden in the Rio Grande Valley in 1600 revolutionized agricultural production of Puebloan farmers. (Courtesy Museum of New Mexico, Santa Fe.)

80

attendant forms of ritual, art, and architecture as well as its own code of morality; new craft techniques, such as those involving blacksmithing and carpentry; new methods of preparing food and of curing; new music and musical instruments, including the double-headed hide drum; and a new, more profit-driven, economy. Also affected were clothing and personal adornment; family structure, with the occurrence of intercultural marriages; and occupational roles. Spaniards employed or pressed Native Americans into service as cooks, maids, carpenters, herders, gardeners, commercial weavers, gleaners of pinyon nuts, salt bearers, and laborers of other kinds. And in Pueblo communities they unilaterally appointed governors, lieutenant governors, sheriffs (*aguaciles*), ditch bosses (*mayordomos*), councilmen (*principales* or *regidores*), church wardens (*fiscales*), and even bell-ringers.[35]

Another institution that characterized contact between Indian and non-Indian in Nuevo México, beginning with Juan de Oñate and persisting into the seventeenth century, was that of *encomienda*. Historian Simmons explains:

> To reward conquistadors in the New World, the king assigned them one or more Indian towns in trusteeship, or encomienda, meaning the colonist (called an *encomendero*) was allowed to collect and use the tribute that otherwise would have gone into the royal treasury. The encomienda grant was highly coveted, not only because it represented a steady source of income, but because it conferred upon the holder exalted status, marking him as a select member of the colonial aristocracy.[36]

Encomenderos, in return for the privilege of being able to exact tribute from the natives, were expected to help protect those natives from enemies. They were further obliged to respond to the provincial governor's call to arms, to live in Santa Fe, to ride escort, to serve as guards, and when necessary to command lesser colonists and native auxiliaries in the colony's defense. Customarily designated as "captains" by the governor, they and the colonists and natives who fought under them took the place of regular troops in seventeenth-century Nuevo México. Their numbers in this far northern frontier came to be limited by the viceroy to thirty-five.[37]

The natives of seventeenth-century Nuevo México found themselves the objects of conflicting demands for their time and labor on the part of Spanish civil and religious authorities. Politically appointed governors and encomenderos expected Indians to work for them. So did the Franciscan missionaries who were trying to establish economically viable mission communities. Civil authorities accused the missionaries of abusing their Indian neophytes; the missionaries returned the favor by hurling similar accusations at those in charge of governing the province's secular affairs. From the point of view of Puebloans as well as from that of Spanish officials sent to the frontier to investigate the causes of dissension between civil and religious authorities, a pox should have been laid on both their houses.[38]

81

It is possible to examine events in Nuevo México of the seventeenth century from many different viewpoints. The outlooks from Pecos and from the Salinas Pueblos, as well as from the engravings in the sandstone cliffs at El Morro, however, provide a reasonable glimpse of the human drama as it unfolded elsewhere on this Spanish frontier that was, in the words of Spanish-born don Diego de Vargas, "remote beyond compare."[39]

Pecos Pueblo was with its two thousand residents among the largest of all Puebloan communities in the early seventeenth century. It early became one of the richest encomiendas in the new province.[40] It was 1617, however, before Franciscans began their sustained efforts toward evangelization there. It was possibly on her feast day, August 2 of 1617 or 1618, that Fray Pedro Zambrano Ortiz bestowed the patronage of Nuestra Señora de los Ángeles de Porciúncula on the community's first European living quarters, a convento for the friar. It was built just beyond the confines of the pueblo, a city state whose seed had been planted about A.D. 1400 or 1450. Much later, in 1769, the same patronal name was to be given to a river in Alta California where a great city, Los Angeles, was destined to grow. Nuestra Señora de los Ángeles de Porciúncula near Assisi in Italy was the mother house of the Order of Friars Minor (Franciscans).[41]

The Salinas pueblos—so named by Spaniards for the nearby salt lakes (*salinas*)—were by no means overlooked. A mission begun at Chililí in 1613 or 1614 was followed in 1622 by one founded at Abó, one of three units within the modern Salinas Pueblo Missions National Historical Monument. The other two pueblo units preserved within the monument, Quarai and Las Humanas (Gran Quivira), had missions begun within their midsts in 1626 and 1629, respectively.[42]

Cancerous jealousies and struggles for prerogatives between religious and civil authorities quickly manifested themselves at Pecos. Governor Juan de Eulate, who took office in 1618, was anxious to curry favor with the Puebloans. He was accused by the friars, who were trying to overturn the Puebloans' "idols" and to undermine the authority of the native religious hierarchy, of encouraging paganism. A native interpreter in the employ of the governor went about assuring the people, including those at Pecos, that newly converted Indians need relinquish neither their native idols nor their concubinage. The governor, furthermore, was accused by the missionaries of condoning forced labor, slavery, and the kidnapping of "orphans."[43]

In 1620 Mexican-born Fray Pedro de Ortega became Zambrano's successor as the missionary at Pecos. Like Zambrano before him, Ortega made it his business to destroy the religious paraphernalia—objects of clay, stone, and wood—of the Pecos people, their "pagan idols," whenever he found them. Although he is not credited with having built the first church at Pecos, discounting a brush *jacal* that must have served the purpose, Fray Ortega likely had a hand in the beginnings of the "convento and most splendid temple of singular construction and excellence" erected by his successor, Fray Andrés Juárez, between 1621 and 1625. Based on sheer size alone,

82

the first real church at Pecos, the ruins of which are now preserved in Pecos National Historical Park, qualifies as one of the most ambitious buildings ever constructed under Spanish auspices in North America. Historian Kessell describes it well:

> The Pecos project was monumental. The pueblo's size, consequence, and self-respect dictated that its church be the best in the land. Plans called for a nave as wide inside as the largest available pine beams would span, forty-one feet at the entrance, tapering to thirty-seven and a half feet at the sanctuary. Height of ceiling would approximate width. The number of Pecos Indians, that is the size of the potential congregation, determined length—a remarkable one hundred and forty-five feet from entrance to the farthest recess of the apse. Wall thickness varied from eight to ten feet down the sides between the buttresses, to twenty-two feet at the back corners where two of the planned towers would rise. Outside, the massive structure, with its rows of rectangular ground-to-roof buttresses up the lateral walls, its six towers, and its crenelated parapet would look as much like a fortress as a church—a reflection not of Father Juárez' fear of attack, but rather of European heritage.
>
> Such an undertaking laid a heavy burden on the Pecos. Each sun-dried mud block, about 9 1/2 by 18 by 3 inches, weighed forty pounds or so. Gray to black in color and containing bits of bone, charcoal, and pottery, the earth must have been dug from trash mounds that had accumulated along the edge of the mesilla. The job would require 300,000 adobes. While the men hauled earth and water and the great quantity of wood needed for scaffolding, the actual laying up of walls in Pueblo society was women's work. "If we force some man to build a wall," wrote Fray Alonso Benavides, "he runs away from it, and the women laugh."[44]

The eighteenth-century church of Mission Nuestra Señora de los Angeles de Porciúncula visible at Pecos National Historical Park, New Mexico, was built over the rubble of an earlier and much larger structure, which was destroyed in the 1680 Pueblo Revolt. (George H. H. Huey.)

This tremendous building was architecturally unique. Built of adobe, field stone, and wood, it was a far northern-frontier version of the masonry fortress-churches erected in Europe and in Nueva España in the sixteenth century. Lauded by chroniclers as a "magnificent temple," it served the Pecos peoples until the general Pueblo Revolt of 1680. Its full dimensions were not understood in modern times until 1967, when National Park Service archeologist Jean Pinkley uncovered its massive foundations underlying "the smaller, cruder eighteenth-century church built right on top of its crumpled ruins."[45]

While building was underway at Pecos, Fray Francisco Fonte began in 1623 to plan a permanent church for the Tompiro-speaking natives of Abó. The settlement had been here since at least A.D. 1100. The prehistoric ruins as well as those of Father Fonte's mission of San Gregorio are preserved within Salinas Pueblo Missions National Historical Monument. Far more modest in size than the monument simultaneously being erected at Pecos, Father Fonte's church and convento featured a novel bit of architecture for a mission complex: a circular kiva, or Puebloan underground

This pottery candlestick was excavated from the seventeenth-century ruins of Las Humanas pueblo, Salinas Pueblo Missions National Monument, New Mexico. (Lawrence Ormsby.)

ceremonial chamber, within the mission's courtyard. Archeologist and architectural historian James Ivey writes, "Since it appears to have been built during the major construction effort on the church, Fonte must have approved of it. It may have served as the temporary church during the construction of the full-sized church, helping the Indians in the transition from their kivas to the above-ground churches typical of Catholicism."[46] If Ivey is correct, Father Fonte appears to have been far ahead of his time in terms of tolerance of native religious beliefs and practices.

Construction of the first church of San Gregorio de Abó was completed about 1627. Between 1640 and 1651, a later Franciscan, Fray Francisco Acevedo, greatly enlarged and altered the church and convento at Abó. In the reverse of the situation at Pecos, where a smaller mission had been erected on the ruins of a larger one, at Abó the later and larger mission concealed the presence of the earlier and smaller church until Ivey, in his role as archeologist, uncovered the buried evidence in March 1987.

Alterations on the church and convento at Abó continued until the time of its abandonment about 1673. Survivors gave up their ancient village to take refuge among towns to the west along the Río Grande. Apache raids and, above all, a drought and resulting famine of 1667-72 had been too much for them.[47]

The ruins of Abó and land surrounding them became a New Mexico State Monument in 1938. During that year and the next archeological investigations were carried out at the site; the massive walls of the later church were stabilized and, to some extent, reconstructed. Further stabilization and alterations took place in 1958 and 1971-72. In 1981 the National Park Service took over management of Abó under the 1980-created Salinas National Monument, today's Salinas Pueblo Missions National Monument, and stabilization efforts in 1983-84 brought the ruins to their present magnificent appearance, a great monument still "in the midst of a loneliness."[48]

The beginnings of the pueblo of Quarai date to the start of the fourteenth century A.D. By the time in 1626 when Fray Juan Gutiérrez de la Chica arrived on the scene, it was probably inhabited by peoples speaking a Tompiro language. Southern Tiwa-speakers, with whom the settlement has been most frequently identified, may have been brought here by friars in the seventeenth century.[49]

Father Gutiérrez began to build his mission of La Purísima Concepción de Cuarac (Quarai) in 1627. The church, convento, and courtyards were probably ready for dedication about 1632. As at Abó, later friars made various repairs and changes to the church and complex, including the addition of second-story rooms above the sacristy.[50]

Quarai was abandoned by friars and natives alike, probably about 1677. A community that had been in place more or less continuously since A.D. 1300 was unable to withstand oppressive demands made on it by conflicting interests of Spanish authorities of church and state, effects of the drought and famine of 1667-72, and the effects of Apache raids and epidemic diseases. Survivors went to live with their cultural kinsmen in villages along the Río Grande and elsewhere.[51]

The ruins of Quarai had brief periods of reuse and reoccupation in the mid-eighteenth and nineteenth centuries, and early in the twentieth century a Mr. Baca lived in the convento. In 1913, 1935-36, 1939-40, and 1958 archeologists working variously under the auspices of the Museum of New Mexico, the Civilian Conservation Corps, the Works Projects Administration, and the National Youth Administration carried out archeological investigations at the site. In 1981 Quarai State Monument was transferred to the National Park Service and is now a part of Salinas Pueblo Missions National Monument.[52]

About 1300, at the same time people were beginning to settle Quarai, still others were beginning to construct a large circular pueblo at a place known at least since the nineteenth century as Gran Quivira. The ruins of this and later pueblos at the site, as well as of two churches constructed here under Franciscan auspices in the seventeenth century, now constitute the Gran Quivira unit of Salinas Pueblo Missions National Monument. Spaniards knew this place, called by its inhabitants Cueloce, as the Tompiro community of Las Humanas. In the seventeenth century, it was the largest of the Salinas pueblos.[53]

The Tompiros of Las Humanas were targeted for conversion with the arrival there in 1629 of Father Francisco Letrado and the Franciscan lay brother Diego de San Lucas. The two friars negotiated successfully with the natives for usable rooms within the existing pueblo and for land on which a church could eventually be built. They repainted the walls of one of the rooms, placed an altar in it, and used it as a temporary place of Christian worship, one probably dedicated to San Isidro. In 1630, after spending the winter in Santa Fe, the two men returned. With the help of a pro-Spanish faction in the village, they began to build a church. Father Letrado was reassigned to the Zuni pueblo of Hawikuh in 1631 and killed there in February 1632. But Brother San Lucas, working under direction of Father Francisco de Acevedo who had been sent to Abó, remained to oversee completion of the structure in 1634 or early 1635. By then the status of Las Humanas had been reduced to that of a *visita*, a mission with no priest in residence.[54]

As for the martyred Father Letrado, a record of his demise survives in the rocks. On the north cliff of Inscription Rock at El Morro is an engraved inscription which reads, "se pasaron a 23 de Marzo de 1632 anos a la benganza de muerte del Padre Letrado. Luhan" [They passed on March 23, 1632, to the avenging of the death of Father Letrado. Luhan (who was presumably a soldier)].[55]

The first church at Las Humanas—whether dedicated to San Isidro or to San Buenaventura remains a question—underwent various repairs and revisions until construction began on a new church in 1660. Foundations for this more ambitious building were laid by Fray Diego de Santander, who worked on the building until his

A seventeenth-century Spanish leaf-shaped lance blade. (George H. H. Huey from the Enrique E. Guerra collection.)

85

transfer to San Marcos in the Galisteo Basin in 1662. His two successors attempted to complete the job, but time ran out on Humanas. In 1670 Apaches struck the pueblo with a vengeance, sacking the San Isidro church in the process. The general famine affecting the whole province began here in 1669, and in 1671 friars and the pro-Spanish faction of the pueblo left the ancient settlement. They probably moved to Abó before moving again to pueblos on the Río Grande. Las Humanas was left to collapse into rubble. By the nineteenth century it had become an archeological site.[56]

In 1909 Las Humanas became the Gran Quivira National Monument. Although limited stabilization of the ruins occurred earlier, major archeological and stabilization efforts were carried out from 1927 to 1932. More work was done in 1938-1940, 1942, 1948, 1962, 1965-1968, 1976, and 1978-1981. The end result, with Abó and Quarai, is the most compelling modern evocation of those troublous times in seventeenth-century Nuevo México to be seen anywhere. They make Salinas Pueblo Missions National Monument one of the most dramatic parks in the United States.[57]

Buildings aside, what of the effectiveness of the message of redemption and religious salvation extolled by the friars? Father Juárez and all who followed him at Pecos and in the other pueblos became fully aware that the governors appointed by Spaniards were merely figureheads in their respective communities, people who became middlemen in brokering relations between Puebloan peoples and outsiders to the culture. Internally, the real power remained in the hands of persons whom the Spaniards called *caciques*, the "priests of the idols," as they were labeled by one Franciscan. These men were the stubborn guardians of ancient tradition, and try as the missionaries might to shred it—then as now—the fabric of native social and religious organization remained intact. The virgin Mother of God was added to Corn Mother; the role of governor, while made permanent, failed to displace the role of cacique.[58]

Situated as it was next to the Great Plains, since time immemorial Pecos had been a trading center for Puebloans and peoples who dwelled to the north and east. By the sixteenth century Apachean-speaking Native Americans were among the principal trading partners of Pecos residents. The plains people were able to offer Alibates flint knives; flint and bone scrapers and other tools; buffalo hides and buffalo leather goods; jerked and powdered meat; tallow; tanned skins of antelope, deer, and elk; salt; and an occasional Caddoan-speaking slave from farther east. In return, the nomads received corn, other agricultural products, pottery, local turquoise, and cotton blankets. Pecos became middlemen in these exchanges, passing along, especially, the much-needed skins to other Puebloans and to Spaniards. The latter used the skins for everything from clothing and sacks to tents, breastplates, and footwear.[59]

After 1630, and with even more intensity after 1650, Franciscans—frustrated in their attempts to suppress native religious practices—began to make more direct assaults on native religious practices and practitioners. Imprisonment, torture, and public flogging of recalcitrants became a common mode of discipline. Alleged Indian sorcerers were occasionally hanged by civil authorities.[60]

Adding to tensions between Spaniards and Puebloans was the fact that the Spaniards' desire for slaves eventually disrupted what had been peaceful trade relationships between plains-dwelling Apaches and Comanches and Puebloans at such places as Pecos and the settlements of Las Humanas, Abó, and Quarai. By the 1670s Apaches were themselves being taken as slaves for Spaniards' homes; what had once been amity between Puebloans and plains peoples turned to enmity, with Puebloan settlements on the eastern fringes being subjected to steadily increasing raids by their newly horse-mounted neighbors. The Apaches helped force abandonment of several Pueblo towns. It was harvest time in 1670 when they overran Las Humanas, sacking the church of San Isidro, killing eleven residents, and taking thirty-one captives.[61]

If these were not woes enough, the years between 1667 and 1672 were times of severe drought throughout Nuevo México. Famine took its toll on Spaniards and Native Americans alike, with no crops harvested between 1665 and 1668. The numbers of dead were in addition to those of people swept away by European-introduced diseases. Smallpox, measles, whooping cough, and cholera were grim reapers. In 1640 smallpox killed three thousand Native Americans, nearly ten percent of the entire Pueblo population at the time. More epidemics ravaged the populace in the 1660s.[62]

The Hopi pueblo of Mishóngnovi in northern Arizona, typical of the communities to which many Puebloans of New Mexico's Rio Grande Valley fled in the wake of the 1680 Pueblo Revolt. (Ben Wittick photo courtesy Museum of New Mexico, Santa Fe.)

All these events culminated in 1680 in a well-planned and well-coordinated rebellion by most Puebloans against their Spanish oppressors. One of the leaders of the rebellion was Popé, a Tewa religious leader from San Juan Pueblo who had been flogged by the Spaniards in 1675 for his participation in efforts earlier in the decade to reinvigorate native religious practices. Popé directed efforts of his fellow Puebloans from Taos Pueblo.[63]

In 1680 the 2,350 Spaniards living in Nuevo México, including thirty-three Franciscan missionaries residing in native settlements, were outnumbered along the Río Grande and at Ácoma Pueblo by 25,000-30,000 Native Americans. Most of the former were living in Santa Fe and vicinity, and when the rebellion began, a force of Tanos besieged the capital. Except at Isleta Pueblo and in the Piro missions, residents killed the missionaries and any other Spaniards they could find. Within a matter of days, all the missions had been destroyed, and twenty-one missionaries and nearly four hundred colonists had been killed.

Governor Antonio de Otermín was allowed to lead the surviving Spaniards and their Indian sympathizers south from Nuevo México all the way to El Paso. Although

87

at least two attempts were soon made by Spaniards to regain the lost province, it was not until 1692 that Spanish forces led by don Diego de Vargas were able to effect a reconquest. For a dozen years the Puebloans were left largely to their own devices, their rebellion against the Spaniards marking one of the rare times in history that Native Americans were successful through their own efforts in ridding themselves of what they clearly regarded as Spanish oppression.[64]

By 1680 the Salinas pueblos had been abandoned. But the Towas at Pecos were still very much alive and in place. Internally divided between an anti-Spanish faction and another that, if not pro-Spanish, was at least neutral on the subject, the Pecos behaved with some duplicity. They did not kill their minister, the aged Fray Fernando de Velasco, but instead sent him off to Galisteo, where the Tanos promptly killed him instead. At least twenty days before the event, they revealed to a Spaniard plans for the uprising. So did they reveal the plans to Father Velasco. This gave them time to warn Governor Otermín of impending events, however useless the warnings proved to be. The people at Pecos did, though, kill a young lay brother, Juan de la Pedrosa, as well as two Spanish women and three Spanish children. And while there were Pecos residents who helped besiege Santa Fe, not a single person from Pecos is mentioned as a rebel in Spanish records of the 1680s.[65]

What is clear from the physical evidence is that someone—the people of Pecos later accused the Tewas—laid waste to the monumental church at Pecos. Everything in it made of wood, including the massive roof, was torched. "It was," writes historian John Kessell,

> like a giant furnace. When the fire died down, the blackened walls of the gutted monster stood still. To bring it low, Indians bent on demolition clambered all over it, like the Lilliputians over Gulliver, laboriously but jubilantly throwing down adobes, tens of thousands of them. Unsupported by the side walls, the front wall toppled forward face down, covering the layer of ashes blown out the door. With an explosive vengeance, the Pueblos had reduced the grandest church in New Mexico to an imposing mound of earthen rubble.[66]

It is almost impossible today, standing on the very site now serenely silent except for the happy voices of fellow visitors to Pecos, to imagine the fury and hatred that created such awesome ruins.

Almost as if to commemorate the two hundredth anniversary of Columbus's bold move to America, in 1692 don Diego de Vargas launched his successful reconquest of Nuevo México from his post in El Paso. Early during the reconquest he marched on Pecos. He found it deserted. Soon, however, two Pecos people, an old man and an old woman, were found nearby and taken prisoner. Both told the same story: the young people had fled when they heard that Vargas was at Santa Fe and had rejected a proposal by male elders to go to Santa Fe to sue for peace. Vargas released the old man as an emissary to tell the others that Vargas had come to pardon the people of Pecos in the name of the king. Ultimately, the plan worked. The Towas returned to their pueblo and Vargas departed in peace.[67]

The closing years of the seventeenth century at Pecos, as elsewhere in Nuevo México, were neither uniformly peaceful nor trouble-free. Although the new Spanish administration was perhaps more enlightened than had been those of the pre-revolt years, Christian religious practices were again imposed on the natives. Missionaries baptized persons born since 1680. And Vargas installed as officials at Pecos a governor, lieutenant governor, alcalde, aguacil, fiscales, and war captains elected by the Indians themselves. The old dual system of governance had returned.[68]

In 1693 the newly elected governor of Pecos, Juan de Ye, warned Vargas of a plot he said was being fomented by Tewas and Tanos along with people at Picurís and Taos pueblos to prevent Spanish colonists from reoccupying Santa Fe. With Juan de Ye and some forty Pecos warriors to aid him, Vargas and his own soldiers forcibly recaptured the Spanish capital and moved in. By thus currying Spanish favor, the people of Pecos hoped once again to establish their pueblo as the profitable gateway of trade between the plains and Río Grande Valley.[69]

In 1694 Vargas installed Father Diego de Zeinos as the missionary at Pecos. In less than three weeks he had overseen construction of a temporary church, one that incorporated the huge, still standing north wall of the convento and which lay on top the leveled mound covering the wall of the pre-1680 structure. The new building measured about twenty by sixty or seventy feet. It would do until a new church was begun some eleven years later.[70]

Father Zeinos accidentally shot and killed one of his Pecos servants in 1695, with the result that he was sent away from the pueblo to be replaced by fathers Juan Alpuente and Domingo de Jesús María, neither liked by the Pecos. Adding to the Pecos' discontent was the fact that the winter of 1695-96 was again a time of drought aggravated by a plague of worms the previous growing season. Hardest hit were the new Spanish colonists, and their food shortages placed increased demands on the Puebloans. His parishioners threatened Father Domingo, and it appeared that a repeat of 1680 was about to take place.[71]

The ax came down on June 4, 1696. The Tewa, Tiwa, and Tano pueblos of the north as well as Jémez rebelled, killing twenty-one Spanish settlers and five Franciscan friars who were dispatched to their greater reward. Again, Pecos remained divided into factional camps. Its people took no direct part in the rebellion, which Vargas was able to put down within six months, and the pro-Spanish faction hanged four leaders of the anti-Spanish faction within the pueblo.[72]

Despite the show of loyalty to the Spaniards, Vargas ordered everything of value removed from Pecos. He told the people it was to protect the goods, church furnishings included, from rebel attack from outside. Since Vargas had been able to quell the

89

general uprising, the resolve in Mexico City became stronger than ever to hold this far northern province at all costs. A repeat of the 1680 fiasco might cause native uprisings along the entire northern frontier, the reasoning went, so more settlers, livestock, provisions, and tools were poured into the enterprise. The 1696 rebellion had precisely the opposite effect than that desired by its fomenters.[73]

Vargas was replaced as governor and captain general of Nuevo México by Pedro Rodríguez Cubero in 1697, although the reconqueror remained in this land so distant from his home in Spain until his death in 1704. Six Franciscans took turns administering to Pecos between 1697 and 1700, most often visiting there from Santa Fe. At the end of the century and the beginning of the next one, Pecos was a pueblo divided. "The fatal rift at Pecos," Kessell tells us,

> betrayed only vaguely in the years before, broke wide open under the stress of revolt and reconquest. Pecos turned on Pecos. None would forget the executions of 1696. For whatever reasons, some had committed themselves to the Spaniards' presence—at a later date they would have been styled Progressives—while others—the Conservatives—resisted it just as grimly.
>
> Rent from within . . . the fortress at the gateway between pueblos and plains stood less firm before the Comanches and the epidemics to come.[74]

To the west, a few seventeenth-century Spaniards—in addition to Oñate and the troops en route to avenge the death of Father Letrado—left their names and messages on the cliffs at El Morro. On July 29 in what appears to be 1620, for example, an inscription was engraved that says, in translation, "I am the captain General of the Provinces of Nuevo México for the King our Lord, passed by here on the return from the pueblos of Zuni on the 29th of July in the year 1620, and put them at peace at their humble petition, they asking favor as vassals of his Majesty and promising anew their obedience, all of which he did, with clemency, zeal, and prudence, as a most Christian-like (gentleman) extraordinary and gallant soldier of enduring and praised memory."[75]

The irony in this inscription is that the captain general and governor of Nuevo México at the time was don Juan de Eulate. Kessell once more tells us about the governor:

> In testimony . . . which eventually found its way to the Tribunal of the Holy Office in Mexico City—the Franciscans and their allies damned Eulate on a variety of counts, making him out a blaspheming ogre, a mortal enemy of the church, the faithful, and the Indian. To ingratiate himself with mission Indians and loosen the friars' hold, the governor deliberately encouraged these natives to continue their pagan ways. . . . Eulate protected and favored Pueblo ceremonial leaders, "idolaters and witches . . . because they trade him tanned skins."

90

The governor paid no heed to Indian rights, charged the missionaries, only to Indian exploitation. He condoned forced labor, slavery, and even the kidnapping of "orphans." As a reward for loyalty to him, Eulate issued to his henchmen licenses on small slips of paper, *vales*, entitling them to seize one or more orphaned Indian children, a practice [Father] Zambrano witnessed at Pecos. "Like black slaves," these children, the friars averred, ended up perpetual servants in Spanish homes. The slips merely read: "Permit for Juan Fulano to take one orphan from wherever he finds him provided that he treats him well and teaches him the Christian catechism."[76]

Nor was this all. Eulate had declared in front of a priest and others that marriage was a better state than that of celibacy. Religious men, moreover, did nothing but sleep and eat, while married men went diligently about their work. The outraged priest responded that "the sleep of John had been more acceptable to Christ Our Lord than the diligence of Judas," but the response fell on deaf ears.[77]

Relieved as governor at the end of 1625, Eulate was arrested by civil authorities when he reached Mexico City on charges of Indian slave trading and of having used several wagons to haul goods to Nueva España duty-free.[78] None of this seems to describe a "most Christian-like (gentleman) extraordinary and gallant soldier of enduring and praised memory."

In 1629 someone carved the only poem ever to appear on Inscription Rock when Governor Manuel de Silva Nieto and his party passed by on a journey during which they stationed new missionaries at the pueblos of Ácoma, Zuni, and Hopi. The poetic inscription, the only record of this journey, reads:

(George Grant photo courtesy National Park Service Western Archeological and Conservation Center, Tucson, Arizona.)

Aqui [obliterated] y Governado

Don Francisco Manuel de Silva Nieto

Que lo ynposible tiene ya sujeto

Su braco yndubitable y su Balor

Conlos carros del Rei Nuestro Senor

Cosa quesolo el Puso en este Efecto.

De Agosto 5 seiscientos Beinte y Nueve Que se

bien a Zuñi pasa y la Fe lleve.

91

The unrhymed translation is:

> Here [passed] the Governor
>
> Francisco Manuel de Silva Nieto
>
> Who has done the impossible,
>
> by his invincible arm and his valor,
>
> with the wagons of the King our Master,
>
> a thing to which he alone put into effect
>
> August 5, 1629, that one may pass to
>
> Zuni and carry the faith.[79]

Other names of seventeenth-century Nuevo Mexicanos also appear on the sandstone: Juan Gonsales (possibly 1629); Captain-Sergeant-Major Juan de Arechuleta and the Adjutant Diego Martín Barba and the Lieutenant Agustín de Ynojos (1636); Juan Garsya (1636); Luys Pacheco; Antonio de Zalas; Juan de Godoy (1640); Bartolomé Romero (1641); Juan del Castillo (possibly 1646); Francisco Luxán de Jurado (1660 or 1666); Bartolomé de Sisneros; and Antonio González (1660 or 1667). The latter was secretary to the Father Custodian of Nuevo México's Franciscans, Fray Alonso de Posada. Sometime during his 1661-64 tenure as governor of Nuevo México, the infamous Diego Dionisio de Peñalosa, who later tried to sell his services to England and to France in their competition with Spain, denied Father Posada and his secretary, Gonzáles, proper military escort for a visitation to the Zuni and Hopi pueblos.[80]

One of the most historically significant seventeenth-century inscriptions at El Morro reads in translation: "Here was the General Don Diego de Vargas, who conquered for our Holy Faith, and for the Royal Crown, all the Nuevo México, at his expense, Year of 1692." It was in Vargas's journal that the term El Morro first appeared. The inscription could have been fashioned here on his first visit, November 8, 1692, or on his return trip from Hopi and Zuni after November 27 of that year. And while the legacy of Vargas is often said to be the continuing Spanish presence in New Mexico, "the only physical marks of his you can see today are the words scratched into the rock at El Morro."[81]

PIMERÍA ALTA

Most of us who live in the United States do not know that a region encompassed by what since the mid-nineteenth century has been "southern Arizona" was once considered by Spaniards to be the northern half of the Pimería Alta, its southern half

92

today comprising a large area of northern Sonora, Mexico. The whole of the Pimería Alta, since 1854 divided by an international boundary, lies within the Sonoran Desert. It is a land famed for its saguaros and other columnar cacti as well as for its paloverdes, mesquites, Gila monsters, and horned rattlesnakes.

In the late seventeenth century, this northern reach of Nueva España was vaguely conceptualized as a part of the province of Nueva Vizcaya, New Biscay, or perhaps as part of the province of Ostimuri or of an ill-defined Sonora. Earlier, in the sixteenth century, it had merely been a part of America Septentrional, a land in the northerly direction of the constellation of the seven plow oxen.[82]

The Pimería Alta received its name soon after the arrival there in 1687 of a Jesuit missionary, visionary, and cartographer, Eusebio Francisco Kino. Father Kino and other Spaniards were aware that the Native Americans who lived there spoke mutually intelligible dialects of a language common to others farther south in Nueva España, a tongue labeled by Spaniards as Pima. To distinguish these northern Piman speakers from those in the south, their homelands came to be known respectively as the Pimería Alta and the Pimería Baja—the lands of the northern and southern Piman Indians. That the natives referred to themselves as the O'odham, or dialectical variations of that term, failed to interfere with the labeling propensities of the conquerors.

In subtle ways, the Pimería Alta has managed to persist as an environmental, historical, and cultural entity to the present. Although the land is now intersected by the United States and Mexico boundary, southern Arizonans living south of the Gila River and Sonorans living in Hermosillo and northward have strong ties to one another socially and economically. There is manifested a realization, however slight, of a shared historic and cultural heritage.

Although the cultural heritage began in prehistoric times with the O'odham, several thousand of whose descendants continue to live in southern Arizona, it was a heritage that became enlarged with Father Kino's arrival in 1687 at the O'odham (Piman) village of Cosari on the headwaters of the Río San Miguel in what today is northern Sonora. Kino had come to the region to start cattle and horse ranches as a means of supplying the Jesuits' mission enterprise in Baja California. When he rode out of the Opata mission settlement of Cucurpe and headed a few miles northward to Cosari, he entered among Native Americans who as yet had had no intimate, prolonged experience with non-Indians. He and his horse crossed an invisible line which historian Herbert Bolton poetically named "the Rim of Christendom."[83]

Between 1687 and his death from natural causes in Magdalena, Sonora, in 1711 at the age of sixty-five, Father Kino founded more than two dozen missions and visitas among the northern O'odham. In the process, he introduced to the region a new religion, architecture, settlement pattern, economy, political system, language, music, and a whole panoply of domestic plants and animals. Before his arrival, the O'odham—like many Native Americans elsewhere in North America—raised only

Father Eusebio Francisco Kino, S.J., pioneer Jesuit missionary in the Pimería Alta, founded more than two dozen missions and visitas between 1687 and 1711. This equestrian statue by Mexican sculptor Julian Martinez is located in Tucson, Arizona. (Edward McCain.)

93

Sunrise on the ruins of the Pimería Alta church of Mission San José de Tumacácori, now preserved at Tumacacori National Historical Park, Arizona. (Randy Prentice.)

squash, corn, beans, and cotton. Their only domestic animal was the dog. Before the advent of Kino, there was no such thing in the Pimería Alta as literacy; the years had no numbers and the days neither hours nor minutes. What food was available was shared rather than hoarded.

Over many centuries the O'odham had evolved cultural mechanisms that took fully into account the stern realities of the Sonoran Desert and its many microenvironments. People adapted to their surroundings instead of struggling to mold their surroundings "nearer to the heart's desire." Father Kino, on the other hand, arrived in this arid country with the vision of Moses' Promised Land before him, "a land of brooks of water, of fountains and depths that spring out of valleys and hills; a land of wheat and barley, and vines, and fig trees and pomegranates; a land of olive oil and honey; a land wherein thou shalt eat bread without scarceness. Thou shalt not lack anything in it."[84]

None of the many churches built by Father Kino during his lifetime continue in use. Those very few that remain are essentially archeological ruins. But later Jesuits rebuilt churches in settlements where Kino had planted the seeds of Western culture and, after them, Franciscans did the same in many of the same locations. The modern result is that there are eighteenth- and early-nineteenth-century missions still standing in northern Sonora and southern Arizona referred to as part of "the Kino chain," and three of these are now preserved as units of Tumacacori National Historical Park. They are the standing ruins of missions los Santos Ángeles San Gabriel y San Rafael de Guevavi, San José (originally San Cayetano) de Tumacácori, and the visita of Calabazas. The now-preserved Tumacácori ruins are on the site of an O'odham village relocated long after Kino's death, and Calabazas was unknown to Kino in his lifetime. The adobe ruins of Guevavi, those of a church built in 1751, may or may not be in the same location as Kino's Guevavi. All three, however, are directly attributable to his pioneering missionary endeavors.

It was 1691 when Kino, accompanied by a fellow Jesuit, took his first ride into what today is southern Arizona. He had been enticed to the large village of Tumacácori by its O'odham residents, who had sent messengers asking him to come there. Leaving Tumacácori, Kino and his companions rode southward up the Río Santa María, today's Santa Cruz River. They passed through the village of Guevavi en route to the founder's headquarters mission at the village of Cosari, the place he had dedicated to Nuestra Señora de los Dolores, Our Lady of Sorrows.

The tireless missionary made no fewer than thirty-six extensive journeys throughout the Pimería Alta, parts of at least fifteen of them within the boundaries of today's southern Arizona. In addition to about a dozen additional visits to Tumacácori and Guevavi, Father Kino and his European traveling companions became the first non-natives known to have ascended and descended the north-flowing Santa Cruz River between, even though somewhat remote from, the east and west units of the modern Saguaro National Monument, a natural-history preserve created to protect the indigenous saguaro and other plants native to the Sonoran Desert. The historic record offers no evidence concerning whatever opinion the peripatetic Jesuit may have had of this giant, visually dominating cactus. Written descriptions of plants and animals were not Father Kino's concern. People, and how to extend the reign of God over them, were.[85]

So far as is known, Kino was also the first European to set eyes on the enormous prehistoric mud ruins of today's Casa Grande Ruins National Monument. With his Indian servants and guides, he arrived at the Casa Grande, great house, for the first time on November 27, 1694. He later penned a description:

> The casa grande is a four story building, as large as a castle and equal to the largest church in these lands of Sonora. It is said that the ancestors of Montezuma deserted and depopulated it, and, beset by the neighboring Apaches, left for the east or Casas Grandes [of Chihuahua], and that from there they turned toward the south and southwest, finally founding the great city and court of Mexico. Close to this casa grande there are thirteen smaller houses, somewhat more dilapidated, and the ruins of many others, which make it evident that in ancient times there was a city here.
>
> On this occasion and on later ones I have learned and heard, and at times have seen, that further to the east, north, and west there are seven or eight more of these large ancient houses and ruins of whole cities, with many broken metates and jars, charcoal, etc. These certainly must be the Seven Cities mentioned by the holy man Fray Marcos de Niza. . . . The guides or interpreters must have given his Reverence the information which he had in his book concerning these Seven Cities, although certainly at that time and for a long while before they must have been deserted.[86]

The myth of Aztlán, concerning the Aztec founders of Mexico City, was clearly alive and well in Kino's time. And neither had the legend of the Seven Cities of Cíbola died with the death of Vásquez de Coronado.

Who, in fact, had built the Casa Grande? Archeologists tend to agree it was constructed around A.D. 1300 or soon after by peoples whom prehistorians have labeled Hohokam. Whether or not they were the ancestors of the historic O'odham, which seems highly unlikely, remains a matter of debate and conjecture. Also conjectural is the use to which the multistoried structure was put, although religious purposes seem the most probable. Writer Rose Houk gives her imagination free rein:

> The priest emerged from the cool recesses of the Great House. With long strides he crossed the plaza, nodding in recognition to the villagers who were anxiously waiting for the ceremony to begin. In the corner of the plaza a group of men were gambling, women hurried to finish preparing the food for the feast, and a clutch of young women coyly smiled at the young men who had come for the festivities. . . .

95

He had spent the last four days inside the Great House, seated on a stone chair before a window on the west wall of the top floor. Before the altar to the God of the Sun, he sang the songs and recited the chants that he had learned from his father. Each morning he and his assistants smoked tobacco in cane cigarettes, blowing the smoke to the East where White Mocking Bird lives.

For four days he had been watching the sun set through a window in the Great House. Each evening it had disappeared at the same place on the horizon. This event was to cue him that he should go out among his neighbors and announce that the rains should be coming soon and that they should prepare their fields for planting. The women must know also, because the fruit of the Green Spirit, the saguaro cactus, would soon be ripe, and they must take their long sticks and willow baskets to the hills and collect it.[87]

It may have been a century and a half before another priest made use of the Casa Grande, and this time it was a black-robed representative of the crown of Spain. Before an improvised altar erected in honor of God the Father, God the Son, and God the Holy Ghost, he intoned the words of a religious rite that for more than a millennium had been part of his cultural heritage. Father Kino was back at the ruins of Casa Grande toward the end of 1697, this time in the company of Captain Juan Mateo Manje, Lieutenant Cristóbal Martín Bernal, Alférez Francisco de Acuña, Sergeant Juan Bautista de Escalante, and twenty soldiers. On November 18 Kino, perhaps unwittingly emulating an ancient tradition, resurrected the ruins of the Casa Grande as a church. "After four leagues," wrote Captain Manje, "we arrived at midday at Casas Grandes, inside of which Father Kino said mass even though we had traveled without eating until then."[88]

Picking up on the oral traditions of local O'odham, Manje asserted,

> All those buildings were built by people whose chief was called *el Siba*, which in their language means "The cruel and bitter man." Because of the bloody wars waged against them by Apaches and 20 allied nations many were killed on both sides. Some of the Indians left, divided themselves and returned to the north, from whence they had come in previous years; but the majority went to the east and south. From all this information we judge it is likely they are the ancestors of the Mexican nation.[89]

Both Manje and Lieutenant Martín added to the physical description of the ruins. Wrote Martín:

> We saw all the rooms of the building, which is very large, four stories high, the walls forming a square, and very thick, about two yards in width, of the previously mentioned white clay. Although the heathens had burned it at different

times, the four stories can be seen with very good rooms, apartments and windows, curiously plastered inside and out in such a way that the walls are washed and smoothed with a somewhat red clay, the doorways similarly. There are also in the immediate area outside eleven somewhat smaller houses built with the peculiar curiousness of the large high one. Also it is seen that it was greatly populated and that they had a government and in a large area is seen a lot of broken, painted pottery. Also is seen a main irrigation canal, ten yards wide and four deep and with very thick sides made of the same earth, which goes to the house through a plain.[90]

Kino, this time with Captain Diego Carrasco as his military escort, was back within view of the Casa Grande at the end of September 1698. And he and Manje passed nearby once again—for their final time—in March 1699. On neither occasion did the missionary and his companions pause again for a closer inspection.[91]

Father Kino's end-of-life tenure in the Pimería Alta was not altogether a peaceful one. By 1694 many northern Pimans, and especially those who lived in the upper Altar River Valley of today's northern Sonora, had become resentful of floggings and even of killings of some of their number by Spanish soldiers. Their resentment spilled over into open rebellion in the spring of 1695 precisely at the time General Juan Fernández de la Fuente was in the north with several cavalry units to eradicate threats from Jocomes, Janos, Sumas, and Apaches who were making hostile incursions ever deeper into eastern Sonora.

The 1695 Pima uprising, which resulted in the martyrdom of Father Javier Saeta, a Jesuit recently stationed at Mission Caborca, as well as in the deaths of at least five non-local Native American employees of the missionaries at Tubutama and Caborca, was soon brutally put down by a superior Spanish military force as well as by force of persuasion by Father Kino. Kino was able to succeed in his mission of peace despite hatred engendered by a horrible massacre inflicted by Spanish soldiers on forty-eight O'odham who had assembled peacefully to hold a dialogue with their oppressors. The location of the massacre, in today's northernmost Sonora, came to be known as La Matanza, The Slaughter. There was an echo here of what Spanish Catholics had inflicted on French Protestants on the east coast of La Florida a little more than a century earlier. And so were there similarities to a massacre inflicted on Sioux Indians by American soldiers at a place called Wounded Knee nearly two centuries later.[92]

Once the Pima matter was resolved, General Fernández, General Domingo de Terán, General Domingo Jironza Petris de Cruzat, and a formidable army of more than three hundred regular troops, militiamen, and Indian allies set out to the north to punish the Apaches, Jocomes, Sumas, and Janos. And punish them they did, killing sixty Indians, either in battle or by hanging or clubbing prisoners, and bringing back seventy women and children who were distributed among the soldiers as spoils of war.

97

Not that the Spanish "victory" was one-sided. The army, struck down by an illness presumably resulting from the men's having drunk bad water—poisoned by Indians, some believed—lost large numbers of its own. Among them was General Terán, whose death seems to have occurred somewhere toward the north end of the Chiricahua Mountains. This was the same Terán who as governor of Coahuila had led Father Damian Massanet on a mission-founding expedition into eastern Texas in 1691.[93]

During the course of this campaign the Spanish troops had made their way through a pass at the northern end of the Chiricahua Mountains in today's southern Arizona, one they christened San Felipe. In later years it would briefly be called Puerto del Dado and, finally, Apache Pass. Its important springs and the ruins of its nineteenth-century American fort are now protected and interpreted by the National Park Service as Fort Bowie National Historic Site. Spaniards, fighting Apaches, had preceded Americans, fighting Apaches, in this place by some 165 years.[94]

Not since 1540 had any European challenged the desiccated trails of today's southwestern Arizona. It was then that Melchior Díaz had gone in futile search of Hernando de Alarcón on the lower Colorado River.

Father Kino, he of insatiable curiosity about the geography of the land, reentered the region in the late seventeenth and early eighteenth centuries. He made three treks along the Camino del Diablo, part of which delineates a portion of the modern boundary between Arizona and Sonora, through Organ Pipe Cactus National Monument, in 1699, 1701, and 1706. He also visited the oasis at Quitobaquito, inside the monument's present boundaries, in October 1698, and he was at the O'odham village of Sonoídag (the present Sonoyta, Sonora, a Mexican settlement near the southeastern corner of the monument) in 1698, 1699, 1702, and 1706, and twice in 1701.[95]

Kino jotted a few remarks describing his initial visits to Quitobaquito and Sonoídag:

> In the afternoon [of October 7, 1698] we left for the good place [Quitobaquito] which we named San Serguio and another four leagues along the *arroyo* [Sonoyta River] which goes to the sea. It has water which runs in many places, *carrizales* [canes], *tulares* [bulrushes] and ducks and birds from the marshes, and excellent pasturage for the cattle. From San Marcelo [Sonoyta, Sonora] there are irrigation canals and flat, level lands for planting, although this year they had not sowed these except for many squashes.[96]

Quitobaquito continues to boast running water, marshes, canes, bulrushes, ducks, and other water birds, but cattle—a part of Spain's continuing legacy in the Sonoran Desert—are now prevented from drinking and pasturing here.

As for the O'odham living at Sonoídag in the late seventeenth and early eighteenth centuries, these were uniformly described by Father Kino and his fellow Europeans as being exceptionally poverty-stricken and hunger-ridden. Except for the Sonoyta River and rare artesian oases like that at Quitobaquito, the country is one of extreme aridity, even for a desert. That people were able to live here permanently is strong testimony to their genius, perseverance, and intimate knowledge of all the plants and animals in their environs as well as of the possibilities of domestic horticulture even in stressed circumstances.

During a February 1694 journey into westernmost Pimería Alta south of the present international boundary, Captain Manje—admittedly heavily influenced by his European background—wrote, "The Indians went about naked, covering their bodies only with small pieces of fur hares. . . . We gave them a supply of food since they were poor and hungry, living on roots, locusts and shell fish." And later, in March: "[The Indians were] poor people who lived by eating roots of wild sweet potatoes, honey, mesquite beans and other fruits. They traveled about naked; only the women had their bodies half covered with hare furs."[97]

Unknowingly, when he baptized two dozen children at Sonoídag in 1698, Father Kino set the slow fuse on a bomb —that of the Pima Rebellion—timed to explode in the middle of the next century with tragic consequences for Sonoídag's Jesuit missionary.

It may have been with greater awareness that he and his cohorts became the first people to commit to writing descriptions, however inadequate, of today's Hiached O'odham, the so-called Sand Papagos. They continue to live in southwestern Arizona as twentieth-century citizens of the United States, and some of their deceased occupy a cemetery inside of Organ Pipe Cactus National Monument.

Father Eusebio Kino's name is memorialized in 3,197-foot Kino Peak in the Bates Mountains within the monument's boundaries. It is a fitting remembrance for a man who more than any other set the stage for European beginnings in this part of the world.

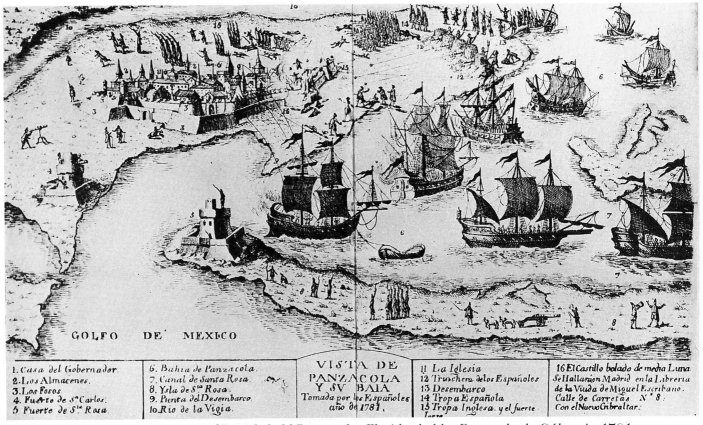

The successful Spanish invasion of British-held Pensacola, Florida, led by Bernardo de Gálvez in 1781, aided the fledgling United States by eliminating the British threat from the south and west. (Courtesy John C. Pace Library Special Collections, University of West Florida, Pensacola.)

As the curtain fell on the seventeenth-century act in the continuing drama of North America, Spain's position among competitors for religious, political, and economic dominance over the vast region was not unlike that of an aging agave in the Sonoran or Chihuahuan desert. For eight to twenty years this remarkable plant, which can take root in almost any soil, grows slowly, building up its energy. Then, on cue, its stored up energy explodes in a treelike stalk, its inflorescence, which blooms briefly before the plant dies.[1] The eighteenth and early nineteenth centuries were for Spain in North America a period of inflorescence that culminated, at last, in final blossom and death. The crown's resources were unable to match its desires.

In La Florida, England was becoming more than a mere competitor. Her avaricious Carolina traders and, later, Georgia colonists showed signs of taking over—although a narrowed portion of territory defined by the modern Florida would rest precariously in Spanish hands for most of the ensuing dozen decades. Louisiana, large expanses of the northern Gulf Coast, and lands along the Mississippi River and its tributaries were conceded to France for much of the century. All lands at the head of the Gulf Coast had been labeled Amichel in 1519 by Francisco de Garay. Although the label changed through time, the idea persisted in the mind of Spain.

Only toward the west, in Tejas, Nuevo México, Sonora (southern Arizona), and along the length of the Pacific Coast from Alta California to Alaska did Spain take a more determined stand, seeing this vast region as a more direct, overland extension of northern Nueva España and as a bulwark against those who would challenge her connections to the Pacific Islands and Asia. Determination aside, the eighteenth and early nineteenth centuries, while destined to mark the years of Spain's full bloom, would also witness her demise in North America.

ADIOS HISPANIA: LA FLORIDA'S FAREWELL TO SPAIN

As the eighteenth century dawned, Spaniards had become reasonably secure in San Agustín and were attempting to anchor themselves in Pensacola. Even so, Florida continued to be regarded elsewhere in New Spain as a poverty-stricken and undesirable outpost. It was neglected by the crown and by viceregal authorities more often than otherwise. Desirable or not, Spaniards were obligated to maintain the region as partial protector of Nueva España's vital shipping route to Spain along the Florida Straits and Bahama Channel. The north-flowing Gulf Stream was the propellent that sent them sailing on their way.

If higher Spanish authorities harbored any serious doubts concerning the strategic importance of La Florida in terms of its location next to the north-bearing currents of the Gulf Stream, occasional wrecks of treasure-laden ships just off the peninsula's east coast served as harsh reminders there were no convenient alternatives to the route. Such a reminder was delivered on July 31, 1715, when a hurricane struck

Sixteenth-century Spanish rosary. (George H.H. Huey from the Enrique E. Guerra collection.)

101

eleven ships of a Spanish fleet offshore from today's Canaveral National Seashore. Ten of the eleven vessels were sunk and a thousand of the 2,500 people on board were killed. A similar disaster struck a fleet of twenty-three ships in 1733. The vessels were wrecked along the Florida Keys from the present city of Marathon to Key Biscayne. At least one of these ships, the *Nuestra Señora del Populo* (*El Pinque*), went down inside today's Biscayne National Park, where in 1984 it was located and surveyed by National Park Service personnel.[2] There was the added consideration that in the hands of foreign powers, San Agustín could provide a base from which enemy ships might attack. As for Pensacola, Spanish presence there served to block French designs on the eastern head of the Gulf.

Earlier, Spain had found it necessary to strengthen her island holdings in the Caribbean. Not only did these islands generate products of their own, but they also were crucial springboards between Old World and New. In Puerto Rico, Juan Ponce de León's capital at Caparra had been moved to San Juan in 1521, the year he died. The second capital's San Felipe del Morro Castle, a fortification begun in 1589, had been largely built by the mid-seventeenth century. Now protected as part of San Juan National Historic Site, it was completed between 1775 and 1787, roughly as it now appears.

The nearby fortress of San Cristóbal, heralded as "a masterpiece of military engineering," was begun in 1634 and had reached its full size thirty-four years later. Its finishing touches, seen in today's imposing structure, were applied between 1766 and 1783. San Cristóbal successfully withstood a British siege of 1797. And the small fort of El Cañuelo, opposite El Morro and also within San Juan National Historic Site, was built of wood in 1610 but was burned during a Dutch siege of 1625. Stung by the Dutch success, Spaniards rebuilt the fort of masonry in the 1660s even as in 1633 they began the task—one carried on intermittently for a century and a half—of erecting massive walls around what today is El Viejo San Juan, the old city.[3]

The construction of fortifications in San Juan paralleled to some extent Spaniards' similar endeavors in La Florida. Although Castillo de San Marcos had been built during the second half of the seventeenth century, it was the eighteenth century before it took the form now to be appreciated within Castillo de San Marcos National Monument. In 1702 England declared war against France and Spain (Queen Anne's War, or the War of Spanish Succession) and hostilities erupted between Spain and England on the Carolina-La Florida border. Governor James Moore of Carolina set out with a force of 500-600 Carolina militiamen and 300-600 Indian allies to capture San Agustín. The town, with its church, Franciscan friary, and some nine hundred inhabitants, was not well fortified. The stone Castillo de San Marcos, however, was another matter. Learning in advance of the British attack, Governor Joseph de Zúñiga y Cerda ordered the townspeople to take refuge inside the fortress. While the British destroyed the town, the Spaniards inside the castillo were able to withstand

Cannonballs stacked at the seventeenth and eighteenth-century fortress of San Cristóbal, at San Juan National Historic Site, Puerto Rico. The fortress was regarded in its day as "a masterpiece of engineering." (Frank Balthis.)

the siege until four Spanish warships arrived to block Moore's escape by sea. He burned some of the ships of his small fleet and abandoned others before marching overland to the mouth of the St. Johns River, where he embarked for Carolina before the last day of the year. Discredited for the moment, Moore resigned his governorship.[4]

Castillo de San Marcos historians Arana and Manucy tell what happened next:

> In the two decades that followed 1702, out from the Castillo went strong earthworks and palisades, buttressed at strategic points with redoubts. These made St. Augustine a walled town, secure against invasion as long as there were enough soldiers to man the walls. But in those dark days who could be sure of tomorrow? In 1712 came *La Gran Hambre*—the Great Hunger—when starving people ate even the dogs and cats. The war [with England] ended at last in 1714. The hostile noose around St. Augustine slackened, but it was an uneasy peace with many "incidents." In 1728 Colonel William Palmer of Carolina marched against the presidio. The grim walls of the fort, the unwinking readiness of the heavy guns, and the needle sharp points of the yucca plants lining the palisades were a powerful deterrent. Palmer "refrained" from taking the town. For their part, the Spaniards set off their artillery, but they made no sorties.[5]

Palmer's audacious foray was followed in 1733 by the founding of the utopian colony of Georgia with headquarters at Savannah by a thirty-six-year-old nobleman named James Edward Oglethorpe, a person "with a thin but stubborn strain of self-righteousness and hypocrisy. He denied to others what he desired for himself. Though he strictly prohibited rum in his colony, he drank countless bottles of it himself, together with much wine and beer. . . . He forbade slavery in Georgia, saying it was against the gospel while enriching himself as director of the Royal Africa Company."[6] Oglethorpe's colony, awarded by the English crown a grant of land stretching between the Savannah and Altamaha rivers and in theory westward all the way to the Pacific Ocean, largely comprised otherwise respected citizens who had been confined to debtors' prison in the wake of a great economic depression in the mother country.

With an eye on the possibility of Spaniards' asserting their claim to what had become de facto a kind of no man's land, the new colony's leader sailed down the coast in 1734 to an abandoned St. Simon's Island off the south Georgia coast looking for a likely place to build a fort. In 1736 he returned with forty-four men—chiefly craftsmen—and seventy-two women and children to construct Fort Frederica. He named it for Frederick, the Prince of Wales and the only son of King George II. The site, abandoned peacefully in 1755, remained free of later development. Its pristine location and few standing ruins are now beautifully preserved and interpreted as Fort Frederica National Monument.

Isolated and forbidding, Florida's Castillo de San Marcos continues to command a view of St. Augustine and of the sea passage to the rest of the world. (Joseph L. Fontenot.)

103

Three years after his founding of Fort Frederica, Oglethorpe found himself with an excuse to move on San Agustín:

> In 1739 the English precipitated the War of Jenkins' Ear in doubtful defense of a smuggler by that name who claimed his ear had been cut off by Spaniards when his vessel was overhauled on the Florida coast some nine years earlier. It soon became a part of the European war of Austrian succession (King George's War in America), which lasted until 1748 with no important changes in the position of the powers in the New World. . . . In January 1740 [Governor Oglethorpe] sailed up the St. Johns and took the small [Spanish] forts Pupa and Picolata. Oglethorpe, in planning to attack Saint Augustine, also gained control of the sea and by May 1 had 1,600 men on seven warships carrying forty dugouts to landing operations. On May 12, the invaders took Fort San Diego eighteen miles north of Saint Augustine on the coast. Four days later, they reached Moosa, a fortified Negro village one mile north of the city, where they seized thirty houses in the deserted settlement. Discouraged by incessant rains and dysentery, the Georgians withdrew to recover and regroup, but were back at San Diego by the end of May and prepared to encircle the city [San Agustín] on June 6. A week later the siege of the fortress began in earnest. Again the English guns proved to be too light for the task of reducing the fort. The Spanish defenders were better prepared than at any previous time. There were 613 men in Saint Augustine and another eighty in Apalachee. They could not match Oglethorpe in manpower, but at midnight on June 25 a Spanish force of 300 men moved out of the fort and surprised their old enemy, Colonel John Palmer, who was camped at Moosa, and killed eighty-seven whites [including Palmer and twenty-two of his Scotch Highlanders] and thirty-five Indians. In July, when seven heavily armed Spanish warships appeared, Oglethorpe abandoned the siege and returned to [Frederica].[7]

During the course of the 1740 siege the strategic importance of Matanzas Inlet, an opening to the inland waterway south of San Agustín, was demonstrated beyond all doubt. Through this inlet Spanish ships laden with food were able to supply the beleaguered subjects at the provincial capital. Castillo de San Marcos, which had added arched bombproofs, a new roof that could be used as a gun deck, and a tall watchtower and new parapets before the English attack, had done its job again.

A "clumsy Spanish reprisal" led by La Florida Governor Manuel de Montiano was attempted in 1742, when in June an invasion force of some thirty-six ships and thirteen hundred men sailed from San Agustín for St. Simons Island and Fort Frederica. The Englishmen, after a decisive battle fought with the invaders in a meadow later dubbed Bloody Marsh, now a detached unit of Fort Frederica National Monument, forced the Spaniards to retreat and return to San Agustín. Fort Frederica had been saved and, with it, English rule in Georgia and the Carolinas. Indeed, "By this victory, Oglethorpe saved the thirteen colonies for England and so preserved the nucleus of the United States for English civilization."[8]

In 1743 Oglethorpe made one more try at dislodging the Spaniards from San Agustín, but to no avail. He returned that same year to England where he lived until his death in 1785, enjoying "his pleasant estate, his English beer, and his literary friends, including Dr. Johnson, Boswell, and Oliver Goldsmith."[9]

Spurred on by their realization of the importance of Matanzas Inlet, between 1740 and 1742 the Spaniards erected a stone fort on the Matanzas River near its mouth. The restored structure and its historic vista are now maintained and interpreted by the National Park Service as Fort Matanzas National Monument.[10]

Although the immediate threats of invasion abated, Spaniards periodically repaired Castillo de San Marcos. Modernization work begun in 1739 was completed in 1756, an event marked with installation over the main gate of the royal coat-of-arms—which can still be seen—and a suitable inscription. Further work ceased when money ran out, but commenced again in mid-1762. Spain's efforts at maintaining the mighty fortress, however, abruptly came to an end in 1763. And the reason had nothing to do with San Agustín itself.[11]

What brought about the British takeover of La Florida was the Treaty of Paris signed in 1763 to settle the Seven Years' War, the final phase of a century-long global struggle between England and France for colonial supremacy. In North America, and starting two years earlier, this same phase of the international contest was known as the French and Indian War. In Europe, Spain had weighed in on the side of France at the last moment in what proved to be a losing cause. Under terms of the 1763 treaty France ceded her claim to nearly all of Canada to England. She also gave England her lands east of the Mississippi River even as Spain ceded La Florida to England for the return of Havana which had been captured by the English in 1762. The so-called Isle of Orleans, on the other hand, which included the city of New Orleans, as well as France's possessions west of the Mississippi River, had been secretly relinquished by France to Spain in 1762. It was two years before the French colonists in Louisiana learned of the transfer, and in 1768 a group of angry Frenchmen drove out the Spanish governor. It was 1769 before Spain was able to take charge of Louisiana west of the Mississippi. She regarded control of this vast region as a means of protecting her valuable Nueva España possessions against encroachment from the east.[12]

Built by Spain to ward off a threat to La Florida from England, Castillo de San Marcos, with its torreon *and cannon, stands as a reminder of that bygone era. (Bill Keogh.)*

The Florida that England acquired in 1763 stretched from the East Coast on the Atlantic all the way to the Mississippi River. It included former Spanish Pensacola and former French-held Mobile and Natchez. England had wanted Florida for several reasons. Possession of her lands consolidated British holdings along the Atlantic Coast of North America. It gave England ready access to crucial sea lanes; it offered forests of pine and oak useful in shipbuilding; it opened new opportunities for trade with Native Americans; and its climate and soils offered the promise of good production of citrus, sugar, and indigo.[13]

At the time of their wholesale departure from Florida in 1763, Spanish subjects in San Agustín numbered a mere 3,046 persons of whom 89 were Christian Indians later settled outside of Havana, 95 free Negroes, and 315 Negro slaves. By contrast, even as early as 1688 there were more than 300,000 English settlers on the eastern seaboard of North America, many of them pushing southward into the Carolinas.[14]

On the western side of Florida, at Pensacola, the fledgling Spanish settlement found itself to be the most insignificant of pawns in an international game of chess. Two centuries of Hapsburg rule of Spain ended with the death of Carlos II in 1700 and succession to the Spanish throne of Philip V, a grandson of the Bourbon "Grand Monarch" of France, Louis XIV. The first of Spain's Bourbon rulers, like his successors, was ever challenged by England in its quest for empire. And because of their common Bourbon connection, Spain and France became uneasy allies. Pensacola had been founded in competition with the French who had gained a foothold at neighboring Mobile (1702) and Biloxi (1717) and who in 1718 would found New Orleans. Now, however, with a Bourbon monarch on the Spanish throne and sharing the common threat of English aggression, Spaniards and French living at the head of the Gulf became warily reliant upon one another.[15]

The numbers of people living at Pensacola's fort of San Carlos de Austria—the site of which almost certainly lies somewhere within the Pensacola Forts area of Gulf Islands National Seashore—varied between a hundred and three hundred. "In 1713," write the Colemans,

> 212 persons were reported [here], including twenty-five women. Civilians at the post included carpenters, blacksmith, some Indians, and, occasionally, chaplains and medico-friars. The task of provisioning these people was never adequately solved. The area itself was not fertile enough for large crops, and food staples had to come from Mexico. Several times the French forts to the west sent supplies to San Carlos de Austria in order to prevent starvation. Despite these conditions, Spain maintained the fort.[16]

The little fort, about a hundred yards square, and its twenty-eight guns (eight- and ten-pounders) suffered many calamitous fires as well as heavy storms. In 1707 Indians succeeded in making off with four horses, clothing, and other hard-to-come-by items. When a new commandant took over in 1718, he found San Carlos de Austria without an exterior ditch or parapet and most of its guns in useless condition.[17]

As early as 1693 don Carlos de Sigüenza y Góngora had urged construction of a fortification at the west end of Santa Rosa Island to cover the inlet to Pensacola Bay. His recommendation had been ignored in favor of a site on the *barranca* (bluff) on the opposite mainland. But in 1718 Spaniards at Pensacola worked to strengthen San Carlos de Austria even as they began to fortify Sigüenza Point, the western tip of

Santa Rosa Island. The new fortification, as well as the old one, were soon to be put to the test.

When Philip V disregarded his pledge to renounce any claim to the throne of France (he was, after all, a Bourbon), between 1719 and 1721 France and Spain found themselves at war once again. In May 1719 a French fleet sailed into the bay and captured the small garrison at Punta Sigüenza. San Carlos de Austria was taken next, and the Spanish personnel of both places were allowed to go to Havana.

Between 1719 and 1722 Pensacola changed hands more than once. Finally, thanks to the treaty which ended the War of the Quadruple Alliance, France gave up its claims to Pensacola Bay and its former Spanish possessors took over again. The entire settlement was moved to Santa Rosa Punta de Sigüenza and its fortification was christened Presidio de Principe de Asturias.[18]

Appointed to take charge of the new Pensacola was don Alejandro Wauchope. He carried out orders to evacuate the sixty Spanish soldiers and their supplies from St. Joseph's Bay (southeast of today's Panama City, Florida) and to bring them to Santa Rosa Island. By 1723 the men had used logs and boards to build a warehouse; powder box; powder magazine; captain's house; paymaster office; eight large houses for officers; two dozen small dwellings for "workmen, convicts, and other persons of the populace"; a bake oven; and a lookout tower. This unlikely assemblage constituted Pensacola for nearly three decades.[19]

The entire site, at least as an archeological feature, would lie protected on Santa Rosa Island had it not been for storms and high tides. A hurricane and tidal waves struck in November 1752, drowning many of its inhabitants, washing much of it into Pensacola Bay, and leaving the rest uninhabitable. Survivors scattered throughout the bay region, a few remaining on Santa Rosa Island where they built a blockhouse on higher ground. Still others settled around a tiny Indian mission called San Miguel near present-day Seville Square, the nucleus of modern Pensacola.[20] In 1964 archeological investigations revealed traces of Santa Rosa Punta de Sigüenza on Santa Rosa Island east of Fort Pickens, near Battery Worth.[21]

By the time Great Britain took over Pensacola under terms of the 1763 Treaty of Paris, Spain had squandered more than $36 million (1978 value) to further the vain dream of a Gulf Coast empire. Its most recent fort, San Miguel de Panzacola, was in terrible condition. As recently as 1761 the little community had been besieged by Creek Indians, and when the 1763 evacuation came, there were hardly eight hundred residents. The prize won by the English consisted of a dilapidated stockade and about a hundred huts and hovels, hardly the stuff of empire.[22]

A proclamation of October 1763 divided England's newly occupied territory into East Florida and West Florida, the latter extending all the way west to the Mississippi River but excluding New Orleans. Her occupation of both halves proved to be brief:

twenty-two years in the former and eighteen years in the latter. The 1783 Treaty of Paris, signed at the conclusion of the Revolutionary War, formally returned both Floridas to Spain. By then West Florida had already seen its English population shipped out to New York, but in East Florida it was November 1785 before the last British vessel departed carrying her subjects.[23]

Short-termed as it was, the British impact on Florida proved to be a lasting one. England introduced changes in the nature of government, land tenure, Indian relations (most Indians under direct Spanish control had evacuated Florida with the Spaniards), and economic relationships that returning Spaniards could not undo. The British, for example, made no serious efforts to effect the religious and cultural conversion of the Indians. They licensed traders to deal with them instead and gave the Native Americans gifts when expediency demanded it. They also allowed a traffic in firearms and rum and favored conferences over force when differences had to be ironed out. These were policies that Spaniards later followed among Florida's surviving Native Americans.[24]

As soon as the British moved into San Agustín in July, 1763, the town became St. Augustine and Castillo de San Marcos was Anglicized to Fort St. Mark. Little or nothing was done to improve this imposing structure until 1775, when British subjects at Lexington and Concord showed by force of arms that they desired to be left alone by King George. As the capital of East Florida, St. Augustine assumed new importance and its various defenses, including the fort, were repaired and improved in 1775 and 1776.[25]

The situation to the south at Fort Matanzas was similar. After installing armaments in 1765 to replace those the Spaniards had taken when they withdrew, little was done at the rectangular masonry fort other than to station an artilleryman there with a small garrison, a personnel complement which changed on occasion. But after the onset of the American Revolution, when British loyalists began to seek refuge in East Florida from rebelling American colonists, more attention was paid to Fort St. Mark as well as to Matanzas. In fact, American troops tried unsuccessfully to take East Florida from the British in 1777 and 1778.[26]

After Spain entered the Revolutionary War on the side of the American colonists in June 1779, the size of the British garrison at Matanzas was increased and a few improvements may have been made on the structure. But to no avail. Treaties between England and France, England and Spain, and England and the new United States concluded in 1783 momentarily brought their conflicts to an end. And Florida was formally ceded once again to Spain.[27]

An unusual episode with a Hispanic twist unfolded in British East Florida between 1768 and 1777. A Scottish physician and would-be colonizer named Andrew Turnbull hoped to induce Italians and Greeks to work for him as indentured servants on the east coast of Florida in a projected agricultural enterprise involving cotton, indigo, and silk-worm production. The staging area was the city of Mahón on the Balearic island of Minorca, whose Catalán-speaking populace was then under England's control in spite of the island's proximity to the eastern Spanish coast.

Although Turnbull preferred Italian and Greek colonists, a great majority of the 1,403 persons who signed on as indentured servants were Minorcans. During the eighty-day trip to Florida, some 148 colonists died, as did 500 Negro slaves who went down in a single ship. In spite of this, 1,255 men and women—including Father Pedro Camps (Turnbull's wife was a Roman Catholic, as were the Minorcans)—made it to St. Augustine. From there they headed south to found a colony opposite Mosquito Inlet at the northern entrance to today's Canaveral National Seashore. Turnbull called it New Smyrna after the birthplace of his wife.

The lot of the colonists was malnutrition, disease, and unrest. Three hundred Italians rioted and in the first year 300 adults and 150 children died of sickness and starvation. Finally, in November 1777 New Smyrna gave up the ghost and its survivors, Minorcans among them, made their way to St. Augustine.[28]

The details of history in British West Florida and at its capital of Pensacola are somewhat different than those in East Florida. By the time of the British takeover of Pensacola in 1763, Spanish occupation had become confined principally to the mainland rather than to Santa Rosa Island. And it was on the mainland that the British concentrated their activities, although during a smallpox epidemic in 1770 unfortunates who got the disease were sent to the island until they recovered or died.[29]

After France formally became an ally of the American revolutionaries in 1778 and Spain did likewise in 1779, the situation at Pensacola and other British holdings on the Gulf Coast, such as those in British West Florida at Mobile and Natchez, became extremely precarious. In 1777 a youthful, bright, and energetic Spanish colonel with previous field experience in Nueva Vizcaya, Bernardo de Gálvez, had become governor of Spanish Louisiana. His father was Matías de Gálvez, later to become viceroy of Nueva España, and his uncle was José de Gálvez, royal visitor general to Nueva España from 1765 to 1772.[30]

Almost immediately after Spain's declaration of war on England, Gálvez moved on Natchez and Baton Rouge from his capital in New Orleans, capturing both of them before the end of 1779. In early 1780 he took Mobile from the British and prepared to go after Pensacola.[31] In the meantime, the British did what they could to fortify Pensacola further against impending Spanish attack. They constructed Fort George, Queen's Redoubt, Prince of Wales Redoubt, and the Royal Navy Redoubt at Red Cliffs. All of these stood on the mainland, the latter within the boundaries of today's Pensacola Forts area of Gulf Islands National Seashore.[32]

However, British efforts were to no avail. Between March 9 and May 8, 1781, Gálvez and his men laid siege to Pensacola, taking the capital and the last bastion of British presence on the Gulf Coast on May 9. When the Spanish invasion began in

March, the Spaniards' first camp was on Santa Rosa Island. After the British surrender, Spanish soldiers immediately took possession of the Royal Navy Redoubt.[33]

Among the troops of Gálvez were free black militiamen, both *pardos libres* of mixed parentage and *morenos libres* of pure African stock. They were members respectively of the Compañía de Voluntarios de Pardos Libres and the Compañía de Voluntarios de Morenos Libres, and enjoyed all the privileges of any Spanish soldier. Thousands of free black soldiers served in many Spanish posts in the Americas, and theirs was a crucial role in the history of Spanish North America that has all too often been ignored.[34]

The war for West Florida was over in 1781. Thanks to the 1783 Treaty of Paris, control of all of Florida—including an additional strip along the Gulf stretching to the Mississippi River—was returned to Spain for the final time. The 1781 Spanish success against the British had temporarily won for them effective control of Mississippi south of the 32nd parallel. The northern portion became an American possession. In 1795 Spain and the United States agreed in the Treaty of San Lorenzo, the so-called Pinckney's Treaty, to a line at the 31st parallel demarcating Spain's northern boundary in the region. The U.S. Congress organized the Mississippi Territory in 1798, but it was not until 1803 and the Louisiana Purchase that Americans came into possession of all of Mississippi as it appears today, including the area in today's Mississippi District of Gulf Islands National Seashore. For all practical purposes, Spain was in control of these particular islands between 1780 and 1803 (on paper, from 1783 to 1800).[35]

The capture of Pensacola by Spaniards in 1781 is shown in this 1784 French engraving. (Courtesy John C. Pace Library Special Collections, University of West Florida, Pensacola.)

It was as a result of all these contentions that beginning in 1801 an overland highway was built connecting Nashville, Tennessee, with Natchez, the capital of Mississippi Territory and located on the east bank of the Mississippi River north of the 31st parallel. Thanks to Pinckney's Treaty, the Spaniards had allowed "right of deposit" at New Orleans. This was an arrangement by which Americans living in the west could float their products down the Mississippi and store them in New Orleans under bond and without penalty until an ocean-going ship could pick up the goods to be carried to an American or foreign port. But Americans were nervous that the right of deposit might be withdrawn. Moreover, it sometimes took as long as three months to get mail in Natchez from the nation's capital in Philadelphia when letters had to come by sea and up the river. It was clear a road must be opened.[36]

The final result, which generally followed a Native American trail known as the Chickasaw Trace, was a "wilderness artery" that came to be known as the Natchez Trace, whose heyday was between 1801 and 1821. For the young United States, it was the pioneer federal internal improvement project, and today it is interpreted by the National Park Service as the Natchez Trace Parkway. Although never officially a

Spanish route, it was the Spanish presence in Florida and Louisiana that inspired its construction.[37]

Just as the Spanish settlers, soldiers, and loyal Native American allies had departed from Florida after the English takeover in 1763, so did the English subjects leave their new homeland after 1781 and 1783. St. Augustine was formally returned to the Spaniards in July 1784, but it was November of the following year before the British were completely gone. More than 16,000 of them left East Florida alone, and by 1787 there were only about 900 white persons and 490 Negro slaves in the entire former British province. Most of them, including 469 Catalán-speaking Minorcans and a few Italians and Greeks who had once been the colonists of Dr. Turnbull's New Smyrna, lived in San Agustín. Pensacola had a mere 265 residents.[38]

Spain's second period of rule in Florida could only be characterized as inglorious. Historians Arana and Manucy explain:

> They came back to an impossible situation. The border problems of earlier times were multiplied as runaway slaves from Georgia found welcome among the Seminole Indians, and ruffians from both land and sea made Florida their habitat.
>
> Bedeviled by these perversities and distracted by revolutionary unrest in Latin America, Spain nevertheless did what had to be done at the [Castillo de San Marcos]: repairs to the bridges, a new pine stairway for San Carlos tower, a bench for the criminals in the prison. . . . In 1785 Mariano de la Roque designed an attractive entrance in the neoclassic style for the chapel doorway. It was built, only to crumble slowly away like the Spanish hold on Florida.[39]

In San Agustín itself, a singular event occurred under the sponsorship of Father Thomas Hassett, an Irish priest who on his arrival there in 1779 had just finished studies at El Real Colegio de Nobleses Irlandeses, the Irish College at Salamanca in Spain. Father Hassett opened a school for the children of Minorcans in 1787, and in doing so founded what is regarded as the first free school within the boundaries of today's United States.[40]

Fort Matanzas fared no better than Castillo de San Marcos. A Spanish engineer declared it to be in sufficiently good condition that nothing more need be done to it than routine maintenance and repair. Features such as the entrance ladder and a wood pipe drain were replaced with new ones. By 1796 the fort was troubled by the erosion of its foundations and soon after by a leaking roof. Repairs were made in 1799, but by 1810 part of the second-story floor near the chimney had given way and the structure was on its way to collapse. By 1821,

> Fort Matanzas [had] faded into the oblivion of history. Vegetation overran the terreplein and the roof of the tower, each of these features shear-cracked vertically

111

in two places. The southwest angle of the terreplein listed forward because its foundation was undermined. The sentry box, except for its base, the central merlon of the south parapet, the wooden drain pipe and well curb of the cistern, the stairways, doors and windows, the roof hatch cover, and the chimney, all disappeared.[41]

Pensacola's second Spanish period, which began with the stunning military victory of Bernardo de Gálvez over the British in 1781, was as lacking in glory as the same period for San Agustín. The town was the responsibility of the Spanish administration in Louisiana, although it had a local civil and military commandant. Its streets were left unpaved; the two hundred houses, largely one-story, were built of wood; and several wharves which ran into the harbor were allowed to fall into ruin. Huge amounts of money were spent on repairing and improving the community's military defenses, but with uninspiring results.[42]

The Royal Navy Redoubt within the Pensacola Forts area of Gulf Islands National Seashore was renamed Fuerte San Carlos de Barrancas. Life for the soldiers garrisoned there was less than healthful, a condition attributed by a 1792 visitor to the post to "inordinate Use of Ardent Spirits and bad Wine, superadded to high seasoned Meats and promiscuous Intercourse with lewd women."[43] What had precisely three centuries of a Columbian legacy fostered?

A gun battery at Punta Sigüenza at the western tip of Santa Rosa Island was completed after 1793. And in 1793 plans were made for a substantial structure, a water-level battery, just below San Carlos to be named Batería de San Antonio. The conclusion of the French Revolution and the execution of Louis XVI in January 1793 stimulated this activity. Spain turned on its former ally in a war that lasted until peace was negotiated in 1795. Although the late eighteenth-century French and Spanish conflict saw no action on the Gulf Coast, prudence had dictated that Spaniards there should prepare for the worst.[44]

Prudence additionally dictated that after war broke out between Spain and England in 1796 further defensive measures be taken. The seven-gun battery at Punta Sigüenza was enclosed and construction on the Batería de San Antonio which had gotten underway in 1793 was pushed forward. The Colemans explain:

> Of masonry construction, [Batería de San Antonio] was planned as a seven-gun medialuna [half-moon shaped structure] with a counterscarp. There were three rooms or bombproofs to the rear. One of these was used as a magazine, the other two as storage areas and shelter for the garrison. The structure was stuccoed and embellished with ornamental architectural detailing [some of which can still be seen]. In time, it was connected to the upper fortification [Fuerte San Carlos de Barrancas] by a passageway. When San Antonio was built the harbor was much closer to the counterscarp than it is today. The battery was probably designed by Francisco P. Gelabert, who drew a plan for it and also one for Fort San Carlos de Barrancas in 1796. The present form of the battery conforms to this plan.[45]

In 1796 Spanish engineers used the parapets and moat of the Royal Navy Redoubt in laying out a new Fuerte San Carlos de Barrancas, built of logs, timbers, and sand, behind San Antonio.[46]

That year the new governor of West Florida, don Vicente Folch y Juan, arrived in Pensacola. Between his arrival and 1797 he laid out a town about a quarter of a mile east of the Batería de San Antonio, one which included a church dedicated to San Carlos, a Plaza de Armas de San Fernando, and six named streets. In 1798 about 160 people lived here, including whites, black slaves, free blacks, and free mulattos and including workmen, officers, and soldiers.[47]

In 1800 Napoleon Bonaparte persuaded Spain to cede Louisiana to France under terms of the Treaty of San Ildefonso. Provisions of the treaty were kept secret for months, and the Spanish governor-general in New Orleans continued to administer affairs for West Florida until October 1802, when he was ordered to turn the colony over to its new proprietor. The order was not carried out until the following year, 1803, when France sold the Louisiana Territory to the United States for $15,000,000.[48] The former Spanish governor-general in New Orleans became the provincial commandant of West Florida, answering to the governor-general of Cuba. Pensacola, with its western boundary again the Perdido River, was made the provincial capital.[49]

Dissolute living conditions continued among the troops at San Carlos de Barrancas after 1796. Bootlegging soldiers supplied their fellow soldiers with *aguardiente de caña*, a homemade rum distilled from sugar cane, and drunks stole, set fires, and brawled. Men tried and convicted for wounding someone else were sentenced to jail in the Batería de San Antonio whose casemates were used for the provincial prison.[50]

Although Spain had played a leading role in helping North Americans win their independence from England, by 1803, with the new United States as an immediate neighbor, tensions between the two groups mounted in West Florida. The situation worsened during the War of 1812 between the United States and England. In 1814 the British forced the powerless Spaniards at Pensacola to allow the landing of some two hundred troops as well as arms and supplies for Britain's Indian allies. General Andrew Jackson was in nearby Mobile when he learned of the British action, and with 3,000-4,000 soldiers he marched on the West Florida capital. Before the action was over, Jackson had taken the town but the British had escaped by sea leaving behind a blown-up Fuerte San Carlos de Barrancas, spiked guns at Batería de San Antonio, and a destroyed gun battery at Punta de Sigüenza on Santa Rosa Island. In December 1814 the War of 1812 came to an end and the Americans departed.[51]

Because privateers became a growing threat along the Gulf Coast, in 1817 the Spaniards used pine stakes to build a new Fuerte San Carlos de Barrancas near the site of the one destroyed by the fleeing British. It came into use in 1818 when Andrew Jackson, who believed Spaniards were encouraging Indians to attack Americans in

Scrolled bas-relief designs on the façade of the Batería de San Antonio at Fuerte San Carlos de Barrancas, Gulf Islands National Seashore, Florida, betray its late eighteenth and early nineteenth century Spanish origins. (Connie Toops.)

113

Georgia, returned with an army—this time without either official presidential or congressional authorization. The Spanish commander pointed the guns of San Carlos and of the Batería de San Antonio at the attackers, but without success. The Americans occupied Pensacola, established a military government, and commandeered its forts. An American captain named James Gadsden—who later would play a vital role in Mexico's final cession to the United States—surveyed the Pensacola defenses and wrote a report about them.[52]

Although the United States briefly returned the captured posts to Spain, it became clear to the mother country it could no longer hope to keep La Florida as its own. On February 2, 1819, the Spanish Minister to the United States, don Luis de Onís, and American Secretary of State John Quincy Adams signed the Transcontinental Treaty which, after the U.S. Senate's final ratification on February 22, 1821, and the president's approval on February 21, transferred all of La Florida to the United States. At the same time, Spain relinquished to the United States all of its former claims to vast expanses of land between the Columbia River and northern Alta California and south of the Missouri River to northern Utah, New Mexico, and Texas.[53] "What began for Pensacola with the arrival of Tristán de Luna in 1559," writes historian Jack Holmes, "ended with Old Hickory in 1821."[54]

More than that, it was what began for all of La Florida in 1513 with Juan Ponce de León that came to a conclusion in 1821. But like most conclusions, this one was tentative. The Hispanic tie between Florida and islands in the Caribbean, Puerto Rico and Cuba included, continues to the present. Spanish remains a strong voice in our southeasternmost state. And while visual reminders of the early years are few, there are interpretive programs and there remain historic vistas, restorations, or ruins at such places as Biscayne National Park, Canaveral National Seashore, Cumberland Island National Seashore, De Soto National Memorial, the western shores of Everglades National Park, Fort Frederica National Monument, Fort Caroline National Memorial and Timucuan Ecological and Historic Preserve; Dry Tortugas National Park, Gulf Islands National Seashore, and Ocmulgee National Monument.

In three places, the once imposing presence of Spain can still be seen in forts. Most awe-inspiring is that at Castillo de San Marcos National Monument. Perhaps the moodiest is the stabilized and restored structure at Fort Matanzas National Monument. The most interesting in some respects may be the carefully maintained Batería de San Antonio in the Pensacola Forts area of Gulf Islands National Seashore. Surrounded as it is by present-day Pensacola Naval Air Station, there is a sense here of military continuity.

114

PORTFOLIO

Mission Nuestra Señora de los Angeles de Porciúncula, Pecos National Historical Park, New Mexico.
(George H. H. Huey.)

*Mission San José de Tumacácori, Tumacacori
National Historical Park, Arizona.
(Edward McCain.)*

*Eighteenth-century bulto
of Jesús, southern Texas.
(George H. H. Huey photo
from the Enrique E. Guerra
collection.)*

Mission San Juan Capistrano, San Antonio Missions National Historical Park, Texas. (JC Leacock.)

Top Mission San Buenaventura and Las Humanas Pueblo, Salinas Pueblo Missions National Monument, New Mexico. (Tom Danielson.)

Bottom Mission Nuestra Señora Purísima Concepción de Cuarac, Salinas Pueblo Missions National Monument, New Mexico. (George H. H. Huey.)

*Above Grizzly bears,
Katmai National Park
and Preserve, Alaska.
(Jim Bones.)*

*Right Fairweather
Range, Glacier Bay
National Park and
Preserve, Alaska.
(Carr Clifton.)*

Ajo Range, Organ Pipe Cactus National Monument, Arizona. (Carr Clifton.)

Chisos Mountains, Big Bend National Park, Texas. (Carr Clifton.)

Martinez Adobe, John Muir National Historic Site, California. (George H. H. Huey.)

Redwood Creek, Redwood National Park, California. (Carr Clifton.)

Above Padre Bay, Glen Canyon National Recreation Area, Arizona/Utah.

(George H. H. Huey.)

Right Gunsight Butte and Navajo Mountain, Glen Canyon National Recreation Area, Arizona/Utah. (George H. H. Huey.)

Far Right Grand Canyon National Park, Arizona. (Carr Clifton.)

Far Left Chisos Mountains, Big Bend National Park, Texas. (Carr Clifton.)

Left Narbona Expedition pictograph, Canyon de Chelly National Monument, Arizona. (George H. H. Huey.)

Below Petroglyphs, Big Bend National Park, Texas. (Carr Clifton.)

Far Left Otter Cliffs, Acadia National Park, Maine. (Carr Clifton.)

Left Castillo de San Marcos National Monument, Florida. (Bill Keogh.)

Above Batería de San Antonio, Fuerta San Carlos de Barrancas, Gulf Islands National Seashore, Florida. (Connie Toops.)

Glorieta Mesa from Pecos National Historical Park, New Mexico. (George H. H. Huey.)

LOUISIANA

On paper, at least, King Charles III of Spain acquired the vast reaches of Louisiana from his Bourbon cousin, Louis XV of France, by a secret treaty signed at Fontainebleau on November 3, 1762. Through this acquisition Spain hoped to buffer its Mexican possessions against encroachment by other European powers. Terms of the treaty were not made public until 1764, however, and it was 1766 before the first Spanish governor, don Antonio de Ulloa, arrived in New Orleans to assume the new charge. Although there were attempts by French residents to oust the Spanish administration, Ulloa and his successors persisted until 1803 when the region reverted to France for a few months before being sold to the United States. Spain had actually secretly retroceded Louisiana to France in 1800, but it was 1803 before anything was done about it. The story of the 1766-1803 Spanish administration of New Orleans—and in particular its "French Quarter," now a National Historic District—is interpreted today in the French Market area of the city at the Visitor and Folklife Center of the French Quarter unit of Jean Lafitte National Historical Park and Preserve.[55]

Spain faced tremendous problems in Louisiana. She needed to gain the trust of the region's many tribes of Native Americans, most of them distrustful of the new rulers. Adding to Spanish concerns was the presence of aggressive British traders on the northeast boundary just across the Mississippi, men with no fondness for Hispania. Moreover, the non-Indian population of Louisiana was overwhelmingly French and would remain so for the entire period of Spain's rule.

To cope with these problems, Spain dealt with the Native Americans as France had done: by distributing presents and becoming involved in the fur trade. French traders already involved in these activities were generally employed to do the job. And while key French officials were replaced with officials more likely to be loyal to the new government, many of the replacements were themselves ethnically French.[56]

Spain's administration of Louisiana can best be described as having been largely indifferent until the appointment in 1776 of Bernardo de Gálvez as its new governor. Gálvez assumed the post at the start of 1777 and, in the face of British threats from West Florida, began a slow buildup of troops, artillery, and munitions.[57]

To help with the buildup, the Spanish Crown ordered the governor and commandant general of the Canary Islands to enlist seven hundred men for Louisiana service. By mid-1779, six ships carrying 2,010 so-called Isleños had left the islands for Louisiana via Havana. These included 600 soldiers, 444 of them with families. A large number, however, failed to reach Louisiana. Many stayed to live in Cuba and others, especially infants, died on the Caribbean island.[58]

The Isleños settled in various areas of Louisiana, but one group that arrived in 1778 was settled the following year at Barataria within what today is the Barataria unit of Jean Lafitte National Historical Park and Preserve. Some 150 people lived there initially, and it came to be known as the Bayou de Familles after the Isleño families who resided there. Thanks largely to floods and hurricanes, by 1796 Barataria was deserted save for a couple of holdouts. One of them, María Olivares, remained until she died in 1807, four years after Barataria had become a part of the United States.[59]

A continuing influence in New Orleans and elsewhere in Louisiana—one whose beginnings lie in Louisiana's period of Spanish rule—is exerted by its Cajun population. These Acadians, "Cajuns," had been expelled from Nova Scotia by the British in 1755. Some were detained in England before being sent in 1758 to France, where they languished until the Spanish government in Madrid paid the costs of bringing them to Louisiana in 1785 to join other Acadian settlers who had arrived two decades earlier.[60]

Another important Spanish contribution to New Orleans lies in the architecture of many of the buildings in the French Quarter and in Jackson Square. Much of the French Quarter was built during Spain's rule of Louisiana. Among the many period structures to be seen today are the Cabildo, built in 1795; the Presbytère, begun in 1795 (completed in 1847); and Madame John's Legacy, a house on Dumaine Street, dating from 1788. The French Quarter unit of Jean Lafitte National Historical Park and Preserve offers regular ranger-guided tours of the district.[61]

North of New Orleans along the Mississippi and some of its tributaries, including the Missouri River and extending to St. Louis, was the region of Upper Louisiana. One of its remote outliers was that on the lower Arkansas River begun in the late seventeenth century as a French trading post. Now preserved and interpreted at Arkansas Post National Memorial, it was five years after her takeover of Louisiana before Spain began to exercise control of this distant trading station/fort. Its former French commander and a delegation of Quapaw chiefs had tried to forestall the change in administration, but in 1768 Alexander de Clouet, a French officer in service to Spain, arrived at Arkansas Post to take charge. He was met there by eighty-five white civilians; thirty-five black, mulatto, and Indian slaves; and eighteen military personnel, all of whom were required to swear allegiance to Spain.[62]

Subsequent events at Arkansas Post offer a case study in problems faced by Spain in dealing with Indians in Upper Louisiana and in relationships with French and other unregulated traders, with the British, and, finally, with Anglo-Americans of the new United States. When it became inevitable that a Spanish administration would take over at Arkansas Post, many of its residents deserted and joined a French Canadian outlaw who operated far upriver on the Arkansas. A traveler at the time described the river as

the asylum of the most wicked persons without a doubt in all the Endes [sic]. They [the outlaws] pass their scandalous lives in public concubinage with captive

Indian women who, for this purpose, they purchase among the heathen, loaning those of whom they tire to others of less power . . . [for] quieting their lascivious passion; in short they have no other rule than their own caprice and . . . [conduct] themselves like brutes.[63]

These renegade French owed allegiance to no one and added to their mischief by allying themselves with Osage Indians, longtime rivals of both France and Spain, encouraging them to capture and enslave women from among the Caddo. Osage men lived in the Missouri country but often hunted—and robbed—in the Arkansas region. Many legitimate trappers were killed by Osage within the jurisdiction of the soldiers stationed at Arkansas Post.

To counter Osage problems, Spaniards persuaded the Quapaw to wage war against them. A great many scalps were taken and hung on public display at the fort at Arkansas Post. Finally, tired of hostilities with the Quapaw, the Osage petitioned for peace in 1777.[64] Simultaneously, on the east side of the Mississippi where lands still belonged to England, British traders urged Chickasaw Indians to harass hunters heading in their direction from Arkansas Post. These same traders, moreover, were able to offer goods—including liquor—to Indians at cheaper prices than were the Spaniards and were able to win Quapaw loyalty. The British also hunted and trapped in Spanish territory with impunity.[65]

Although Spain did not officially join Americans against the British in the Revolutionary War until 1779, as early as 1776, the year of the Declaration of Independence, Spanish-allied Native Americans at Arkansas Post were raiding British hunting and trapping camps along the Arkansas and Mississippi rivers. Among these were Kaskaskia Indians who had moved into the Arkansas country to escape Iroquois incursions in their native Illinois homelands.[66]

During the course of the Revolutionary War, in 1779, Arkansas Post was relocated to a higher, drier site upriver on the north bank. When word arrived that Spain was formally at war with England, the post's commander crossed to the eastern side of the Mississippi with a detachment of soldiers and civilian witnesses where, meeting no opposition, he "took possession of the left bank of the Mississippi River opposite to the Arkansas, White, and St. Francis Rivers, as far as the limits of the Natchez garrison as dependencies and jurisdictions of this post." All of which helped legitimize Spain's post-war claim to the east bank of the Mississippi in this northern area.[67]

The post's only military involvement in the revolution was tangential. Its residents fought against an Englishman named James Colbert who had rebelled against the Spanish occupation of Natchez, escaped, and vowed with the help of Indian allies to disrupt Spanish commerce on the Mississippi as a means of effecting the release of some of his companions whom the Spaniards had imprisoned in New Orleans.

117

In April 1783 Colbert and some hundred companions, including Chickasaws, Natchez rebels, and his eleven half-Indian sons, raided the new Arkansas Post settlement and its Fort Carlos III, completed in 1781. Before they were driven off, the attackers succeeded in killing two Spaniards and wounding a third while suffering one dead and one wounded.

Four and a half months later, on September 3, 1783, the Treaty of Paris ended the Revolutionary War, bringing to an end England's occupation of lands east of the Mississippi. These now belonged to the United States and, arguably in some reaches, to Spain.[68]

It soon became apparent that American citizens of the fledgling United States were bent on expanding their territory toward the west. To forestall the advance, in 1783 Spain concluded formal peace agreements with the Chickasaw and Choctaw Indians who stood between the Spaniards' eastern and Americans' western frontiers. Spanish friendliness toward Native Americans attracted to Arkansas displaced Delawares in 1786 and Miami-Piankashaw peoples in 1789. But opportunities for trade were also a magnet for growing numbers of Americans.[69]

In an effort to bring contraband trade between Americans and Spain's Indian allies to a halt, Captain don Joseph Vallière was dispatched to Fort San Carlos III and Arkansas Post as commandant in 1787. He assumed leadership of 32 soldiers and counted 119 civilians, many of them hunters and some of them discharged Spanish veterans—not exactly a commanding presence in this wilderness outpost of Spain's far-flung American empire. Even so, Vallière and his successors did their best to keep the Americans in check. Between 1791 and 1792 a new fort, San Esteban, was built at Arkansas Post to replace Fort San Carlos III, which by then had fallen victim to the Arkansas River. Nothing in the record suggests that the dedication of San Esteban included mention of what Christopher Columbus had begun exactly three centuries earlier.[70]

In 1794 twenty-seven-year-old Captain Carlos de Villemont became Spain's longest-tenured and final commandant at Arkansas Post. In 1800 he married a local woman and eventually raised six children there before dying in his adopted land. It was under his watch in July 1795 that Spain, fearing a war with the United States, through Pinckney's Treaty gave up its claim to the east side of the Mississippi between the mouth of the Yazoo River to the 31st parallel north of New Orleans, thus making the 31st parallel the southern boundary of the United States. Pinckney's Treaty also gave Americans free navigation on the Mississippi as well as a three-year right to deposit cargo at New Orleans. The agreement opened a hole in the dike which marked the beginning of the end for Spanish Louisiana.[71]

Spanish officials in Louisiana had hoped to stem the tide of United States' expansion by populating the province with new settlers. "Ironically," as historian Roger Coleman notes, "because Spanish subjects preferred to settle elsewhere, Louisiana officials had to rely on Americans—the very people she sought to exclude—to settle in Louisiana. The governor instructed Commandant de Villemont to invite Americans from Vincennes and Detroit to settle in Arkansas."[72]

Men with such surnames as Winters, Stillwell, Hubble, Russell, Carr, and Price became homesteaders in Spanish Arkansas. And in 1800, Spain—by then having decided Louisiana was a luxury it could no longer afford—agreed to transfer Louisiana to France in exchange for a Tuscan kingdom for indigent relatives of King Charles IV. France reneged but demanded the retrocession of Louisiana nonetheless. A powerless Spain complied, and on October 15, 1802, orders reached New Orleans that the colony should be turned over to French officials. It finally happened in a ceremony held in New Orleans on November 30, 1803. Twenty days later, there was a second ceremony when a French agent turned Louisiana over to American representatives. France had sold all of Louisiana—which included the Arkansas Post and St. Louis—to the United States for $15,000,000, the renowned Louisiana Purchase.[73]

A month later, in January 1804, Captain Villemont transferred the fort at Arkansas Post to Lieutenant James B. Many. Fort San Esteban became Fort Madison, and the relentless march of Americans toward the Pacific continued.[74]

The most important non-Indian settlement in Upper Louisiana, or Spanish Illinois as it was often called, became St. Louis. It was founded in 1763 as a trading post on the Missouri River by Frenchmen who had no knowledge at the time that Louisiana, thanks to the 1762 secret Treaty of Fontainebleau, had become a part of Spain. By the time the French commander relinquished control of St. Louis to newly-appointed lieutenant governor don Pedro Piernas in 1770, St. Louis had become a thriving trading center, "a commercial place with money behind it." In 1763, Pierre Laclede Liguest of the mercantile company of Maxet, Laclede, and Company had selected the location for St. Louis. Clearing of the site began early in 1764, and by August 1766 fifty families lived in forty houses in an area occupied today by the Gateway Arch of Jefferson National Expansion Memorial.[75]

Somewhat larger was the slightly older farming, lead-mining, and salt-making community of Ste. Genevieve. But St. Louis, partly because of its location

Most of western North America is conceived as "Louisiana" in this map by Samuel Lewis in the New and Elegant General Atlas, *1804. (Courtesy Huntington Library, San Marino, California.)*

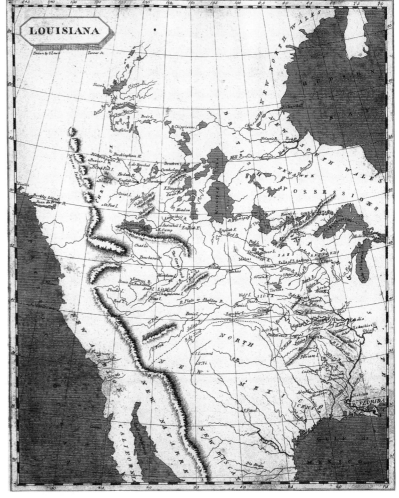

on higher ground, became the capital of Upper Louisiana and headquarters of the Spanish lieutenant governor. Also because of its location, it became the principal trading center for the entire region. Indians from throughout the Missouri and Upper Mississippi valleys poured into St. Louis in May and June to trade their furs and other goods to local merchants and to pick up gifts—items such as blankets, cloth, fancy garments, plumed hats, mirrors, combs, sewing needles, thimbles, ribbons, vermilion, hoes, axes, knives, wire, kettles, muskets, gunpowder, tobacco, and, occasionally and illegally, brandy—bestowed on them annually by the government. Spanish St. Louis was colorful at the very least.[76]

After Spain's 1779 entry into the Revolutionary War on the side of the Americans, the British lieutenant governor in Michigan authorized a trader, Emanuel Hesse, to recruit Indians for a proposed assault on Spanish positions in Upper Louisiana. Learning of possible attack, Fernando de Leyba, who had been lieutenant governor since 1778, oversaw construction of four stone towers at the corners of the St. Louis settlement. One tower, which housed the cannons, was called Fort San Carlos. When Hesse and his combined force of British and Indians attacked in May 1780, the guns were waiting for them. The attackers fled, but not before they had killed, wounded, or captured seventy-nine of the village's seven hundred people.[77]

De Leyba's successor at St. Louis was don Francisco Cruzat, a popular man who had previously been lieutenant governor in 1775-78. Cruzat used money from the royal treasury to build a line of fortifications surrounding the town, and in 1781, on his own initiative, he sent Captain Eugene Pourré and the 2nd militia company of St. Louis on a northerly expedition. On February 12, 1781, Pourré, his troops, and Indian allies made a highly successful attack on the British fort at St. Joseph, Michigan—probably the closest any official Spanish force ever got to the Great Lakes. The raiders were feted as heroes when they got back to St. Louis in early March. Had it been there at the time, the Jefferson National Expansion Memorial would have provided its visitors with an unobstructed view of the celebration.[78]

With St. Louis as the center of fur trade over a vast region, it is not surprising that at least one of its residents and a subject of Spain, Santiago la Iglesia (Jacques d'Église), got as far afield as present-day North Dakota, where he contacted the Mandan Indians. His 1790 journey marked Spain's deepest overland penetration toward the Pacific Northwest.[79]

Efforts after the Revolutionary War to protect Louisiana from a takeover by American frontiersmen were capped by Spanish concessions to the United States made in 1795 in Pinckney's Treaty.[80] England and Spain were soon at war again, and to head off British attack from the north, the Louisiana governor, Francisco Carondelet, dispatched Lieutenant Colonel don Carlos Howard and a large expeditionary force to St. Louis in 1796. Not only did the Irishman Howard oversee construction of new fortifications in Upper Louisiana's capital, but in 1797 he also led

120

his troops and some Sac and Fox warriors on an unsuccessful raid on the British establishment at Prairie du Chien in southwestern Wisconsin.[81]

Believing that American settlers would help defend Upper Louisiana from the British, the Spaniards circulated handbills encouraging Americans to move into the territory. After 1796 nearly all new settlers were American rather than French or French Canadian. When Spain assumed control of Upper Louisiana in the 1770s, there were about a thousand non-Indian inhabitants. By 1804, when the United States formally took control, more than three-fifths of its 10,350 non-Indian inhabitants were Americans. While Spanish officials had come and gone, the remainder of the population was either French or black, both black slaves and free blacks accounting for 15 percent of the population.[82]

Ironically, St. Louis, as part of the Louisiana region upon which Spain had counted to buffer its Nueva España possessions from advances of competing national powers, was soon to become a gateway to the west. One of its trails was destined to lead to Santa Fe—a story interpreted today at Jefferson National Expansion Memorial in this great Missouri city. From a Spanish point of view, Louisiana had become its first major North American "borderland in retreat."[83]

TEJAS

Spanish interest in Tejas, like that in Louisiana, grew largely out of a concern for protecting what the crown regarded as its national right from competing European monarchies. Tejas lay strategically located between Nueva España and the areas of French incursion at the head of the Gulf Coast. Added to these political motivations were religious ones: Franciscans were anxious to get on with the business of bringing the good news of Christ to uninitiated Native Americans.[84]

The earliest missions to be established within the modern boundaries of Texas—although they were in southernmost Nuevo México at the time—were those founded in west Texas on the Río Grande in the aftermath of Nuevo México's Pueblo Revolt of 1680. To accommodate Puebloan peoples who had, for whatever reasons, gone south with the Spaniards to El Paso—and to further missionary work among local Native Americans—the missions of Corpus Christi de la Ysleta and Nuestra Señora de la Concepción del Socorro were founded between 1680 and 1682. The church at Ysleta del Sur Pueblo, now within the corporate limits of El Paso and adjacent to the Tigua Indian Reservation, continues to serve descendants of the Native Americans for whom it was begun. Ysleta del Sur boasts that it is the oldest community within today's Texas. Both Ysleta, where the present church was built after 1908, and Socorro, whose church now in use was built in 1843 and which has a handsome flat ceiling of carved and decorated *vigas* (beams), are not far downstream from Chamizal National Memorial.[85]

121

But the beginnings of missionary efforts among the Indians of what in the late seventeenth and early eighteenth century was Spanish Tejas lay in the efforts of Franciscan friars Damián Massanet and Francisco Casañas de Jesús María. In 1690 they founded the missions of San Francisco de los Tejas and Santísimo Nombre de María among the Caddoan-speaking Tejas and Hasinai Indians along the Trinity River in present-day Houston County in eastern Texas. Those initial efforts were short-lived. In 1693 a combination of floods and threats from the Tejas had forced the missions' abandonment.[86]

Later efforts followed in eastern Tejas with the early eighteenth century founding of such missions as those begun, for example, in 1716: Purísima Concepción, Nuestra Señora de los Nacogdoches, San José de los Nazones, San Miguel de los Linares de los Adaes, and Nuestra Señora de los Dolores de los Ais.[87]

In 1718, with the founding of Mission San Antonio de Valero—later to become famous in Texas history as the Alamo—Franciscans began a concerted proselytizing campaign among Native Americans along the San Antonio River in the immediate region of today's San Antonio, Texas. The Native Americans resident here were originally almost exclusively Coahuiltecan speakers, and a form of that language came to be the lingua franca used by later arrivals in the missions. The Coahuiltecans were represented by an almost bewildering array of variously named bands. But during the eighteenth century, the missions also served Native Americans whose linguistic affiliation is now impossible to determine as well as lesser numbers of Apaches, Caddoans, Comanches, Karakawans, Tonkawans, and Cotonames. The pre-mission lifestyle of most of these people, and especially of the Coahuiltecans, was geared to the semi-nomadism of a hunting and gathering subsistence.[88]

The founding of Mission San Antonio de Valero on May 1, 1718, by Fray Antonio de San Buenaventura y Olivares and three other friars from the Apostolic College of Santa Cruz de Querétaro in Mexico was followed four days later by the founding by Governor Martín de Alarcón of the nearby Presidio of San Antonio de Béxar and its immediately adjacent town, the Villa de Béxar. The development of San Antonio's missions and of what evolved into the modern city of San Antonio occurred side by side throughout most of the eighteenth century.

Just as three missions were destined to be relocated to the San Antonio area in 1731, that same year the small civilian and military population of its presidio and town were augmented by a group of fifteen families of Isleños, Canary Island farmers whose immigration had been sponsored by the crown. Their arrival marked the formal beginnings of the Villa de San Fernando de Béxar, predating by forty-seven years the arrival of Canary Islanders at Barataria in Louisiana.[89]

A new edifice for the church of San Antonio de Valero was built beginning about 1755. What remains of it, now regarded as the most famous shrine in Texas, is preserved as the Alamo by the Daughters of the Republic of Texas because of the role it played in the 1836 war by Texans for their independence from Mexico. And in a very

122

real sense, the modern San Antonio, Texas, is in its entirety a living monument to the memory of the 1718 villa of San Fernando and presidio of San Antonio de Béxar.[90]

In the fall of 1719 Indian refugees from the eastern missions who were fleeing attacks from eastern Apaches and escaping the chaotic conditions in that area occasioned by that year's outbreak of war between Spain and France, began to arrive in San Antonio in large numbers. With them was Fray Antonio Margil de Jesús, a member of the Apostolic College of Guadalupe de Zacatecas in Mexico. To accommodate the refugees, and because they preferred not to live among the Native Americans already at San Antonio de Valero, in 1720 Father Margil established the mission he named San José y San Miguel de Aguayo, thereby honoring the Tejas governor, Marquis de San Miguel de Aguayo. He located the church on the east bank of the San Antonio River about four and a half miles downstream from de Valero. In 1721, there were 227 Native Americans in residence.[91]

Mission San José is today one of four San Antonio missions whose history is interpreted as a part of San Antonio Missions National Historical Park. It was relocated near its present site on the west bank of the river sometime between 1724 and 1727. An epidemic of smallpox and measles raged through the area in 1739, and most people either fled or died, leaving a congregation of forty-nine men, women, and children. The church was afterward moved to higher ground and construction of the first permanent buildings began in the 1740s. A visitor in 1757 described eighty-four flat-roofed Indian homes; parapets and battlements; soldiers' quarters; carpentry; granary; textile workshop; sugar mill; corral; cemetery; friary; and a church.[92]

San José reached its peak of Indian population, 350, in 1768, the same year construction began on the stone church that remains in use today. In 1777 Father Juan Morfi called it "the first mission in America" in terms of its beauty, strength, and plan. He characterized it as "the Queen of the Missions."[93]

Father Morfi also described San José's farm, one that was fenced and that covered two and a half square miles. Water for the crops, he wrote, "is taken from the San Antonio River and is distributed by means of a beautiful irrigation ditch to all parts of the field, where corn, beans, lentils, cotton, sugar cane, watermelons, melons, and sweet potatoes are raised. It has a patch for all kinds of vegetables; and there are some fruit trees."[94]

The Indian population at San José, never more than 350, fluctuated with the times. A virulent epidemic in 1783 helped reduce the number to 128, but three years later it was back up to 189 before dropping again in 1789 to 138, increasing by the end of 1790 to 144 and dropping in 1791 to 106. In 1794, when San José underwent partial secularization and the former mission lands were divided among the Indians, there were twenty-eight heads of Christian families or adult single persons. In 1804 a count showed fifty-seven Native Americans; in 1809 fifty-five; and in 1815 forty-nine. At that, it was always the most "thriving" of the San Antonio missions.[95]

Franciscan missionary Antonio Margil de Jesús founded Mission San José y San Miguel de Aguayo in 1720. (Anonymous portrait courtesy Harry Ransom Humanities Research Center Art Collection, University of Texas, Austin.)

123

Reasons for the decline of San José as well as of the other San Antonio foundations were numerous. Among them was a decree issued in 1777 by Teodoro de Croix, Commandant General of the newly-formed Provincias Internas (Interior Provinces)—which included Texas—declaring that all unbranded cattle were property of the government. Croix's decree was confirmed by royal order in 1787. Since the missions' great herds were largely unbranded, this deprived them of their principal means of support for their Indian neophytes and converts. Epidemics also proved to be devastating, as did the effects of periodic raids on the missions and their livestock by Comanches and Apaches. Spanish soldiers and settlers were also inclined to help themselves to mission livestock, often taking away whole herds.

The result was that Indians either died or left the missions. With little or nothing there to entice them to stay, and with the military refusing to offer the Franciscans escort to seek new recruits, decline became inevitable toward the end of the eighteenth century. The Spanish crown did little or nothing to reverse the trend. Missions were a drain on the royal exchequer since missionaries' salaries were paid out of the royal treasury. And after Louisiana was ceded to Spain in 1763, France no longer appeared to pose the threat to Nueva España that it had at one time.[96]

Unlike the missions Spaniards had founded in Nuevo México and, to some extent, in La Florida and Sonora—where churches were built and missionaries ensconced themselves in the midsts of sedentary Native American communities—the missions in Tejas were *reducciones*, or "reductions." The former were termed *conversiones*, "conversions."

Reducciones were deemed necessary by the missionaries where the native population was widely scattered and seasonally mobile. Such people tended to be either semi-nomadic hunters and food collectors or farmers who lived in such marginal areas that their means of subsistence made it impossible for them to congregate year around in large, fixed communities. To succeed with a program of conversion and assimilation, the lands over which they wandered necessarily had to be "reduced." In the Spanish mind, people who roamed over large tracts of territory were especially uncivilized.

In northern Sonora, parts of which eventually became southern Arizona, when the original Native Americans living in conversiones died as a result of epidemics, replacements from other areas were occasionally forcefully recruited by Jesuit missionaries to settle in the depopulated communities, thus making them de facto reducciones.

In the legal theory of Spain, Native Americans were to become loyal, Spanish-speaking, clothes-wearing, tax-paying, Roman Catholic subjects of Spain within ten years from the time they were first contacted by missionaries. This was to be brought about in stages, starting with that of *misión*, or "mission," followed either with reducción or conversión, depending on the type of settlement and subsistence means

124

of the natives. The second stage was to be followed by that of *doctrina*, or "doctrine," the religious supervisor or *doctrinero* of which might be either regular (missionary) or secular clergy. Members of a doctrina were already professed Christians. The final stage, that of *curato*, or "curacy," would be called a secular parish and would be overseen by a secular parish priest, not by a member of a religious order. In the church, the act of secularization meant a switch from mission status to that of parish or curacy. And more importantly from the perspective of the royal treasurer, secular clergy—diocesan priests—were supported by their parishioners rather than by the crown. Regular clergy, on the other hand, received a royal stipend. Moreover, parishioners were subjects of Spain and liable for taxes; Indians under the supervision of regular clergy were neither.[97]

In Spanish North America there were virtually no instances in which missionaries succeeded in bringing about the religious and cultural conversion of Native Americans within ten years. And more often than not, secularization was not a sign of missionary success. It indicated instead the arrival of non-Indians who by then had come to outnumber the tragically decimated native populations—although there were indeed Native North Americans who became wholly assimilated into the mainstream of frontier Spanish culture and who lost their Indian identity in the process. Many such persons who became successfully assimilated did so via intermarriage.

Mission San Antonio de Valero was completely secularized in 1793, its chapel no longer used for services by Christian Indians and its properties turned over to the pastor of the secular San Fernando parish of the Villa de San Antonio. In 1794 the other four missions of the San Antonio area—all now a part of San Antonio Missions National Historical Park—were secularized, but only partially. Some of the irrigated fields and mission properties were turned over to Christian Indians; Indians' houses became their own; and a so-called justice was appointed to manage the temporal affairs of the former mission community. But because there were still Indians under instruction in these four places, the Franciscan friars remained at their posts in a dual role as pastor to Christian Indians and missionary to the neophytes. Because of the shortage of priests, the friars stationed at San José and at San Francisco de la Espada in 1794 also began to take care of missions Nuestra Señora de la Concepción de Acuña and San Juan Capistrano, respectively.[98]

Although by then the Tejas missions should have seen the handwriting on the wall, in 1793 the Apostolic College for the Propagation of the Faith of Guadalupe de Zacatecas sent friars Manuel de Silva and José María Francisco de la Garza to eastern Texas where they founded what was to become the last Tejas mission, Nuestra Señora del Refugio.[99] As for San José and its neighboring three missions, Zacatecan friars continued to serve them for three decades after the 1794 secularization decree. By 1801 San José's Native Americans were working at looms that wove cloth and blankets as good as those produced in Querétaro in Nueva España. The parish

125

church-mission was also producing wheat flour ground from locally grown crops in an ingenious mill devised by pastor and missionary Father José Manuel Pedrajo. In 1955 Dr. Paul Czibesz wrote about this remarkable mill, which is now restored and can be seen at Mission San José:

> The hydraulic machinery of the San José Mission mill is living proof that the impulse-turbine was invented a long time before Pelton had published his invention. . . . It is not an ordinary water-wheel. It is really a turbine-runner. Water-wheels work on gravity force or they use the velocity head of the water flow. The turbine wheel of the San José mill utilizes, obviously, the impulse energy. . . . Old fashioned water-wheels utilized the weight of water on overshot wheels or they used the velocity of the flow by undershot assembly. Both methods could use only one-tenth of the available water power. Pelton's impulse wheel works on impact and impulse energy, and utilizes at least three-fourths of the hydraulic power available. It would appear that the San José Mission mill is nothing less than the ancestor of Pelton's turbine.[100]

Other authorities who have examined the mill have said it is a so-called Norse mill, already in existence in the days of Pliny (A.D. 23-79), and a similar eighteenth-century mill has been observed near Mexico City.[101]

In early 1807 Lieutenant Zebulon Pike, with no official authorization, entered Spanish land in Nuevo México where he was taken into custody by Spanish troops and conducted to Santa Fe. From there he was taken as a prisoner to Chihuahua, where the Spanish commandant general ordered him to leave Spanish territory and return to the United States in the Louisiana Territory. En route from Chihuahua to the United States, he paused at Mission San José for a friendly visit in June 1807. He remarked in his diary that he had been treated with the kindest hospitality by the priest, Fr. Bernardo Vallejo.[102]

While the end for missions must clearly have been in sight, in 1817 Fr. José Antonio Díaz de León arrived at San José from the Zacatecas college as the mission's last Spanish-period friar and, in fact, as the last missionary in Texas in its pre-republic period. Since 1810 Mexicans had been battling for their independence from Spain, and in September 1821 a triumphant Agustín de Iturbide entered Mexico City and eleven years of war drew to a close. The Empire of Mexico replaced that of Spain. And on the frontier, the few remaining missions in Tejas became Mexican rather than Spanish, a final nail soon to be hammered into the proselytizing arm of Christ.[103]

The story of the other three missions of San Antonio Missions National Historical Park parallels almost precisely that of San José, except that they did not arrive on the San Antonio River until 1731. Another difference is that all three were founded by friars from the Apostolic College of the Holy Cross at Querétaro rather than by friars from the Zacatecan college. In 1772, however, the Querétarans—since 1768 busy

Mission San José y San Miguel de Aguayo, one of four preserved in San Antonio Missions National Historical Park, Texas. Construction on this famed stone church began in 1768. (JC Leacock.)

126

with a new mission field in Sonora where they had replaced the expelled Jesuits—turned their Texas missions over to the Zacatecan Franciscans.[104]

Founded originally in 1716 among the Tejas, Mission Purísima Concepción moved once from its original site before coming to rest on March 5, 1731, in its present location as Nuestra Señora de la Purísima Concepción de Acuña, named partially in honor of Juan de Acuña, the Marqués de Casafuerte, the viceroy who had authorized the relocation. Its Coahuiltecan population of about 300 had dropped to 250 by 1738 before taking a plunge to 120 in the wake of a 1739 epidemic. After 1740 the number leveled off at 210.[105]

The beautiful stone church of Concepción, the oldest unrestored church in the United States where many interesting interior painted designs survive, was dedicated in December 1754. The following year the friary was under construction, but a carpentry, granary, and smithy were already in place inside the plaza in front of the church. Most of the Coahuiltecans lived in adobe houses, but a few lived in *jacales*, huts of wood and reeds.[106]

As elsewhere in mission communities, friars at Concepción instituted political status positions based on the Spanish model. Missionaries appointed an Indian superintendent (*mayordomo*), superintendent's assistant, *fiscal*, overseer, and a head groom to care for the horses. And Native Americans were instructed in more than a dozen occupations foreign to their indigenous culture, trades such as musician (European instruments), fieldhand, cowboy, oxen drover, woodcutter, blacksmith, gardener, carpenter, shearer, soapmaker, carder, weaver, comber, spinner, saddler, and shepherd. Barbers, candlemakers, tailors, and laundresses were hired from the non-Indian populace of the presidio when those tasks had to be accomplished.[107]

Concepción, like other San Antonio missions, sent an annual requisition list to the apostolic college. Once a year a supply train would arrive carrying beads, necklaces, ribbons, rosaries, brushes, shoes and other garments, hats, spurs, bridles, copper pots, saddles, griddles, kettles, and iron tools. And also at Concepción, the friars had introduced the dance of the *Matachines*, a contra-dance performed by costumed dancers to the accompaniment of violins, and which continues today to be popular in many Indian and non-Indian communities throughout Mexico and in the southwestern United States.[108] Concepción underwent the same process of semi-secularization in 1794 that San José had undergone. By that year, its numbers had been reduced to thirty-eight. It was placed under the administration of the priest at San José.[109]

When the Mexican War of Independence began in 1810, San Antonio had a large number of republicans, people sympathetic to the cause of Mexican independence, as well as royalists, those who favored the continuation of Spain's rule. Among the republicans was Juan Bautista de las Casas. His revolutionary coup, as well as an 1812-13 invasion of Texas and San Antonio by some fourteen thousand Mexicans, Indians, and American filibusters led by José Bernardo Maximiliano Gutiérrez de Lara and

Mission Nuestra Señora de la Concepción de Acuña was dedicated in 1754. The oldest unrestored church in the United States, it is now part of San Antonio Missions National Historical Park, Texas. (JC Leacock.)

127

Augustus Magee, disrupted the city for several months. Las Casas' insurgency was put down and he was executed, and in 1813 General Joaquín Arrendondo defeated the filibusters and restored Spanish rule in Tejas. Soon after, in 1815, Spanish official José Antonio Huízar was awarded a grant of land at Concepción that had first been approved in 1806 but which the illness of another official and the insurgency and invasion had delayed. By about 1819 services were no longer held in the church, its former parishioners attending services at San José. On the eve of Mexico's takeover in 1821, it was for all practical purposes abandoned.[110]

Mission San Juan Capistrano had begun its life in eastern in Texas in 1716 as Mission San José de los Nazonis. It ceased operations in 1719 but was reestablished in 1721 before moving in 1731 to San Antonio. Since there was already a mission San José at San Antonio, the relocated mission was given the patronage of the four-teenth- and fifteenth-century Franciscan saint John Capistran, who had directed the Catholic campaign against the Turks. He had been a general of the Order of Friars Minor (Franciscans).[111]

Historians Leutenegger and Perry summarize its first ten years:

> Hampered by Apache raids, obstructionist tactics of Governor Carlos Benites Franquís de Lugo (1736-1737), and the great epidemic of 1739, the mission made slow progress during its first decade. The Governor's attitude encouraged recalcitrance among the resident Indians (*reducidos*) who alleged mistreatment by the missionaries. Orderly mission life broke down and construction came prac-tically to a standstill.[112]

A population of 169 Native Americans in 1740 increased to 203 by 1762. And in the meantime, by 1756 the mission had a stone church and sacristy. By 1762 there was a large stone granary; the textile shop had three looms "and a well-equipped weaving and spinning room where blankets and cloth were woven from cotton and wool pro-duced from the mission's farm and sheep"; a dozen ox carts were available for haul-ing stones; carpenters and masons were well supplied with the necessary tools; and three well-armed Spanish soldiers lived at the mission for its defense.[113]

In 1794, when the missions were semi-secularized, the priest in residence at Mission San Francisco de la Espada doubled his duties by also taking over at San Juan. A devastating flood of the San Antonio River in 1819 seriously damaged the fields of both Indian and Spanish farmers at missions San José, Capistrano, and Espada. In March 1820 Fr. Miguel Muro—who at the moment was the sole mission-ary in San Antonio—distributed fifty-peso donations to each of the three places. A year and a half later they would come under Mexican jurisdiction.[114]

San Francisco de la Espada was the descendant of the abandoned eastern Texas church of San Francisco de los Tejas, the first mission to have been founded in what was then, in 1690, regarded by Spaniards as Texas. It was 1731 when San Francisco was moved for its final time to the San Antonio River and renamed "de la Espada."[115]

Espada, the southernmost of the San Antonio missions, was the most exposed to attack by Apaches. Its chapel was the first to have been built of stone. By 1758 its roof had apparently collapsed. In 1765 Indian houses were starting to be built of stone. Seven years later, when its administration was turned over by the Querétarans to the Zacatecan friars, a new church, also of stone, was under construction. The building described in the 1772 report was the sacristy which was then being used for services in anticipation of completion of the entire building. And in 1777 the old church lay in ruins as construction continued on the new one. Major building efforts went ahead about 1780.[116]

Espada, like the other missions, was reasonably productive. In 1765, there were three looms whose weavers were making cotton blankets and cloth for wearing apparel; the mission's farmlands grew corn, beans, cotton, watermelons, and cantaloupes; there was a blacksmith's forge; and there were plenty of good farming tools on hand. The same report listed 700 head of cattle, 950 small stock (sheep and goats), 50 horses, 52 mares, and 50 hogs. Where the latter were located is not stated explicitly, but the likelihood is that they were at the mission's outlying ranch, which came to be known as Rancho de las Cabras ("Goat Ranch"). The 1772 inventory mentions a peach orchard as well as an extensive network of *acequias*, irrigation canals as well as a dam. The inventory also notes a feature not mentioned for other missions, a kiln for firing bricks and floor tiles. So were there a peach orchard and an imposing acequia, an irrigation canal that spanned Piedras Creek on a stone-arched aqueduct and whose water was lifted from the river with the help of a stone dam. Both acequia and dam, still in operation and within the boundaries of San Antonio Missions National Historical Park, may represent the oldest continually used water system in the United States.[117]

Rancho de las Cabras, the ruins of which are located near Floresville, Texas, and which is now a part of San Antonio Missions National Historical Park, was begun by the Querétaran friars sometime in the mid-eighteenth century as Espada's ranch. By 1762 there was a stone house somewhere on the property, and ten years later the ranch headquarters were enclosed by a stone wall. After the Zacatecans took over from the Querétarans, major work at Las Cabras got underway between 1775 and 1780. The shape of the ranch compound was altered and two bastions for defense were added. The complex eventually included a chapel, a possible well, various stone rooms, *jacales*, and a lime kiln. The ranch served Espada at least until the semisecularization of the missions in 1794, after which, in 1809, its lands and buildings were possibly deeded to Ignacio Calvillo. He was the husband of Antonia de Arocha, a member of one of San Antonio's 1731 Canary Island families.[118]

This beautiful quatrefoil arch embraces the entrance to the stone church of Mission San Francisco de la Espada, San Antonio Missions National Historical Park, Texas. (JC Leacock.)

129

Espada shared the fate of the other San Antonio missions. When Tejas became a part of Mexico in 1821, it had only three years before its bones would be picked clean by a decree of final secularization.

Although the story of Spain's missions in Tejas came to an end in 1821, descendants—cultural as well as biological—of the men, women, and children who peopled the missions and who dealt with them as neighbors during the viceregal period continue to give Texas, especially southern Texas, a distinctive character. Historian Arnoldo de León reminds us that the actors in the colonial theater of Tejas were not merely Spanish padres or Spanish military aristocracy. Indeed, the majority of them were mixed-bloods of every conceivable description. The residents of San Antonio, Goliad, and Nacogdoches, the only centers of civilian population in eighteenth century Tejas, included Mexican Indians, black slaves, free blacks, mulattos, and mestizos, the people who were the tailors, merchants, butchers, bakers, candlestick makers, blacksmiths, servants, barbers, packers, and ranch hands. These were the very backbone of Spanish expansion and were often joined by local Native Americans who chose either to marry or otherwise to lose their identities among the newcomers.

They evolved a frontier culture that was in many respects uniquely their own. And if de León is right, they

> mustered up a resilience that would allow Mexicans to resist the hostile forces of Anglo American racism after the Texas Revolution of 1836. . . . Importantly, when the political world of Texas-Mexicans crumbled, their culture was pliable enough that it could adjust to the circumstances and continue on its own terms. This adaptive capacity blunted the bane of racism and colonialism and helped make the transition without loss of identity. . . .

> Tejanos [Texas Mexicans] were able to resist imposed standards from outside their own cultural milieu and succeeded in carrying on traditions and beliefs that were an integral part of their community. The mission institution, the center of Spanish-Texan society in the beginning, helped prepare Chicanos so they could live in white society on their own terms while moving in and out of that culture and protecting and preserving that which they held dear. As such, the missions of the Spanish period were significant as they acted as centers of socialization for a manner of living that would ward off annihilation once Anglo Americans arrived.[119]

Because of Spain's late seventeenth- and early eighteenth-century suspicions concerning the intentions of her French neighbor to the east, not only did she establish a buffer of missions, but she created presidios, military posts, as well. In addition to that at San Antonio, at least half a dozen presidios were founded in the early part of the eighteenth century in eastern Tejas. And immediately south of the Río Grande in Coahuila, the presidio of San Juan Bautista del Río Grande, southwest of San Antonio, was established in 1703.[120]

Throughout virtually all of the eighteenth century, troops in these places were engaged only against Native Americans. This is in spite of the fact that the principal reason for their establishment was to head off French encroachment, exemplified by the abortive late seventeenth-century efforts of La Salle and France's subsequent occupation of Louisiana.[121]

In the early nineteenth century Spanish attention in eastern Tejas shifted to the Americans who had purchased the Louisiana Territory in 1803. President Jefferson and other Americans contended that the western boundary of Louisiana was the Río Grande from its source to its mouth. Spain countered that the western boundary was much farther east: from Natchitoches on the Red River and then by a line southward to the Gulf of Mexico on the Calcasieu River. While diplomats failed to resolve the problem immediately, the Spanish and American military commanders in the field, after coming close to a hostile engagement between their troops, agreed to the creation of a Neutral Ground between the Arroyo Hondo just west of Natchitoches west to the Sabine River and, farther south, between the Calcasieu and Sabine rivers. The matter was finally officially resolved by the February 1819 agreement between Spain and the United States—ratified in February 1821—known as the Adams-Onís Treaty. The eastern boundary of Texas, as it is today, was set at the mouth of the Sabine River north to the 32nd parallel, due north to the Red River, up the Red River to the 100th meridian at the Arkansas River, and then north from the headwaters of the Arkansas to the 42nd parallel. This left the Panhandle of today's Oklahoma as well as the western and southern three-fourths of Colorado in Spanish hands as well as all of today's Texas.[122]

In the eighteenth century the political boundaries within Nueva España of what today is the Big Bend region were ill defined. The area north and south on the Río Grande from near the modern Lajitas southeast to the mouth of the Pecos was regarded as a part of Nueva Vizcaya, while the Coahuila line entered the Big Bend at its southeastern end.[123] Spaniards showed little interest in these arid lands until Brigadier General Pedro de Rivera reported on his frontier inspection of 1724-28. Rivera proposed a careful exploration of the country between the presidio of San Juan Bautista near the modern Piedras Negras, Coahuila, and just south of Eagle Pass, Texas, to La Junta at the mouth of the Río Conchos on the Río Grande at today's Ojinaga, Chihuahua, opposite Presidio, Texas. This stretch of the Río Grande includes both the Amistad National Recreation Area and Big Bend National Park. The purpose of the proposed exploration was to locate a suitable site for a new presidio.[124]

The soldier who drew the assignment from Rivera was Captain José de Berroterán. His 1729 expedition began in Nueva Vizcaya on the Río Conchos south of Chihuahua City, proceeded to San Juan Bautista, and headed up the Río Grande on its south side to the western end of Amistad National Recreation Area before crossing the river near the mouth of the Pecos and going to the vicinity of the modern Dryden, Texas, where

131

he gave up the search for a suitable presidio location. His failure, like that of others who followed him, left an enormous expanse of country in western Coahuila and eastern Nueva Vizcaya between San Juan Bautista and El Paso an open door for Apache raids into Spanish and Christian Indian settlements in the south.[125]

The Berroterán expedition was repeated in 1735 and early 1736 in one led by Coahuila Governor Blas de la Garza Falcón, which included his son, Miguel, and Captain José Antonio de Ecay Múzquiz. Presumably, they also skirted Amistad National Recreation Area, and they located a site for Presidio de Sacramento on the Río San Diego about twenty miles south of modern Ciudad Acuña, opposite Del Rio, Texas.[126]

In yet another effort to plug the huge gap in the northern line of defense, in 1747 the viceroy sent three military expeditions into the region to locate a presidio site. One of these was headed by the new governor of Coahuila, Pedro de Rábago y Terán. His assignment, successfully carried out, was to cross the great desert country between Coahuila and La Junta. In the process, on December 2 he and his men crossed to the north side of the Río Grande, probably in the vicinity of Mariscal Canyon—and became the first Spanish expedition known to have entered the confines of today's Big Bend National Park. Although Rábago strongly urged that a presidio be built at La Junta, it was 1760 before its Nuestra Señora de Belén, or Presidio del Norte, became a reality.[127]

In 1766-67 María Pignatelli Rubí Corbera y San Climent, son of the lieutenant general of the Kingdom of Aragón and ambassador to France and of the second Marquesa de Rubí and Baroness of Llinas, made a careful inspection of the entire northern frontier of Nueva España to advise the viceroy concerning present and future defenses. Happily for history, he is known more simply as the Marqués de Rubí and his remarkable feat as "the Rubí inspection."[128]

Rubí's 7,500-mile journey bypassed the Big Bend country. But the engineer and lieutenant who accompanied him during the long journey, Nicolás de Lafora and Joseph de Urrutia, used their own observations and those of others to map the entire frontier. The 1771 Lafora map is the first to identify the Big Bend region. It is correctly depicted as mountainous and occupied by Mescalero Apaches.[129]

The Rubí inspection also resulted in the Royal Regulations of 1772, which among other points embodied Rubí's recommendations for the relocation of new presidios along the entire northern frontier. The man assigned by Viceroy Antonio María Bucareli to carry out the reorganization was Colonel Hugo O'Conor, a red-headed Irishman. In 1773 O'Conor rode upstream along the Río Grande from Del Río and the environs of today's Amistad National Recreation Area before making his way into the Big Bend region. He ordered the establishment of presidios in the area—although not within the park's boundaries, insisting that the Big Bend country needed to be covered because it offered main trails for Indians attacking Spanish settlements farther south.[130] It was, parenthetically, this same Hugo O'Conor who in 1775 ordered that the Spanish presidio of Tubac be located north to Tucson, an action which made him the founding father of the modern non-Indian Tucson, Arizona.

Once the line of presidios was nearly in place, in 1775 O'Conor ordered a general campaign to drive Apaches north of the Río Grande beyond the reach of Coahuila communities. Leading one force of troops in the campaign was Coahuila Governor Jabobo de Ugarte y Loyola who, with a force of 184 men, campaigned without much success in the general vicinity of the modern Amistad National Recreation Area. More than once they were at the mouth of San Pedro Canyon at the recreation area's east end as well as at the mouth of the Pecos River at the other end. The hapless Spanish troops remained in the field until January 1776, the Apaches clearly the winner in the contest. A similar campaign in the same area by Colonel Juan de Ugalde in 1777 yielded equally dismal results.[131]

The following year, Teodoro de Croix, commandant general of the 1776-created Provincias Internas, and Father Juan Agustín Morfi, who at the time of his death in 1783 was working on a history of Tejas, set out as commander and chaplain on another inspection trip. Apache raids had increased rather then decreased after O'Conor's line of presidios had been established, and both men needed to know what should be done. Their tour of inspection took them through the lower end of today's Big Bend National Park.[132]

Spain's entry into the Revolutionary War on the side of the embryonic United States in 1779 precluded that nation's spending large sums of money defending its northern frontier. Furthermore, it was Croix's opinion that a line of defense farther to the south made more sense than one so far from Spanish settlements. Thus in 1782 he ordered the abandonment of the presidios of San Vicente and San Carlos, both occupied in 1773 at Colonel O'Conor's command.[133]

Between 1779 and 1783, when Spain was preoccupied with its conflict with England, efforts to seal off the Big Bend area to protect the south against potential raiders lay largely in the hands of Juan de Ugalde, now the Governor of Coahuila. He and his troops conducted five successive campaigns in the general region of the Big Bend each year from 1779 to 1783. Four years later, in 1787, Ugalde and his troops set out in the January snow, reaching the abandoned San Vicente in March. He crossed the Río Grande and attacked Mescaleros under chief Zapata Tuerto in the Chisos Mountains inside today's Big Bend National Park. Then he marched to San Carlos where he was told he was in Nueva Vizcaya beyond his Coahuila jurisdiction. Regardless, Ugalde attacked a Mescalero camp, killing one person and taking six captives before heading home.[134]

Don Hugo O'Conor, ca. 1775, was the Irish-born inspector of Nueva España's northern frontier. (Drawing by José Cisneros courtesy University of Texas, El Paso.)

133

Caravels like these linked Imperial Spain with possessions in the Americas. (Public domain.)

134

Toward the end of the 1780s the Comanches were pushing down from the north on both Mescaleros and Spaniards. Depending on the exigencies of the moment, Spaniards found themselves negotiating with either Comanches or Apaches and agreeing to protect one group against the other. Ugalde continued his forays, breaking up large concentrations of Native Americans wherever he found them. In 1789-90, the governor spent two hundred days in the field. And in 1791, when the viceroy offered Apaches a promise of peace, they readily accepted, especially since Spaniards offered them food, farm tools, and seeds as well as protection from marauding Comanches.[135]

Soon after 1791 Spain withdrew from the Big Bend. "The Spaniards," writes historian Ronnie Tyler, "were never interested in the Big Bend for any reason other than peace; it was an obstacle to overcome in establishing a secure frontier. But their peace did not last. The hostile Comanches continued their southward migration, soon presenting an even more serious threat that the Spaniards would not be around to answer."[136]

The late seventeenth-century flurry of Spanish interest in the west Gulf Coast area occasioned by Sieur de la Salle's abortive effort to found a French colony had been followed in the early eighteenth century with the Spaniards' founding of missions in eastern Tejas. In 1721 the Marqués de Aguayo established the Royal Presidio of Nuestra Señora de Loreto on the site of La Salle's 1685 fort St. Louis. Even so, by the mid-eighteenth century the entire region between the mouth of the Río Pánuco at today's Tampico, Mexico, to the mouth of the San Antonio River in Tejas for 150 miles inland had remained a *despoblado,* a wilderness, in Spanish eyes. The Tejas portion of this country had persisted as the undisturbed domain of its Native Americans, Karankawan and Coahuiltecan-speakers prominent among them.[137]

Before 1746 the area bordering southeastern Texas within what today is Mexico's northeasternmost state, Tamaulipas, had no Spanish settlements. Between 1746 and 1752, however, it was organized as the province of Nuevo Santander and was colonized by several thousand Spanish families from all areas of Nueva España, especially from Nuevo León, Querétaro, San Luis Potosí, Huasteca, Charcas, and Coahuila. This colonization effort was headed by José de Escandón. Although he was expected to establish colonies in the lower Río Grande Valley in Tejas, the five principal major settlements resulting from his efforts were on the south side of the river at Camargo, Reynosa, Mier, San Fernando, and Revilla.[138]

In 1747 Captain Joaquín Orobio y Basterra, who was then stationed at the 1721-founded presidio of Bahía del Espíritu Santo on the lower San Antonio River in Tejas, made an exploratory trip with Escandón down the river to its mouth at el Bahía del Espíritu Santo (San Antonio Bay). From here Orobio proceeded south along the coast all the way to the Río Grande. En route he became the first person to explore fully and to describe Corpus Christi Bay, and he reported that from Baffin Bay—inland rom Padre Island—to the Río Grande there was no "sweet water." Orobio became he first Spaniard of record to have explored the inland shore opposite the length of Padre Island since Alonso de León had accomplished the feat in 1682.[139]

The Rancho Real de Santa Petronilla was located in the mid-eighteenth century on he El Chiltipin Grant of Nuevo Santander some fifteen miles northeast of the modern Kingsville, Texas, and about twenty miles inland from Padre Island. Its grantee was Blas María de la Garza Falcón, and the ranch became the major link between the presidio at La Bahía and settlements to the south on the Río Grande. It was garisoned with royal troops who patrolled a wide area, Padre Island included.

In 1766 don Diego Ortiz Parrilla, whose earlier stormy career had included a stint as governor of Sonora during some of its most troublous times as well as command of San Sabá presidio in 1758 when that Tejas mission was destroyed and its missionaries martyred, paid a visit to Rancho Petronilla. From the ranch he headed to the coast where he named the bay at the mouth of the Río Nueces Corpus Christi. He sent a troop of soldiers and Indians across the Laguna Madre to the south end of Padre Island. He later reported it was a poor place for a military post since it lacked sufficient fresh water, grass for livestock, and building materials.[140]

Although cattle may have been grazing on Padre Island before the end of the eighteenth century, it was not until 1805 that Padre Nicolás Ballí and his nephew Juan José Ballí established Rancho Santa Cruz de Buena Vista on South Padre Island. Padre Ballí, holder of other land grants on both sides of the Río Grande near today's Brownsville, Texas, was the son of colonists José María Ballí and Rosa Hinojosa Ballí who had arrived in the region with Escandon's first colonists and who were themselves holders of several land grants. When the Mexican War of Independence began in 1810, Padre Ballí, a royalist, fled to his Santa Cruz Ranch for safety. Because the war ended successfully in Mexico's favor in 1821, Padre Ballí and his nephew had to reapply for confirmation of their grant. It was 1828 before their claim to "Padre's Island" was granted, the secular priest thus having lent part of his name to Padre Island National Seashore.[141]

In 1821, when Padre Island was becoming Mexican rather than Spanish, a merchant ship from Louisiana wrecked off the south tip of the island outside the boundaries of the national seashore. Five survivors of its crew of Americans, Spaniards, and mulattos made their way northward on Padre Island to a ranch near Corpus Christi, where they were taken captive by Karankawa Indians tending cattle. The Karankawans took them to Mission Refugio, where the captives were killed outside the mission's compound by a group of angry mission Indians. Spain's empire along the entire Gulf Coast, of "Amichel," tenuous as it may always have been, had come to a sorry end.[142] In the process, it helped set the stage for Mexico's brief appearance in the drama of a westward-expanding United States.

135

A seventeenth-century drawing depicts a properly equipped Spanish cavalryman. Gear included leather jacket (cuera), broadsword, lance, musket, pistols, shield, and riding boots. (Courtesy Archivo de Indias, Seville, Spain.)

ust as Manifest Destiny ultimately moved the United States on a relentless march from east to west across the face of North America, in earlier times the same urge propelled Spain from south to north from Mexico City, Puebla, Tlaxcala, Veracruz, Oaxaca, and Chiapas to the head of peninsular Alaska. While her ventures in La Florida, Louisiana, and Tejas had been important ones, her activities among the northern frontier provinces of Nuevo México, Sonora, and Alta California during the eighteenth and early nineteenth centuries occupied much of the attention of successive viceroys. And it was more than mere curiosity that sent a Spanish tentacle far up the Pacific Northwest in the later years of the 1700s.

Spain's Final Century In Nuevo México

"The historian Bancroft," we are told by Warren Beck, "claims that 'from 1700 New Mexico settled down into that monotonously uneventful career of inert and non-progressive existence which sooner or later is to be noted in the history of every Hispano-American province.'"[1]

Although Bancroft's stereotypical and prejudiced views of Hispano-American culture are betrayed in this remark, certainly eighteenth-century Nuevo México was a sea of calm—although not uneventful—when measured against the maelstrom of the Pueblo Revolt and other momentous happenings of the preceding one hundred years. Lives for settlers and Puebloans alike moved slowly ahead toward one of accommodation. Whatever dreams Spaniards may have had of cities of gold or of other mineral riches evaporated in the face of reality. They gave way to a more practical view of subsistence, a livelihood based largely on farming and on livestock raising, especially sheep but including cattle. And while there were disputes over land and religion, Puebloan and Spaniard, ever segregated in their own communities, nonetheless began to evolve a common society based on dependency relationships.

Additional flames in the forge used to weld a common society came in the form of less than fully sedentary Native American cultures who were neighbors to the Río Grande heartland: Comanches, Apaches, Utes, and Navajos. While alliances shifted throughout the eighteenth century, the bottom line is that most Puebloans and Spanish-speaking peoples in Nuevo México were as often as not the objects of raiding and killing by the mounted warriors of these disparate tribesmen. The resulting fear and misery shared by Pueblo and Spanish peoples often made for common bonds between them.

Historian John Kessell characterizes post-seventeenth century Nuevo México as a place where "the tide of the future ran on toward the mundane, toward colonial rivalry, solicitation of sex in the confessional, and even constitutions. . . . Friars no longer dictated the affairs of the colony. The primary concern of the Spanish Bourbon kings and their colonial bureaucracy were defense and revenue, not missions."[2]

Bulto *of San Francisco de Asís from Pecos National Historical Park, New Mexico. Franciscan missionaries bequeathed a lasting cultural legacy to the American Southwest (George H. H. Huey.)*

137

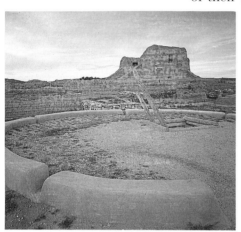

The old religion and the new are exemplified by the Puebloan kiva (foreground) and ruins of the Spanish mission church at Pecos National Historical Park, New Mexico. (JC Leacock.)

Changing throughout the eighteenth century were the attitudes of Franciscan missionaries—as well as of some secular officials—toward the native religious practices of their Puebloan charges. In 1714, Nuevo México's Governor Juan Ignacio Flores Mogollón had heard the rumor that the natives of Pecos had built a semi-subterranean kiva on the pretext that it was a women's spinning room. Flores had also heard of the "great superstitious and idolatrous abuses" committed in kivas, and ordered that if such existed at Pecos that it be "demolished immediately."[3]

Fifty-three years later, in 1777, Fray Francisco Atanasio Domínguez reported there were nine kivas in this very village. His view of kivas, however, was neither one of approbation nor of suspicion. More objectively, he said of them that they "are the chapter, or council, rooms, and the Indians meet in them sometimes to discuss matters of their government for the coming year, their planting, arrangements for work to be done, or to elect new community officials, or to rehearse their dances, or sometimes for other things."[4] Franciscans themselves held chapter meetings among their members, and often in a large room at a mission dedicated especially to that purpose.

Even when Franciscans wanted to suppress native religious practices, it was physically impossible. In 1776 there were twenty missionaries in communities totaling 18,261 native parishioners, or 913 persons per friar. Nor were Franciscans any longer the only Catholic priestly presence in Nuevo México. Three Bishops of Durango made visitations respectively in 1730, 1737, and 1760, and the first of them, Bishop Benito Crespo, appointed don Santiago Roybal, born in Nuevo México, as his vicar and ecclesiastical judge in Santa Fe, thus giving secular clergy an unwelcome foot in the Franciscans' door.[5]

In 1705, the year after the death of don Diego de Vargas, don Francisco Cuervo y Valdés was appointed his temporary successor. He went to Santa Fe in March, and by the end of 1705 he had recruited enough settlers to begin a new villa in the Bosque Grande de Doña Luisa, the future Albuquerque, today the largest city in New Mexico. Pecos Pueblo was among the Native American communities that in 1706 joined in a petition asking that Cuervo be made permanent rather than provisional governor.[6]

In 1706 it was reported that Fray José de Arranegui was building a new church of Nuestra Señora de Porciúncula at Pecos, to replace the chapel built after the original, enormous edifice was destroyed in the 1680 Revolt. Construction was completed by 1717. It had a total of sixty-eight roof beams, "well wrought and corbelled." It covered some three thousand square feet of floor space, far less than the more than five thousand square feet of Fray Juárez's church over whose ruins the new one was constructed. This was the fourth and final church at Pecos, whose ruined adobe walls command the scene at today's Pecos National Historical Park.[7]

Franciscans may have provided themselves with a church and living quarters at Pecos, but their ministry was less than successful. Part of the reason lay in the rapid turnover of religious: at least fifty-eight priests between 1704 and 1794. Few, if any, learned to speak Towa. And as priests came and went, Pecos seem simply to have gone. Seven or eight hundred people at the beginning of the century had become a mere ninety-eight adults and forty-four children in 1792.[8]

The record of late-seventeenth- and early-eighteenth-century Pecos cannot be fully appreciated without a knowledge of the community's most influential member vis-à-vis the conquering Spaniards. His story exemplifies that of hundreds of other Native Americans throughout the Spanish New World like him who found status and power in the new social order that developed between aboriginal communities and those of foreign rulers. He was known to Spaniards as Felipe Chistoe.

Chistoe's name comes to historical light during the 1696 abortive rebellion staged by a segment of the Puebloans. He emerged in the immediate aftermath of the rebellion as the pro-Spanish governor of the pueblo, the head of one of two sharply-divided factions at Pecos. To prove that the people—his people—were steadfast in their loyalty to Spain, Chistoe, his war captains, and a hundred auxiliaries showed up in Santa Fe in 1696 at the request of don Diego de Vargas. Chistoe was with Governor Vargas when the latter rode out to inspect the damage inflicted in various pueblos during the uprising. Once back in Santa Fe, Chistoe requested—and received—the governor's permission to execute his principal rivals in the pueblo.[9]

As 1700 drew to a close, families of the men slain by Chistoe and his accomplices as well as others at Pecos tried to entice the whole pueblo to rebel and kill him. The would-be rebels were arrested and sent to prison in Santa Fe. They soon escaped and joined the Jicarilla Apaches. Others continued to oppose the Chistoe faction, but always on the losing side. They finally petitioned Vargas to be allowed to move into the abandoned pueblo of Pojoaque. Whether they did so or not is unclear, but they disappeared—probably some among Apaches and some in other pueblos.[10]

When Cuervo replaced the fallen Vargas as governor of Nuevo México one of his first acts was to give loyal Pueblo leaders, Chistoe among them, "suits of fine Mexican cloth like that used by the Spaniards [and] white cloth for shirts, as well as hats, stockings, and shoes." The Spanish-speaking Chistoe became a Cuervo supporter.[11]

The 1707 successor of Cuervo's as governor of Nuevo México was don José Chacón Medina Salazar y Villaseñor, Marqués de la Peñuela. He declared war on kivas and native religious ceremonies and ordered one of his men to lead troops in destroying kivas in the pueblos and pronouncing against native dances. Later, in 1711, when Peñuela's administration was under attack, Chistoe sided with the governor and said no harm had been done—which was true in the case of Pecos. The kiva destroyers had not gone there. And Chistoe further sided with the governor in a dispute with the Franciscan custos over the transfer of a popular missionary from Pecos and his

139

replacement by a younger man. Chistoe went so far as to assert that he and his people would have to flee for the mountains unless the new Franciscan were removed from his post.[12]

The viceroy of Nueva España conferred on Felipe Chistoe the title of native governor and captain general of the Pecos, Tanos, Southern Tiwas, and "the frontiers and valleys of the east." The Franciscan custos, however, was able to withhold the title because of the Pecos governor's opposition to the transfer of clergy in the village.[13]

It was under Chistoe's watch, in 1714, that the new governor, Flores Mogollón, ordered the destruction of the rumored kiva at Pecos. Four of them were located and destroyed while Chistoe acquiesced.

> Felipe Chistoe cannot have watched the rape of his peoples' sacred places without regret. But he said nothing. Life would go on. They would build new kivas. This vicious act by the Spaniards did not justify war or flight. Chistoe and the Pecos had too much to lose. The Spaniards had made him what he was, the most important Pueblo leader on the eastern frontier. They led the campaigns in which he and his auxiliaries profited from booty. And of course they supplied many of the trade goods that lured the Plains people to Pecos every year. Life would go on.[14]

In 1714 the governor made the decision to disarm Nuevo México's Pueblo allies in accordance with royal regulations. But Chistoe, who held a patent from former viceroy Conde de Galve to carry a firearm, got his gun back.[15]

Given the lack of other kinds of riches in Nuevo México, the labor and products of the Puebloans continued to be, in the words of one friar, "the rich mines of this kingdom." Their weaving, buffalo hides, and tanned animal skins became the chief source of wealth for a parade of Spanish governors. And while many Puebloans suffered under such a regime, there were always those like don Felipe Chistoe, governor of Pecos Pueblo, who managed to thrive in the new system. He remained steadfast until his death in the mid-1720s.[16]

As one stands today amid the ruins of Pecos, one might reflect on the meaning of the life of Felipe Chistoe. Whether traceable to Spanish introduction or not, factionalism—"progressives" versus "conservatives"—remains a fact of life in virtually every Pueblo community today. These ruins may represent one possible result. Remote though it may have been from Mexico City, Madrid, London, and other centers of world power, Pecos was by no means insulated against the effects of decisions made in these distant places by total strangers. Throughout the empires of Spain, France, England, Portugal, and Holland, Native Americans found themselves forever embroiled in "storms brewed in other men's worlds."[17]

For Pecos, one such storm was brewed in the international competition between Spain and France. The ill-fated colonization attempt of Sieur de la Salle on the Texas coast in 1685 had gotten the Spaniards' attention, and in 1695 Diego de Vargas used

ague reports of French designs on the Nuevo México colony as a means of wresting
more military aid from the crown. The French had come into possession of the
Mississippi Valley and tributary river valleys in the late seventeenth century, and
from Missouri to northern Nuevo México was not such a great distance. Plains
Apaches complained to Spaniards they were being pushed ever westward and southward by Comanches and Utes, Jumanos and Pawnees, and by westward-moving
Frenchmen who supplied the Apaches' enemies with firearms. In 1719 Nuevo México
Governor Antonio Valverde led an army of sixty presidial soldiers, forty-five settlers,
and 465 Puebloan auxiliaries onto the Plains all the way to the Arkansas River in
search of Apache enemies, although they eluded him. Valverde returned to Santa Fe
with stories told to him by Apaches about French forts, weapons, and military advis-
ers among their Pawnee adversaries.[18]

In 1720 an expedition commanded by Pedro de Villasur went onto the plains to
check on rumors of French intrusion. He and his troops were attacked by Pawnees at
the North Platte River in Nebraska and, it was alleged by the few survivors,
Frenchmen. The Spanish party was all but annihilated.[19]

By the 1730s and '40s, whatever official fears there may have been of French
expansion into Nuevo México were overcome by more practical considerations: trade.
As early as 1739 seven or eight French traders came down from the Illinois country
and entered Nuevo México at Taos and, after unloading their contraband goods, were
riotously entertained before most of them departed. One who left through Pecos carried a message from the vicar in Santa Fe to his French counterpart in New Orleans
inviting trade.[20]

*Using buffalo hides
as a canvas, an
anonymous artist
depicted Pawnee
Indians, allied with
the French,
attacking the 1719
expedition of Pedro
de Villasur at the
junction of the
Platte and Loup
rivers in what is
today Nebraska.
Although the artist
included French
troops in the scene,
none actually
participated in the
battle. (Photo of
Segesser II courtesy
Museum of New
Mexico, Santa Fe.)*

In 1744 a lone Frenchman from the Illinois country wandered into Pecos and was taken as a captive to Santa Fe, interrogated, and presumably released. More French traders appeared on the scene in Nueva España from time to time in the mid-eighteenth century, including four who appeared at Pecos in 1750 and two more who showed up in 1752 leading a pack train loaded with "all manner of dry goods, hardware, and fancy items, from silk garters and lace, hawk bells and mirrors, to embroidered beaver skin shoes and ivory combs." The latter professed to have been unaware that trade between France and Spain was illegal, an excuse not good enough to prevent their goods from being sold at public auction and their being shipped off to Spain. "Their attempt to open the Santa Fe Trail had been precisely seventy years too soon."[21] The takeover of Louisiana by Spain in 1763 alleviated Spaniards' fear of the French in Nuevo México just as it had in Texas. Attention could be paid to other matters.

Because of the strategic position of Pecos at the gateway between plains and pueblos, it had long been a center of economic and military importance. Vásquez de Coronado had discovered in 1540 that the people of Pecos had for many years been involved in commerce with people on the plains, the latter regularly coming to trade there. Their most valued goods in the eyes of Puebloans, but especially of Hispanos, were captive children and young women: Apache, Navajo, Ute, Comanche, Wichita, or Pawnee. Descendants of these captives came in Nuevo México to be known as *genízaros*.

Most of the trade at Pecos, as at Taos Pueblo, was with Plains Apaches, and the annual fall trading sessions, called *rescates* or *ferias* ("fairs"), persisted as long as Plains Apaches did. In addition to captives, the Puebloans at Pecos as well as Spaniards who came there received buffalo meat and hides, lard, buckskins, and elk skins in exchange for horses, bridles, tobacco, and metal awls.[22]

The first two Pecos deaths attributed to Comanches took place in 1739. Until then, Comanche presence on Puebloan perimeters had not particularly been a threat. But increasingly in the 1740s it became apparent that Comanches, for whatever reasons, were bent on the destruction of Pecos and Galisteo pueblos. Comanches mounted a major assault on Pecos in 1746, killing a dozen inhabitants, kidnapping a boy, and stealing the village's horses. A Spanish punitive expedition sent after them found the body of the boy and managed to kill some sixty Comanches, but they suffered a loss of nine soldiers and a civilian.[23]

In 1748 a second major attack was carried out by some 130 mounted Comanches against Pecos, and devastating though it may have been, it paled in comparison with the effects of an assault launched in that same year by an unnamed disease. At least fifteen children and three single males died during the epidemic, one which swept all the pueblos as well as Santa Fe. Indeed, during the recorded life of Pecos, there were major epidemics in nearly every decade: 1696, 1704, 1728-1729 (measles), 1738 smallpox), 1748, 1759, 1780-1781 (smallpox), 1800 (smallpox), 1816 (smallpox), and 1826. Deadly diseases killed far more people at Pecos than did Plains Indian raiders.[24]

Little could be done to defend against epidemics, but Spaniards could, and did, station soldiers at Pecos to aid in its defense. A so-called presidio at Pecos west of the convento, nothing more than a structure to accommodate a fifteen-soldier guard, was probably built in the 1740s or '50s. Earthworks as well as towers at the gates were built by 1750.[25] The mid-eighteenth-century policy of Governor Vélez Cachupín toward Comanches was one of delicate diplomacy and of trade backed, when necessary, by an iron fist. He dealt with refugee Plains Apaches by allowing them to settle within sight of Pecos. The policy worked well but was shattered by his successor as governor, Marín del Valle. Apaches departed from Pecos and Comanches began their raiding once more. As Comanche hostility increased, trade at Pecos and elsewhere with Apaches lessened. So did the population at Pecos plunge, from 344 to 269 between 1760 and 1776. Pecos was at a virtual state of war with Comanches during that whole period.[26]

The year 1776 was a fateful one in the history of North America. In the east, Americans declared their independence from Britain. In what today is the American Southwest and Mexican north, the military administration of the Provincias Internas, of which Nuevo México was one, was created. And in Nuevo México, two Franciscan friars and eight fellow Spaniards set out from La Villa de Santa Fe on July 29 on what turned out to be a fruitless search for an overland route from northern Nuevo México to Monterey and the recently established missions in Alta California.

Although they failed in accomplishing their goal, fathers Francisco Atanasio Domínguez and Francisco Silvestre Escalante succeeded during a five-month period in exploring a vast expanse of what until then was for Spaniards a *tierra incógnita*, an unknown land. Juan Rivera had explored parts of northern Colorado in 1765, searching for the headwaters of the Río Colorado and a rumored deposit of free native silver. But Rivera's journal was not widely circulated and much of the land trod by Escalante and Dominguez in 1776 was new to Spain.

From Santa Fe the route of Escalante and Dominguez lay northwestward into today's Colorado; northward nearly the length of Colorado; westward into northern Utah; and southward in central Utah to today's northern Arizona border. They headed east along the strip country north of the Grand Canyon, finally crossing the Río Colorado on November 7 after leading their horses to its northern edge down a canyon named for them: Padre Creek Canyon. A short distance from the mouth of the canyon they were able to ford the river, El Vado de los Padres, "The Crossing of the Fathers." The site today is submerged beneath 450 feet of water in Lake Powell behind Glen Canyon

Sonoran-born New Mexico Governor Juan Bautista de Anza and his troops traveled to southern Colorado in 1779 in search of the notorious Comanche warrior Cuerno Verde, "Green Horn." The Spaniards' passed near the dunes of today's Great Sand Dunes National Monument on their return. (George H. H. Huey.)

143

Dam in the Utah portion of Glen Canyon National Recreation Area. By January 2 they were back in Santa Fe. For the first time since 1540, when Vásquez de Coronado's men had been stopped at the south rim of the Grand Canyon, a Spanish expedition had explored lands on its northern side.[27]

In 1778 Sonoran-born, seasoned frontiersman Juan Bautista de Anza, who knew well the overland route from Sonora to Alta California, arrived in Santa Fe as Nuevo México's new governor. He took to the field soon afterward, in 1779, determined to bring to heel Cuerno Verde ("Green Horn"), the most formidable of the Comanche foes who had been making life miserable for northern Nuevo Mexicanos. Anza's force, including Spaniards, Puebloans, Utes, and Apaches, encountered Cuerno Verde in the Wet Mountain Valley of Colorado and succeeded in killing not only him but also his first-born son, four of his captains, a medicine man who professed immortality, and ten others. The Spaniards' return route to Santa Fe took them via Sangre de Cristo Pass, just a few miles south of the dunes whose natural history is interpreted today at Great Sand Dunes National Monument.[28]

Its population dwindling, Pecos was officially reduced in 1782 to the status of mission *visita*, a place without a resident priest. It would be cared for from Santa Fe. And in 1785, the Comanches became serious about wanting peace with the Spaniards. While there were a few bumps along the road to that particular destination, the arrangements produced by Anza and his successors worked. Before it was over, peaceful trade with Comanches was a thriving enterprise and the former enemies pitched their tents without fear in sight of Pecos. Indeed, Pecos, as the port of entry and trade for Comanches, took on the air of an agency town with resident interpreters.[29]

The unsuccessful 1776 attempt to open a direct route from Santa Fe to Monterey in Alta California was followed at the end of the eighteenth century with Spanish officialdom's directing some of its attention toward opening routes of commerce connecting its other centers in the west: Tucson, San Antonio, St. Louis, and Santa Fe. The Camino Real from Chihuahua City north to Santa Fe had been a well-established road at least since the late sixteenth-century days of Juan de Oñate, but linkages in the other directions were tenuous at best. In 1795, for example, Captain José de Zúñiga of Tucson had led an expedition to attack Indians presumed to be hostile and open a route tying northern Sonora to Nuevo México. Their seven-week round trip took them as far as the Zuni villages but no farther, and the course they followed never became heavily used.[30]

In 1786 French-born interpreter-scout Pedro Vial—who had spent years living among Native Americans in the southern plains—was commissioned by Texas Governor Domingo Cabello to explore a direct line of communication between San Antonio and Santa Fe. Although the route ended up being anything but direct, Vial managed to make the journey, arriving in Santa Fe in late May 1787 after having been out for nearly nine months. José Mares was dispatched to find a way to shorten he distance, if such were possible, and Vial was sent by Governor Fernando de la Concha on a 1788-89 journey to Natchitoches, San Antonio, and back to Santa Fe. In 1792-93 he made the round trip to St. Louis, although there were no direct results from his adventure-filled outing. All such explorations came and went through northern Nuevo México's springboard of Pecos.[31]

Late in 1794 a group of Santa Fe Spaniards petitioned the governor for vacant lands on the Río Pecos at a place called El Vado ("The Crossing"). When the San Miguel del Vado grant became settled, it relieved Pecos of its "gateway" status and set the pueblo on its road to extinction. Plains traders and hunters, *comancheros* and *ciboleros*, made their new headquarters at San Miguel. And though by then Pecos was again a full-fledged mission rather than a *visita*, its population was 180 Native Americans, some of whom were Tanos rather than Towas. During the remainder of Spain's presence in Nuevo México, for Pecos it would simply be a matter of hanging on.[32]

The hanging on was done in the company of non-Indians. In 1799, Pecos was inhabited by 159 Native Americans and 150 people non-natives. Five years earlier, its population had been wholly Indian. But after San Miguel del Vado was settled, it blossomed as Pecos continued to wither. The decline at Pecos took place just as other Native Americans in the region, those who had never been under the tutelage of missionaries, were causing problems for the entire province.[33]

Navajos—now well mounted on horses—became especially troublesome. In 1805 Antonio Narbona, who had been born in Mobile in Louisiana (later, Alabama) in 1773 when it had been an English possession, led three hundred troops and Opata Indian auxiliaries on a punitive expedition that set out from Zuni Pueblo. They caught up with a group of Navajos near Canyon de Chelly and killed 155 warriors, women, and children. It has been suggested that a spectacular red and white painting on a cliff in Canyon del Muerto in today's Canyon de Chelly National Monument depicting a Spanish cavalcade may be a Navajo pictorial version of the 1805 Narbona expedition. One horseman wears a cloak bearing the cross of the military order of Santiago. Could this be a likeness of Narbona come to rest on a cliff? From eighteenth-century Mobile to immortality in the heart of Navajo country is a considerable distance by anyone's measure.[34]

Although documentation is scanty, it is believed that "during the early 1800s, Spanish sheep ranchers explored and named features of the countryside" around today's El Malpais National Monument in western New Mexico.[35]

While most eighteenth- and early-nineteenth-century Spanish attention in Santa Fe was directed toward the south and down the Río Grande and Camino Real, Zuni and the lands to the west were not, as the Narbona expedition of 1805 suggests, altogether

In 1805, Antonio de Narbona and his Spanish soldiers attacked and killed 155 Navajo warriors in Canyon de Chelly. This pictograph in Canyon del Muerto, part of Canyon de Chelly National Monument, is believed to depict that expedition. (George H. H. Huey.)

145

neglected. Proof of this assertion remains engraved in sandstone at El Morro. Although lacking names as famous as those who preceded them to the adjacent water hole in the seventeenth century, the cliff's face nonetheless speaks of continued journeys by Spaniards moving along this east—west corridor to the end of Spain's rule over the region.

In 1700 Fray Juan de Garaycoechea was sent to Zuni where he was able to persuade the people to move out of their hiding places at Corn Mountain and to resettle their abandoned pueblo of Halona. Scratched onto the face of Inscription Rock are the names of Phelipe García and Cristóbal Pérez, both possibly a part of Father Garaycoechea's escort. Soldier Felipe de Arellano "signed" the rock in September 1700 and, apparently, again in December 1701 during a tour of inspection. In 1701 Governor Pedro Rodríguez Cubero made a trip to the Hopi country with an armed force, one of whose members may have been Captain Juan de Uribarri, a man whose inscription appears on the cliff in 1701 and again in 1709.[36]

Joseph Domínguez, an aid to Captain Rael de Aguilar who, among other positions, served as Protector General of the Indians and as Adjutant General to Governor Félix Martínez, passed by El Morro in 1708 and at another time. His second inscription is undated. And in June 1709 Ramón Garzía Jurado (or Jurtado) "passed by here on the way to Zuni" for reasons not stated. Juan de la Rivas, whose name is on the rock, was with Uribarri at El Morro in 1709.[37]

The stubborn and independent Hopi Indians of today's northern Arizona refused to submit to domination by Spaniards, missionaries or otherwise, even in the aftermath of the reconquest of Nuevo México by Diego de Vargas in 1692. In 1680 they had killed the four Franciscans living among them, and in 1700, disturbed by the willingness of people living at the Hopi pueblo of Awatovi to allow Franciscans again to work in their midst, other Hopis destroyed the village.[38]

Fray Francisco de Yrazábal replaced Fray Garaycoechea at Zuni in 1716 and began at once to urge Nuevo México Governor Félix Martínez to do something about Hopi resistance. The governor, resolved to settle the Hopi "problem" once and for all, outfitted a sizeable expedition in Santa Fe and marched to Hopi via the Zuni settlements. On the way, on August 26, they left two inscriptions on El Morro [in translation]: "Year of 1716 on the 26th of August passed this way Don Feliz Martinez Governor and Captain-General of this realm to the reduction and conquest of Moqui [Hopi] and . . . Reverend Father Friar Antonio Camargo Custodian and Vicar." The other reads, "[Captain] Juan Garsia de la Rivas, senior magistrate of the council of the Villa de Santa Fe and constable for the Holy Office of the Spanish Inquisition [was here] on August 26, 1716."

The expedition reached the Hopi towns after a pause at Zuni, and the Hopis again refused to be told by Spaniards what to do. Spaniards pulled Hopi crops out by the roots and drove Hopi livestock off before returning to Santa Fe.[39]

Ten years later, a soldier treated the Santa Fe council to an outing. Inscribed at El Morro are the [translated] words: "There passed by here the Lieutenant Don Joseph de Paybe Basconzelos the year that he brought the council of the realm, at his expense, on the eighteenth of February of the year 1726." Their inscription was followed by one simply stating, "Casados 1727," and in 1736 Inscription Rock produced the only known record of what was probably a formal tour of inspection to the Zuni area: "The day 14th of July of 1736 there passed by here the General Juan Paez Hurtado, Inspector, and in his company the Corporal Joseph Truxillo."[40]

Perhaps the most noted eighteenth-century personage to have endowed Inscription Rock with a record of his visit was Father Martín de Elizacochea, Bishop of Durango. He was the second of three bishops of Durango to pay Nuevo México a visit—a journey made after 1733, when the viceroy of New Spain had upheld the bishop's claim to Nuevo México as part of his jurisdiction, but before 1738, when the claim was upheld by the Council of the Indies. He and his secretary made a trip to Zuni via El Morro, where the bishop may have requested his secretary to leave the engraved messages (in translation): "The 28th day of September of the year 1737 there arrived here the very illustrious Señor Doctor Don Martin de Elizacochea Bishop of Durango and on the 29th went on to Zuni." This was accompanied by, "The 28th day of September of the year 1737 there arrived here the Bachelor [of Laws] Don Juan Ignacio de Arrasain." No other details of this episcopal journey are known.[41]

In 1742 the Franciscans, concerned that Jesuits pushing up from northern Sonora might claim the territory, sent Fray Carlos Delgado to Hopi to bring back to Sandía Pueblo on the Río Grande 441 Tiwas who had fled to Hopi during the 1680 Pueblo Revolt. A faint inscription at El Morro may relate to this episode: "Francisco Lopes Palomino . . . passed by here as guide for the friars from Moqui [Hopi]."[42]

By the third quarter of the eighteenth century travel toward the west from Santa Fe apparently slowed down. Missionaries remained active at Zuni, but otherwise there was little in this region to draw the attention of anyone other then Native Americans who lived, hunted, gathered, and traded in the region. There are only three dated inscriptions at El Morro for the remainder of the Spanish period, by Pedro Romero in 1751 and again in 1758, and a final one by Andrés Romero dated 1774. Whether the same person or not, a Pedro Romero was "Lieutenant of the Jurisdiction" of the western Keres-speaking Ácoma and Laguna pueblos in 1750.[43]

In May 1805 Zuni's Franciscan minister had left and "the Indians had lapsed into paganism." There was at least one later replacement, however, because "On July 27, 1821, Fray Antonio Cacho, missionary at Zuni, notified Governor *ad interim* Facundo Melgares that he had left the pueblo, with the consent of the Father Custodian, because of imminent danger of Navajo attack. On the letter is a note by the Governor, dated July 28: 'I implore, and charge, the Father Custodian not to abandon Zuni'. . . ." Not only was Zuni abandoned, but in a sense, so was Nuevo

México. "On September 11, 1821, the Governor took an oath of allegiance to the Government of the Mexican revolutionary, Iturbide. Spanish dominion was ended."[44]

With the United States' acquisition of the Louisiana Territory in 1803, the Spanish of northern Nuevo México had found themselves with new distant neighbors. St Louis was then becoming even more of a springboard than previously, and in 1804 Lewis and Clark were there getting ready for an expedition to the Pacific. It did not help matters between the United States and Spain when in 1807 the peripatetic Zebulon Montgomery Pike was taken prisoner in Nuevo México, subsequently to become a guest of the friars at Mission San José in San Antonio. Spanish concern with American intrusion in Nuevo México would remain to the very end.[45]

The year 1821 marked finality of Spain's dominion over Nueva España—Nuevo México, Tejas, and La Florida included. Nuevo México became a part of Mexico. By then, what had been the great Pecos Pueblo was up for land-grant grabs. And it almost happened:

> Evidently Santa Fe promoter Esteban Baca, who rounded up sixteen willing dere-licts in 1821, would have moved right into the pueblo [as a grantee]. In his appli-cation for a settlement grant, which seems to have been lost in the independence shuffle, don Esteban did not mince words. He understood that there were now only eight or ten Pecos Indian families left, and all that land going to waste. Their church was falling down. Their minister had abandoned them. Because they were so few, "and having no title," the Pecos were plainly in peril. Besides, the king wanted vacant lands peopled and planted. Therefore, reasoned Baca, his people, "leaving to the Indians whatever land they can cultivate," would move in, reverse the downward population trend, rebuild the church, and bring in a minister. It was, if nothing else, a very good try.[46]

And if it was sad beginning of the final chapter for a viable Pecos Pueblo, so was it a sorry conclusion to the story of Spanish rule.

NORTHERN SONORA

After the 1711 death of the Jesuit missionary Father Eusebio Kino, except for Father Agustín de Campos who was stationed at Mission San Ignacio until 1736, there was little continuity in the Jesuit effort among the northern Piman Indians of the region. Before Kino died, Father Juan de San Martín had become the first resident minister at the village of Guevavi, which Kino had first visited in 1691. The ruins of a later construction at Guevavi are now one of three units of Tumacacori National Historical Park, Tumacácori and Calabazas being the others. Father San Martín managed to build a house and a small church at Guevavi before having to vacate his post before

The partially restored ruins of the early nineteenth-century Franciscan church of Mission San José de Tumacácori are the centerpiece of Tumacacori National Historical Park, Arizona. (Laurence Parent.)

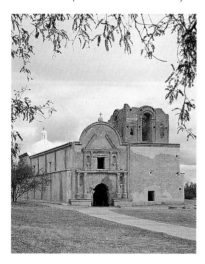

148

February 1703 because of illness—a common enemy among missionaries and Native Americans along the Río Santa María, today's Santa Cruz River.[47]

Except for occasional visits by the indefatigable Father Campos, the Northern Piman settlements of Guevavi and Tumacácori joined most such villages in northern Sonora in remaining without priests until the arrival of Jesuit reinforcements in 1732—the year the joint governance of Sonora and Sinaloa was created by royal order. Three newly arrived Jesuits were installed in their headquarters: Father Ignacio Xavier Keller at Santa María Soamca (today's Santa Cruz, Sonora); Father Johann Baptist Grazhoffer at Guevavi; and Father Philipp Segesser von Brunegg at San Xavier del Bac. Included within San Xavier's jurisdiction was Casa Grande, twenty leagues to the northwest.[48]

When Austrian-born Johann Baptist Grazhoffer was assigned to Guevavi as its resident priest, Tumacácori became one of its visitas. Father Grazhoffer died at Guevavi within the year and was replaced by Father Philipp Segesser von Brunegg, a Swiss who, like Grazhoffer, had come to New Spain under the authority and aegis of the Spanish crown and who had initially served at San Xavier del Bac.[49]

In July 1734 the O'odham (Pimans) at Guevavi as well as at the more northerly Bac (Wa:ak) and more southerly Santa María Soamca deserted their villages, stealing or damaging mission property in the process. Frightened by a rumor that Captain Juan Bautista de Anza was coming to kill them, they had fled to the hills. By the time Anza arrived on the scene, the padres were already negotiating the peaceful conclusion of what could have become a rebellion. And before the year was out, Father Segesser became ill, as had Father Grazhoffer before him. He survived, however, and was ultimately transferred to a more healthful post farther to the south in the Pimería Baja.[50]

While Guevavi was going through a period when it had only visiting, rather than resident, missionaries, silver was discovered just to the south in 1736. So remarkable was the discovery, in fact, that some, or most, of the silver (*plata*) was near the surface of the ground in chunks (*bolas*) or slabs (*planchas*). It appeared to chief justice Captain Juan Bautista de Anza the elder, father of the Anza who would later be Governor of Nuevo México and leader of an expedition of colonists to Alta California, that the silver had already been mined and processed. If so, the king would be entitled to half of it rather than to the mere twenty percent were it newly-mined ore.

This discovery—in today's northernmost Sonora—was made at a place named by the *alcalde mayor* of Sonora, Captain Gabriel de Prudhon Heider Beltrán y Mújica, the "Real de Arizonac." More than a dozen decades later the name he chose, "Arizonac," would become the "Arizona" eventually designating the forty-eighth state of the United States of America.[51]

The year 1736 was noteworthy for another reason. It was then that Father Ignacio Xavier Keller, who had arrived in the Pimería Alta in 1732 to be stationed at Mission

149

Santa María Soamca, set off on a journey of exploration to the north. He got as far as the Gila River, visiting the Casa Grande and contacting Native American communities along the Gila and Verde rivers. In 1737 he made a similar journey, this time becoming the first European known to have seen the junction of the Salado (Salt) and Verde rivers.[52]

After Father Segesser's departure from Guevavi, its next Jesuit resident was Father Alexandro Rapicani, a blond and blue-eyed native of the Duchy of Bremen, who took over in 1737. He left Guevavi in 1741 and was replaced that year by a *criollo*, a Spaniard born in Nueva España (Puebla), Father Joseph de Torres Perea. By the time Father Torres Perea arrived at Guevavi he found within his jurisdiction a goodly number of Spanish-speaking non-Indian families, "the loose human scraps of a mineral-oriented society." They were *gente de razón*, "people of reason," with such surnames as Ortega, Tapia, Grijalva, Bohórquez, Gallego, Samaniego, and Covarrubias. The reason for their presence—and their numbers doubtless included mestizos, mulattos, and others of varied racial backgrounds—was the planchas de plata find at Arizonac in 1736. In this sense, Mission Guevavi became the first church to serve Arizonans.[53]

In 1741 or 1742 a royal cédula directed that the Jesuits were to contact and convert the Hopi Indians, the Franciscans of Nuevo México having so far failed in the task of their conversion. Father Keller, who had previously been at least as far north as the Gila River, drew the assignment. Leaving his mission at Santa María Soamca with an escort of nine soldiers in July 1743, he may well have visited the Casa Grande once again en route to the unknown mountains to the northeast. Somewhere beyond the Gila his little party encountered hostile Apaches who stopped their further progress, and Keller was forced to return to Soamca.[54]

It was also in 1743 that Jesuit missionary Jacobo Sedelmayr, who had arrived in the Pimería Alta in 1736 for an assignment at Mission Tubutama on the upper Altar River, ventured west to the place where in 1701 Father Eusebio Kino had overseen the cutting of twelve small beams "for the little church of Nuestra Señora de Loreto de San Marcelo." This was the O'odham village of Sonoyta, Sonora, immediately adjacent to the southeastern corner of today's Organ Pipe Cactus National Monument.[55]

In 1744 Father Sedelmayr was allowed by his superiors to try where Keller had failed and to effect the conversion of the Hopis. He set out from his mission at Tubutama in October for the Pima villages on the Upper Gila Valley. Although he could not get guides to take him north toward the Hopi, and his efforts like those of Father Keller ended in failure, Father Sedelmayr left posterity an account of the Casa Grande which he supposedly visited on this trip. Unfortunately, nearly his whole description is plagiarized from that by Captain Juan Mateo Manje of 1697. His own observations of the ruins, assuming he actually saw them, were possibly superficial and he may have felt those of Manje were more suitable for an official report intended for the viceroy, Conde Fuenclara.[56]

150

At Guevavi, Father Torres Perea was replaced in February 1744 by Father Ildefonso de la Peña, who remained only until May. The mission was temporarily abandoned once more, visited once in awhile by Father Keller and one time by a secular priest, don Joachín Félix Díaz, curate of Nacozari, Sonora.[57]

On his death in 1739, don José de la Puente Peña Castrejón y Salzines, Marqués de Villapuente, a Spaniard who had made a fortune in the New World, had provided for an endowment of as much as twenty thousand pesos for the establishment of two new missions in the Pimería Alta: Sonoyta, renamed San Miguel in accordance with the wishes of the marqués, and Saric on the upper Río Altar.[58]

Partly to help with the decision about where to found the two new missions, the ever-wandering Jacobo Sedelmayr set off once more for the west from his mission at Tubutama on a trip during October and November of 1748. He appears not to have visited San Marcelo de Sonoitac on this entrada, although he notes having seen Sonoyta earlier and assured his superiors that it "is suitable for founding another mission for the many *rancherías* and people in the vicinity."[59]

In November 1750 Father Sedelmayr returned for a visit to Sonoyta, probably his second, en route to the Colorado River. His path lay along the Camino del Diablo. At Sonoyta itself Sedelmayr, Lieutenant Colonel Diego Ortiz Parrilla, and twenty-nine soldiers found "the ranch of Captain Cipriano where there is an abundance of water for all and broad acres for raising crops. There are many [additional] Indians here, too, who were gentle and tractable. They assisted the Father Visitor [Sedelmayr] and were obedient to the soldiers. . . . There is a good house here made up of three rooms and a kitchen. There are ruins of a smaller house where Father Kino used to come to say Mass, so far as these Indians were able to remember."[60]

In a letter written by Sedelmayr to Father Juan Antonio Baltasar, the Jesuit Father Provincial, in early January 1751 he elaborated even further concerning Sonoyta. He hoped to found the mission here dedicated to San Miguel as the marqués had stipulated. "All the conditions are right for the new Sonoyta mission," he wrote. The house with three rooms and a kitchen "was built by the deceased Indian captain of Caborca, but his children are not living in it and it will be easy to buy from them. Because I have no doubt a missionary will come, I am presently making preparations and have ordered Father Tomás Tello [of Caborca] to have a field of grain planted in Sonoyta for the new father. I have already sent some there. . . . I also think that initially the padre in Sonoytac will need about two soldiers. . . ."

In the same letter, Father Sedelmayr reported that the O'odham chief from a village near the Casa Grande had paid a visit to Tubutama.[61]

Four days later, the Jesuit padre penned another letter to Father Baltasar with still more news about Sonoyta and the village near the Casa Grande:

151

> I think it was about the 9th of this month, three Yumas from San Miguel de Sonoytac came here to bring me a few horses that had strayed from me on the Colorado as well as some stirrups that a soldier had unfortunately lost there. This is no small matter for gentile Indians to travel 50 or more leagues to deliver something that belongs to someone else.
>
> Also, a Papago chief asked me for grain and took it to sow in Tussonimo, a ranchería on the Gila River near Casas Grandes where a branch of the Pimas live with their chief, Jabanimo. By their way of asking, I became aware of their desire that one of the two new missions be established there. . . .
>
> A report also came from San Miguel de Sonoytac that they are already preparing a field for the new missionary.[62]

In 1751 Father Sedelmayr was able to use some of the money of the marqués to install thirty-three-year-old, German-born Father Heinrich [Enrique] Ruhen as missionary at Sonoyta. There, next to the abundant organ pipe cacti among the rocky slopes of adjacent hills, the stage was set for a major disaster for Jesuits and Spaniards in northern Sonora.[63]

At faraway Guevavi, Sardinian-born Joseph Garrucho had been installed as resident missionary in 1745. By the time of his arrival the Northern O'odham population of Guevavi and of other settlements along the river had declined precipitously, sometimes requiring military persuasion to bolster the numbers of people living in the mission community. Between 1732 and 1744 there had been a mere 978 baptisms. Only twenty-three families had been in residence in 1744, and those numbers were falling. Much of this was the result of disease, but the Jesuits believed infertility was another factor.[64]

During Garrucho's six-year stay at Guevavi, at least three murderous epidemics of measles and smallpox struck Guevavi. "Heathens and [backsliding] Christians" were brought out of the desert hills and mountains by military force and the persuasion of Piman converts to replace natives who had died. Father Garrucho put them to work as "foremen and vaqueros, shepherds and oxherds, mule boys, plowmen, irrigators, gardeners, and a cook and a baker."[65]

The year 1751 proved to be momentous in the life of Guevavi in more ways than one. Father Garrucho hired don Joachín de Cásares, a master builder from Arizpe, Sonora, to oversee construction of a proper house of worship.

> Plans called for, or at least came to include, a rectangular church whose inside dimensions were not particularly impressive, about fifteen by fifty feet. The new structure was to be built on the extreme east edge of the mesilla with its long axis lying roughly north-south and its main doors facing south onto the village plaza. Tabular slabs of local conglomerate rock cemented with mud mortar, Don Joachín and Father Joseph agreed, would provide a solid foundation. The walls of

sun-dried adobes set in mud mortar were to be all of three feet thick, plastered with mud, whitewashed, and finally decorated inside with various colors. The flat roof would rest on *vigas*, large beams spanning the building's short axis. A door through the west wall of the church was to lead out into a patio enclosed on the other three sides by rooms one deep with their doors opening onto the patio. In this *convento*, measuring overall some 90 by 105 feet, Father Joseph would have his quarters, perhaps a small personal chapel, the Indian school, a kitchen, refectory, and whatever storage and work rooms space permitted. Here at Guevavi Joseph Garrucho would leave, if nothing else, a house of God where none comparable had previously stood.[66]

And, indeed, he succeeded. The adobe ruins of Father Garrucho's church are now preserved as the Guevavi unit of Tumacacori National Historical Park.

On September 29 a great fiesta was held at Guevavi in honor of San Miguel. There were dancing, singing, drinking, and a bullfight. People dressed up in their best clothes, ate candy, exploded fireworks. Gente de razón as well as Indians for leagues around gathered at the mission. The only really sour note had been the arrival there of an O'odham troublemaker known as Pedro Chihuahua, the right hand man of another O'odham whom the Jesuits mistrusted, Luis Oacpicagigua of the village of Saric near the head of the Río Altar in Sonora.

Without consulting the missionaries, Governor Diego Ortiz Parilla had elevated Luis to the exalted rank of captain general of the Northern O'odham, and both he and Pedro Chihuahua came to be regarded by the Jesuits as overbearing. Father Keller, it was asserted, had even called Luis "a Chichimec dog whose proper attire was a coyote skin and a loincloth and whose proper pastime was chasing rabbits and rodents in the hills." As for Chihuahua, Father Garrucho had taken from him his baton of authority and ridiculed the Indian before the assembled crowd, snarling that if Pedro set foot in Guevavi ever again he would be rewarded with a hundred lashes."[67]

The resentment of these O'odham and of their followers grew. Perhaps, in fact, it had been growing in ethnic memory since the *matanzas* of 1695, a recollection bolstered by floggings, intimidation, appropriation of land and resources by growing numbers of gente de razón, and the Jesuits' resort to *reducción*. Whatever the case, on Sunday, November 21, 1751, Luis Oacpicagigua and like-minded Northern O'odham gave violent vent to their feelings. A beaten and bloody Juan de Figueroa, the mission foreman living at the village of Tubac, stumbled into Guevavi with the announcement that the Indians had gone crazy and had tried to club him to death. Rumor had it that the nearby settlement of Arivaca was a scene of death and destruction. The O'odham of Guevavi grabbed their weapons and fled, entreaties of Father Garrucho notwithstanding. The Pima Revolt was in full swing.[68]

The same day, November 21, O'odham killed Father Tomás Tello at the western Sonoran mission of Caborca; the next day, they made a martyr of Father Enrique Ruhen at his remote outpost at Sonoyta next to today's Organ Pipe Cactus National

153

Monument. The Indians tore down the Sonoyta church and the priest's dwelling an[d] "conceived such an aversion for Christianity that on no account did they wish ev[er] again to tolerate a missionary among them."[69]

Father Juan Nentvig, stationed at Saric, and Father Sedelmayr at Tubutama man[-] aged to escape after holding off attacking O'odham in a pitched battle at Tubutam[a]. At San Xavier del Bac, missionary Francisco Xavier Pauer escaped with his life, bu[t] the villagers at Bac totally destroyed the chapel and the padre's house. Fath[er] Garrucho, although alive, would never return to Guevavi. His church had bee[n] sacked; religious statues and paintings that had not been packed out to safety wer[e] destroyed; the tabernacle was ruined; the padre's house was vandalized; and eve[n] Garrucho's chickens and pigeons were wantonly killed.[70]

In early January 1752 Luis and his fellow O'odham suffered a stunning defeat at th[e] hands of Spanish soldiers in a fight near Arivaca. By the time Spaniards negotiated peace with Luis on March 18, just short of four months after the revolt had begu[n], two Jesuits, at least forty-five Spanish settlers, and an unknown number of India[n] allies of the Spaniards had been slain. An uncounted number of rebellious O'odha[m] had also been killed, at least forty in the battle in early January. The organize[d] O'odham revolt was finally over, but Spaniards and later missionaries would contin[-] ue to feel the wrath of rebellious O'odham individuals for much of the remainder o[f] the century.[71]

In the wake of the revolt, for Jesuits it became simply a matter of holding on. [A] succession of four missionaries stationed at Guevavi between 1753 and 1767— Francisco Xavier Pauer, Miguel Gerstner, Ignaz Pfefferkorn, and Custodio Ximeno— succeeded in repairing most of the damage done to the church and living quarter[s]. And a year earlier, in 1752, a garrison of regular soldiers had been activated in th[e] Pimería Alta. By April 1753 they had found a permanent presidial home at Tubac the village north of Guevavi. It was a help, but not a cure.[72]

In all probability, Tumacácori was another of the villages heavily affected by th[e] influence of missionaries and gente de razón that was destroyed in the general upris[-] ing of 1751. Situated in Father Kino's day on the east bank of the Río Santa Marí[a] (the later Santa Cruz River), in 1753—if not earlier—it was relocated to the wes[t] bank where it is situated today as the Tumacacori unit of Tumacacori Nationa[l] Historical Park. The old *visita* had been christened San Cayetano by Father Kin[o] but since the move to the new site took place on about March 19, the patronal feas[t] day of San José, the name of the husband of the Virgin Mary was bestowed on it. Thi[s] relocation also placed San José de Tumacácori and the new presidio of Tubac on th[e] same side of the river about three miles apart.[73]

In 1756 Guevavi's Father Pauer saw to the removal of seventy-eight O'odham fro[m] their village of Doacuquita to a place called Las Calabazas on a terrace just above th[e] east bank of the Río Santa María immediately south of the mouth of Sonoita Cree[k]

A little more than a quarter century after the Pima Revolt of 1751, Franciscan friars erected for the O'odham what is arguably the most beautiful Spanish structure in today's United States, Pimería Alta's Mission San Xavier del Bac. It is one of a group of churches of which missions Tumacácori, Guevavi, and Calabazas were once a part. (John P. Schaefer.)

154

and north of the mouth of Potrero Creek. Tumacácori's former patron, San Cayetano (Saint Cajetan), was given to the new settlement. San Cayetano de Calabazas joined Tumacácori and Los Santos Reyes de Sonoita (as distinct from the western San Marcelo, or San Miguel, de Sonoyta) as *visitas* of Guevavi. Calabazas today is a unit of Tumacacori National Historical Park.

It was also 1756 when Father Ignaz Pfefferkorn, a newly-arrived Jesuit missionary, was sent to Sonoyta to replace the murdered Father Ruhen. The O'odham would have none of him.

> The Pápagos [Hiaced O'odham], as newcomers, were [in 1751] but meagerly grounded in Christianity and had little inclination for its tenets. Their life, unbridled from youth, was much more to their liking than that taught by Gospel, and since they had already been five years without a spiritual guide and without instruction, they had again lapsed into their former savage existence. . . . Since the situation was so very difficult, everyone considered it expedient to await another time when it should please Providence to reveal the ways and means through which the conversion of these peoples could be undertaken anew, with greater success.[74]

Whether during his 1756 visit to Sonoyta, as is likely, or a year later, Father Pfefferkorn "had the fortune, after six years, to give decent burial to [Father Enrique Ruhen's] still unburied corpse, with its blood-stained skull." And so did he unknowingly give burial to all future efforts by Spaniards to station a missionary among these recalcitrant and independent O'odham, a people whose sphere of hunting, gathering, and dwelling included the region north of the international boundary now enclosed by Organ Pipe Cactus National Monument.[75]

By July 1757 Father Pauer, working from his *cabecera*, or headquarters mission, at Guevavi, had managed to direct construction of a new adobe church on the west bank at Tumacácori. It would have to serve until the next century, when Franciscan friars would erect an edifice almost twice as large to accommodate the community's O'odham congregation. The ruins of the Jesuit structure lie exposed in outline just to the east of the larger ruins of the later Franciscan church at Tumacácori. And in 1758 an epidemic hit Tumacácori, striking down thirty-six people, twenty-one of whom were laid to rest in its new temple.[76]

The Calabazas *visita* of Guevavi had stood without so much as a house, church, or cemetery since its founding in 1756, but by May 1761 Guevavi's missionary, Miguel Gerstner, had seen to it that a house for the visiting padre was built there and that foundations were laid for a chapel.[77]

During Father Ignaz Pfefferkorn's term at Guevavi interim Sonora Governor don Joseph Tienda de Cuervo ordered Captain Francisco Elías González de Zayas to relocate the eastern riverine O'odham, whom the Spaniards called Sobaípuris, from their

The tiled floor and new roof help protect the original adobe and plaster fabric of the nave of Arizona's early nineteenth-century Mission San José de Tumacácori. (George H. H. Huey.)

155

ancient homelands along the San Pedro River. In March 1762 Captain Elías counted 250 of them before resettling most at Tucson and the others at Soamca and the Guevavi *visita* of Los Reyes de Sonoita. Although intended as a move to strengthen defenses against Apache raiding from the east, which was growing in intensity, it had precisely the opposite effect. The eastern O'odham had formed the eastern bulwark against Apache incursions, and now that wall was gone. Hostile O'odham apostates were replaced as the principal enemy of the Spaniards and their missions by the raiding and warring Apache.[78]

The last Jesuit to serve Guevavi as well as its *visitas* of Calabazas and Tumacácori arrived there in the spring of 1763. He was the Aragón-born Custodio Ximeno and he had been sent to relieve the ailing Father Pfefferkorn. He came upon a scene in which the native population had been in sharp decline. At least twenty people had died in one four-month period at Tumacácori during Father Pfefferkorn's tenure, and that literary Jesuit had baptized barely half as many people as he had buried. When the native governor of Tumacácori had died, O'odham neophytes who had been recruited from the western desert had fled to their aboriginal haunts.[79]

Nearly three years after his arrival at Guevavi, Father Ximeno was able to enumerate only fifty-one persons at his *cabecera* at Guevavi and ninety-one and eighty, respectively, at his *visitas* of Calabazas and Tumacácori.[80]

On December 5, 1766, a group of riders were headed in the general direction of the Santa Cruz River in what today is southern Arizona when they camped for the night at a place they called El Paraje de Sauz ("Willow Place"). "Shortly before that," wrote the chronicler of this expedition, "we had on our left Chiguicagui [Chiricahua Mountains], the usual exit for the Tesocomachi and Mababe Indians. They go by way of Agua Verde from El Dado pass, situated at the northern point of the sierra."

El Dado pass—the pass of the dice or plinths, possibly after some pedestal-like or cube-shaped rock formation—is known today as Apache Pass and is the location of Fort Bowie National Historical Site. And the riders were those in the party of the Marqués de Rubí during the 1766-67 course of their inspection of all of Nueva España's presidios, a journey which took them to the frontier provinces of Sonora, Nueva Vizcaya, Nuevo México, Coahuila, and Texas.[81]

Two weeks later, on December 19, Rubí and his entourage arrived at Mission Guevavi, surely a big occasion for Father Ximeno. Among those who visited Guevavi that day were Captain Nicolás de Lafora, the expedition's chronicler, and a young mapper named Lieutenant Joseph de Urrutia. Thirty-two years later, Urrutia would be posing in the Court of Madrid for his portrait by Francisco José de Goya—an honor accorded the Captain General of all the Spanish Armies.[82]

The curtain came down on the last Jesuit act in the Pimería Alta, and indeed for Jesuits in Spanish possessions everywhere, in 1767. For reasons King Carlos III reserved to himself, he ordered the removal of Jesuits from all his lands. The decree of expulsion was carried out by the Spanish military at the end of July. Father Ximeno was led away from Guevavi by soldiers from the presidio at Altar. And thus ended the Jesuit period for missions Guevavi, Tumacácori, and Calabazas as well as all those other foundations laid as a result of the pioneer efforts of Eusebio Francisco Kino. In a little less than a year, Black Robes were replaced by Greyfriars.[83]

For several months after the Jesuits' expulsion there were no religious to oversee affairs of the Pimería Alta missions. It was necessary for Spanish officials to appoint temporary royal managers, *comisarios*, to tend to the missions' temporalities, which is to say their common lands, herds, and other assets; to pay debts and to collect monies that were due; and to secure property belonging to the Native Americans. Appointed as comisario for Soamca, San Xavier, and Guevavi (including Tumacácori and Calabazas), don Andrés Grijalva discharged his responsibilities in the most direct way possible. He simply rode to these mission communities and told the resident O'odham that everything was now theirs to do with as they saw fit, and he gave them the keys to the granaries.[84]

Juan Bautista de Anza, son and namesake of a previous famous frontier presidial commander, had become commander of the presidio of Tubac early in 1760 when he was a mere twenty-four years old. And now, at age thirty-one, he was less than pleased with Grijalva's method of carrying out his assignment. Anza retrieved the keys to the Tumacácori granary where already huge quantities of corn as well as large numbers of livestock had disappeared without accounting. Thanks to Anza, something would be left at Guevavi and the other missions on the arrival there in the summer of 1768 of Friar Juan Crisóstomo Gil de Bernabé, O.F.M., a grey-robed Franciscan from the Apostolic College of Santa Cruz de Querétaro in Nueva España.[85] Other former Jesuit *cabeceras* in the Pimería Alta were also resupplied with Franciscan replacements in that summer of 1768, with Fray Francisco Garcés the last, arriving at San Xavier del Bac in late June.[86]

Father Gil soon rode out from his new post at Guevavi, where the Jesuit-built church remained in remarkably good repair, to inspect his three *visitas*. The church begun earlier at Calabazas was still not finished and stood roofless. And at Tumacácori he found the Jesuit church intact as well as a community comprised of O'odham who had returned to this part of the valley after the 1751 revolt: Papagos, natives dispossessed of their lands at Tubac, and residents of the former Tumacácori when it had been on the east bank of the river. At Sonoita, a few O'odham remained in the face of danger from Apaches, but not for long. By 1774 it was abandoned along with Guevavi itself.[87]

Father Garcés, who was never one to sit still, had been at San Xavier del Bac only two months when he set out on his first journey of exploration. Traveling with four O'odham companions and, despite instructions, no military escort, he left on August 29 heading west all the way to Sonoyta. He remained mute on the reception given

This image of Santa Teresa de Ávila appears in the west transcept of Mission San Xavier del Bac. (Helga Teiwes.)

157

him there by the western O'odham, but it could not have been hostile or he would have said so. From Sonoyta he went north to the Gila River and to the O'odham village of Pitiaque near the Casa Grande. Before he returned to his mission at Bac, he had probably gotten his first look at these great prehistoric ruins.[88]

In 1770 or 1771 Father Gil de Bernabé elected to move from Guevavi. Epidemics and Apaches had been too much for it. He moved his *cabecera* downstream to Tumacácori, from then until the end of its mission life a *cabecera* with a Franciscan in residence. By 1773 Guevavi, now a *visita*, was down to nine families.[89]

Responding to a call from the Gila River O'odham in 1770 to come baptize their children, who were dying from a measles epidemic, Father Garcés rode out from San Xavier once more, leaving on October 19. And once more he may have visited the Casa Grande ruins. After a journey of 250 miles among the O'odham and their neighboring Yuman-speaking peoples, he was back at San Xavier by November 2.[90]

In 1771 the irrepressible Garcés was off again. This time it was to seek a viable overland route to the Colorado River and, hopefully, beyond to California. Although he may have known that Jesuits who had preceded him in the region had accomplished the task before, he also wanted to reconnoiter sites for new missions. Leaving San Xavier August 8 with three O'odham, he headed west into the heart of the riverless land today encompassed by the main portion of the Papago Indian Reservation, home of the Tohono O'odham Nation. On August 15 he met the native governor of Sonoyta somewhere in the desert, and the two men became friendly traveling companions. They arrived at Sonoyta that night. Garcés made a mental note of the ruins of the church where Father Ruhen had been killed in 1751, and he inquired of the Sonoyta O'odham about the possibility of paying a visit to the Yuma Indians (Quechans) living on the lower Colorado. Although there were some objections to his attempting the journey, on August 17 he set out with two local O'odham as guides. Their route was the Camino del Diablo. In the vicinity of the Tinajas Altas Mountains, they headed north to the Gila River and down the Gila to the Colorado. After a sojourn among the Yuman-speaking peoples of the lower Colorado, he returned to San Xavier over the Devil's Highway by which he had come, once again skirting the southern edge of Organ Pipe Cactus National Monument. On October 23 he reached Sonoyta, even visiting the ruins of the Jesuit mission "where the people gathered to be happy with him at his safe return." And by October 26, 1771, when his diary of the journey ends, he was at the mission at Caborca.[91]

Back at Tumacácori, Father Ximeno was joined by the end of 1772 by Father Francisco de Clemente. For the first time in the mission's history, two priests were in residence rather than one. The pair teamed up to build proper adobe living quarters for the O'odham at Tumacácori as well as a wall around all the mission grounds. And before the year was out, they had a consecrated cemetery at Calabazas as well as a roof on the village chapel, thereby completing its delayed construction.[92]

In 1769, largely at the instigation of José de Gálvez, Visitor General of Nueva España, the decision was made to push the reach of empire and, hopefully, of revenues for the crown, northward along the Pacific coast from Baja California. There was also royal concern that Russia might try to extend her 1728 and 1741 explorations of the Alaska coast to found settlements there and to push them southward down the Pacific slope. Under the Gálvez proposal, one California would grow into two, an upper (*alta*) and a lower (*baja*). Gálvez planned a four-pronged peaceful assault on Alta California: two groups of soldier and artisan settlers would go by ship from the mainland to Baja California before sailing on to Alta California; two other groups, each with a Franciscan from the Apostolic College of San Fernando, would travel via ship to Baja California and then overland to Alta California. The Franciscans were to begin a program of missionization of the northern province's Native Americans. Leader of this "sacred expedition," as president of the missions of Alta California, would be Fray Junípero Serra.[93]

Although the two land expeditions and two ships reached their destination as proposed, subsequent events did not go well. In 1773 Serra composed a memorial outlining the sorry plight of the Alta California establishments, a report which made clear to viceregal authorities the need to open a reliable land route from Mexico through Sonora to California. The person to open such a route was Captain Juan Bautista de Anza of the royal presidio at Tubac.

Although they left no personal record of their having done so, two Native Americans especially important in the Spanish-period history of Sonora made the trek across the Camino del Diablo in 1773. These were Sebastián Taraval, a Cochimi native to northern Baja California but who had lived in Alta California since 1769, and the Yuma (Quechan) leader Salvador Palma. Captain Juan Bautista de Anza met both of them at the presidio of Altar, Sonora, and knew that in addition to Father Garcés, he now had someone who could help guide him to Alta California via an overland route. Palma returned to his home on the lower Colorado; Taraval went with Anza to the latter's post at Tubac to await the journey.[94]

The long trek began in Tubac on January 8, 1774, and included thirty-four men: fathers Garcés and Juan Díaz; Taraval; an O'odham interpreter; servants; soldiers; muleteers; and a carpenter. The first leg of their trip took them to Caborca. By January 28 they were at Sonoyta where, Garcés said, "the people are very much scattered," and where Anza observed only six families, the rest said to be out gathering wild plant food. From Sonoyta they again ran parallel to the south end of Organ Pipe Cactus National Monument, eventually emerging on February 9 at the Colorado.[95]

Before the 1774 expedition ended, the friars and Anza reached San Gabriel in southern Alta California. Garcés and Díaz got to San Diego while Anza went all the way north to Monterey. On their return trip, after crossing the Colorado at the Yuma Crossing, they followed the Gila from its mouth eastward to the Gila River O'odham

159

Don Juan Bautista de Anza's career included the governorship of New Mexico (1778-88) and command of the 1775-76 overland expedition to California that resulted in the founding of San Francisco. (Annonymous portrait courtesy Museum of New Mexico, Santa Fe.)

villages and to the Casa Grande ruins. Visiting them on May 24, Anza said they were known as the "Palace of Montezuma," and that while the material of the buildings was purely of earth, "they also contain a mixture of small stones or coarse sand, which appears by its consistency like the finest mortar or cement, a better test of which is that it still endures after the many years which they estimate it has lasted."[96]

From here the party dropped south to Tucson, San Xavier del Bac, and Tubac, thereby avoiding Sonoyta and the Camino del Diablo. The way had been set for a colonization expedition to Alta California of major proportions soon to take place.

In September 1771 don Antonio María Bucareli y Ursúa replaced the Marqués de Croix as viceroy of Nueva España. It was during his viceregal administration that rumors were heard in the Spanish court that both England and Russia had designs on the region of the Pacific Northwest as far south as Alta California. Spain became determined to take whatever measures were necessary to forestall their expansion into lands regarded by the crown as properly belonging to it.[97]

These concerns had led to the Anza and Garcés overland expedition to Alta California in 1774 and in 1775 brought about the far more ambitious effort to take people from northwestern Nueva España overland as colonists for the new province. Charged with the task of leading the expedition and of seeing to the arrangement of its details was Juan Bautista de Anza. In the midst of all these preparations, in August 1775, the Sonoran frontier was visited by commandant-inspector Hugo O'Conor, who in 1773 had ordered that new presidios be placed on a line along the Río Grande in southern Tejas to shield Spanish settlements to the south from incursions of marauding Native Americans. As if Anza did not have enough to occupy his time, O'Conor signed an order on August 25, 1775, directing that Anza's presidio at Tubac be transferred north to Tucson.[98]

Difficulties aside, by September 29, 1775, some 240 persons, many of them recruited from Sinaloa and southern Sonora, set out from San Miguel de Horcasitas in Sonora headed for California "for the reinforcement of the royal presidio of San Carlos de Monte Rey, and for the establishment of the port of San Francisco"—part of which is today's Golden Gate National Recreation Area. Their eventual numbers, augmented by more colonists picked up at Tubac, included Anza; the Franciscans Pedro Font, Francisco Garcés, and Tomás Eixarch; alférez don José Joachín Moraga; soldiers and their families; cowboys; muleteers; servants; a commissary; and volunteers and relatives or servants of soldiers "of both sexes and all ages." And to help them along, there were 302 beef cattle as a walking larder, 140 pack mules, and 340 saddle animals. Never before had northern Sonora (southern Arizona) witnessed such a sight, nor would it again.[99]

The route of the expedition led it northward through the present-day international boundary crossing at Nogales, Sonora, and Nogales, Arizona. They followed Potrero

Creek to its junction with the Santa Cruz River. Father Font and four soldiers had ridden ahead to this point, and here on October 15 at the mission *visita* of Calabazas he celebrated Mass with Fray Pedro Antonio de Arriquibar who, with Fray Gaspar de Clemente, had recently taken over at Tumacácori. From the sixteenth through the twentieth of October, while Lieutenant Colonel Anza made final preparations at the Tubac presidio, Father Font rested at Tumacácori in companionship with Arriquibar and other friars. In addition to Father Garcés, who had ridden down from San Xavier to join the expedition, there were Father Félix de Gamarra, who was to fill in for Garcés at San Xavier during the latter's absence, and Father Eixarch. By this time Guevavi, the former *cabecera* and *visita*, had been abandoned. Only two of the three units of Tumacacori National Historical Park remained active in the fall of 1775.[100]

From Tubac, the expedition continued northward through San Xavier del Bac and Tucson to the Gila River. Here on October 31, while most of the party rested, Anza and fathers Garcés and Font paid a visit to the nearby "Casa Grande de Moctezuma." Font carefully mapped the major ruin with the walled enclosure around its courtyard, and Font provided a detailed description—clearly not one plagiarized from earlier sources—in his diary:

Ruins of the "Great House," or Casa Grande, ca. 1900. This edifice, which fascinated Spaniards from at least the late seventeenth century, is now protected as part of Casa Grande Ruins National Monument, Arizona. (Courtesy Arizona Historical Society, neg. # 92004.)

> We went to [the Casa Grande de Moctezuma] after Mass and returned after noon, accompanied by some [Gila River O'odham] Indians and the governor of Uturituc, who on the way recounted us the history of tradition which the Gila Pimas preserve from their ancestors concerning this Casa Grande. It all reduces itself to fables, confusedly mixed with some Catholic truths. . . .
>
> The Casa Grande, or Palace of Moctezuma, must have been built some five hundred years ago, according to histories and the scanty notices of it which exist and are given by the Indians, for apparently it was founded by Mexicans when in their migration they were led by the Devil through various regions until they reached the Promised Land of Mexico, and when during their stops, which were long, they established settlements and erected edifices. . . .
>
> All this region is scattered with pieces of ollas, jars, plates, etc., some ordinary and others stained with various colors, white, blue, red, etc., an indication that it was a large settlement and of a people different from the Gila Pimas, for these do not know how to make such pottery.

[Here follows a minute description of the Casa Grande, including its size, numbers of and dimensions of rooms, thickness of walls, building materials, sizes of doors, etc.]

161

Judging from what can be seen the timbers were of pine, although the nearest mountain which has pines is distant some twenty-five leagues. There is also some mesquite. The whole edifice is built of earth. . . . To furnish light to the rooms nothing is to be seen except the doors, and some round holes in the middle of the walls which face the east and the west. The Indians said that through these holes, which are rather large, the prince, whom they call The Bitter Man, looked at the sun which it rose and set, in order to salute it. No signs of stairs were found, from which we conclude that they were of wood and were destroyed in the fire which the edifice suffered from the Apaches.[101]

Font's account concludes with a version of O'odham myths telling how Bitter Man built the great house and how after his departure a man called The Drinker arrived and fashioned human beings out of mud. The Drinker also created saguaro cacti out of people with whom he was angry, and he made the sun come close to the earth—which is why it's so hot in the summer.[102]

Although in his own account of this visit Father Garcés defers to the report of Father Font, he later speculates on the ruin's origins. He does so in an effort to explain his rejection by Hopis whom he had managed to contact at Oraibi Pueblo on July 3, 1776. In view of the fact that many Hopis today as well as a few archeologists believe that at least some of the Hopis are descended from some of the prehistoric Hohokam people of southern Arizona, Father Garcés's speculations and reports of what he had been told take on new meaning:

[T]he trouble was . . . with the chief or chiefs, who ordered them that they should give me neither food nor shelter; which (mandate) they punctually obeyed. Various other reasons, besides their unwillingness to be baptized, or even to admit Españoles in their land, could there be for this order; such are, their having learned that I came through the Jamajabs [Mohaves] their enemies, and that I had gone with Españoles among the Yumas, friends of the Yabipais Tejua [Yavapais] and of the Chemeguaba [Chemehuevi], with whom the Moquis [Hopis] are at war; so that they suspected my coming as that of a spy. Also they knew that I was padre ministro of the Pimas, who likewise are their enemies. This hostility had been told me by the old Indians of my mission [San Xavier del Bac], by the Gileños [Gila River O'odham], and Cocomaricopas; from which information I have imagined . . . that the Moqui nation anciently extended to the Rio Gila itself. I take my stand . . . in this matter on the ruins that are found from this river as far as the land of the Apaches; and that I have seen between the Sierras de la Florida and San Juan Nepomuzeno. Asking a few years ago some Subaipuris Indians [eastern riverine O'odham] who were living in my mission of San Xavier, if they knew who had built those houses whose ruins and fragments of pottery . . . are still visible—as, on the supposition that neither Pimas nor Apaches knew how to make (such) houses or pottery, no doubt it was done by some other nation—they replied to me that the Moquis had built them, for they alone knew how to do

162

such things. . . . Also have the Pimas Gileños told me repeatedly that the Apaches of the north came anciently to fight with them for the Casa that is said to be of Moctezuma; and being sure that the Indians whom we know by the name of Apaches have no house nor any fixed abode, I persuaded myself that they could be the Moquis who came to fight; and that, harassed by the Pimas, who always have been numerous and valiant, they abandoned long ago these habitations on the Rio Gila . . . and that they retired to the place where they now live, in a situation so advantageous, so defensible, and with such precautions for self-defense in case of invasion.[103]

The Anza expedition followed the Gila from Casa Grande to its mouth at its junction with the Colorado River. In early December the main body of the expedition continued to Mission San Gabriel in southern Alta California and ultimately to Monterey, where they arrived on March 10, 1776. Along the way, they skirted the eastern edge of Santa Monica Mountains National Recreation Area. Font, Anza, and eighteen soldiers, muleteers, and servants made a reconnaissance of the San Francisco Bay region, part of which—including Fort Point and the beach south of Point Lobos and Seal Rocks—today is the Golden Gate National Recreation Area. It is believed Anza may have camped next to Mountain Lake, now within the boundary of the San Francisco Presidio unit of the recreation area. His expedition started from Monterey on March 22 and returned there April 13. It was June 27, however, before the northwest Mexicano colonists whom Anza had brought to Monterey moved north to become the founders of what evolved into today's city of San Francisco.[104]

On February 24 the expedition members passed along the California coast south of Santa Barbara within view of the islands of today's Channel Islands National Park, and Font commented on them in his diary. During the return trip—comprising only Anza, Font, and twenty-seven other persons as an escort, the colonists having been safely deposited in Monterey—the greatly reduced entourage passed the Channel Islands on April 26. Wrote Font,

Today we were able to see the islands of the Channel, which hitherto, neither going nor returning, had we been able to see clearly, but only very confusedly and indistinctly, because of the fogs which are almost continuous in this sea. With this opportunity I sketched them according to the front view which they presented from this place of La Assumpta [Carpinteria]. . . . I noted that looking southward from this place, the largest island, which is that of Santa Cruz, lies to the southwest, and the rest follow after it toward the south. And I may remark that all these islands are some six or eight leagues out at sea and are the ones which form the Channel.[105]

163

On its way to California, the expedition left fathers Garcés and Eixarch behind at the Quechan (Yuma) villages on the Colorado River. Father Eixarch stayed there living with the Quechan chief Palma until Anza and Font returned on May 11. Father Garcés, in the meantime, had characteristically ventured off by himself with some Native American guides on a journey of exploration up the Colorado River to the Mohave country; west across the deserts and mountains to Mission San Gabriel; over the mountains north into Alta California's San Joaquín Valley; back over the desert to the Mohaves; and from there to the Hopi village of Oraibi where he was turned back on July 4, 1776. Garcés was again at the Yuma Crossing on August 27, more than three months after the others had already passed by on their way home. From Yuma he ascended the Gila River to the O'odham villages, possibly seeing the Casa Grande one more time before going south to arrive on September 17 at his mission of San Xavier del Bac.[106]

Anza, Font, Eixarch, and the others took the most direct return route to San Miguel de Horcasitas by traveling south from the Gila River to the Camino del Diablo and then going east on a line parallel with the southern edge of today's Organ Pipe Cactus National Monument to Sonoyta where they saw some twenty families of western O'odham and passed the ruins of San Marcelo de Sonoyta, where Father Ruhen had been killed twenty-five years earlier. Anza and Font reached Horcasitas on June 1.[107]

They had no way of knowing at the time that in the summer of 1781 the Quechans (Yumas) would rebel against the Spanish colonists who in 1780 had settled in their midst at Yuma Crossing, killing fathers Garcés, Juan Díaz, Joseph Matías Moreno, and Juan Antonio Joaquín de Barreneche as well as a former California governor, Captain Fernando de Rivera y Moncada, and some thirty Spanish soldiers. Only the women, children, and a few men were spared. This so-called Yuma Massacre struck a fatal blow to Spain's plans to open a permanent overland route from Mexico to the Californias. The Quechans had barred the crossing—except briefly later in 1781 and in 1782 when Spanish punitive expeditions operated in the area. The natives would continue to close the route for the remainder of Spain's days in North America. California, while not geographically an island, might just as well have been one. After 1781 its Spanish presidios and towns became largely dependent either on goods produced at the missions or on supplies brought in once or twice yearly by ships that had embarked from the port of San Blas in Nayarit.[108]

Hugo O'Conor's order to move the presidio at Tubac north to Tucson was carried out sometime in 1776, the year Sonora joined Tejas, Nuevo México, and the Californias as one of the newly formed Provincias Internas. Neither action did much to quell increased raiding by Apaches, Seri Indians, and backsliding Christian O'odham. Just before Christmas of 1776 the raiders cleaned out all the stock belonging to Mission Tumacácori and in June 1777 "sacked and set fire to . . . [Calabazas], burning all the houses, the church, and the granary with more than a hundred fanegas of maize. The mission Indians put up a stiff defense killing thirteen of the enemy at a cost of seven of ours gravely wounded with little hope of survival."[109]

Troops stationed at the Presidio de Terrenate, which in 1780 had moved from its former location on the San Pedro River in today's southeastern Arizona to Las Nutrias near Cananea in today's northern Sonora, continued in their largely futile efforts to subdue Apaches. In the fall of 1780 don Joseph Antonio de Vildósola, commander of the presidio, "detached Lieutenant Don Pablo Romero with an ensign and fifty men, including twenty Opatas to examine La Tinaja Colorado, and its Sierra de Chiricagui [Chiricahua], along the western part and return through the Puerto del Dado as far as San Simón." While snow and freezing weather drove the troops back, and little or nothing came of their efforts, the expedition represented yet another Spanish use of the place now called Apache Pass.[110]

When word of the 1781 Yuma Massacre reached headquarters of the Provincias Internas in Arizpe, Sonora, Lieutenant Colonel Pedro Fages was ordered by commandant general Teodoro de Croix to advance on the Quechans with his company of Catalonian volunteers to recover the captives and to negotiate a peace. His expedition, which succeeded in recovering the hostages and burying the dead but which failed to negotiate a settlement with the Quechans, lasted from September 16 through December 30, 1781. During the course of the campaign, Fages withdrew from Yuma to Sonoyta—the ransomed women, children, and the few men who had been spared in tow—to rest his pack and saddle horses and to wait for needed supplies to arrive from the Altar presidio. In reaching Sonoyta, they had followed the Camino del Diablo on October 26-27. While Fages waited in Sonoyta, the rescued captives—mostly widows and fatherless children—were sent to the safety of Altar.

On November 23 Fages and his troops set out again to go after the Quechans, trailing once more from Sonoyta over the Camino del Diablo to the Gila River and to Yuma. After retrieving the bones of the four murdered Franciscans and failing to engage the Quechans in a decisive battle, Fages backtracked to Mission Caborca—again along the Devil's Highway through Sonoyta. This December 15-20, 1781, journey was not the last time the Spanish empire would pass this way. Concern with the Quechans, lasting for nearly another year, would keep Sonoyta and the Camino del Diablo busy.

After a series of military conferences held in the winter of 1781-82 it was decided that Fages should take his Catalonian Volunteers to Alta California to join forces with that province's governor, Felipe de Neve, for an assault on the Quechans from the west. Simultaneously, Captain don Pedro de Tueros of the Altar presidio would advance on the lower Colorado from the east. The pincers would close on April 1.

As a result of these plans, on February 27, 1782, some thirty-nine soldiers under Fages's command left the mission community of Pitiquito near Altar presidio, passing through Sonoyta March 2 before going over the Camino del Diablo on the way to the Yuma Crossing and west to the California missions, where they rendezvoused at

Fray Junípero Serra as depicted on the frontispiece engraving from Relacion historica de la vida y apostolicas tareas del Venerable Padre Fray Juípero Serra, *1787, the first book published in Alta California. Serra was the Franciscan missionary responsible for what eventually became a chain of twenty-one Alta California missions. (Courtesy Bancroft Library, University of California at Berkeley.)*

Mission San Gabriel on March 26 without having contacted the enemy. At San Gabriel, Neve decided the attack should be postponed until September 15, when the water in the Colorado would be lower.

In the meantime, however, Captain Tueros had started out on schedule. To let Tueros know the campaign was postponed until mid-September, Fages and twenty soldiers rode for Yuma, meeting the Altar captain there on April 15. There were some minor encounters with Quechans, but both troops returned the next day in the directions from which they had come, Tueros back through Sonoyta to Altar and Fages to California.

At last, in late August, Fages and Neve headed eastward from San Gabriel with a combined force of fifty-nine mounted and well-armed men. And from Altar, captains Joseph Romeu and Pedro Tueros led their mounted troop of some one hundred men, including Pima auxiliaries, toward the west. Their route was through Sonoyta and over the Camino del Diablo.

Before reaching the Colorado River, Fages received word he had been made governor of California while Neve had been promoted to Inspector General of the Provincias Internas. Governor Fages left immediately for Monterey to assume his new duties, while Neve, perhaps less enthusiastic, continued to the rendezvous with Romeu and Tueros on September 16. The Sonoran detachments did most of the fighting, none of it too successful, and Neve called off the campaign on October 3. The California soldiers returned to the coast while Neve, with an escort of thirty men, headed southeastward over the Camino del Diablo after ordering Romeu and Tueros to linger a bit longer in search of Quechans. Neve paused long enough at Sonoyta on October 17 to compose a report of the entire campaign to Teodoro de Croix, perhaps the only official Spanish military communique ever composed at this remote settlement.[111]

By 1787 the *visita* of Calabazas had become virtually abandoned, while Tubac, abandoned in 1783, was reoccupied that year by Piman Indian auxiliary troops. This meant the missionary in charge at Tumacácori, Baltasar Carrillo, had only to concern himself with a mission and a presidio, the latter largely O'odham like his mission community. This seems to have remained the situation until 1807 when Juanico Legarra, the Papago (O'odham) native governor at Tumacácori, was granted 6,770 acres in behalf of his fellow O'odham. The lands stretched from Tumacácori in a ten-mile long, half-mile wide strip southward up the Santa Cruz River past Calabazas to the north edge of Guevavi. This Tumacácori Grant of 1807 was intended to insure the O'odham's right to graze livestock and to farm. Their farming and stock-raising effort at Calabazas appears to have lasted at least until 1821, when Sonora became a part of Mexico. As late as August 1823 Calabazas was apparently still an occupied settlement, if only barely so.[112]

In 1795 the College of Querétaro, whose friars manned the missions in the Pimería Alta, dispatched Fray Diego Miguel Bringas de Manzaneda to the region to deal with personnel matters among the missionaries and to rekindle zeal in their vocation of bringing the O'odham to vassalage and Christianity. Carrying out his visitation, Fray Bringas succeeded in reaching O'odham villages on the Gila River, visiting the Casa Grande ruins as he did so. Bringas, perhaps impressed by the fortress-like appearance of the great house, proposed in his later report to the king that a "presidio should be located near the ancient edifice known as the house of Moctezuma." He carefully located the ruin on his excellent map showing his travel route in the Pimería Alta. His visit to Casa Grande may not have been the last by a Spanish subject (actually a criollo born in Sonora) in the period of the viceroyalty of Nueva España, but it was the last of record. The northern frontier, unbeknownst to Bringas and his contemporaries, was in retreat.[113]

In 1803, the year sovereign control of Louisiana went from Spain to France to the United States, a report was made on the missions of the Pimería Alta. At Tumacácori "a church was being built anew." And about time. The Franciscans had been making do with the adobe structure built by Jesuit missionary Francisco Pauer in 1757.[114]

Construction had actually gotten underway in 1802 when the settlement's population consisted of seventy-six O'odham and 102 "Spaniards." The plan for the church was ambitious: a cruciform structure with brick vaults and dome modeled after that at Mission San Xavier del Bac. Building bumped fitfully along until 1810, when Mexicans began their revolution for independence from Spain. After 1814 the royal subsidy for Tumacácori was cut off. That same year, however, Yaqui Indians were employed in working a gold mine at the abandoned Guevavi, which had long ceased to be a mission. When Tumacácori's minister, Fray Narciso Gutiérrez, died on December 13, 1820, he was buried beneath the floor of the old Jesuit church. When the new mission was completed, it would be under the regime of an independent Mexico rather than that of Spain. General Juan de O'Donojú, sent to Nueva España as its Captain-General, signed a treaty with soon-to-be Emperor Agustín de Iturbide on August 24, 1821. The highest-ranking Spanish officer in Nueva España had recognized Mexican independence. Sonora and the rest of Spain's former northern frontier were changed forever.[115]

ALTA CALIFORNIA

It had been 167 years since Sebastían Vizcaíno had sailed past Point Loma and the site of today's Cabrillo National Monument into a bay he christened San Diego. But now, on April 11, 1769, another ship flying the Spanish flag, the packet boat *San Antonio* and her captain Juan Pérez, sailed past Point Loma and dropped anchor in the harbor. No explorers these, but missionaries and soldier-settlers come to stay. Eighteen days later, the little vessel was followed by another ship of Spain, the *San Carlos.* All but two of its 26-man crew had died of scurvy during the 110-day journey from the tip of Baja

California, but its most distinguished passenger, engineer and diarist Miguel Costansó, survived. And while no one on board the *San Antonio* had died, everyone was sick or disabled except the two Franciscan chaplains, friars Juan Vizcaíno and Francisco Gómez. It was a tentative beginning for what proved to be Spain's final effort permanently to expand its over-extended empire into North America.[116]

On May 14 the beleaguered survivors of the sea voyages were joined in San Diego by an overland expedition from Baja California led by Mexican-born Captain Fernando de Rivera y Moncada, who later would be military governor of California and who was destined to die in 1781 at the hands of Quechan Indians on the lower Colorado River. Rivera was accompanied by twenty-five *soldados de cuera* (leather-jacket soldiers), and by three muleteers and—at the start, at least—forty-two Hispanicized Christian Indians. The chaplain and diarist of the expedition was Father Juan Crespí.

With pick, ax, shovel, and crowbar, Rivera opened the way for the overland expedition behind him, that led by the Catalán governor of Baja California, Gaspar de Portolá. With Portolá were Fray Junípero Serra, another Catalán, chosen to head Franciscan mission efforts in Alta California, as well as nine or ten soldiers, a pair of servants, and a dozen Baja California Native Americans. Forty-four Indians had started the trip, but thirty-two either died along the way or deserted. The Portolá party joined the others in San Diego on July 1, and the great California effort began in the place first seen by Cabrillo more than two centuries earlier.[117]

The founders of Spanish Alta California, like settlers who followed them, were typical of founders of virtually the whole northern frontier of Nueva España from La Florida to the Pacific Coast. Collectively, these Spanish-speaking pioneers were of ethnically and racially mixed backgrounds. Not only did "Spaniards" include Cataláns and Basques, to say nothing of Irishmen, but so were there criollos, "Spaniards" born in the New World who frequently were of mixed racial heritage. Persons who in Alta California came to be known as *californios*, and many of their descendants—much like descendants of Hispanic pioneers—stress their Spanish, as opposed to their Mexican, heritage.

> The recognition of the role that colonial Mexicans—that is, the role that the persons of mixed blood—played in settling the Borderlands and especially California does not reject the essential part that Spaniards performed in the exploration, colonization, and missionization of the Southwest. Spanish *peninsulares* [Spaniards born in Spain] overwhelmingly were the *adelantados*, the officials, and the priests who explored, governed, and served settlers. But to claim that the settlers were preponderantly Spaniards—as the *californios* assert—must be rejected as historically untenable. These settlers, as the study of California settlement shows, were not Spanish, but overwhelmingly mixed-bloods from Indian, Spanish, and also Negro stock.

168

Although the Mexican mixed-bloods and the Baja California Indians constituted the vast majority of the permanent soldiers and colonists of Alta California, the Spaniards—with extremely few exceptions—planned and encouraged the development of the new colony. The Spanish Franciscans not only established twenty missions but also insured California's permanent settlement and economic development. Spanish officers erected [four] presidios [San Diego, Santa Barbara, Monterey, San Francisco], [four associated] presidial towns, and [three] civilian pueblos [Los Angeles, San José, Branciforte]. It was also these officers who initiated the *rancho* system by making the first land grants to retired Spanish soldiers. Yet, as important as Spanish leadership was, without those of mixed-blood, Alta California could neither have been occupied nor colonized.

The Mexican mixed-bloods, in addition to being the pioneer soldier-settlers who garrisoned presidios, guarded missions, carried the mail, erected buildings, farmed, and even took care of flocks, soon became the main source of "Spanish" population for securing the territory [as exemplified in the colonists brought to California in 1775 by Juan Bautista de Anza].[118]

The Franciscans, as guardians of conservative and fundamentalist Catholic dogma, frequently spoke out against the civilian and military establishments. The friars objected to what they saw as "the fun-loving and unchaste behavior of the religiously lax soldiers and settlers, a behavior that was far from edifying to the California mission Indian."[119]

The complaint echoes one registered by Father Pedro de Arriquibar in 1795 concerning peaceful Apaches living in Bacoachi, Sonora: "In the conference I had with them on the afternoon of my visit, when I played a game of chance with them (to which they are highly addicted, and chiefly the 'boys' and even the women), they told me that this and the other card games they play is the first milk they sucked from the Christians; that in their country they knew nothing of this. They made the same statement about dances, swearing oaths, obscene language and other vices which they have, i.e., that they learned all this from the Christians of Bacoachi."[120]

With the seeds of the typically heterogeneous colony planted in San Diego, Portolá set out for the north with a small party to locate the harbor at Monterey. Father Serra stayed in San Diego to direct the construction of Mission San Diego de Alcalá, the first in what eventually would become a chain—and Native Americans would find "chain" to be an appropriate choice of words—of twenty missions, *reducciones*, along the Pacific slope founded between 1769 and 1817 by Franciscans of the College of San Fernando. The twenty-first and northernmost of the Alta California missions, San Francisco Solano (Sonoma), was founded in 1823 when California was a part of Mexico.[121]

The Portolá expedition to find Monterey Bay—whose location was known from Vizcaíno's reports—overshot the mark all the way to Half Moon Bay. From here they

Lupine graces the shoreline at Drake's Bay, Point Reyes National Seashore, California. Drake's Bay was first called the Port of San Francisco by Spaniards in the early 1770s, but the name was transferred southward after the infinitely larger bay was explorered in 1775. (Larry Ulrich.)

169

sighted the Farallones, islands today administered with their surrounding waters as the Gulf of the Farallones National Marine Sanctuary, as well as Point Reyes and Drake's Bay, both within Point Reyes National Seashore.

Although the men knew they had gone beyond Monterey, Portolá sent his chief scout, a criollo sergeant named José Ortega, ahead to try to reach Point Reyes:

The church at Mission San Carlos Borromeo de Carmelo, California, founded in 1771, still serves the seaside community of Carmel. (Painting by Orianna Day, gift of Eleanor Martin, courtesy M. H. de Young Museum, San Francisco, neg. # 37566.)

Next day [November 4, 1769], food nearly being exhausted, some hunters struck into the mountains northeast of the camp to look for game. The chase, or perhaps only the hope of it, led upward until presently they came out on a clear height [Sweeney Ridge] and beheld a great quiet harbor to the east and north. These hunters were the first white men to report a glimpse of San Francisco Bay. Ortega returned a few hours behind the hunters, with the news that his way to Point Reyes was cut off by a roadstead that led into the estuary described by the hunters—a noble harbor that was almost land-locked, so near together stood the two titanic pillars of its one gate, open to the sunset ocean. [Father] Crespí, who saw it the next day, had a sense of its importance. "In a word," he said, "it is a very large and fine harbor, such that not only all the navy of our most Catholic Majesty but those of all European could take shelter in it."[122]

Incredibly, and notwithstanding the many sea voyages that had sailed past the Golden Gate, this land expedition presumably became the first European-Mexican sighting of the great bay. The place from which the sighting is believed to have occurred is now protected and interpreted as the Sweeney Ridge unit of Golden Gate National Recreation Area.

Down from the ridge, Ortega and eight men were sent out to try to reach Point Reyes—where Indians had told them a Spanish ship was anchored—by circling around the "estuary." "The worthy scout explored the bay to its southern extremity, but he succeeded in getting north only to the neighborhood of Hayward. Either from this point or while on the Peninsula Ortega saw the passage through the Golden Gate and the three islands within the strait, Alcatraz, Yerba Buena, and Angel."[123] Today, Alcatraz—now famed for its 1934-63 federal penitentiary—is maintained and interpreted as a unit of the Golden Gate National Recreation Area.

Failing to locate Monterey on this first try, Portolá and his men returned to San Diego. Although the Spaniards there were in desperate straits, they managed to survive until a ship brought relief supplies. In 1770 the overland journey to Monterey was successful, and both a mission and presidio were founded as one—and in 1777 Monterey became the capital of California for the entire Spanish and Mexican periods of its history. In 1771, the mission left the presidio chapel for its own new quarters at Carmel. This second of the California chain of twenty-one missions was dedicated by Father Serra to San Carlos Borromeo, but it is best known today as Mission Carmel.[124]

The foundation of three other missions followed in rapid succession: San Antonio de Padua (1771), San Gabriel Arcángel (1771), and San Luis Obispo de Tolosa (1772). But matters were not going well in the new province for either the military establishment or Franciscans. The Fernandinos got a little boost when they were relieved of the responsibility for the Baja California missions in 1772, that field being turned over to the Dominicans. Even so, it took a trip by Father Serra to Mexico City to confer with Viceroy Bucareli to bring improvement in Alta California's provisioning. More important, perhaps, were reports of increased Russian activity in the north. Whatever the impetus, decisions made in 1773 brought Anza to California in 1775-76, leading a party of colonists.[125]

In 1770 Pedro Fages—who in 1781 would lead rescue and retaliatory expeditions against the Quechans on the lower Colorado River—led a small party of lancers and muleteers to San Francisco Bay, camping on the East Bay in the vicinity of Alameda before turning back. In 1772 he conducted a more thorough survey of the bay, one that provoked more interest in the region. Father Serra wanted two missions established at what he called the Port of San Francisco (the name then applied to what came to be known as Drake's Bay), a cause he promoted with the viceroy. The viceroy responded by ordering that two missions and a presidio be established there. Rivera y Moncada, who in 1774 replaced Fages as military commander of Alta California, reconnoitered the San Francisco region, perhaps getting as far as Point Lobos.[126]

While San Francisco awaited its founding, in 1775 an old Spanish tradition was activated in Alta California: the granting of land to individuals. It was then that a retired soldier, Manuel Butrón (or Buitron) was encouraged to accept title to a few acres near Mission San Carlos Borromeo not far from the presidio and capital at Monterey. It was Spain's method of encouraging people to remain in its far-flung provinces and to increase the productivity of the land. Although Butrón and his Indian wife left their grant three years later, theirs was the first such offering of acreage that would become a near flood in California during the Mexican regime.[127]

It was 1784 when the first individual grants for ranchos were given, huge tracts of land suitable for grazing livestock. One such Spanish-period grant—although its size was less than grand, a mere three square leagues—was the Malibu Rancho grant awarded to José Bartolomé Tapia in 1804. U.S. government surveyors later calculated there were 13,315.70 acres in the original survey. The Tapia heirs held the grant, which was also known as the Topanga Malibu Sequit, to the end of the Mexican period in 1848. A patent for the land was issued in 1872 to Matthew Keller, and today it is a part of the Santa Monica Mountains National Recreation Area.[128]

Additional grants which lay within the boundaries of today's Santa Monica Mountains National Recreation Area included one of eleven square leagues and eventually

171

confirmed by the United States as 48,671.56 acres, El Conejo grant issued in two parts in 1802-03 by Governor Arrillaga to Ignacio Rodríguez and José Polanco. Adjacent to it on the east was El Paraje de la Vírgenes grant of two square leagues granted in 1810 to Miguel Ortega. With the later addition of two Mexican-period grants (1837), that of Rancho Cañada de Triunfo and another issued to J.M. Domínguez, it was patented by the United States in the amount of 8,884.04 acres.[129]

Only about twenty-five grants for ranchos were given during the whole of Spain's control of Alta California (1769-1821). Throughout the Spanish period, the best lands over which Spaniards exercised control were those held by the Franciscans in trust for Native Americans. Considering that by 1784 there were only a few hundred Spaniards and as many as a quarter million Native Americans, this is not surprising. Nor is it surprising that as time moved on, Spanish military and civil authorities pressed ever harder for the secularization of the missions, although without success.[130]

When it became definite that Anza was going to bring colonists to California, thirty-year-old naval officer Juan Manuel de Ayala was ordered to take his packetboat *San Carlos*—also called the *Toison de Oro* ("Golden Fleece")—from the Pacific port of San Blas to Alta California with supplies for the new settlers. He was further ordered to make an exploration of San Francisco Bay by ship, a feat which he and first pilot José Cañizares accomplished over a forty-four day period starting August 5, 1775. Cañizares had entered the bay first in a longboat before being followed that evening by Ayala in the *San Carlos*. The *Golden Fleece* had entered the Golden Gate, at last opening a parade of ships that would follow from that day to this, vessels now viewed everywhere by visitors to the Golden Gate National Recreation Area. Native Americans, of course, had long paddled the Bay's waters in their canoes and rafts.[131]

The story of Anza's expedition, his exploration of the bay region, and the subsequent arrival of the soldier-colonists at San Francisco has already been told. It seems to have been Father Pedro Font who in 1775 was the first unequivocally to apply the name of San Francisco to the bay that still bears it.[132]

On June 27, 1776, Lieutenant don José Joachín Moraga arrived in the Bay Area from Monterey, pausing at the site where two days later Father Francisco Palóu celebrated the first Mass at Mission San Francisco de Asís (Mission Dolores). With Moraga, besides Father Palóu as their chaplain, were thirty-five soldiers and the military storekeeper and their families, a total of 179 men, women, and children. Also with him were at least twenty-two non-military settlers, *pobladores*. While they awaited the arrival of the *San Carlos* to bring them needed supplies, Moraga scouted the region carefully and selected the place where, on July 26, the main force was assembled to begin to build a chapel and some crude shelters. Moraga's choice of a site for el Presidio de San Francisco—different from that originally selected by Anza—was affirmed by Palóu and the captain and pilot (Cañizares) of the *San Carlos* after the supply boat arrived on August 17. It was situated somewhere within the confines of today's Presidio of San Francisco, now being relinquished by the United States Army to the National Park Service as a part of the Golden Gate National Recreation Area. Cañizares devised the original formal plan, one calling for a church, royal offices, warehouses, guardhouse, and houses for the soldier-settlers.[133]

To expedite construction, a squad of sailors and two carpenters joined in to complete a warehouse, the *comandancia*, and a chapel, while the soldiers worked on their own dwellings. On September 16, 1776, with sufficient progress being made, *San Carlos*'s crew joined the soldiers and [non-military settlers] and four missionary priests at a solemn high mass, then performed the ceremony of formal dedication, followed by the singing of the *Te Deum Laudamus* ["We praise Thee, O God"], "accompanied by the peal of bells and repeated salvos of cannon, muskets, and guns, whose roar and the sound of the bells doubtless terrified the heathen, for they did not allow themselves to be seen for many days."[134]

Although Father Palóu had celebrated the first Mass at the mission site on June 29, it was October 9 before a wooden church plastered with mud and roofed with tules was ready for services. Another noisy dedication ceremony ensued, and San Francisco had its mission and presidio.[135]

Despite the fact it was now in place, the presidio was anything but rich nor were the lives of its soldier-settlers those of opulence. Supplies were always short, and even the decade of the 1780s saw few if any improvements either in structures at the presidio or in the quality of lives of its inhabitants. Matters were not much better in the 1790s, although by the end of 1792 there had been a few renovations and a new wall had been built. It was also in 1792 that an unidentified ship appeared in the harbor, provoking the presidio's commander to fire a salvo at it. This may have been the only time the presidio's lone cannon was used for anything other than ceremony, and the effects were equally harmless. The ship sailed away untouched, never to be heard from again.[136]

On November 14, 1792, the cannon was fired in recognition of the landing at the presidio of a distinguished visitor, Captain George Vancouver, who had arrived in H.M.S. *Discovery*. Vancouver, who had recently been involved in negotiations with Spaniards at Nootka Sound concerning the boundary separating the two nations, was not looked upon as an enemy but as a gentleman and an officer. Thus he received a warm welcome rather than a hot one. Vancouver's description of what he saw at San Francisco is edifying:

We soon arrived at the Presidio, which was not more than a mile from our landing place. Its wall, which fronted the harbor, was visible from the ships; but instead of the city or town, whose lights we had so anxiously looked for on the

This lithograph by V. Adam of the Presidio of San Francisco, ca. 1816, is based on a drawing made by Louis Choris. (Courtesy California Historical Society, San Francisco, neg. # FN-25092.)

night of arrival, surrounded by hills on every side, excepting that which fronted the port. The only object of human industry which presented itself, was a square area, whose sides were about two hundred yards in length, enclosed by a mud wall, and resembling a pound for cattle. Above this wall, the thatched roofs of their low small houses, just made their appearance. On entering the Presidio we found one of its sides still unenclosed by the wall, and very indifferently fenced in by a few bushes here and there, fastened to stakes in the ground. The unfinished state of this part, afforded us an opportunity of seeing the strength of the wall, and the manner in which it was constructed. It is about fourteen feet high, and five feet in breadth, and was first formed by uprights and horizontal rafters or large timber, between which dried sod and moistened earth were pressed as close and as hard as possible; after which the whole was cased with earth made into a sort of mud plaster, which gave it the appearance of durability, and of being sufficiently strong to protect them, with the assistance of their firearms, against all the force which the natives of the country might be able to collect.[137]

Vancouver realized the presidio could not withstand an artillery assault, and he further observed that it was manned by only thirty-five soldiers, their families, and a few servants. He also described the post's interior, including the soldiers' houses, the chapel, and commandant's house—all with windows "destitute of glass." Before he sailed away on November 26, he found time to visit Mission Dolores as well as the more southerly Mission Santa Clara, which had been founded by Father Serra in 1777.[138]

Right after Vancouver's departure, the Spanish commandant at the San Francisco presidio began to get some action on his many requests to improve the region's defenses. Efforts were begun north of San Francisco at Bodega Bay, adjoined by Tomales Point at the northwest edge of Point Reyes National Seashore, to start a Spanish settlement. The project, however, was abandoned after two weeks. The supplies were used instead to erect a proper fortification for San Francisco. This fort, built of timbers and masonry and well-supplied with cannons—the site of which is also situated within the grounds of today's Presidio of San Francisco—was finished in December of 1794 and dedicated as the Castillo de San Joaquín. It was supplemented in 1797 by construction of a gun battery, the Batería de San José, east of the harbor's entrance near where Vancouver had anchored his ship in 1792.[139]

While attack by foreign invaders was always a concern, the reality is that most garrison duty involved efforts to round up Native Americans for the missions, either Indians who had fled the missions or who had never been brought into them. This was the Spanish military's role in effecting *reducción*. The success of the soldiers at San Francisco in this regard seems generally to have been indifferent, although not entirely without success.

In 1806 San Francisco became the setting for one of the most romantic tales in the history of Spanish North America. The story begins in 1805 when Nikolai Petrovich

174

ezánof, imperial inspector and plenipotentiary of the Russian American Company, rived in Sitka, Alaska—the location of the modern Sitka National Historical Park— inspect and improve the Russian colony there. He reached Sitka at a time of severe mine for the Russian settlers. They were eating "eagles, crows, devil-fish, and almost nything that teeth could bite, and, as a result, scurvy and death had made their ppearance."

Just when the need appeared to be the greatest, an American Captain Wolfe landed Sitka in his ship *Juno.* Rezánof bought the entire vessel from keel to crow's nest and cluding its cargo. Those provisions exhausted, with naturalist and physician Dr. eorg Heinrich von Langsdorf, he set out for Alta California in the *Juno* to get relief upplies, leaving Sitka in early March 1806. On April 5, in violation of Spanish direcves, the ship sailed into San Francisco Bay and anchored at the presidio's harbor.[140]

The Spaniards had earlier been told to expect a visit from a Russian scientific expedition, and to receive them courteously. The result is that Rezánof was welcomed by lférez Luis Argüello, son of commandant José Darío Argüello, who happened to be way at the time. Padre José de Uría of Mission San José, who was visiting in San rancisco, was able to carry on a conversation in Latin with Langsdorf since the paniards knew no Russian and the Russians, presumably, no Spanish.

Young Argüello invited the Muscovites to his home for dinner at his parent's home. angsdorf was impressed:

> Madame Argüello had had fifteen children, of whom thirteen were at the time living; some of the sons were absent upon military services, others were at home. Of the grown up unmarried daughters, Donna Conception interested us more particularly. She was lively and animated, had sparkling love-inspiring eyes, beautiful teeth, pleasing and expressive features, a fine form, and a thousand other charms, yet her manners were perfectly simple and artless.[141]

y the time the Russians' six-week visit had ended, Rezánof had ingratiated himself ith the Argüello family as well as with Governor José Joaquín de Arrillaga, and he nd the beautiful sixteen-year-old María de la Concepción Argüello—in spite of difrences in religion, the fact that he had been widowed four years, and the great disarity in their ages (he was fifty-eight or -nine)—had become betrothed. He had also anaged to load the *Juno* with Spanish-produced grain, flour, and other foodstuffs. ezánov promised to return within two years' time to be married. On May 21, the hip set sail for Alaska, but not before stopping at Alcatraz Island to retrieve the otential deserters he had deposited there to make sure he had enough crew to man he ship on its return voyage.[142]

What happened afterward was immortalized in a poem by Francis Bret Harte. ezánof returned to Alaska to unload the relief supplies before returning to Russia.

175

On his way from Siberia to European Russia, he became ill, fainted, fell from his horse, and was struck in the head by one of its hooves. His death left the world forever to wonder whether his involvement with Concepción Argüello had been born of love or impurely of expediency. As for Concepción, she remained steadfast to her betrothed, awaiting his return. No word came.

> At length she took the robes of a nun, and devoted herself to a life of charity. When her father became governor of Baja California, she went there too for several years, probably from 1815 to 1819. For a while she was back in Alta California, and went then to Guadalajara. In 1829, now thirty-eight years of age, she returned to Alta California, and thereafter remained, living for the most part with the De la Guerra family of Santa Barbara. Not until 1842, thirty-six years after Rezánof's departure, did she at last get word of the way in which he died. Sir George Simpson of the Hudson's Bay Company is said to have informed her. . . .

> In 1857, at the [Dominican] Convent of Saint Catherine, Benicia [the first convent in California], Concepción Argüello died. Her life had been famous not only for its romance but also for its kindliness and charities, so that she was venerated by all. Thus passed away the most cherished figure in the romance of Alta California history.[143]

On September 16, 1810, a fifty-eight-year-old Mexican curate in the town of Dolores in Mexico rang the bells of church in an act of defiance that would lead eventually to the downfall of Spain in California as elsewhere in her northern New World possessions. The priest was Miguel Hidalgo y Costilla, and just as the shot fired at Lexington was heard 'round the world, the bells of Father Hidalgo's church rang in ascending crescendo for the next eleven years until Spain cracked apart in the unbearable pitch.

In California in 1810,

> insurgents on the high seas captured supplies and equipment destined for California. From this date until the end of the Spanish period in California the soldiers never again saw their pay [nor missionaries their royal stipends]. The semi-annual supply ships rarely made the trip to California, dictating that the presidios had to rely on foodstuffs from the missions. The governor gave drafts on the royal treasury in exchange for the food, but never repaid the debts. These circumstances forced Governor Arrillaga to ignore his orders to forbid foreign trade in order to supply the province with necessities.[144]

As elsewhere along the Spanish northern frontier, necessity dictated the opening of California's gates to the Trojan horse of foreign intervention—although that is not what eventually brought Spanish California to a close. What began as a drizzle in Spanish California ended as a torrent in Mexican California.

176

Part of the drizzle manifested itself in occasional Russian and American sailors as well as in Alaskan Native Americans, Aleuts included. In 1810 Corporal Francisco Josef de los Dolores Soto—the first Hispanic to have been born in San Francisco—and two other soldiers captured three Russian-directed Indian fur traders near Mission San José. Simultaneously, many small vessels, canoes or perhaps Aleut kayaks (*baidarkas*), were in San Francisco Bay, those in them going after sea otters. Spaniards also investigated a report of a sailing vessel in Bodega Bay, part of which is within the northwesternmost portion of Point Reyes National Seashore. They found a small American ship there with several small boats used in hunting sea otters, and they saw Alaskan Indians as well.[145]

Early in 1811 many more Russian-directed Native Americans appeared in the Bay region. As many as 130 canoes were seen involved in hunting fur seals, and Russian supply ships connected with this effort were anchored in Bodega Bay. In mid-year the ships and Indians disappeared, but they were back in mid-1812, some of them seen as far east as Carquinez Strait and others as far south down the San Francisco peninsula as San Mateo. A Spanish reconnaissance discovered a Russian brigantine lying just off the shore about eight leagues north of Bodega Bay. It had brought some eighty men from Unalaska and Kamchatka to a site where a small fort was under construction. Ivan Alexander Kuskov, their leader, had explored the coast in 1808 and now was back to settle it. The post would come to be known as Fort Ross, and it was destined to last well into the Mexican period until sea otters were hunted into near extinction. The colonists withdrew in 1839 and the fort was sold in 1841 to a Swiss who had settled in Mexican California, John Augustus Sutter.[146]

Although Fort Ross should have been construed by Spaniards at the San Francisco presidio as a threat, relationships between Russians and Spaniards, cordial at the outset, remained that way. In 1813 trade between the two places was initiated when Lieutenant Gabriel Moraga drove twenty cattle and three horses to Fort Ross to be turned over to the Russians. And in 1815 at least three Russian shiploads of goods were traded for foodstuffs at San Francisco. The following year, the presidio played host to Lieutenant Otto von Kotzebue and his crew on board the *Rurik*, a ship of the Russian Imperial Navy embarked on a scientific expedition. It turned out to be a gala occasion for all concerned and, thanks to the scientific observers sailing with Kotzebue, left posterity a fine written and pictorial record of the presidio and of the natural history of San Francisco and environs.[147]

The reach of Alaskan natives, whether Aleuts or Eskimos, involved in the early nineteenth-century trade in furs from sea otters and seals is truly amazing. If one account can be credited:

In 1811 a ship belonging to Pope and Boardman of Boston, brought about thirty Kodiaks [Pacific Eskimos known as the Koniag] from Russian Alaska to San

177

Nicolás Island to hunt otter and seal. They were left there with provisions to be picked up again in about a year, the ship meanwhile sailing farther south. Meanwhile a feud broke out between the native Indians [Gabrieleños] and the Kodiaks. The majority of the native men were killed by the newcomers and the island women were forced to live with the invaders. It was about this period that Juana María was born and she may have been an offspring of Kodiak and Indian parents.[148]

In 1835 a ship was sent to the island to bring the Indians and Eskimos still living there to the mainland. Except that one person, a woman, was somehow overlooked the effort was successful. Eighteen years later, in 1853, she, too, was retrieved and brought to Santa Barbara where she died of natural causes within the year and was buried in the Mission Santa Barbara cemetery.[149]

San Nicolás Island is one of the Channel Islands, although it is not included within Channel Islands National Park. And while other versions of this affair variously identify Anacapa and San Miguel islands—both of which are in the park—as the place where it occurred, San Nicolás is almost certainly the correct location.[150]

Spain's last three decades in North America, California included, were characterized by efforts to consolidate and to defend lands already occupied rather than to extend the limits of an already over-extended empire. The Spanish-Anglo Convention of 1790, often referred to as the Nootka Convention, amounted to an admission to England by Spain that she could no longer defend what she had regarded as her rightful territories in the Pacific Northwest and elsewhere. In signing this agreement, Spain in effect consented not to extend her boundaries northward or southward from already established settlements. In the case of Alta California, this effectually meant San Francisco, although the Spaniards still had a small post at Nootka.[151]

Concerned that England might try to force her way into Alta California, in 1792 Viceroy Revillagigedo instructed the governor to be especially on the alert with regard to British intrusions (an exception being made of Vancouver). One result was the shoring up of presidial defenses at San Francisco, Monterey, and San Diego including construction of shore batteries. The 1794 Castillo de San Joaquín and Batería de San José at San Francisco were among the fruits of this policy. At the same time, the Spanish program of consolidation resulted in the founding of five new missions in the decade of the '90s and in the 1797 founding of the pueblo of Branciforte near Mission Santa Cruz.[152]

The fortification constructed to augment the defensive capabilities of the San Diego presidio was a gun battery sited at the harbor's entrance at Punta de Guijarro, an appendage of Point Loma and not far from today's entrance to Cabrillo National Monument. Construction on the battery and attendant buildings began about 1794 and was completed by 1797. Like the castillo built at San Francisco, the facility at Guijarros was dedicated to San Joaquín. Its "guns saw action only twice. In March

803, they were fired on the American brig *Leila Byrd*, which returned fire to the fort, an event that has been termed the 'Battle of San Diego Bay.' In July 1828, the American ship *Franklin* was fired upon by the battery. Both vessels sustained minor damage."[153]

Financial hardships notwithstanding, in 1815—and partially in response to the Russian presence at Fort Ross—work got underway at the San Francisco Presidio. The original Castillo de San Joaquín gave way to a whole new horseshoe-shaped fort. The old chapel was torn down in 1815 and replaced by a new one in 1817. It may have been during this period that at least one adobe wall presently incorporated within the Presidio's Officers' Club was constructed. In the 1930s a WPA-built Spanish revival addition enveloped the Spanish commandant's house while leaving an original wall on view.[154]

In 1818 the San Francisco presidio was put on alert, as were all other Spanish installations on the California coast. An American ship's captain had warned the governor, Pablo Vicente de Solá, that two ships manned by Argentine insurgents were on their way to promote the cause of Mexican independence in his province. Earlier, in 1816, Argentineans had freed themselves of Spain and the Viceroyalty of La Plata and had organized the independent United Provinces of La Plata. Now some of these same revolutionaries were said to be en route to California to liberate it—whether *californios* desired independence from Spain or not.

The ships were under the command of a French-born privateer—a polite word for "pirate"—named Hippolyte de Bouchard. Although he never attacked San Francisco, on November 20 Bouchard put in at Monterey which he easily seized and spent a week ransacking before sailing south to sack the Ortega rancho at Refugio just north of Santa Barbara. He helped himself to whatever he wanted at San Juan Capistrano, leaving California in mid-December. Earlier, about December 5, Bouchard had landed on Santa Rosa Island in today's Channel Islands National Park to take on wood and water.[155]

The attacks by ships flying the flag of Buenos Aires brought reinforcements to California in the summer of 1819 in the form of two hundred men with arms, ammunition, and artillery pieces. Some were accompanied by their wives and children. Forty foot soldiers of the San Blas infantry were assigned to the presidio at San Francisco, "but they proved more of a liability than an asset. Most of them had been kidnapped by press-gangs or recruited from jails in Nueva Galicia. Unruly and refusing to conform to military discipline, the newcomers caused considerable trouble."[156]

To accommodate the guns brought by the arrivals from San Blas, more construction was done at the San Francisco presidio. While no one knew it at the time, the flag flying over the post was soon to change—although it was January 1822 before *californios* were informed that Spain had relinquished her claim to their province in 1821. Thus Alta California remained loyal to her mother country until April 11,

1822 when Spanish officials in Monterey took the oath of allegiance to Mexico, an occasion for "religious services, cheering, the firing of guns, music, and illuminations."[157]

The nationality of California had changed, but it took longer for changes in official personnel. Governor Solá remained in his post as the first Mexican governor until November of 1822. During the interim, there was some excitement at the San Francisco presidio when rumors reached the governor that Americans or Britons had infiltrated Spanish territory in the north. Solá ordered presidial commandant Luis Antonio Argüello to investigate the rumors. He set off on October 18, 1822, with a small cannon, a herd of beef, Franciscan Fray Blas Ordaz, English-speaking interpreter-guide John Gilroy who had been in California since 1814, two ensigns, a cadet, and a strike force of fifty-two cavalry and mounted infantrymen from the Monterey and San Francisco garrisons. They saw neither Americans nor Englishmen over the next four weeks, but they managed to explore a lot of terrain no Spaniard—or Mexican—had previously set eyes on.

Their route took them to the Sacramento River, whose course they followed upstream to Cottonwood Creek. Although the precise line of travel is vague after this, they rode up the creek to its source before heading to the coast via the Trinity, Eel, and Russian rivers, crossing the Trinity Mountains in the process and heading south along the Coast Range to near Fort Ross before reaching the Marin shore south of San Rafael and taking boats across the Golden Gate to San Francisco. And while it is by no means certain, they may well have passed through a region today inundated by a man-made lake and surrounded by mountain forests now set aside as the Whiskeytown-Shasta-Trinity National Recreation Area.[158]

Spain had tried. However, any objective assessment of her brief period of hegemony in Alta California would probably agree with that of historian Bernard Bobb:

> Few were the benefits which either Spain or New Spain derived from the settlements of California, although politically it may have had a certain value as a factor in the international rivalry with England and Russia. Financially, it was a drain on an already heavily-burdened treasury. Administratively, it was one more problem for a harassed executive. Commercially, it produced nothing of notable value. Its defensive worth was dubious. It did not become a land of opportunity for great numbers of the lower classes. Only to the church was it fruitful through its containment of a considerable number of unsaved souls.[159]

Even for the church, the effort cannot be counted as a total success. Although Christianization and partial or total assimilation of Native Americans did indeed occur among a comparative few in California, for others who became ensnared in the program of mission *reducción*, the results were, quite simply, death. As in other

180

places where Europeans came into contact with Native Americans in the New World, and even where they didn't, introduced Old World diseases against which the native populations had no immunity exacted a staggering toll. Precisely how staggering is a subject of ongoing debate, but all sides agree the numbers were grim. The mission system had its unintended consequences. Writing specifically about the Franciscans' objectives at Mission San Diego, historian Robert Archibald has summarized the situation well: "The principle emerges that decent peoples whose motives as judged by their own standards are excellent, have frequently violated other people who live by different standards."[160]

The Franciscans would continue their efforts to improve the standards of their native charges under the Mexican regime, but not for long.

THE PACIFIC NORTHWEST

The concern with Russian and British encroachment that had fostered the Spanish move into Alta California also sent Spanish ships, and Spaniards, moving into the Pacific Northwest in the eighteenth century.

Although Alta California, with its fine harbors at both San Diego and San Francisco, was closer to the scene of operations in the Pacific Northwest, the principal port of embarkation, as it was for California, was the port and shipbuilding settlement of San Blas on the Gulf of California about 140 miles west of Guadalajara. While San Blas was convenient to Alta California and Sonora and had a sheltered harbor as well as a year-round supply of freshwater and hardwood, it was in a region of the Tropic of Cancer inflicted from June to October with heavy rains and plagues of disease-carrying mosquitoes.[161]

It was from the port of San Blas that the intrepid ensign, Mallorcan-born Juan José Pérez Hernández, set out in the frigate *Santiago*, alias the *Nueva Galicia*, at the end of January 1774, bound for Alta California and beyond past Strait Juan de Fuca to 55° 30' north latitude, in the vicinity of Prince of Wales Island in southeastern Alaska. This was the same Pérez who had commanded the packet boat *San Antonio* on her voyage to Alta California in 1769. His orders were to make a careful exploration of the entire Pacific coast from 60° north latitude—the neighborhood of Yakutat Bay, Alaska— south to Monterey. He was to go through the formalities of the official act of possession at each place he found suitable for settlement, including erecting a large wooden cross at the site. He was to avoid conflict with the natives, dealing with them fairly, and to make observations concerning them and their possessions and resources.

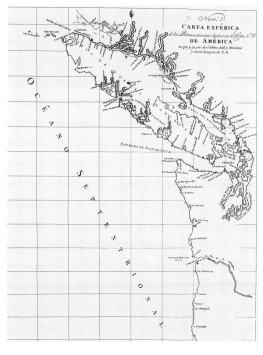

A charter showing discoveries on the northwest coast of America indicates results of the 1792 circum-navigation of Vancouver Island by Dionisio Alcalá Galiano and Cayetano Valdés in the Sutil *and* Mexicana. (From Relación del viaje hecho par las goletas Sutil y Mexicana en al año 1792, *courtesy Special Collections, Library of the University of British Columbia, Vancouver.)*

The *Santiago* got as far north as 55° 30' before turning southward while hugging the coast. During the return voyage, Pérez put in at Nootka on the west side of Vancouver Island, where he bartered with the friendly natives. Continuing south, he sighted the distant Sierra Nevada de Rosalía, the nearly 8,000-foot-high Mount Olympus in the heart of today's Olympic National Park. Before the year was out, the *Santiago* was back at San Blas having accomplished little beyond making preliminary contact with the Nootkan Indians on Vancouver Island.[162]

Because Pérez had not managed any landings or acts of possession, another sea expedition was sent out in 1775 to lay claim to this vast and still largely uncharted region. Three vessels sailed out of San Blas on March 16, but one, the *San Carlos,* was a supply ship scheduled to go only as far as Monterey. The *Santiago* and *Sonora,* by the time they reached California, were commanded by a twenty-five-year-old Basque, Bruno de Hezeta, and a thirty-two-year-old Peruvian-born *criollo,* Juan Francisco de la Bodega y Quadra.

Hezeta and the *Santiago* succeeded in getting as far north as somewhere off the west coast of Vancouver Island before turning back, while Bodega and the *Sonora* got as far as 58° 30' north latitude, or in the region of today's Glacier Bay National Park and Preserve in Alaska. During its journey, the *Sonora* lost a landing party to the Quileutes in the Hoh River area of the southern coastal portion of Olympic National Park.

It was only because of dangerous inshore winds and the fact that most of his crew was suffering from scurvy that Hezeta halted his northward voyage and turned back south. On the return trip, on October 3, he discovered what he called Puerto de la Bodega on the California coast, a place now known as Tomales Bay. Years later his name for what came to be known as Tomales Bay was confused with a smaller inlet to the north, today's Bodega Bay.

After a stop at Monterey, where Bodega and the *Sonora* caught up with Hezeta and the *Santiago*—which had preceded them to the California capital by five weeks—both vessels returned to home port at San Blas, arriving there November 20. No Russians had been seen, but the mouth of the Columbia River, El Río de San Roque, had been discovered by Hezeta. Bodega had also planted a cross on the west coast of Prince of Wales Island, but the Indians had carted it off.[163]

Since no Russians or Englishmen had been seen during these first two voyages of exploration, Spanish interest may have waned had it not been for the fact that in 1778 James Cook, searching for the elusive Strait of Anian that would offer a northern passage between the Atlantic and Pacific oceans, landed on the west coast of North America at a cape on the Oregon coast he named "Foul Weather," perhaps today's Cape Perpetua. He had somehow gotten a copy of a journal of the Hezeta-Bodega voyage of 1775. Sailing northward while keeping a journal and making charts of his own and exploring the region of the Bering Sea, Cook satisfied himself that the Northwest Passage was a myth before he sailed to the Hawaiian Islands where the natives killed him in 1779.[164]

Responding to the threat implied by Cook's voyage, in 1779 two more vessels were sent from San Blas to the far north: the flagship *Favorita*, commanded by Ignacio de Arteaga, and the *Princesa*, whose captain was Juan Bodega. The frigates left port on February 11, and once west of Baja California, they remained far out at sea planning to hit the coast at a high latitude. The vessels came to shore at Bucareli Sound on the west coast of Prince of Wales Island, and while anchored there and trading with the natives, a smallpox outbreak struck the crew of the *Princesa*—which may ultimately have been responsible for a devastating smallpox epidemic that ravaged the entire coast, killing a large percentage of its native population.[165]

Arteaga continued his northward voyage, sailing past the sites of today's Glacier Bay National Park and Preserve and Wrangell-St. Elias National Park and Preserve before reaching Port Etches on Hinchinbrook Island at the mouth of Prince William Sound. On July 22, 1779, he sent a party ashore to erect a cross and, naming the port the Puerto de Santiago de Apostól (Saint James the Apostle), he claimed the land for Spain. This was "the northernmost point at which possession was ever executed by Spanish subjects in America." Spain, however briefly, had reached her outer limit in the New World.[166]

From Hinchinbrook Island the seamen followed a southwesterly course to the tip of the Kenai Peninsula where they made another act of possession, sailing past the modern Kenai Fjords National Park on the way.[167]

Because the Arteaga expedition found no Englishmen and because it was discerned that Russian activities were confined to the Aleutian Islands, the Spanish crown assumed it could rest on its laurels, especially since it had now made formal acts of possession as far north as near the 61st parallel. Furthermore, Spain found itself involved in a war with England on the side of the infant United States and there were other global concerns that seemed more pressing.[168]

In the early 1780s word got out concerning the bounty of valuable sea otters on the Pacific coast of North America, and the rush was on, this time led by the Russians and English but followed tentatively by the Americans and French. In 1784 the

To counter possible Russian expansion, Spaniards sent sea expeditions northward as early as the 1770s, past places such as Muir Inlet in today's Glacier Bay National Park and Preserve. (Carr Clifton.)

Russians planted their first fur trade outpost on Kodiak Island, followed by another on the nearby mainland in 1786. Britishers began to arrive at Nootka in 1785. In 1786 Jean François Galaup, Comte de la Pérouse, landed at Alaska's Lituya Bay and calling it Port de Français, claimed it for France. Lituya Bay is within Glacier Bay National Park and Preserve. Two years later the American John Kendrick put in at Nootka and rode out the winter in the sound. While all this was happening Spaniards contented themselves with the less valued sea otter pelts that could easily be obtained off the coast of Alta California.[169]

Finally, in 1788 two more vessels set sail from San Blas bound for Alaska: the flagship *Princesa*, commanded by Esteban José Martínez Fernández y Martínez, and the *San Carlos*, commanded by Gonzalo López de Haro. As ordered, they made their way to Prince William Sound. Near here they separated, running their individual courses southwestward, both doubtless sailing past Kenai Fjords National Park as well as south of Aniakchak National Monument and Preserve on the Alaska Peninsula before rendezvousing at the Russian outpost at Dutch Harbor on Unalaska Island in the Aleutian chain. The Russian operating the post remarked on the dark complexions of his welcome visitors, and Martínez explained to him that most of his crew were either blacks, Indians, or mulattos. After a few weeks the two ships made their way back to San Blas, López de Haro getting there in October and Martínez in December. Based on what they had learned, it was Martínez's recommendation that Spain permanently occupy Nootka ahead of other foreign powers.[170]

Partly on the strength of his own recommendation, in 1789 Martínez was sent back to Nootka on the *Princesa* and López de Haro on the *San Carlos*. During their stay there were non-violent confrontations with ships flying the flags of England, the United States, and Portugal, the Spaniards' consistently asserting their claim by right of prior discovery. They underscored their claim by confiscating four English ships and appropriating their mixed crews of "assorted Europeans, Hindus, Filipinos, Malays, Hawaiians, and Chinese." Nootka was nothing if not cosmopolitan. And the Spaniards erected a fort, San Miguel, on the island.

While all of this was taking place, Captain José de Cañizares—he who with Ayala had mapped San Francisco Bay in 1775—arrived in Nootka on board the *Aranzazu* with word that Charles III had died the previous year and that Viceroy Manuel Antonio Flores had ordered the abandonment of Nootka before winter. Martínez reluctantly complied and returned to San Blas in early December with many Chinese artisans in tow.[171]

A new viceroy, the Conde de Revillagigedo, sent more expeditions northward in early February 1790 in an effort to hold the territory. Francisco de Eliza, who had taken part in the Spanish capture of Pensacola, sailed on the *Concepción*. He was to be the new commander at Nootka. Also going to the north was Salvador Fidalgo on he *San Carlos* and Manuel Quimper on the *Princesa Real*. Eliza was to build a new ort at Nootka to be manned by Catalonian volunteers.

From Nootka, Salvador Fidalgo set out to assess the nature and extent of the Russian presence in Alaska, sailing to Prince William Sound where he left on the map he names Córdova and Valdez, the latter to honor Antonio Valdés y Bazán, minister of marine and the Indies. From Prince William Sound the men rounded the Kenai Peninsula into Cook Inlet, possibly pausing to examine more closely one of the fjords in today's Kenai Fjords National Park. From the head of Cook Inlet Fidalgo reversed his route, sailed to within sight of the Russian settlement on Kodiak Island, and then all the way back to San Blas. If his course lay down the western side of Kodiak Island, he passed today's Katmai National Park and Preserve.[172]

What happened subsequently is described by historian Warren Cook:

> Events at Friendly Cove [Nootka] in 1789 generated a crisis that took Madrid within a hair's breadth of war, but Carlos IV and [cabinet head] Floridablanca eventually backed away from a conflict in which there was no likelihood of assistance from any useful ally. Distressing circumstances in Europe, rather than particular assets and liabilities of Spain's position on the northwest coast, determined the outcome. Madrid's yielding had little to do with the validity of Spanish claims to the area in question; the consequence was a matter of which contender could marshal the most coercive power in Europe. . . .
>
> The Nootka Convention of [October] 1790 gave Britain her first internationally recognized title of access to a portion of the Pacific coast of North America. Its terms made an irreparable breach in Spain's claim to exclusive sovereignty along that coast.[173]

This first of what proved to be three Nootka conventions by no means laid to rest Spain's immediate interest in the region.

The official accounts of the voyages of Cook and of La Pérouse had fired the imaginations of the European public as well as of official planners. Spain's response was to outfit a scientific expedition of its own, one commanded by Alejandro Malaspina and accompanied by naturalists, astronomers, and artists. The twin corvettes of the expedition, the *Descubierta* and *Atrevida*, sailed from Cádiz on July 30, 1789. They traveled around Cape Horn to Acapulco, making extended visits and scientific observations and collections at Trinidad, the Río de la Plata, Chile, and Peru as they went. Leaving Acapulco in May 1791, the vessels headed directly to the Alaskan coast at Cabo Engaño near the head of the Gulf of Alaska. From here they sailed northward and westward along the Gulf before turning back to the mouth of Yakutat Bay next to today's Wrangell-St. Elias National Park and Preserve, whose largest

185

body of ice now bears the name of the expedition's leader, Malaspina Glacier. At Yakutat Bay, the men collected native artifacts and artists Tomás de Suría and José Cardero made drawings of the coastal Tlingit people living there.[174]

From Yakutat, Malaspina's expedition headed southward within sight of land past Glacier Bay National Park and Preserve to Nootka. From there the route lay down the Washington, Oregon, and California coasts with a stop at Monterey before continuing to Acapulco. After a further voyage that would take them to Manila, Australia, and New Zealand before reversing direction around Cape Horn and back to Spain, the ships arrived at Cádiz in September 1794 to a gala reception. Artist Cardero had been left in Mexico.[175]

Under terms of the first Nootka convention, Spain had not relinquished total claim to Nootka and environs. She had simply relinquished exclusive sovereignty over Nootka Sound, recognizing the right of Englishmen to be there as well. Commander Eliza and his fort remained in place.

The year 1792 became the most active for Spain in the Pacific Northwest when she dispatched four expeditions to explore and to help set a definite boundary demarcating the competing claims of the English and Spanish crowns. The first of these expeditions, to set the boundaries, was headed by Juan Bodega y Quadra on board the frigate *Santa Gertrudis* followed by the brigantine *Activa* and the *Princesa*. With Bodega when the ships left San Blas early in 1792 were José Mariano Moziño Suárez Losada, a naturalist who would leave posterity with an invaluable account of the Nootka region and its native inhabitants, and artist Atanasio Echeverría y Godoy, whose depictions of plants, animals, people, and scenes in and around Nootka have since become famous.[176]

The other three major expeditions in 1792 were those of Jacinto Caamaño, who concentrated his explorations between Prince of Wales Island in southeastern Alaska and Nootka; of Salvador Fidalgo, who established a Spanish settlement, Núñez Gaona, at Neah Bay on the south side of the mouth of the Strait of Juan de Fuca; and of Dionisio Alcalá Galiano and Cayetano Valdés, assisted by their scribe and artist José Cardero. Their ships were the *Sutil* and *Mexicana*. The latter, on their return to California from Nootka in September 1792, followed the coast from Cape Mendocino in the north until the men sighted Point Reyes before heading directly to Monterey. Thanks largely to the observations and depictions by José Cardero, this expedition has achieved considerable status among historians of Alta California's late colonial period.[177]

When Bodega went to Nootka in 1792 it was as a commissioner to negotiate the Spanish side in the dispute with England over the location of boundaries. His British counterpart in these negotiations was George Vancouver, who arrived at Nootka with the *Discovery* and the *Chatham* in August of that year. Bodega and Vancouver were unable to agree on terms, Bodega being willing to relinquish only Nootka while

186

Vancouver wanted everything north of San Francisco. They agreed to refer the problem to their respective sovereigns. Bodega sailed south to Monterey, where he remained from October 9, 1792 to January 13, 1793. Vancouver also sailed south, visiting the San Francisco presidio before stopping at Monterey, where he met again with his diplomatic adversary. When Bodega left Monterey it was to sail to San Blas; Vancouver went to the Hawaiian Islands before returning to the Northwest for further explorations and to await instructions from London.[178]

A second Nootka convention was signed between Spain and England in 1793 in which Spain agreed to pay for lands, ships, and cargoes seized by them at Nootka in 1790. But it was 1794 before the third and final convention settled the major issue concerning Nootka: whether or not Spaniards had a right to maintain their post there. Until 1794 Spain was de facto the master at Nootka. But the 1794 convention called for the "mutual abandonment of Nootka" by both countries.

Charged with seeing to the formal abandonment was the new commandant of San Blas and commissioner for Nootka, Brigadier General José Manuel de Álava. He left for the north with Salvador Fidalgo in mid-June on board the *Princesa*, which by then must have known the way by heart. Álava met with Vancouver at Nootka on the first day of September 1794, but both had to wait for specific instructions from their respective nations concerning how finally to settle the issue. The Iberian Álava, on seeing the country, wondered aloud how the region "could ever have been the object of contention between our respective sovereigns."[179]

Word failed to reach the two commissioners as they waited in the north, so in mid-October they set sail for the south. The Spanish general left behind a permanent marker, however: his family name. It survives as Cape Alava on the coast of Olympic National Park near the northern boundary of its Ozette unit and the southern edge of the Ozette segment of the Makah Indian Reservation. Half the cape is in the park; the northern half is on the reservation. The waterlogged portion of the Ozette archeological site in the vicinity of Cape Alava provided its investigators with extraordinarily well-preserved wooden, woven, and fiber objects dating from shortly before A.D. 1500, when a clay slide buried a portion of the village.[180]

In 1795, when Nootka was finally evacuated, the British commissioner was Lieutenant Thomas Pearce; Álava continued as Spain's commissioner. As provided in the 1794 convention, the Spanish fort was dismantled and evacuated. The native Nootkans soon reclaimed the site and returned it to its pre-Spanish appearance.[181]

Although Nootka was abandoned, Spain was still not finished with its concerns for the Northwest. Between 1804 and 1806 four successive Spanish expeditions were sent out from Santa Fe in efforts to intercept and halt the United States expedition led by Meriwether Lewis and William Clark to the Pacific. The Americans, however, managed to reach the mouth of the Columbia River in 1805 unmolested by Spaniards.[182]

Until as late as 1819 there remained Spaniards who believed their nation had a legitimate claim to what by then had become conceptualized as Oregon Country. England, the United States, and Russia laid the same claim. American John Jacob Astor had founded his fur-trading post in Astoria in 1811. And earlier, in 1792, American Robert Gray had sailed into the Columbia River. The activities of Gray, Lewis and Clark, and Astor had given the United States a voice in the region.

Insofar as Spain was concerned, the matter was finally put to rest in the wake of the Adams-Onís, or Transcontinental, Treaty of February 22, 1819. Using the 1818 edition of John Melish's "Map of the United States and the Contiguous British and Spanish Possessions" as their guide, American and Spanish negotiators resolved disputes not only over the boundaries of Texas, Louisiana, and West Florida, but also on Spain's northern boundary in the west. A line was drawn along the 42nd parallel from the headwaters of the Arkansas River to the Pacific Ocean. Thus the northern boundaries of what today are the states of California and Nevada were agreed upon with Spain left in possession of lands to the south. This line also conceded Spanish ownership of all of today's Arizona, Utah, New Mexico, Texas, a strip along the southern Wyoming border, nearly three-quarters of Colorado, the southwestern corner of Kansas, and the Oklahoma Panhandle. It was February 1821 before ratifications were exchanged and this treaty between Spain and the United States went into effect.[183]

In the end, nearly its whole American enterprise crumbling, Spain's hopes for the far northwest, whatever these may have been, were erased by reality. Events beginning in Mexico in 1810 would ensure it forever. But the mark of Spain in the Pacific Northwest—if only in names on the land, the California and Oregon boundary, and in the words of historians—has been a lasting one. The names and the words recall the distant reach of a once mighty empire.

188

Federal Mexico as symbolized by the Mexican eagle above a prickly pear cactus, each pad of which represents a state or territory of the new republic as defined by the Constitution of 1824. (From Vito Alessio Robles, Coahuila y Texas des de la consumación de la independencia *[2 vols] Mexico, 1945-46. Courtesy David J. Weber.)*

190

Nations are not a fact of nature. They exist nowhere outside the perceptions of people. In 1821 Agustín de Iturbide's perception of the new Mexico was, like that of Spain from which independence had just been won, as an empire. But three years later, in 1824, Iturbide's empire gave way to the Estados Unidos Mexicanos, the United States of Mexico, and a republic with nineteen states and four territories came into being.[1]

The fledgling Mexico was a country of disparate parts and peoples. From tropics to snow-capped mountain peaks; from mountain masses to valleys, plains, and coastal shorelines; and from temperate zones to North America's driest deserts, her population consisted of Native Americans who spoke dozens or even hundreds of mutually unintelligible languages; of Spaniards, both *criollos* and *peninsulares*; of blacks, *mestizos*, *coyotes*, mulattoes, Afro-mestizos, *lobos*, *zambos*, and people of every conceivable mixture of races; and of a relatively small, wealthy aristocracy divided from masses of people at the lowest rung of the socio-economic ladder.

It had been the might of Spain rather than internal cohesiveness that had glued the parts together. Now that the glue was gone, parts were bound to be lost.

[I]n 1821 only few Mexicans could have had premonitions of the drama that was about to unfold. The large majority of the population had not been affected directly by the wars [for independence], and the illiterate masses most assuredly did not know that a change, important at least for those on the threshold of power, had taken place. The nineteenth century would vindicate the general apathy of the rural Mexican, for his life would change little, if at all. The fate of the Mexican Indian continued to rest totally in the hands of others, as it had for the last three hundred years. His privations went unnoticed. He could take little solace in the fact that the politically articulate groups in Mexico City that completely overlooked his interests demonstrated precious little ability to govern even themselves.[2]

TEXAS

The first of Spain's former northern possessions to fall from the hands of Mexico was Tejas.

Just before Mexico declared her independence from Spain, a Connecticut-born entrepreneur named Moses Austin received permission from the last Spanish governor, Antonio María Martínez, to establish a colony of three hundred families in the province. In this role, Austin was regarded as an *empresario*, or contractor, and his grant and similar ones which followed were known as empresario grants. The senior Austin died before he could start his project, but his son, Stephen, took over.

MEXICO

An 1830s painting by Lino Sánchez y Tapia of an ideally-outfitted Mexican presidial soldier. (Courtesy Thomas Gilcrease Institute of American History and Art, Tulsa, Oklahoma.)

No sooner had he begun work on the colony when Tejas changed hands. The younger Austin had to go to Mexico City, where early in 1823 he got the necessary approval. By the late 1820s Austin had issued 297 grants. In the meantime, the granting system was broadened in 1825 by a law which allowed grants to go directly to individuals rather than through an empresario. That same year, the Mexican Congress combined Tejas and Coahuila into a single state, Coahuila y Tejas, and Tejas lost some of the autonomy it had enjoyed briefly under Iturbide's "empire." Tejas had only one representative in the new state government, increasing to two in 1827.[3]

Thanks to a liberal policy of granting lands to foreigners, who overwhelmingly were Americans, it was not too many years before Mexicans, or *Tejanos*, were vastly outnumbered in their own state. Suspicious of American plans for Tejas, Mexico banned the empresario system and further Anglo-American immigration in 1830. But because of the protests of Texans, primarily Anglos but including a significant number of Tejanos, the ban was lifted in 1834. That year and in 1835, the Mexican government began selling Tejas land directly to individuals, thereby saving profits for itself and eliminating the middlemen.[4]

The partial secularization of the remaining Tejas missions in San Antonio that had begun in 1793-94 became total secularization under republican Mexico in 1823 and 1824. The church structures at former missions San José, Concepción, Capistrano, and Espada—all units of San Antonio Missions National Historical Park today— were turned over to the secular pastor of San Fernando de Béxar, the Reverend Refugio de la Garza, and his assistant, the Reverend José Antonio Valdez—the only two priests then in the San Antonio region. The churches "were completely neglected during the remaining years of the Mexican regime and of the first years of the Republic of Texas."[5]

Among other things, secularization meant that the town council, or *ayuntamiento*, of San Antonio's civil settlement, San Fernando de Béxar, became solely responsible for handling disputes among individuals concerning what formerly had been mission lands and water. The town council, depending on the period, consisted of a mayor/ judge, four alderman who were also inspectors and tax collectors, and a city attorney. Voting rights were limited by law to a small proportion of the male population.[6]

After the partial secularization of the missions in 1794, mission Indians who remained in their communities became *vecinos*, which in theory made them citizens of the town and put them on equal footing with non-Indian residents. Previously, the Franciscans had managed mission lands and water as trustees on behalf of their Native American neophytes. With partial secularization, "partial" because Franciscans remained as pastors and teachers in the four churches, vecinos' rights to their lands and allotments of irrigation water from the Río San Antonio were recognized. The lands included agricultural fields (*labores*), garden patches (*fanegas*) and pastoral ranchos.[7]

Lino Sánchez y Tapia based this painting of Lipan Apaches near Laredo, Texas, on an 1828 sketch by a relative. (Courtesy Thomas Gilcrease Institute of American History and Art, Tulsa, Oklahoma.)

When *vecinos* found themselves in disputes over land, water, or other property with citizens, the matter was adjudicated by the town government. Traditionally, resolution of problems called for testimony from all concerned parties. Decisions were rendered based in part of the judge's knowledge of the claimants, a system that worked reasonably well in small communities in which most people knew one another on a face-to-face basis. Moreover, "the focus of Spanish and Mexican law was on the resolution of conflict and the accommodation of conflicting interests, serving the greatest interest in the community and its harmony," rather than on "common law ideas of absolute rights . . . serving the interests of the individual."8

Nonetheless, "it is fairly safe to generalize that the former mission Indians (recategorized as vecinos), uncertain of the intricacies of law and taxation, became displaced as property owners by avaricious townspeople who were more knowledgeable in the acquisition of real estate."9

The irony is that a similar fate would befall the new Hispanic owners of former mission properties in an Anglo-American Texas after 1836. Historian Almaráz summarizes the effects of mission secularization on Native Americans:

Comanches in Mexican-period Texas, as documented by Lino Sánches y Tapia. (Courtesy Thomas Gilcrease Institute of American History and Art, Tulsa, Oklahoma.)

In the formative years of independent Mexico, the national government generally respected the temporal properties in the care of frontier missionaries, particularly the churches. When the final secularization of the [San Antonio] missions occurred in 1823 (completed in 1824), national authorities delegated responsibility for carrying out the mandate to state and local officials. Although Mexico's national colonization law of 1824 protected mission properties from widespread encroachment, the process of alienating the irrigable lands had already begun under the supervision of municipal officials. In 1825, the legislature of the dual state of Coahuila y Tejas authorized the governor to "alienate the lands that pertained to the extinguished missions." In San Antonio the result was merely a confirmation or reaffirmation of what already had transpired at the former Franciscan missions, especially the two within geographic proximity to the corporate limits of the city, namely, [San Antonio de] Valero [i.e., the "Alamo"] and Concepción. . . .

In [the] latter [1823-24] period [of secularization] there did not seem to be any overt concern about respecting property rights of previous [Native American] owners at the missions. In the meantime, the principle of entail (limiting the inheritance of landed estates to a specific line of heirs) had come under criticism in Spain by politicians of liberal persuasion. Accordingly, if entail had been jealously defended as a prerogative by American-born Spaniards [criollos], how could the privilege by shared with mission Indians? Without either experience or understanding of the legal process to protect private property, it is conceivable that many mission *vecinos* disposed of their newly acquired land holdings for a pittance. Also, they possibly became indebted to some individuals who petitioned

193

the state to award the real estate as satisfaction of an outstanding mortgage. When [after 1793-94] the second distribution transpired (1823-1824), the land around the missions was the same; only the names of grantees had changed [from those of Indians to those of non-Indians].[10]

Although alienation of lands at Mission Concepción occurred more slowly than elsewhere, between 1806 and 1829 gente de razón with such surnames as Huízar, Beramendi, Castillo, Calvo, Montes, and Ruiz became the primary recipients of former mission and vecino holdings. At Mission San José y San Miguel de Aguayo, the town council of San Fernando de Béxar approved twenty-five grants in the immediate wake of the 1824 secularization order, while at San Juan Capistrano, there was spirited competition among both men and women for the mission's fertile agricultural lands. Here, even the mission's walls and ruined structures were given an appraisal based on the value of their stones estimated by the cartload. Many stones were bought and hauled away, some by Bachiller Francisco Maynes, a former military chaplain who had been recently assigned to the San Fernando church.[11]

Mission Espada suffered the same fate as the others. The stones of its twenty-eight structures were valued by the oxcartload, many of them sold and hauled away. Of the twenty-five grantees of the mission's agricultural lands in 1824, sixteen were townspeople or non-mission residents, while nine were owners of mission structures.[12]

Historian Almaráz summarizes the fate of the missions under Mexico:

> Especially during the brief fifteen-year period of Mexican sovereignty, following the inauguration of the duostate of Coahuila y Tejas and the transfer of the political capital from San Antonio to distant Saltillo, the mission churches and ancillary structures endured the ravages of time, weather, and humanity. As a rule, municipal government (initially Spanish- and later Anglo-dominant) viewed the former missions as windfall stockpiles of construction rubble for the convenience of preferred citizens. With subtle twists and pivots, governmental intercession in the mission properties continued throughout the nineteenth century.[13]

The San Antonio missions were destined to play a final role in the history of Mexican Tejas. In early October 1835 a battle was fought between Texans and Mexican military forces at the town of Gonzales in a dispute over possession of a cannon that had been given the citizens of Gonzales to protect themselves against Indian attack. Not only did the Texans keep the cannon, but the attacking soldiers were also forced to retreat to San Antonio. In the days that followed, armed Texans captured Goliad and its supplies and ammunition and held a formal "Consultation of All Texans" in which a provisional state government was formed. They also sent armed men to capture San Antonio, men joined by 135 Tejano troops who also wanted some degree of

utonomy for Tejas. Like the Anglo Americans, they were opposed to the dictator
General Antonio López de Santa Anna who wanted a strong central government.[14]

On October 22 the Texas invaders moved toward the missions along the San
Antonio River. Stephen Austin, who was in charge of the entire Texan army, directed
James Bowie and James Fannin—in charge of the San Antonio operation—to choose
one mission as a campsite that would control the road from Goliad. By late afternoon,
the Texans had driven Mexican sentries away from Mission Espada and had seized
what was left of the buildings. The next day they reconnoitered San José and San
Juan missions, but finding nothing there of use to them they again spent the night at
Espada. On October 24 there was a skirmish at Espada, resulting in the death of one
Mexican forager and the wounding of others, and on October 27 Austin himself
arrived at the abandoned mission.[15]

By that night the Bowie and Fannin contingent of the Texan force was in control of
the abandoned Mission Concepción, and the stage was set for a real battle. The next
day the Texans soundly defeated a force of Mexican cavalry, infantry, and artillery
led by Colonel Domingo de Ugartechea and Lieutenant Colonel don José María
Mendosa. In less than two months, it was over—at least for the time being. General
Martín Perfecto de Cós surrendered on December 11, agreeing to leave Texas and
never to return north of the Río Grande. The missions within San Antonio Missions
National Historical Park had played their final role in the drama of Mexican Texas.[16]

While the downstream churches dropped from Mexican-period history, the north-
ernmost and oldest of the five and the first to have been totally secularized, San
Antonio de Valero, was destined to become a symbol of Texans' identity. General
Santa Anna did not view kindly the revolt of the Texans, and in 1836 he marched on
Texas, arriving at San Antonio on February 23. Here at what once had been Mission
San Antonio but what was by then known as the Alamo, he found the Texans—187
of them combatants, including seven who were Tejanos—fortified within the walls of
the old mission. Although Santa Anna won the battle for the Alamo, he lost a major
engagement on April 21 and was captured. On May 14 the Mexican capitulation was
formalized and the Republic of Texas was born.[17]

From the Tejanos' perspective the victory of the Texans was not an unqualified success. Historians Teja and Wheat provide a view from San Antonio, one that also summarizes the dilemma ultimately shared by Mexicans in the remainder of Mexico's
northernmost states:

The 6 March 1836 assault by Mexican troops on the Alamo in San Antonio, Texas, reinforced the determination of republican rebels elsewhere to fight on for independence. (Painting by Donald M. Yena courtesy Mr. and Mrs. Frank Horlock.)

> The Tejanos of Béxar were caught in the middle of a crisis that they had not cre-
> ated and could not control. The rush of the events of the mid-1830s further iso-
> lated the Bexareños from Mexico and Anglo Texas alike. Finally the great hopes
> Bexareños had nurtured for so long went up in the smoke of the Texas
> Revolution. Though many Tejanos ultimately sided with the revolutionaries

195

against Santa Anna, the independence movement was not only wrested from their hands but also left them outsiders in their own land. Thus the Tejanos of San Antonio de Béxar were forced to seek their own destiny on the margin of a new Texas society.[18]

It was in Texas that the flashpoint of the Mexican War took place in the spring of 1846. United States President James K. Polk sent General Zachary Taylor and 4,000 regular troops to south Texas and the north bank of the Río Grande near present-day Brownsville. After shots were fired across the river and other border skirmishes took place, Mexican President Mariano Paredes ordered General Pedro Ampudia to cross the river and attack Taylor's forces near Fort Brown. "American blood has been shed on American soil," Polk cried, and the war was on.

Th initial battles of the Mexican War were fought on Texas soil, the first at Resaca de la Palma on May 8, 1846 and the second at Palo Alto on the next day. Both engagements were won by U.S. forces and both involved General Taylor and Mexican General Mariano Arista. The Palo Alto National Battlefield near Brownsville is now preserved in its rural setting and its story interpreted by the National Park Service. [19]

NEW MEXICO

When the Mexican Empire assumed sovereignty over Nuevo México in 1821, the once-great Pecos Pueblo was already close to giving up the ghost. The settling of San Miguel del Vado had doomed Pecos's "gateway" status, and the census of 1799 had been the last to show Pecos with more Indians than non-Indians.

Under Mexico's 1824 constitution, Nuevo México was accorded the status of territory rather than that of state—a tacit acknowledgement of its remoteness from Mexico City and its insignificant standing in the new nation's economy and polity. None of this mattered greatly to average Nuevo Mexicanos.[20]

Similarly, formal declarations of mission secularization after 1826 had little practical effect on most missions in Nuevo México. This is because Franciscans moved into existing communities, unlike the situation in Tejas and California where the friars had actually created communities (*reducciones*). As long as Franciscans resided in the missions, they lived in the conventos and consumed the products of one or two fields. But they "owned" nothing. When they departed, ownership was left entirely in community hands.[21]

As early as 1813 assaults by outsiders had begun against Pecos lands. In 1814 because a Spaniard had requested, and received, a grant neighboring Pecos, the Pecos lands had been formally measured. The pueblo, like other pueblos in Nuevo México, was by then entitled to four square leagues, the rough equivalent of twenty-seven square miles. The surveyor had used as the center point of his survey the *cruz mayor* or large cross, in the middle of the community's cemetery which was considerably

196

outh of the pueblo. This had chopped off valuable acreage to the north. The domain f a future Pecos National Historical Park was being shrunk.[22]

Others continued to chop away at Pecos real estate, but it was under Mexico's egime in 1825 that the really serious chopping got underway. Because the handful of ecos still living in their pueblo were unable to work their farms, Governor artolomé Baca declared them vacant and unused and opened most of the village's our square leagues to outsiders.

With or without grants they came. Almost overnight dozens of families settled the "Cañón de Pecos." Beginning with the baptisms of two male Roybal infants in the mission church, April 16, 1825, mention of Hispanos from the Cañón de Pecos became more and more frequent. This in fact was the beginning of the present-day village of Pecos. By the early 1830s, the priest at San Miguel del Vado was listing settlers merely "from Pecos," and in May of 1834, he buried a boy "in the chapel of Pecos." Plainly they were there to stay.[23]

The natives still living in the village protested the alienation of their lands, but to no vail. They may have won their case in court, but the settlers—squatters, actually— emained.[24]

Meanwhile, as soon as word reached Santa Fe in 1821 that Nuevo México was no onger under Spain's control, trade barriers between Nuevo México and foreign powers vere lifted. Poised to take advantage of the situation was William Becknell, a Missouri trader in his early thirties who left Arrow Rock, Missouri, on September 1, 1821, with some twenty men and a pack train of goods for the New Mexican market. Te took a path to Santa Fe whose genesis had lain in the period of Spain's possession of Louisiana and St. Louis, a time when Spain strove to link the commercial centers of its various northwestern possessions.[25]

For Becknell and for the thousands who followed him over the Santa Fe Trail until he coming of the railroad in 1879 lessened the route's importance, San Miguel del Vado "was the port of entry, the ancient pueblo of the Pecos no more than a curious elic up the trail a ways." Twenty-five years after he had first seen Pecos, Becknell published a description of it from memory:

Mexican muleteers prepare for an 1830s trek to Missouri via the Santa Fe Trail. (From Commerce of the Prairies *by Josiah Gregg, 1845.)*

"Day's End at Pecos" depicts Mexican and American Santa Fe Trail traders camping near the ruins of Pecos. (Roy Anderson painting from the collection of Pecos National Historical Park, New Mexico.)

We stopped at night [November 30, 1821] at the ancient Indian village of Peccas about fifteen miles from San Miguel. I slept in the Fort [i.e., the pueblo proper], which encloses two or three acres in an oblong, the sides of which are bounded by brick [stone] houses three stories high, and without any entrances in front. . . . I was informed by the Spaniards and Indians that this town and Fort are of unknown antiquity, and stood there in considerable splendor in the time of the Conquerors. . . . The Indians have lost all tradition of the settlement of the town of Peccas. It stood a remarkable proof of the advance made by them in the arts of civilization before the Spaniards came among them. All the houses are well built and showed marks of comfort and refinement. The inhabitants, who were all Indians, treated us with great kindness and hospitality. In the evening I employed an Indian to take my horses to pasture, and in the morning when he brought them up I asked him what I should pay him. He asked for powder and I was about to give him some, when the Spanish officer forbade me, saying it was against the law to supply the Indians with ammunition. Arms are kept out of their hands by their masters who prohibit all trade in those articles with any of the tribes around them. On the next day in the evening we came in sight of Santa Fe.[26]

The Franciscans had built a chapel at San Miguel del Vado in 1805, and after that, friars stationed there administered to the needs of Pecos so long as those needs existed. The last baptism of an Indian at Pecos was performed on June 2, 1828; by the end of the year, the last Franciscan at San Miguel del Vado had left to be replaced by a secular priest on New Year's Day 1829. An episcopal visitation to San Miguel in 1833 made no mention of Pecos.[27]

Whether the bishop mentioned them or not, about thirty or forty native Towas of Pecos were still there in 1833. But not for long. Pecos had suffered horrendously from smallpox as well as at the hands of other Native Americans. In 1828 they had been raided by Indians who were probably Arapahos and Cheyennes. These calamities, not to mention the appropriation of their property by Mexicans, finally forced them to move away about 1838. The few survivors made their way to Jémez Pueblo where, at least, the natives also spoke Towa. The details of the abandonment—including precisely when it occurred, the numbers of people involved, and the route of travel to Jémez—are obscure and shrouded in romantic fantasy. The outlines, however, are clear. The Pecos survive today in the Pueblo of Jémez and their former home survives as Pecos National Historical Park. "Actually, neither people nor place really died. They simply parted company."[28]

In 1836, two years before the remaining Pecos left their home, someone with the initials "O.R." engraved them with the date on El Morro. The paucity of Mexican-period inscriptions on the face of these cliffs speaks volumes concerning the meanness of life in remote, isolated, and nearly forgotten Mexican-period Nuevo México.[29]

Mexican Nuevo México came abruptly to an end on August 19, 1846, when General Stephen Watts Kearny rode unopposed into the plaza at the capital of Santa Fe and read a proclamation telling people that "New Mexico" had now become a territory of the United States and that its people would henceforth be American citizens. By the time of the Mexican War the commerce of New Mexico had become more closely tied to the United States and St. Louis than to Mexico City via the Camino Real. With few exceptions, its people were in no mood for armed resistance.

Once in Santa Fe, Kearny divided his army into three segments. One, under Colonel Sterling Price, remained in Santa Fe as the New Mexican occupation force. A second, under Alexander Doniphan, patrolled in Navajo country before being dispatched southward in December to Chihuahua City to engage the Mexicans there. His route took him down the Río Grande to El Paso, crossing the river in the vicinity of the present day Chamizal National Memorial. Kearny himself continued his move toward California, leading his men down the Gila to the Colorado and across the Colorado to southern California. They paused along the way at the Casa Grande ruins.[30]

Kearny's proclamation and the New Mexicans' widespread—if not total—acquiescence marked the de facto end for Mexican New Mexico. But not until February 2, 1848 and the signing by the United States and Mexico of the Treaty of Guadalupe Hidalgo bringing a formal end to the Mexican War did New Mexico—as was the case with Alta California—truly become a United States territory. It was a territory that included not only the present New Mexican boundaries, but also large portions of west Texas and southern Wyoming, southwestern Kansas, all but the northeastern quarter of Colorado, the Oklahoma Panhandle, much of eastern Utah, and nearly all of the area north of the Gila River that was to become Arizona. Parts of the southern boundary, the so-called Mesilla Strip adjacent to El Paso and today's Chamizal National Memorial, remained in dispute for another six years. What is not in dispute is the fact that Mexican territorial losses as a result of the treaty, combined with its 1836 loss of Texas, cost the young nation about half of her territory. It was, admittedly, the least populated half and the most remote from Mexican centers of commerce and power. But modern Mexicans have not forgotten the loss of these lands a century and a half ago.[31]

The Hispanic legacy begun in New Mexico with don Juan de Oñate's 1598 colonization has remained strong in the forty-seventh state. Although Hispanos throughout the territory suffered a fate similar to that visited on southern Texans after 1836, with disputes over land and water generally being resolved in favor of Anglo Americans, the Spanish and Mexican presence is more readily apparent throughout today's New Mexico than in any other state in the union. Spanish-surnamed individuals are found in every stratum of modern New Mexican society and in virtually every occupation. New Mexico is a place where language, architecture, food, music, law, general historical awareness of the region's Hispanic past, and social, economic,

199

and political networks persist as forceful reminders of continuity from beginning, ultimately attributable to a time in 1492 when Christopher Columbus found what was for Europeans a whole New World.

SONORA (SOUTHERN ARIZONA)

An engraving of Mission San José de Tumacácori, ca. 1864. (From A Tour Through Arizona 1864 by J. Ross Browne.)

Late in May 1822, when northern Sonora's Mission Tumacácori was a part of Mexico rather than of Spain, Fray Ramón Liberós arrived to take over the post from Fray Juan Bautista Estelric, who had been transferred because of a scandal involving his relationship with a woman by whom, it was rumored, he had fathered two children. Mocking his Franciscan vows of poverty, he had secreted away "in money, in gold and silver blanks, close to a thousand pesos, clothes, and superfluous things."[32]

Scandalous behavior aside, Father Estelric had at least begun a vigorous building program at Tumacácori, during which he worked on the new church by closing off the transepts whose foundations had been laid earlier, raising the walls to their fourteen-foot level, and building a dome over the sanctuary.[33]

Father Liberós carried on. The barrel vault of the sacristy was completed as was the final level of the bell tower. The walls reached their present height; a flat viga-supported roof was put in place; the facade was built as was a cylindrical mortuary chapel; the convento was overhauled; and the sacristy was finished. And sometime before Fray Liberós departed in 1828, he had changed the patronage of the mission from San José to that of La Purísima Concepción. The remains of the church he left behind are largely those seen by visitors to today's Tumacacori unit of Tumacacori National Historical Park. The still-standing ruins of Tumacácori are a Mexican, rather than a Spanish, monument—although the tall, blue-eyed, dark-haired Father Liberós was himself a Spaniard born in Aragón in 1789.[34]

Not that it mattered much on the frontier, but in 1824 the new Mexican government created the State of Occidente in the place of the former State of Sonora, which itself had been created out of the earlier combined State of Sonora y Sinaloa. What did matter was that two years later, another of the many epidemics that periodically ravaged settlements along the Santa Cruz River struck Tumacácori. Identified as measles, the disease hit with a vengeance and left Father Liberós and his mission with only eighteen families and a few children.[35]

In 1826 word also came that a party of thirty-seven foreign trappers led by "Old Bill" Williams and Céran St. Vrain had been seen among the Gila River O'odham villages. They had told the Indians they had permission to trap the Gila and were, in fact, carrying a passport issued by Mobile-born Governor Antonio Narbona of Nuevo México. Theirs was the first recorded visit of American beaver trappers to what later would become southern Arizona, but it would not be the last. They and those who

200

ollowed them on the Gila—including the likes of James Ohio Pattie, Ewing Young, Antoine Robidoux, David E. Jackson, Joseph Reddeford Walker, and Nathaniel Pryor—doubtless saw the ruins of the Casa Grande. In the 1830s one such trapper, "P[auline]. Weaver 183__," engraved his last name and the initial of his first name as well as the year—the last number of which is illegible—on the walls. They are yet preserved at Casa Grande Ruins National Monument.[36]

At the end of 1827 the Mexican Congress passed legislation calling for the expulsion from Mexico of all Spaniards, largely *peninsulares* but also *criollos* and others who for whatever reason remained loyal to Spain. The states followed the federal government's lead in 1828. Spanish Franciscans could in theory be exempted from the expulsion decree by reason of age, poor health, or useful vocation, but most elected to leave Mexico. Legislators in el Estado Libre de Occidente enacted expulsion legislation, and before the end of 1828, Father Liberós and his confreres in the northern missions departed. A few, but not Liberós, would manage to remain on the Sonoran frontier.[37]

The Spanish Franciscan Fray Rafael Díaz got the necessary exemption allowing him to continue service in the Pimería Alta. He had previously served Mission San Xavier del Bac, and now he found himself in the role of circuit-riding priest caring for missions Cocóspera (his headquarters), Tumacácori, and San Xavier as well as the soldiers and their families at the presidios of Santa Cruz, Tubac, and Tucson. The goods belonging to the missions had been turned over to civil administrators and a story familiar in Tejas and Nuevo México repeated itself. In 1831 Sonora again became a political entity when the State of Occidente was divided into the states of Sinaloa and Sonora, so the plundering of mission properties took place under the less than watchful eyes of Sonoran officials—or even with their blessing.[38]

The general neglect by Mexico of the frontier further showed itself in increased attacks by Apache Indians. The raiders terrified Mexicans and O'odham alike. In early 1830 Apaches sacked the mission outlier of Calabazas, which was then being used as a kind of ranch headquarters for the mission. The raiders set fire to its chapel and other buildings and carried off the sacred vessels and vestments. After that, livestock continued to be grazed in the region, but for the next two decades no one felt safe living there.[39]

By April 1854 Federico Hulsemann and Luis Pedro Chambon had moved to Calabazas to operate a ranch on behalf of the firm of Payeken, Hundhausen & Company, a firm associated with off-again and on-again Sonoran Governor Manuel M. Gándara. Taking advantage of President Santa Anna's secularization decree of 1842 and working through his brother-in-law as intermediary, Gándara had purchased the "abandoned" Tumacácori and Calabazas lands in 1844. But Apaches and the governor's preoccupation with other affairs had prevented his stocking the ranch until he was able to strike a deal with the Germans' company in 1852.[40]

201

Hulsemann and Chambon apparently moved into Calabazas soon after the deal was closed, because by April 1854 they had stocked the place with sheep and goats and had repaired the old *visita* chapel as a ranch house. They had also built a large barracks-like structure to the north to accommodate the Mexican workers and their families. The irony in their situation was that in 1853 James Gadsden—who had earlier inspected the military installations at Pensacola—had successfully negotiated with Mexican President Santa Anna on behalf of the United States for the purchase of land south of the Gila River which included the site of Calabazas. The treaty of sale was signed on December 30. In a sense, the Gándara ranch with its German caretaker was actually in the United States rather than in Mexico—although formal ratifications were not exchanged between the two governments until June 30, 1854, and the new boundary dividing the countries was not surveyed and marked until 1855.[41]

Whether in the United States or Mexico at the time, Calabazas witnessed one of the most dramatic moments in its more than century-long history on April 26, 1854. On that day forty "tame" Apaches who had been living peacefully in Tucson and sixty Mexican lancers commanded by Hilarión García and Antonio Comadurán descended on a large group of Western Apaches who had planned to attack Calabazas.

Watercolor painting of an Apache warrior, ca. 1850. Apache raids on the mission communities of the Pimería Alta often provoked merciless retaliation from presidial soldiers. (Courtesy Arizona Historical Society.)

[L]ess than a mile from the [Calabazas] ranch the Mexican cavalry rode into the 200 Apaches—presumably Coyotero and Pinaleño bands of the Western Apache tribe—"lancing and killing the rascals." The Tucson Apaches "butchered and mutilated" the Apache wounded whom the Mexicans failed to kill on the first charge. "The carnage," said [railroad surveyor Peter R.] Brady, "was awful."

The jubilant Hulsemann and his close associates took "a smile or two" from his supply of mescal to celebrate the defeat of the "barbarians." Brady noted there was insufficient liquor for the "common herd, so they had to get drunk on blood and glory." This included attaching the severed head of [the Western Apache named] Romero . . . to a spike driven into the wall outside and near the entrance of a room used as a mess hall.

"They had cut a slit or two in his forehead," [wrote Brady,] "and there it was. . . . The face was sadly altered, but I could recognize the murderous features. [Railroad surveyor Asa B.] Gray could not refrain from a joke. He said he supposed they had hung up the head near the mess room door as a kind of sign, 'hash within.' Captain Garcia wanted to know if this was the head of one of the captives that had acted as interpreter the day before. I replied that I could not swear to it, but that I thought it was, for it was ugly enough for him. Gray said he could not tell . . . but if it really was the head he said it was in such a shape now he did not think his own mother would know him, such a difference does it make to see a man's head off and on his shoulders."

202

Most of the raiding Apaches were lanced in the back by the pursuing Mexican lancers. A few more were shot. The Tucson Apaches dispatched the wounded. Mementos, which Brady mistook at first for dried apples, were kept for eventual shipment to Ures, the capital of Sonora. These were Apache ears, a string of them from two-and-a-half to three-feet long, many still with their copper, shell and button earrings in place.[42]

By July 1, 1854, the ranch at Calabazas had become part of Doña Ana County in the U.S. Territory of New Mexico. Hulsemann and his fellow caretakers remained there until 1856, when the last Mexican troops stationed at the Tucson presidio marched southward across the new international boundary to make way for a peaceful American takeover. What had been northern Sonora was now southwestern New Mexico—and continued as New Mexico until a separate Arizona Territory was created in 1863. The Hispanic-period history of Calabazas had drawn to a close. The *visita's* next tenant would be a major in the United States Army.[43]

As for Tumacácori, it was on the road to extinction. In 1839 Fray Faustino González summarized the situation for all the missions of Pimería Alta. He said that the remaining mission Indians wallowed in misery, vice, and ignorance of God, utterly insubordinate to their ministers. Mission property existed in name only, in hopeless disorder, for everything pertaining to the fields and lands is up for grabs to all.' Thus the economic base of the missionaries' spiritual ministry had crumbled."[44]

Nor was that all. *Mestizaje*, or intermarriage, between O'odham and Mexicans had begun to blur the distinction between the two. "'In these past ten years [1829-39] that they have lived unrestrained,' [Father] González asserted, 'many have died because they left that more ordered life, others are now married to gente de razón, while still others are drifting about or in the employ of gente de razón.' Even the Pápagos who had been congregating in the western missions, since the discovery in the mid-1830s of gold placers near Quitovac and elsewhere in the Papaguería, were now mixed with gente de razón. Given these conditions, there was no hope of turning back the clock."[45]

By 1841 Tumacácori's sole priest—and he had visited only rarely—was Fray Rafael Díaz, stationed at distant San Ignacio lying to the south. He died that summer and was replaced at San Ignacio by Spanish-born Fray Antonio González. On his first visit to his Tumacácori visita, he referred to the church as that of La Purísima Concepción rather than of San José. And before the year was out, lands just south of Tumacácori were surveyed for the so-called Los Nogales de Elías grant; Tumacácori's land documents disappeared in the process.[46]

Fray Antonio and Fray Ángel Arroyo, the last two Quereteran Franciscans in the Pimería Alta, left in mid-1842. When Fray Antonio González returned alone the following year for a brief stay, it was not as a Quereteran, but as a friar attached to the

203

Franciscan Province of Jalisco. From San Ignacio he did his occasional circuit riding only in the company of heavily-armed soldiers. Apaches had put the entire region a great risk. And not only that, the priestless missions were falling into decay.

> At Tumacácori the physical plant was crumbling. On April 3, 1843, the Tubac justice of the peace filed a report on the sad state of the neighboring mission. . . .
>
> The buildings of the mission convento, which he dated 1821, were in 1843 "for the most part fallen down and the rest threatening ruin." Only the church held up. The mission's two former communal fields, immediately south of the pueblo and half a league away across the river, since 1828 had lain "unfenced and abandoned, full of mesquite and other bushes." Because of the shortage of water in the [Santa Cruz] river, the few Indians who remained irrigated only their own small fields. Calabazas, Guevavi, and Sonoita were in ruins with neither buildings nor anything else of value: only a few stray cattle roamed the hills.[47]

When secularization finally came to Tumacácori and the other missions of the Pimería Alta, it "was not by the orderly process set forth in the Spanish Laws of the Indies, not by the Mexican decree of April 16, 1834, which was waived on the Sonora frontier, but by default." After 1843 the signature of Fray Antonio González ceased to appear in the mission registers. Subsequently, the only names were those of secular clergy, like don Francisco Javier Vázquez at Cieneguilla. While Father Vásquez never made it as far north as Tumacácori, Bachiller don Trinidad García Rojas of San Ignacio celebrated baptisms and marriages between 1844 and 1848 for the few O'odham at Tumacácori who had somehow managed to hang on.[48] Unbeknownst to them, in 1844 Governor Gándara had contrived to buy the entire Tumacácori and Calabazas grant. Not that it mattered. Gándara was in no position to take possession

In late October 1848 a column of U.S. Army dragoons passed down the Santa Cruz Valley on its way to California after having fought in Mexico during the Mexican War Among them was a diary-keeper named Cave Johnson Couts:

> We have been marching down the Santa Cruz, since leaving the town by same name, over a good route, and fine little valley, passing several deserted as well as inhabited ranches. The gold mines, near or at Goibaba [Guevavi], are worked at present by some twenty men, and said to be *immensely wealthy*. These miners Mexicans work for $8 per month and their rations. The Apaches are so numerous and severe, however, that the work only goes on at intervals, never over two weeks at a time. As we approached the place yesterday they all broke from the mines for the little Rancho like scared wolves, taking us for Apaches; thought their day had come at last.[49]

204

By mid-1849, their day had come. Or, at least, they had left. Mexican-period history of Guevavi was at and end. Soon to end, too, was the Mexican-period history of Tumacácori itself. Couts visited there as well:

> At Tumacacori is a very large and fine church standing in the midst of a few common conical Indian huts, made of bushes, thatched with grass, huts of most common and primitive kind. . . . This church is now taken care of by the Indians, Pimas, most of whom are off attending a jubilee, or fair, on the other side of the mountain.
>
> No Priest has been in attendance for many years, though all its images, pictures, figures &c remain unmolested, and in good keeping. No Mexicans live with them at all.[50]

The O'odham whom Couts saw at Tumacácori were its last. In December 1848, two months after the U.S. dragoons had gone on their way, Apaches sacked Tubac, stealing, burning, and killing. The surviving people of the former presidio packed what was left of their belongings and headed north to Tucson. The twenty-five or thirty O'odham still at Tumacácori had also had enough. They took the sacred statues from their niches in the church as well as the vestments and sacred vessels and followed the Tubaceños as far as San Xavier del Bac. Here they moved in with their linguistic kinsmen and deposited the mission's belongings for safe keeping. Today, the statues of San Pedro de Alcántara, San Buenaventura, San Cayetano, San Antonio, and San Francisco de Asís which were carried to safety by the O'odham can be seen on display at the Tumacacori unit of Tumacacori National Historical Park. Two others, those of San José and La Purísima Concepción, are objects of religious devotion in niches in the lower registers of the north walls respectively of the west and east transepts of Mission San Xavier del Bac. San Xavier continues as an active parish church for the O'odham of the San Xavier Reservation. Secularization had somehow spared it.[51]

The abandoned Tumacácori still had a few years to go, until June 30, 1854, before it would become a part of the United States of America. Between 1848 and its abandonment the place saw a small parade of curious onlookers, some of whom left their marks on its walls in the form of graffiti. Among them were some of the countless hundreds of Forty-Niners en route to the gold fields of California. One argonaut, H. M. T. Powell, even drew an excellent sketch of the church and its adjoining structures. Nothing of note would happen to Tumacácori until 1908, when President Theodore Roosevelt, by executive order, designated it a National Monument.[52]

Far up the trail from Guevavi, Calabazas, and Tumacácori, there lay the great prehistoric ruins now contained within Casa Grande Ruins National Monument. Although visited little during the Mexican period, between 1823 and 1826 there was a partially successful effort to reopen the overland trail between Sonora and California via the Yuma Crossing, at least to the extent that it could be used as a mail

This bulto *of San Buenaventura was brought to Mission San Xavier by Pimans when Mission San José de Tumacácori was abandonned in 1848. (Helga Tiewes.)*

205

route by Native American runners. In the course of this effort, Father Féli Caballero, president of the Dominican missions in Baja California, made the journe with a small Indian escort from his northern Baja California mission of Sant Catalina across the Colorado River and up the Gila to the O'odham villages an south to Tucson in April 1823. In June of that year, the Dominican friar backtracke to his home base, now escorted by Brevet Captain José Romero, commandant of th Tucson presidio. No mention is made of Casa Grande, although their route betwee Tucson and the O'odham villages on the Gila surely took them very close to it.[53]

In 1823 historian and conservative statesman Lucas Alamán, Emperor Iturbide minister of war, directed Lieutenant Colonel Antonio Narbona, who was then in polit ical control of Sonora, to explore thoroughly the country between Tucson and th lower Colorado River, telling him "to visit, if possible, the ruins of Casa Grande i order to examine the mines said to exist there." Narbona departed Sonora to becom Governor of Nuevo México before making the trip, but in October 1825 General Jos Figueroa, military commander of the Free State of Occidente, set out from Tucson o a similar commission. Although he followed the Gila route to the Colorado River, ther is no mention of Casa Grande in published accounts of the expedition.[54]

The Casa Grande ruins—which had so piqued the curiosity of Spanish-perio Europeans beginning with Father Eusebio Kino and Captain Juan Mateo Manje i the late seventeenth century—did the same for the first Americans to pass by whe the region was still a part of Mexico. Although fur trappers had probably been th first Americans to see the ruins, in 1846 General Kearny's army, guided b Christopher "Kit" Carson, arrived at the site on its march from Santa Fe to Souther California. Both Lieutenant William H. Emory and Captain Albert S. Johnsto described Casa Grande in considerable detail. Johnston and the artist John Mi Stanley sketched the great house.[55]

Although a few thousand Forty-Niners on their way to the gold fields of Californi must have passed within sight of Casa Grande, with at least a comparative few visit ing the ruins, the last detailed Mexican-period description of them was made in 1852 John Russell Bartlett, who was attempting to survey the southern boundary of th United States as negotiated in the 1848 Treaty of Guadalupe Hidalgo, spent part o July 12 making a floor plan of the great house and one of the lesser structures, sketch ing the ruins from the southwest, and taking a lot of notes. "After three hours spent a the ruins, the hottest, I think, I have ever experienced," he wrote, "we set out on ou return to camp. . . . The mercury had stood in the shade, beneath the trees, at 119 Fahrenheit, between the hours of ten and three o'clock."[56] Today the excellent visito center and museum in the Sonoran Desert at Casa Grande Ruins National Monumen is air-conditioned in the summer and heated in the winter, even if the ruins are not.

Also artificially climate-controlled is the visitor center and museum at anothe Sonoran Desert location, Organ Pipe Cactus National Monument. Its Mexican-perio history, like that of the preceding Spanish period, consisted largely of events at th ext-door settlement of Sonoyta—which remains a part of Mexico—and of travelers oming through the southern edge of the monument along the Camino del Diablo. his ancient foot and horse trail linked Altar and Caborca in Sonora with the olorado River crossing at Yuma and with Alta California.

Documentation of visits by non-Indians to this region between 1821 and ratifica- ion of the Gadsden Purchase in 1854 is rare. Lowell Bean and William Mason write f a party of Mexicans who reached Mission San Luis Rey in southern California in 827. Carrying letters from the commander of the Altar presidio and from the padre t Mission Caborca, they sought horses they presumed were running wild and could e had simply for the asking. Having made this long journey in only thirteen days rom Caborca, they almost certainly used the Camino del Diablo.[57]

It may be that quite a few Mexican settlers in the southern California pueblo of Los Angeles came over the Camino del Diablo between 1827 and 1835. The route was eemed sufficiently secure in April 1828 that California Governor José María cheandía asked for a bimonthly mail service—which was never begun—between Altar and San Diego across the Colorado River. And the 1836 Los Angeles census ndicated that a hundred residents, a tenth of its gente de razón, were Sonorans. While a handful had come with Anza in 1776 and a few more by sea in 1832, the najority of Sonorans came overland. Some, at least, had probably taken the shortest ath through the land of organ pipe cactus between Altar and the Pacific Coast.[58]

The early Mexican-period influx of gente de razón into northwestern Sonora rought about by gold discoveries and what appeared to be opportunities to acquire ands for farming and ranching led to inevitable conflict with the O'odham. An offi- ial of Altar explained the situation in an 1838 letter to the Sonoran governor:

> Apart from the numerous reports, I myself have been eyewitness to Papago dis- content in such villages as Quitovac, Sonoyta, Carricito, Soñi, Arivaipa, and Cubó, because of insults and even extortions they have suffered at the hands of unscrupulous Mexican miners and because of the enormous amounts of water taken from them to supply the mining camps. . . . There can be no doubt but what Papago discontent will increase as more and more water and land are taken from them.[59]

The official's prophecy was fulfilled in May 1840, when a badly outnumbered group of O'odham fought a battle with 150 Mexican militiamen at a place called Cóbota, about halfway between present-day Sasabe and Sonoyta. Although they lost the engagement, the enraged O'odham and some Yaqui Indian allies began to attack Mexican settlements. This brought Sonoran regular army troops to the scene in force, and a brief war was fought between O'odham and some 570 armed Mexicans between the summer of 1840 and January 1841. The outcome was inevitable. The O'odham were outgunned and were forced to surrender.[60]

During the course of the campaign, the Mexican army encamped at an apparently deserted Sonoyta toward the end of December. From here they moved northward along the western side of the Ajo Mountains within today's Organ Pipe Cactus National Monument. Historian and former park naturalist Wilton Hoy, drawing on Mexican diary of the campaign, gives details:

> A wet and weary Mexican army now regrouped at the Sonoyta River command post, splashed across the river's shallow waters, and struck a route northeastward to the west base of the Ajos marching ten miles before making camp, possibly at the eastern or southeastern foot of the Diablo Mountains. The next day, December 30, the men entered "a very craggy canyon where it was necessary to carry the three field cannons on mule back." This canyon appears to be the section of the national monument's Ajo Mountain Drive between the Diablo Mountains and the Ajo Mountains with Estes and Boulder canyons on their right. This day's eight-mile march encountered nothing more exciting than rounding up some Papago horses.
>
> The second camp could have been made at the broad outwash plain or bajada of Grass Canyon [near the north end of the Ajo Range]. That evening the Mexican command glimpsed through its telescopes a few fleeing Papagos and their tell-tale smokes high on the Ajo slopes. The Ajo Mountains are doubtless better suited as National Park Service scenery than as a nineteenth-century theater for the pursuit of recalcitrant Indians.
>
> The Mexicans toiled, searched, and camped for five days along its western base. However, the diarist does not complain about the mountain's hostile bajada. . . .
>
> The next morning, on the 31st, "smokes were seen on the peaks of the sierra, on inaccessible heights. Through the telescopes a multitude of Indians was seen making smokes and they had some horses and cattle with them on the heights. There was no way to climb up from this side due to the land slides that crown it. . . ."
>
> The frustrated division made its third camp about six miles away, "at a better site where there was enough water" [and probably outside the monument's boundaries on the northeast side of the Ajo mountains].[61]

Governor Gándara's victorious project ended the next month on the western slopes of the Baboquivari Mountains on today's Tohono O'odham Indian Reservation. His was the only military campaign ever to have been conducted within the boundaries of Organ Pipe Cactus National Monument. And while he won the battles, the peace was not permanent. O'odham raiding continued until Lieutenant Colonel Felipe Flores brought the Indians to heel in June 1843. The peace settlement then became permanent; O'odham never again waged war against foreigners in their lands, although there would be skirmishes.[62]

On the last two days of 1840 a Mexican army pursued a group of O'odham raiders over the Ajo Mountains, now part of Organ Pipe Cactus National Monument, Arizona. (Edward McCain.)

The California Gold Rush of 1849 occasioned a surge of travel over the Camino del Diablo. Unlike Forty-Niners who took the southern overland route through Tucson and down the Gila, there seem to have been few diary keepers among them. Only one such journal, at least, appears to have been published. It was that kept by don José Lías, who set out from Caborca on March 14, 1849 with don Dionisio González. They arrived at Quitobaquito springs inside Organ Pipe Cactus National Monument on March 19. They napped at the oasis before proceeding on their westward way, ultimately to a gold placer on the Stanislaus River.[63]

In 1943 a reminiscent account was published of an 1850 trek over the Camino del Diablo. Seventeen-year-old Francisco Salazar set out with some twenty other Sonorans to seek their fortunes in the Alta California bonanza. When they arrived at the Tinajas Altas, a series of natural granite catchments (*tinajas*) that hold rainwater, they discovered

> a vast graveyard of unknown dead and the road from there to the Colorado was marked the whole way by the dried carcasses of mules, horses, and cattle and the scattered bones of human beings, slowly turning into dust. In such a region but little time can be given to conventional things and the dead were left where they fell to be sepulchered (if at all) by the fearful sand storms that sweep at all times over the desolate waste.[64]

Although Tinajas Altas is well beyond the western boundary of Organ Pipe Cactus National Monument, Salazar's recollection of his Mexican-period sojourn provides a realistic picture of the perils of travel throughout the length of the Camino del Diablo.

Hartmann estimates that as many as four hundred California-bound argonauts died on the Camino del Diablo in the ten years following the start of the rush in 1849:

> In the Southwest, travelers had to choose between the Gila route and the Mexican route. The Gila route was plagued by Apache raiding parties. Many travelers thus attempted the Mexican route, which was relatively free of Indian raiders, especially in the summer. The Mexican route took travelers south and west from Tucson, down Sonora's Altar River valley, and then north from the rough frontier towns of Caborca or Altar toward tiny Sonoita and a dash across the Camino del Diablo. Broiling August continued to be a favored season for travel, not only because of the lack of Indians, but also because of the sporadic summer afternoon rains that, with luck, filled the [granite] tanks. Sonoita and the rock-bound tinajas on El Camino del Diablo were suddenly the focus of life-and-death interest.[65]

Possibly drawn to the region because it became the springboard to Alta California, about 1850 a few Mexican families from Altar and the mining camp of Zoñi founded the first Mexican settlement in the Sonoyta Valley . No longer able to resist as they

209

had in the past, the O'odham of Sonoyta allowed themselves to be eased from their ancient village to about a mile downstream. When the line established by the Gadsden Purchase was finally surveyed in 1855, Sonoyta and its valley remained in Mexico while the United States and New Mexico Territory acquired a cactus wonderland that would one day be preserved for future generations to enjoy.[66]

With the last monument erected along the newly-surveyed line in 1855, the continental United States assumed its present form. Mexico had lost half her lands, but her presence, like that of Spain's before her, remains manifest. Whether Anglo Americans and other non-*mexicanos* who reside in today's Arizona know it or not, Hispanic history and traditions are a part of the region's mutual cultural heritage. It is an inheritance in which each resident shares. Those Mexicans who lived and labored there in the past had no other future than a common present.

The proud owner of a California rancho in the 1830s is portrayed in this painting, "Patrón," by James Walker. (Courtesy Bancroft Library, University of California at Berkeley.)

CALIFORNIA

Although word that Alta California had become a part of Mexico was delayed until 1822 in reaching its northwesternmost possession, the transition was smooth and seems not to have caused any immediate upheavals among the population. Spanish Governor Pablo Vicente de Solá simply became Mexican Governor Pablo Vicente de Solá until the new California governing body sent him away to Mexico City as its deputy in the Mexican Congress. He was replaced in Monterey in November 1822 by the acting governor, Luís Antonio Argüello, who until then had been commandant of the San Francisco presidio.[67]

The historian Chapman has gone so far as to say,

> Strictly speaking, there was no Mexican period of California history. During a quarter of a century the sovereignty of the southern republic was more or less continuously acknowledged, but the actual intervention of Mexico in the affairs of its distant province consisted in little more than the sending of governors and a few score degraded soldiery. These years were therefore more prominently marked by other influences. By far the most important among them was the coming of the Americans.[68]

This, of course, is an outrageous assertion, representing a prejudicial transfer of the Black Legend from Spaniards to Mexicans. While it is true that as happened in Texas there was a relentless movement of Americans into Mexican California, the period is nonetheless characterized by slow but steady growth in the Hispanic population and, as significantly, by intermarriage between Mexican women and American men. It is also the period marking the secularization—and demise—of the missions; a time when California opened its ports to foreign trade and expanded its economy into one of near self-sufficiency; and an era in which land grants greatly outnumbered those issued during the years of Spain's rule and in which cattle ranching extended beyond the confines of mission control.[69]

As with Nuevo México, both Californias were treated after the formation of the United States of Mexico in 1824 as territories rather than as states. But also as with Nuevo México, the practical effects seem to have been few. Mexican California inherited most of the concerns of Spanish California. Spanish fears of further Russian expansion into California became Mexican fears. Bereft of sufficient troops, firearms, and ammunition, San Francisco presidio commandant Luis Argüello, returned from his brief stint in Monterey as acting governor, assumed a posture of, "If you can't fight them, join them." In 1823 Argüello contracted with the Russian-American Company, allowing its people to hunt otters off California's coastline provided the furs were divided evenly between Russians and Californios. Argüello even used his own ship, the *Rover*, to carry the local government's share of pelts to China. In return, he personally received a percentage of the profits.[70]

By 1825 there were some hundred and twenty households and five hundred gente de razón in and near the San Francisco presidio. Nine years later, in 1834, this number of people formed a common council (*ayuntamiento*). Citizens who had once been part of a presidial colony became members of the Pueblo of Yerba Buena. The civil settlement of modern San Francisco, somewhat distant from the presidio, had officially begun.[71]

The presidio had a brief moment of excitement in 1829 when Joaquín Solís, who had been sent to California as a pardoned convict, led disgruntled Mexican troops who had not been paid on a brief revolt against the regime of Governor José María Echeandía. The bloodless revolution began in Monterey, but on November 15 Solís and his rebels appeared at the San Francisco presidio. Support among ordinary soldiers overcame possible resistance by officers, and presidial commandant Ignacio Martínez was dismissed. It was soon after that the rebels scattered and the uprising came to a peaceful end.[72]

In 1833 the presidio was described by an American visitor as a series of "low buildings, with dark tile roofs, resembling prisons more than dwelling houses, and the residence of the Commandant was the most conspicuous among them." He also observed "a few framed houses scattered about outside the square."[73]

Many houses that spilled beyond the immediate confines of the presidio were within the boundaries of today's San Francisco Presidio. The Miramontes family, for example, lived next to El Polin Springs. "Local legend had it that the waters, 'possessed the remarkable power of producing fecundity in women who were childless, and who partook of the waters. . . . In proof it may be mentioned that the Miramontes family, living on the spot, had twenty children.'"[74]

211

In 1833 Apolinario Miranda was given the hundred-vara (1.77-acre) Ojo de Agua de Figueroa grant, a portion of which lies within the presidial boundaries.[75] By the next year, the presidio was close to ruins. Rains had all but washed away the castillo. The presidial commander, Mariano Vallejo, moved the military operations north to Sonoma where Mission San Solano—the twenty-first and last of the Franciscan foundations—had been established in 1823, the only Mexican-period church in the chain. He got permission to sell to private interests everything saleable except a barracks to lodge troops. Vallejo took the presidio's stock north with him. By 1835 what was left of the San Francisco presidio had fallen into caretaker status.[76]

> [T]he Mexican presence, which had never been vigorous, finally slipped away almost entirely. The deserted Castillo, the unmanned artillery, the forlorn cluster of huts called barracks and which housed at best a token garrison, from the late 1830s onward bespoke of the fact that Mexico had neither the treasury nor the troops to guard the Golden Gate. The country's inability to protect the harbor offered an open invitation to foreign seizure. A reply was not long in the coming.[77]

Here was a sorry outcome for what Juan Bautista de Anza had so heroically begun in 1776. Nonetheless, it was on the Spanish and Mexican foundation that the United States would resurrect the post. Even as a unit of Golden Gate National Recreation Area, it will always be The Presidio, a lasting reminder of a Spanish and Mexican past.

In 1821 there were about 3,320 gente de razón in Alta California, two-thirds of whom were women and children. They were outnumbered by mission Indians in a ratio of six to one. By 1845 the total number of *mexicanos* had risen to 7,300. The 120 foreigners living in California in 1830 had become 240 by 1835 and 380 by 1840. In the next five years, the number of foreigners jumped to 680.[78]

Before 1840 there had been very little inducement for Americans or other foreigners to settle in California. The territory was not officially opened to colonization by foreigners until 1828, and until the middle of the 1830s the missions owned or controlled most of the good coastal lands. Outsiders who entered California before 1840, virtually all of them males, married Mexican or Indian women and assimilated themselves into the regional culture.

Believing that if California were to remain a part of Mexico it would have to have a greatly augmented non-Indian population, Mexicans began to repeat the mistake they had made earlier in Texas: they encouraged foreigners to become naturalized Mexican citizens and to remain in California. The process began with the secularization of all twenty-one missions.

Secularization was begun in a tentative way after 1825, when governors allowed select Indians to leave certain missions and gave them land and rights of citizenship. Many Native Americans thus "freed," finding themselves no longer members of iable native societies and ill-equipped to compete in the world of gente de razón, "were reduced to beggary and thieving after having 'gambled away their clothes, mplements, and even their land.' Fray Narciso Durán reported that liberated ndians became 'slaves or servants of white men.'"79

Between 1834 and 1836 all of California's missions were secularized. Historian David Weber provides a summary of what happened:

[M]issions constituted the principal source of revenue for ambitious politicians. Mission overseers . . . sold off cattle, grain, and lands that rightly belonged to the former neophytes, and missions deteriorated under their stewardship. In 1839 Governor Juan Bautista Alvarado tried to check what nearly all writers have termed the "plunder" of the missions, but it was too late. The missions had "entirely gone to ruin," one of Alvarado's agents reported, and non-Indians had moved onto Indian lands. "All is destruction, all is misery, humiliation, and despair," wrote one padre in 1840.

The destruction of California mission properties, however, did not come about solely because of the activities of unscrupulous mayordomos. Mission Indians themselves displayed contempt for the system that had kept them forcibly institutionalized and participated actively in destroying it. Under the padres, many Indians had resisted missionization in subtle ways, and one of every ten had attempted to run away. With the authority of the padres gone in the mid-1830s, most Indians refused to labor for the overseers and showed little interest in acquiring land near the missions; some fled civilization entirely to live among independent Indian societies; others drifted into white settlements where they became laborers or servants; and others went to work on the private ranchos that *californios* had begun carving out of former mission properties. . . .

The last of the missionaries had no missions. In dire need of funds to run his government, Governor Pío Pico had put most of the remaining mission property—including the crumbling buildings and the chapels themselves—up for public auction in 1845. The central government and the Franciscans tried to prevent this sale, but the independent and desperate governor proceeded nonetheless.80

As evident in this 1888 photo, Mission Santa Inés, founded in 1804, suffered from the neglect that befell most California missions after the Mexican War of Independence. (Courtesy California Historical Society, San Francisco, FN-29924.)

This mood in California led to a virtual orgy of land-granting by California governors after 1835. Over the next eleven years some 370 grants, many of them covering huge tracts of acreage, were awarded, Americans getting many of them.[81]

In 1834, before the onslaught began, Governor José Figueroa made a grant of three square leagues to José María Amador, the San Ramón (Norris) grant. At the end of the 1930s playwright Eugene O'Neill bought 158 acres of what had been the Rancho San Ramón, tore down the old adobe farmhouse, and built what he called Tao House, today preserved and interpreted as the Eugene O'Neill National Historic Site.[82]

It was 1835 when Governor Figueroa awarded the three square leagues of the Sausalito grant to José Antonio Galindo. It was awarded once more in 1838, this time by Governor Juan Bautista Alvarado to English-born Guillermo Antonio Richardson who had arrived in California in 1822 and who had married a daughter of San Francisco presidio commandant Ignacio Martínez. The grant overlay lands which now include Muir Woods National Monument and the Marin portion of the Golden Gate National Recreation Area.[83]

In 1836 and again in 1839, James Richard Berry and Joseph Francis Snook were given three grants combined as the Punta de los Reyes grant and totaling a dozen square leagues. The combined grant covered essentially all of today's Point Reyes National Seashore. Snook built a small home for his *mayordomo* (foreman) near Drake's Estero, but seems never to have lived on the ranch himself. He soon traded his property with Antonia María Osio for land in Southern California.[84] Virtually the whole of Santa Cruz Island of present-day Channel Islands National Park was granted to Andrés Castillero in 1839; in 1843 Santa Rosa Island, also within the modern park, was granted to Antonio and Carlos Carrillo.[85] In 1839 as well the El Conejo grant, originally awarded in 1802-03 and within the modern Santa Monica Mountains National Recreation Area, was regranted to José de la Guerra y Noriega. The lands are also known as the Altagracia or Nuestra Señora de Altagracia grant.[86]

First in 1823, again in 1834, and finally in 1842 Ignacio Martínez was awarded the four-square-league Pinole grant, which includes the small plot of today's John Muir National Historic Site. Martínez had been commandant of the Presidio de San Francisco between 1822 and 1828 and acting commandant at various times between 1828 and 1830. He was also its commandant from March 27, 1830, to September 1831.[87]

Although no other California units of the National Park System contain lands that were once all or partially Mexican land grants, the 1844 San Buenaventura grant to Pearson B. Reading lies not too far south of the Whiskeytown-Shasta-Trinity National Recreation Area. Similarly, the 1846 San Lorenzo grant to Rafael Sánchez is south of Pinnacles National Monument.[88]

Among the more interesting "land grants" were those totaling 600,000 acres supposedly issued to José Yves Limantour by Governor Manuel Micheltorena between

842 and 1845. Included were four square leagues south of present California Street San Francisco, much of San Francisco Bay, and all the Farallon Islands. The merican-period Lands Commission upheld Limantour's claims, and on that basis e sold most of them in 1856, fleeing to Mexico in 1857 when the government discovered that the documents were forgeries. Limantour, who was also involved in ipping along the California coast in the 1840s, left his name on Estero de imantour, Limantour Spit, and Limantour Beach south of Inverness Ridge in oday's Point Reyes National Seashore. Limantour Beach is reached by the paved imantour Road—a kind of monument to a Mexican-period swindler.[89]

It was not until 1839 that the Russian seal and otter hunters at Fort Ross abandoned their colony. Until then, sea mammal hunters under Russian auspices continued to ply California coastal waters with devastating effect. Nor were Russians and ieir Aleut, Eskimo, and Indian employees the only hunters. Some were Americans nd others who occasionally plied the same trade. Among these was Tennessee-born ontiersman George Nidever who arrived in California in 1833, having crossed the ierra Nevada with a group of mountain men led by Joseph Reddeford Walker. idever soon went to Santa Barbara, where he immediately started hunting sea tters. His activities came to involve one of the more exciting chapters in the history f Santa Rosa Island of today's Channel Islands National Park.[90] He tells the story imself in his "as-told-to" autobiography:

At that time it was impossible for newcomers to procure a [hunting] license. Capt. [William Goodwin] Denny [Dana], the Capt. of this port, had a license, and Burton, Sparks and other hunters then here hunted under his license, paying him a share of the skins.

We had made the same arrangement with Capt. Denny and 8 or 10 days after I arrived here Sills and I went over to Santa Rosa Island. We had no boats so were obliged to hunt from land. We went over about May of 1835. Two weeks later Sills was taken sick and returned to Santa Barbara. I remained about six weeks longer and killed in all 8 or 10 otters; Sills having got none. I had with me a Kanaka Indian [a Hawaiian native], employed to swim out for the otter killed; at $16 a month.

When Sparks returned from the Lower Coast, he and the Black Steward [i.e., Allen Light, a black man from Boston] and I agreed to hunt together and were taken over to Santa Rosa by the "Peor es Nada." . . .

We remained all winter on the Islands, making our headquarters at Santa Rosa, although hunting on San Miguel and Santa Cruz, as there were very few otters on Santa Rosa. We got altogether on this hunt 60 skins. . . .

About the first of January 1836 we had a fight with N[orth]. W[est]. Indians on the head of Santa Rosa Island.

The living legacy of Spain and Mexico in the United States survives amid a sometimes hostile environment, much like this coastal oak that clings to a rocky cliff on Santa Rosa Island, Channel Islands National Park, California. (JC Leacock.)

215

There were on the island at the time Sparks, Black Steward, and I, hunters of our party; O'Brien, an Irishman, Mathers an American, 3 Kanakas, and Harry Plomer an Englishman, and our cook. Besides our party there was a Portuguese called Manuel, also a hunter, and a Kanaka as help, making in all 12 men.

On the N.E. side of the Island and close to the present [1878] wharf there is a large cave. Its entrance is hardly any larger than an ordinary doorway, but [the cave is] so large inside that a hundred persons could occupy it with ease. Here we kept our provisions and other supplies. About the first of January [1836] Sparks and some of our men saw a brig, one day, in the upper part of the Channel, and remarked casually that they were perhaps N.W. Indians. . . . This appearance of the N.W. Indians would not have surprised us, as we knew they were likely to come at any time, and having talked the matter over long before, we had agreed to fight them at least as long as we could; to this the Portuguese had also agreed. Sparks and Black Steward, while hunting together before, had been driven up into the Island by these Indians and their supplies captured; but we determined to defend ours as long as it could be done.

[A few days later, Nidever and the others were hunting offshore when the "Northwest Indians" were sighted.] Steward called out, "Here come the N.W. Indians." Sure enough, just ahead of us coming out of the fog were 5 or 6 canoes [bidarkas?] pulling with might and main to cut us off from the shore. Each canoe had two Indians and some of them a third. When Black Steward called to us, the foremost canoe was but a few hundred yards away and the other only a short distance in the rear.

The fog had prevented us from discovering them, while our shooting [at otters] had indicated to them our exact position. At the first alarm we made a straight line for the shore and our men needed no urging to exert themselves. We all made for a small cove or bay just below the point and lined with thick bushes. Black Steward was the first to reach the beach. Jumping out as soon as his boat grounded, he turned and fired on the foremost canoe, but the powder having partly escaped from his gun the ball fell short. A moment later Sparks reached the shore and almost at the same time I jumped out on the beach beside him, amidst a shower of buckshot, the Indians already having opened fire. At that moment the first canoe was not over a hundred yards away and the others close behind. Sparks fired at the foremost canoe, wounding one of the Indians, who fell, but raised again just in time to receive my shot, which settled him. This was a reception they little expected and they turned back a safe distance from us, exchanging shots with us in the meanwhile. As soon as each of us fired his first shot, we took refuge in the bushes, under cover of which we soon drove them out of range. We killed 3 and wounded 4 or 5 of them, while none of us received a scratch. . . . The whole number of canoes in the attacking party was 13, each canoe having two men and many of them an extra man. In a canoe there were generally two guns but not unfrequently they carried three. In hunting otter they generally used buckshot, their arms being the old English musket, and this is the reason why they first used buckshot with us. After the first shot they loaded with ball, as they saw we were determined to make a stand. The range of these guns is something incredible. Our men assured us that the bullets from the Indians' guns passed them when they were fully a mile from the beach. The canoes having gotten out of range, they rested for a few minutes then pulled off to the brig, which we could now plainly see about a mile away; the fog having lifted. We then left our cover, drew the boats well up on the beach and buried them in the sand, likewise our provisions, lest the Indians should return. This being done we moved back to a hollow a short distance from the shore, where we could watch the vessel without being seen, and awaited further developments. The rest of the day passed without any further movements on the part of the Indians.[91]

The next day there was another encounter when the unsuspecting Indians came ashore and one of them was shot. The others fled back to their canoes and paddled to the brig. The following day the brig sailed away, "and we never saw them again."[92]

During the 1830s tallow and hide became California's principal export commodities. Cattle had spread like wildfire and were superabundant. Their products were in demand both in England and in New England. The trade began as early as 1822, when two agents for a British company struck a deal with Father President Mariano Payeras of Mission La Purísima Concepción to make contracts with individual missions for their supply of tallow and hides. By the 1840s, with the markets saturated, the trade fell off but did not cease altogether. It is estimated that Boston traders alone may have carried more than six million hides and seven thousand tons of tallow out of California between 1826 and 1848.[93]

The nature of the trade as it was carried on along the California coast was described in a reminiscent account by Prudencia Higuera:

In 1840, when I was about twelve years old, I remember I saw the first American vessel that traded along our shores. One afternoon a horseman came to our ranch and told my father that a great ship, a ship with two sticks in the center, was about to enter our bay to buy hides and tallow.

The next morning my father gave orders and my brothers with the peons, went on horseback to the smaller valleys to round up all the best cattle. They drove them to the beach, killed them there and salted the hides. They tried out the tallow in some iron kettles that my father had bought from one of the Vallejos, but as we did not have any barrels, we followed the common plan in those days. We cast the tallow in round piles about the size of a cheese, dug in the black adobe and plastered smooth with clay. Before the melted tallow was poured into the pit an oaken staff was thrust down in the center, so that by the two ends of it the heavy cake could be carried more easily. By working very hard we had a large number of hides and many pounds of tallow ready on the beach when the ship appeared far out in the bay and cast anchor near a point two or three miles away.

217

The captain came soon to our landing with a small boat and two sailors one of whom was a Frenchman who knew Spanish very well, acted as interpreter. The captain looked over the hides, and then asked my father to get into the boat and go to the vessel. Mother was afraid to let him go, as we all thought the Americans were not to be trusted unless we knew them very well. We feared they would carry my father off and keep him prisoner. Father said, however, it was all right; he went and put on his best clothes, gay with silver braid, and we all cried and kissed him good-by, while mother clung about his neck and said we might never see him again. Then the captain told her: "If you are afraid, I will have the sailors take him to the vessel, while I stay here until he comes back. He ought to see all the goods I have, or he will not know what to buy."

After a little my mother let him go with the captain, and we stood on the beach to see them off. Mother then came back, and had us kneel down and pray for father's safe return. Then we felt safe.

He came back the next day, bringing four boat-loads of cloth, axes, shoes, fish-lines, and many new things. There were two grindstones, and some jewelry. My brother had traded some deer skins for a gun and four toothbrushes, the first ones I had ever seen. . . . After the captain had carried all the hides and tallow to his ship he came back, very much pleased with his bargain, and gave my father, as a present, a little keg of what he called "Boston rum." We put it away for sick people.

After the ship sailed my mother and sisters began to cut out new dresses, which the Indian women sewed. On one of mine mother put some big brass buttons about an inch across, with eagles on them. How proud I was. I used to rub them hard every day to make them shine, using the toothbrush and some of the pounded egg shell that my sisters and all the Spanish ladies kept in a box to put on their faces on great occasions.

Then our neighbors who were ten or fifteen miles away came to see all the things we had bought.[94]

Vessels from all over the world took part in the California hide and tallow trade. Among them was the *Ayachuco*, described in 1834 as "a long, sharp brig of about three hundred tons, with raking masts and very square yards. . . . We afterwards learned that she was built at Guayaquil, and named the *Ayachuco*, after the place where the battle was fought that gave Peru her independence, and was now owned by a Scotsman named Wilson, who commanded her, and was engaged in the trade between Callao and other parts of South America and California. She was a fast sailer, as we frequently afterwards saw, and had a crew of Sandwich Islanders on board."[95]

In 1830 the *Ayachuco* was under the command of Joseph Snook, who would later obtain a land grant at Point Reyes. John Wilson—a Scotsman who had come to California in 1826, married Ramona Carrillo de Pacheco, and considered California is home—was its owner between 1831 and 1836, when he sold it to James McKinley, a Scotsman who had settled in California in 1824.

At last, the *Ayachuco* became the property of the Bordeaux firm of Bizat and Roussell, and French-born Mexican citizen José de Limantour seems to have become their agent. It appears that the inexperienced Limantour himself may have been at the helm when the ship departed Monterey only to run aground at Drake's Bay in the present Point Reyes National Seashore on October 27, 1841. About three-fourths of its $65,000 cargo of French silks, brandy, muslins, and calicos were salvaged. But shortly afterward, the *Ayachuco* went to pieces where it had gone aground to become an underwater archeological site, a very silent reminder within the national seashore of the days of Mexican California when hides and tallow had been the coin of the local realm.[96]

Don Ignacio Martínez, the sometime commandant of the Presidio de San Francisco, was born in Mexico City in 1774 of Spanish parents. He went to California in 1799 and started his military career as a cadet at the Presidio de Santa Barbara. In 1802 he married Doña María Martina Arellanes in Santa Barbara, and it was here the first of their eleven children was born. Long after having received the Pinole land grant, he moved his family to its headquarters at Rancho Nuestra Señora de la Merced in Pinole, where he lived until his death in June 1848.

Even before he had moved to his grant, as early as 1824 Ignacio had sent his sons, Vincente and José, to the ranch to learn the cattle business from *mayordomo* Bruno Valencia. They also planted a pear orchard and vineyards.[97]

When Ignacio died, Mexican California had already become a part of the United States. On July 7, 1846, Commodore John Sloat of the U.S. Pacific squadron had sailed into Monterey Bay, demanding and receiving the surrender of the Mexican officials. By the end of the year the war in California was over. As was the case with New Mexico, California became de facto an appendage of the United States although it would be February 2, 1848, before the signing of the Treaty of Guadalupe Hidalgo would make it official. In 1850, California was taken into the Union as a state.[98]

The defeat of California occurred a year after its population of gente de razón had been counted at 7,300. Some 680, or nine percent, were foreigners, chiefly Americans. When war broke out in 1846, another five hundred Americans were on their way via overland trails.

> As had happened in Texas . . . Mexico failed to people California and New Mexico with substantial numbers of loyal subjects, either Europeans or Mexicans, or to establish effective barriers to keep Anglo-Americans out. That failure contributed mightily to her loss of both [territories] in 1846. More important, however, was the steady political, economic, and social drift of the frontier away from the

219

metropolis. That drift undermined the will of the frontiersmen to follow orders from Mexico City, to oppose American immigration, and to stop distributing land to citizens of a nation that had become what California's delegate to Congress in 1844 termed "our natural enemy."[99]

Vincente Martínez took over one eleventh of the estate willed to his children by Ignacio under the flag of a new nation. The 1,600-acre share of the ranch was along the Cañada del Hambre next to the eastern edge of the ranch.

Vincente had been born on August 8, 1818, at Santa Barbara. When he was seventeen he married Guadalupe Moraga, granddaughter of José Joaquín Moraga, second in command during the 1775-76 expedition to California of Juan Buatista de Anza. Guadalupe died in 1845, and the following year Vincente built a frame house on his Pinole grant lands in what is now called Franklin Canyon. In May 1848 he married sixteen-year-old María Nieves Soto and moved his new wife and family to the Cañada del Hambre. "Some two years later, probably in 1849, Vincente erected the adobe about 20 varas (55 feet) west of the frame structure. . . . [He] occupied the Cañada del Hambre for some seven to ten years."[100] This structure, the Martínez Adobe, is now preserved and interpreted on the grounds of the John Muir National Historic Site.

> Built in 1849 on the large Mexican California Rancho el Pinole, the Vincente Martínez Adobe is a fine example of rural vernacular architecture of the transitional 1840s period, when Mexican architectural traditions were increasingly influenced by European traditions. The story of the adobe comprises a microcosm of American historical development. During the past century and a half, historical evolution of the structure and its setting reflect the transformation of this simple but graceful adobe, built at the far edge of an isolated Mexican rancho, to a modern twentieth century American suburban dwelling. The lives of its owners and residents mirror the history of both Mexico and the United States during a period of extensive political, social, and demographic changes.[101]

Part of that history involves the descent of the Martínez family. Martínez women married men with such surnames as Richardson, Hinkley, Boone, and Tennent. The Moraga and Carrillo and Martínez families joined those of hundreds of other Spanish surnamed Spanish- and Mexican-period pioneers in becoming citizens of the United States and in losing their obvious Hispanic identity. Their assimilation grew out of love rather than by force of arms.

The saga of Spain and Mexico in what today is the United States began in 1493, when Christopher Columbus brought his ship to Salt River Bay on St. Croix Island in the Caribbean. Here the National Park Service interprets the event at Salt River Bay National Historical Park and Ecological Preserve. The other end of this epic tale is

220

nchored in the early American-period Martínez Adobe in John Muir National
Iistoric Site in Martinez, California. What began in violence evolved, at long last,
nto peace.

The story of the entrada of Spain and Mexico in the United States has no ending.
The earlier presence of these nations and their people have inconspicuously become a
part of who we are. Cultural legacies, however shaped and refashioned in the imagination, last for all time.

San Francisco's Fort Point and the Golden Gate appear in the "Presidio House,
1868," by Joseph Lee. (Courtesy Seaver Center for Western History Research,
Natural History Museum of Los Angeles County.)

MAPS

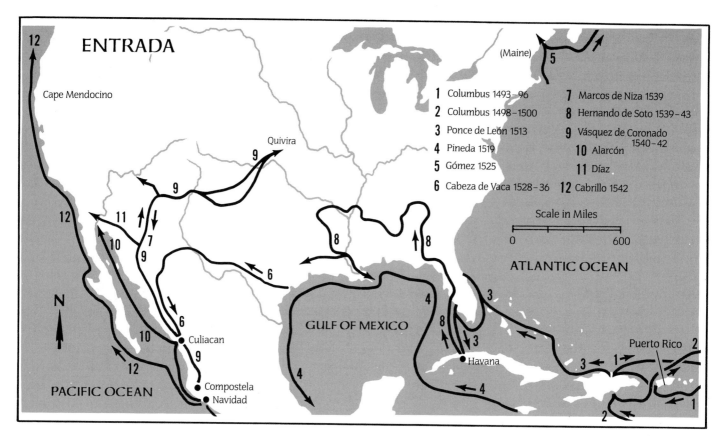

ENTRADA

(Maine)

Cape Mendocino

Quivira

1 Columbus 1493–96
2 Columbus 1498–1500
3 Ponce de León 1513
4 Pineda 1519
5 Gómez 1525
6 Cabeza de Vaca 1528–36

7 Marcos de Niza 1539
8 Hernando de Soto 1539–43
9 Vásquez de Coronado 1540–42
10 Alarcón
11 Díaz
12 Cabrillo 1542

Scale in Miles

0   600

ATLANTIC OCEAN

N

GULF OF MEXICO

Culiacan

Puerto Rico

Havana

Compostela
Navidad

PACIFIC OCEAN

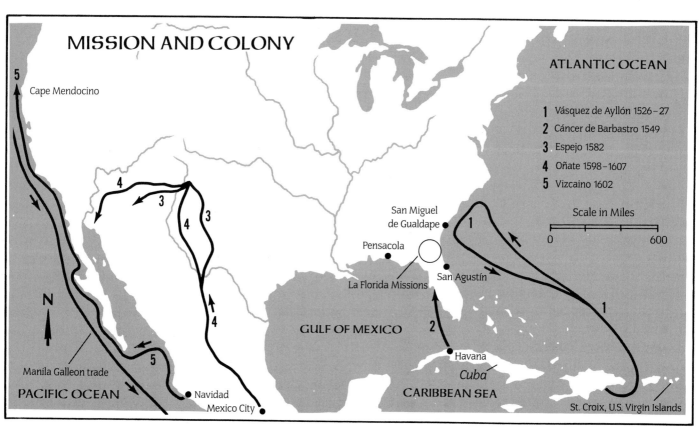

MISSION AND COLONY

ATLANTIC OCEAN

Cape Mendocino

1 Vásquez de Ayllón 1526–27
2 Cáncer de Barbastro 1549
3 Espejo 1582
4 Oñate 1598–1607
5 Vizcaino 1602

Scale in Miles

0   600

San Miguel
de Gualdape

Pensacola

La Florida Missions

San Agustín

N

Manila Galleon trade

GULF OF MEXICO

PACIFIC OCEAN

Navidad
Mexico City

CARIBBEAN SEA

Havana

Cuba

St. Croix, U.S. Virgin Islands

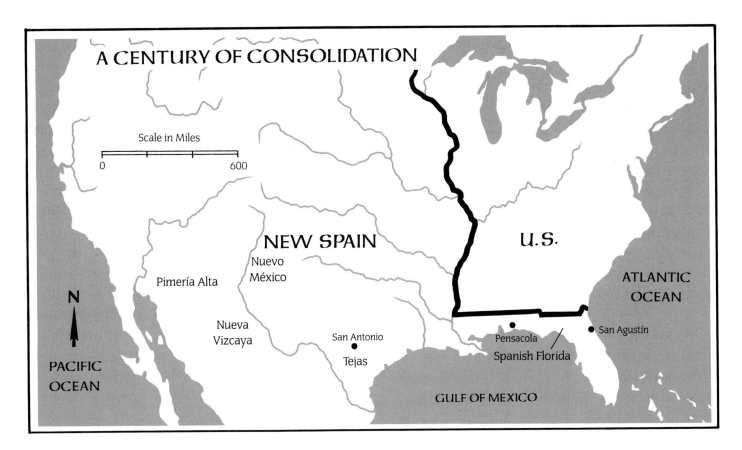

A CENTURY OF CONSOLIDATION

Scale in Miles

0   600

NEW SPAIN

Nuevo
México

Pimería Alta

U.S.

ATLANTIC
OCEAN

Nueva
Vizcaya

San Antonio

Tejas

Pensacola

Spanish Florida

San Agustín

PACIFIC
OCEAN

GULF OF MEXICO

N

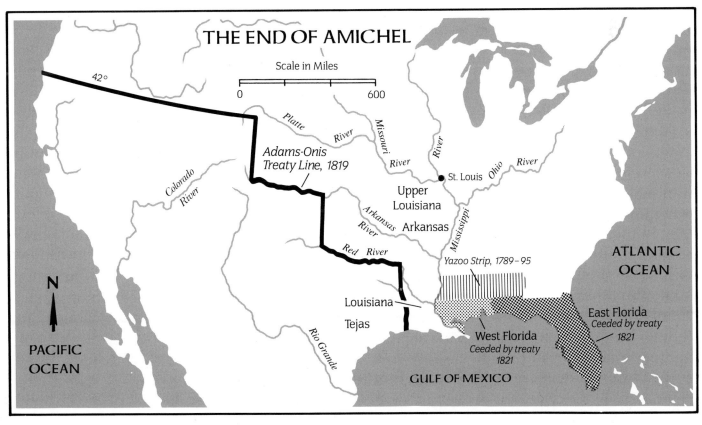

THE END OF AMICHEL

Scale in Miles

0   600

42°

Platte
River

Missouri
River

River

*Adams-Onis
Treaty Line, 1819*

Colorado
River

St. Louis

Ohio
River

Upper
Louisiana

*Arkansas
River*

Arkansas

Mississippi

Red River

Yazoo Strip, 1789–95

ATLANTIC
OCEAN

Louisiana

Tejas

Rio Grande

West Florida
*Ceeded by treaty
1821*

East Florida
*Ceeded by treaty
1821*

PACIFIC
OCEAN

GULF OF MEXICO

N

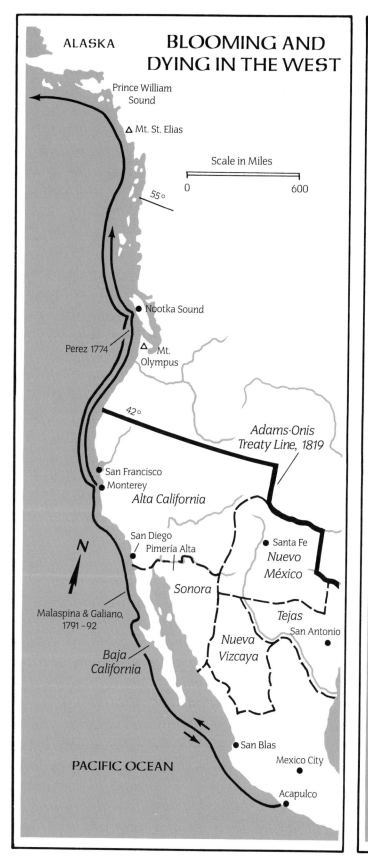

BLOOMING AND DYING IN THE WEST

ALASKA

Prince William Sound

△ Mt. St. Elias

Scale in Miles
0   600

55°

Nootka Sound

Perez 1774

△ Mt. Olympus

42°

Adams-Onis
Treaty Line, 1819

San Francisco
Monterey
Alta California

N

San Diego
Pimería Alta

Santa Fe
*Nuevo
México*

Sonora

Tejas
San Antonio

Malaspina & Galiano,
1791–92

*Nueva
Vizcaya*

*Baja
California*

San Blas

Mexico City

PACIFIC OCEAN

Acapulco

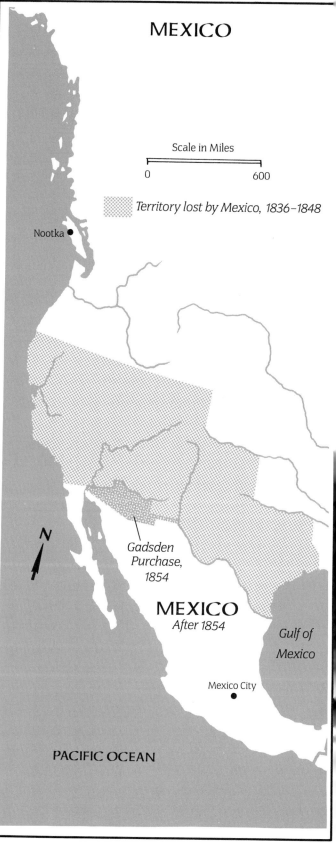

MEXICO

Scale in Miles
0   600

Territory lost by Mexico, 1836–1848

Nootka

N

Gadsden
Purchase,
1854

MEXICO
After 1854

*Gulf of
Mexico*

Mexico City

PACIFIC OCEAN

NOTES

INTRODUCTION

1. Irving (n.d.: 629-630).
2. Irving (n.d.: 631).
3. Morison (1942).
4. This view is best expressed in Sale (1990).
5. Crosby (1972).
6. Dobyns (1983).
7. Thornton (1987).
8. Costo and Costo (1987).
9. Ramenofsky (1987).
10. Reff (1991).
11. Crosby (1990: 7-8).
12. Russell Means, quoted in Gray (1991: 54).
13. Quoted in Booth and Harris (1990: 79).
14. Powell (1971: 4).
15. Juderías (1954: 25-26), quoted in Powell (1971: 11).
16. Powell (1971: 11).
17. Duncan (1991: 30); Powell (1971: 75-76).
18. Duncan (1991: 31).
19. Sánchez (1989: 17. 19); Duncan (1991: 31).
20. Sánchez (1989: 19).
21. Polzer (1991: 20).
22. Stapleton (1960: 7).
23. Uslar Pietri (1989: 13).

ENTRADA

1. Castillo and Bond (1977: 115).
2. Simmons (1991: 58).
3. For one view of the social, political, and economic situation in the Old World which doubtless helped lead to an "Age of Exploration," see Sale (1990: 28-91).
4. Hesiod, quoted in Suárez Barnett (1991: 174).
5. Suárez Barnett (1991: 175).
6. Austin (1983: 26).
7. Lyon (1990a: 283-284).
8. Morison (1974: 112).
9. Brown (1991).

227

10 Irving (n.d.: 217-218).

11 Sale (1990: 131, 132).

12 Morison (1974: 503) is explicit in saying that Ponce de León began his conquest of Puerto Rico in 1506, possibly a misprint. Virtually all other sources consulted give the year as 1508.

13 Quoted in Morison (1974: 503).

14 Weddle (1985: 40). The institution of repartimiento is briefly described in Gibson (1966: 143).

15 Tebeau (1980: 21).

16 Morison (1974: 503-504).

17 Morison (1974: 504-505).

18 Sauer (1971: 27).

19 Weddle (1985: 51-52) summarizes the various hypotheses.

20 Morison (1974: 507).

21 Morison (1974: 507); Weddle (1985: 42).

22 Morison (1974: 507, 510).

23 Dobyns (1983: 152, 157-158); Swanton (1946: Map 11 opp. p. 34, pp. 133, 193).

24 Morison (1974: 510).

25 Landrum (1990: 36); Morison (1974: 510); Weddle (1985: 42).

26 Weddle (1985: 44-45).

27 Weddle (1985: 45).

28 Morison (1974: 511); Weddle (1985: 45).

29 Morison (1974: 515).

30 Weddle (1985: 48).

31 The story of this expedition is in Weddle (1985: 55-65).

32 Weddle (1985: 100). The story of Alvarez de Pineda's voyage along the southern coast of the United States is told here on pages 95-108.

33 There is a discussion of the Cabot voyages in Morison (1971: 157-209).

34 The Verrazzano story is in Morison (1971: 277-325).

35 This is the opinion of Morison (1971: 328). Sauer (1971: 62-63) says the whole journey occurred in 1525 and that Gómez followed the route of Verrazzano, first striking the coast in La Florida and sailing northward along the continent's edge.

36 Morison (1971: 329).

37 The most detailed interpretive summaries of the Gómez voyage, and they conflict in significant details, are those in Morison (1971: 326-331) and in Sauer (1971: 62-69).

38 Judge (1988: 337-339).

39 Weddle (1985: 205).

40 Summary accounts of the Narváez expedition and of that of Núñez Cabeza de Vaca are in Weddle (1985: 185-207); Hudson (1976: 105-107); Morison (1974: 516-525); and Sauer (1971: 36-46, 108-125).

41 Bolton (1964a: 25-26).

42 Sauer (1971: 127).

The literature concerning the Marcos de Niza reconnaissance of 1539 is abundant. In addition to that found in Bolton (1964a: 17-39), the journey, including a good bibliography on the subject, is recounted for in the David Weber-introduced edition of Hallenbeck (1987). Also see Reff (1991: 8-77); Rodack (1985: 163-182); Sauer (1971: 127-129); and Udall (1987: 64-66).

Thrapp (1988: I: 398).

Sauer (1971: 127-128); Weddle (1985: 213).

Weddle (1985: 213).

Morison (1974: 526).

Brain (1985: xx).

Dobyns (1983: 153-154). For less certain ascription, see Bullen (1978) and Smith and Gottlob (1978: 3-4).

Morison (1974: 526); Weddle (1985: 189).

Morison (1974: 527).

Flowers (1991).

Morison (1974: 527-528).

National Park Service, U.S. Department of the Interior, and the Division of Historical Resources, Florida Department of State (n.d.); Hudson, DePratter, and Smith (1989: 78).

This topic is the subject of Dobyns (1983) and of Ramenofsky (1987).

Ewen (1990: 90).

Swanton (1985: 295).

Bolton (1964a: 68); Udall (1987: 72-73).

Bolton (1964a: 69-71); Udall (1987: 72-73).

Bolton (1964a: 139-140).

Udall (1987: 111).

The story of the Alarcón and Díaz trips to the lower Colorado River are recounted in Bolton 1964a: 153-178) and in Udall (1987: 111-112). A careful analysis of the route taken by the men who carried Díaz to his final resting place is that of Ives (1989: 155-166).

These details are found in Udall (1987: 112-129).

Kessell (1979: 12-14).

Bolton (1964a: 201-230). "The Tigeux War," writes Bolton (p. 230), "was a deplorable episode in Spanish empire building, but lest we make invidious comparisons we must not forget analogous chapters in the epic story of our own 'Westward Movement,' which we regard as so heroic."

Sauer (1971: 148). The details of the Coronado expedition are recounted in many publications, including Bolton (1964a); Hammond and Rey (1940); Jones 1929); Sauer (1971: 130-151); Udall 1987: 103-191); and Winship 1896).

Kelsey (1985: 8-9).

See, for example, Morison (1974: 628).

Summary accounts of the Cabrillo expedition are found in Morison (1974: 624-633) and in Sauer 1971: 154-156). The principal full length-treatments are found in Bolton (1925: 13-39) and in Wagner (1929: 72-93, 219-221, 318-323, 330-333, 417-431, 450-453). Also see Moriarty and Keistman (1968).

Heizer (1972).

MISSION AND COLONY

1   Bolton (1960: 4, 13).

2   Salient aspects of the Spanish mission program are discussed in the introduction to Bringas de Manzaneda y Encinas (1977: 1-33).

3   Sauer (1971: 189-90).

4   A detailed account of this affair is in Weddle (1985: 234-46, 248-49); a summary is in Tebeau (1980: 24-25).

5   Weddle (1985: 246).

6   Brown (1991: 52).

7   Weddle (1985: 247-48).

8   Weddle (1985: 248). The most complete accounts of the 1554 wreck of the Spanish flota, including the story of its further salvage by treasure hunters and archeologists in the twentieth century, are in Olds (1976) and in Arnold and Weddle (1978).

9   Weddle (1985: 257-59).

10   Weddle (1985: 259).

11   Weddle (1985: 259-60).

12   Weddle (1985: 267).

13   Weddle (1985: 268-69).

14   Tebeau (1980: 26-27).

15   Weddle (1985: 278).

16   Bearss (1989).

17   The story of permanent Spanish beginnings of La Florida, including Spanish involvement with Indians and the competition with France, are unfolded in the richly illustrated article by Judge (1988).

18   The best and most detailed summary of these events in English is in Lorant (1965: 5-9).

19   Tebeau (1980: 32).

20   Lyon (1982: 4).

21   Lorant (1965: 20-21); Deagan (1983: 22-23).

22   Details of the history of the construction of Castillo de San Marcos are in Arana and Manucy (1977). A later summary, including information on additional Spanish forts, is in Arana (1991).

23   The numbers of French who were killed or captured or who escaped vary in different secondary sources. See Bushnell (1983: 30); Lorant, (1965: 23); and Tebeau (1980: 35).

24   Lorant (1965: 24, 26).

25   National Park Service, U.S. Department of the Interior, Fort Matanzas (1975).

26   Horvath and Smith (1991).

27   Lyon (1982). A more detailed account of these events is in Roncière (1928). A sixteen-page typescript of a 1990 English translation of Roncière by Jean Chastain of the chapter on de Gourgues is on file at Fort Caroline National Memorial and Timucuan Ecological and Historic Preserve.

28 Lyon (1982: 57). Santa Elena, established by Menéndez in 1566, became the capital of Spanish Florida rather than San Agustín. However, after the death of Pedro Menéndez in 1574, the seat of government moved southward to San Agustín. In 1587 Santa Elena was abandoned when its settlers were ordered to move to San Agustín to help protect it against attacks like that perpetrated by Sir Francis Drake. See South (1991: 4) and Bushnell (1983: 35).

29 Lyon (1982: 58).

30 Gannon (1965: 27-28).

31 Dobyns (1983: 284).

32 Gannon (1965: 29, 32). Although Gannon's study of the Catholic church in early Florida is basic, several other works on the subject offer important information. Among these are monographs by Geiger (1937 and 1940); Lanning (1935); and Thomas (1987 and 1988). Also important are the dozen concluding essays in the volume edited by Thomas (1990: 355-580).

33 Gannon (1965: 32-34); Lanning (1935: 37).

34 Geiger (1940: 9).

35 Geiger (1937: 55; 1940: 85).

36 Geiger (1937: 55). The histories of missions San Pedro de Mocamo and San Pedro y San Pablo de Puturibato, as well as of Fort San Pedro, are summarized in Hann (1990: 431, 437, 438-39).

37 Gannon (1965: 39).

38 Geiger (1937: 65; 1940: 51); Lanning (1935: 71).

39 Geiger (1940: 51-52). Details of the Guale attack on Cumberland Island are also in Geiger (1937: 87-88, 100-102) and Lanning (1935: 90-94).

40 Lanning (1935: 79-80).

41 Johnson (1924: 58) and Lanning (1935: 128, 132-33).

42 Gannon (1965: 64); Torres (1977: 15-16).

43 Bannon (1970: 28-29).

44 Bannon (1970: 30); Kessell (1979: 21).

45 Bannon (1970: 31-32); Hammond and Rey (1927: 3-4; 1966: 8); Kessell (1979: 37).

46 Kessell (1979: 38).

47 Kessell (1979: 38).

48 Hammond and Rey (1927: 63), where it is equated with Taos Pueblo; Kessell (1979: 38-39). Hammond and Rey (1966: 59-60) change their minds and identify Nueva Tlaxcala as Pecos.

49 Hammond and Rey (1927: 55); Kessell (1979: 39).

50 Bannon (1970: 32); Hammond and Rey (1966: 18); Kessell (1966: 41).

51 Bannon (1970: 32); Kessell (1979: 41).

52 Hammond and Rey (1966: 22); Kessell (1979: 41).

53 Hammond and Rey (1966: 23-25, 193-94); Kessell (1979: 41-42). The best discussion of Espejo's route in Arizona is Bartlett (1942).

54 Hammond and Rey (1966: 25-26); Kessell (1979: 41-42).

55 Kessell (1979: 42).

56 Hammond and Rey (1966: 27); Kessell (1979: 43). The Pérez de Luxán account of Espejo's expedition is also translated and edited in Hammond and Rey (1929).

57 Kessell (1979: 43).

58 Kessell (1979: 45).

59 Hammond and Rey (1966: 28-29); Kessell (1979: 45, 47).

60 Hammond and Rey (1966: 30-31); Kessell (1979: 47).

61 Hammond and Rey (1966: 33).

62 Kessell (1979: 52).

63 Kessell (1979: 48-62) provides dramatic details of Castaño's ill-fated expedition to New Mexico, emphasizing the story of his capture of Pecos Pueblo. The story is summarized more briefly in Hammond and Rey (1966: 35-39), whereas the same source reprints an English translation of the "Memoria" on pp. 245-95. Another translation and annotation of the "Memoria," one whose interpretation of routes followed differs from that of Hammond and Rey, is Schroeder and Matson (1965).

64 Details are in Hammond and Rey (1966: 39-47).

65 Hammond and Rey (1966: 48-50).

66 The complex story of the incorporation of the Indians of New Mexico and elsewhere in the American Southwest and in northwestern Mexico into the culture of New Spain, a subject beyond the scope of this book, is told in the classic work by Spicer (1962).

67 Simmons (1991).

68 Kessell (1979: 67).

69 Kessell (1979: 69); Simmons (1991: 42).

70 Bannon (1970: 35); Simmons (1991: 4-5).

71 Bannon (1970: 36); Kessell (1979: 70-71).

72 Bannon (1970: 36); Simmons (1991: 87, 96-97).

73 Bragg (1989); Pérez de Villagrá (1933: 129); Simmons (1991: 94-95, 100-101).

74 Pérez de Villagrá (1933: 129-30).

75 Hammond and Rey (1953: I: 335).

76 Simmons (1991: 104-9, 148, 182).

77 Simmons (1991: 106, 125).

78 Kessell (1979: 78).

79 Kessell (1979: 78, 80, 82).

80 Kessell (1979: 82-85).

81 Simmons (1991: 125-27, 132).

82 Simmons (1991: 131-32).

83 Simmons (1991: 140-43, 145).

84 Simmons (1991: 172-75). Also see Murphy (1989: 5-6) and Slater (1961: 7, 98).

85 Simmons (1991: 178-85).

86 Herring (1968: 89).

87 Herring (1968: 135-36).

88 Lyon (1990b: 8-9); Mathes (1968: 7-8); Wagner (1929: 107-17).

89 Lyon (1990b: 11); Mathes (1968: 9-11).

) Mathes (1968: 12-13); Wagner (1929: 133).

4 Wagner (1929: 135).

2 Wagner (1929: 139-40).

3 Mathes (1968: 15); Wagner (1929: 143).

4 Mathes (1968: 15-18); Wagner (1929: 143-51).

5 Mathes (1968: 25).

5 Wagner (1929: 154-55).

7 Wagner (1929: 155, 164).

8 Chapman (1946: 117-18); Wagner (1929: 157-60).

9 Wagner (1929: 158).

00 Wagner (1929: 160, 165-66).

01 Murphy (1984: 29-34); Von der Porten (1972).

02 Wagner (1929: 160-62, 372).

03 Wagner (1929: 162).

04 Wagner (1929: 163).

05 Wagner (1929: 168).

06 Mathes (1968: 30).

07 Wagner (1929: 171-72, 174-76).

08 Mathes (1968: 55-60).

09 Mathes (1968: 89-92, 105-106 n. 58; plate 28); Wagner (1929: 231-34).

10 Wagner (1929: 239, 402 n. 40).

11 Mathes (1968: 94, 98).

12 Mathes (1968: 98-102); Wagner (1929: 249-55, 407 nn. 182, 185, 186).

13 Mathes (1968: 98-104); Wagner (1929: 255-63).

14 Chapman (1946: 142); Lyon (1990b: 8).

A CENTURY OF CONSOLIDATION

Hann (1990: 236-237); Thomas (1987: 82, 90-91, 93).

Hann (1990: 425-426); Thomas (1987: 82, 90).

Gannon (1965: 66-69).

Dobyns (1983: 278-281).

Dobyns (1983: 283); Flowers (1991); Gannon (1965: 75-76).

Gannon (1965: 76-77); Thomas (1987: 90-91).

Arana and Manucy (1977: 10).

Arana and Manucy (1977: 11-12).

Arana and Manucy (1977: 12).

233

10   Arana and Manucy (1977: 11-12).

11   Arana and Manucy (1977: 7-9).

12   Arana and Manucy (1977: 13-14).

13   Arana and Manucy (1977: 14-15).

14   The history of the fort's seventeenth-century construction is detailed in Arana and Manucy (1977: 25-37).

15   This story is told in book-length detail in Dunn (1917). A more recent overview, one which excludes Texas from consideration, is provided by Caruso (1963).

16   Coleman (1987: 3, 6); Tebeau (1980: 60); Thrapp (1988: II: 736-737, 943).

17   Coleman (1987: 8, 11); St. Cosme, quoted in Ramenofsky (1987: 70).

18   Dunn (1917: 13-17).

19   John (1975: 163); Kessell (1979: 267); Thrapp (1988: II: 816-817).

20   Billington (1960: 433).

21   Scurlock and others (1974: 18-19).

22   Jones (1988: 104-105); Weddle (1976: 412).

23   Tyler (1975: 27-29).

24   Almaráz (1989: 4-5); John (1975: 187-192, 207-210).

25   John (1975: 191-192); Morkovsky (1979: 138).

26   Leonard (1974: 13-14). Also see Leonard (1939).

27   Leonard (1974: 22-23).

28   Leonard (1974: 29-31); Tebeau (1980: 61). The story is told in detail by Leonard (1932).

29   Coker (1984: 22-23).

30   Coleman and Coleman (1982: 7, 9).

31   Beck (1962: 61-62). The 1610 date for the departure of Oñate and arrival of Peralta is that given by Simmons (1991: 184-185).

32   Simmons (1991: 182).

33   Simmons (1977: 54).

34   Simmons (1977: 57).

35   Simmons (1977: 56-58); Spicer (1962: 158, 290-291, 390-391).

36   Simmons (1991: 27).

37   Kessell (1979: 99).

38   Spicer (1962: 158-162).

39   Kessell (1989).

40   Kessell (1979: 522-523, n. 41).

41   Kessell (1979: 11, 104).

42   Ivey (1988: 20-21).

43   Kessell (1979: 106-107).

44   Kessell (1979: 112-124).

5   Kessell (1979: 127-129).

6   Ivey (1988: 59).

7   The architectural history of San Gregorio de Abó is presented in detail in Ivey (1988: 55-109).

8   Ivey (1988: 345-353); Toulouse (1949).

9   Schroeder (1979: 241).

0   Ivey (1988: 111-154).

1   Quarai's history is outlined in Wilson (1985).

2   Hurt (1990: 4-8).

3   Ivey (1988: 17, 157).

4   Ivey (1988: 157-171).

5   Murphy (1989: 7-8).

6   Ivey (1988: 178-200).

7   Ivey (1988: 370-379).

8   Kessell (1979: 132).

9   Kessell (1979: 134-137). Plains-Pueblo relationships are analyzed in Spielmann (1989, 1991).

0   Beck (1962: 75-76); Kessell (1979: 226); Spicer (1962: 160-161).

1   Kessell (1979: 221); Spicer (1962: 161).

2   Simmons 1977: 65); Spicer (1962: 162).

3   Spicer (1962: 162).

4   Spicer (1962: 162-163).

5   Kessell (1979: 227-228, 232, 241).

6   Kessell (1979: 239).

7   Kessell (1979: 244-249).

8   Kessell 1979: 251-252).

9   Kessell (1979: 260-263).

0   Kessell (1979: 274, 305).

1   Kessell (1979: 282, 285).

2   Kessell (1979: 287-289). The story of the entire revolt is told in Espinosa (1988).

3   Kessell (1979: 291-293).

4   Kessell (1979: 297).

5   Murphy (1989: 7).

6   Kessell (1979: 106-107).

7   Kessell (1979: 109).

8   Kessell (1979: 138).

9   Murphy (1989: 8).

0   Slater (1961: 9-12).

1   Murphy (1989: 10); Slater (1961: 13-15).

235

82   Almada (1983: 661); Fontana (1990: 452).

83   Bolton (1936).

84   Fontana (1981: 32). This book provides an overview of the history and culture of the Tohono O'odham (Papago Indians). For a summary of the effects of Kino's introductions among the Northern Pimans, see Sheridan (1988).

85   The journeys of Kino are summarized in the biography of him by Bolton (1936). See especially Bolton's map between pp. 594-595.

86   Bolton (1936: 285-286).

87   Houk (1987: 4-5).

88   Manje (1954: 85).

89   Manje (1954: 86).

90   Martín Bernal (1966: 41).

91   Kino (1966: 15); Manje (1954: 124).

92   The story of the 1695 Pima uprising and of La Matanza is summarized in Bolton (1936: 288-317). It is told more-or-less in its entirety in Polzer and Burrus (1971).

93   John (1975: 190-191); Polzer and Burrus (1971: 315-322).

94   Polzer and Burrus (1971: 320-321).

95   These visits are summarized in Hartmann (1989: 36-56).

96   Kino (1966: 21).

97   Manje (1954: 14, 17, 30).

THE END OF AMICHEL

1   Gentry (1982: 30).

2   Skowronek (1984: iii, 22, 25). This volume (pp. 6-18) also has an excellent discussion of Spanish worldwide trade in the eighteenth century, including its legal and economic aspects.

3   Anonymous (1985); Bearss (1989).

4   Tebeau (1980: 63-64).

5   Arana and Manucy (1977: 42).

6   Caruso (1963: 193, 195).

7   Tebeau (1980: 68, 70). The story is also detailed in Caruso (1963: 219-222) and in Arana and Manucy (1977: 46-49).

8   Arana and Manucy (1977: 51); Caruso (1963: 223-226).

9   Caruso (1963: 226-227).

10   For a thorough history of the fort's construction and alterations, see Fort Matanzas Stabilization Team (1980).

11   Arana and Manucy (1977: 51-54).

12   Arana and Manucy (1977: 53-54); Billington (1960: 131); Cowan and others (1983: 24); Stokes and Tregle (1978: 432f); Tebeau (1980: 72).

3   Arana and Manucy (1977: 54); Johnson and others (1978: 265).

4   Leonard (1974: 42-43); Tebeau (1980: 74).

5   Leonard (1974: 35, 37).

6   Coleman and Coleman (1982: 9).

7   Coleman and Coleman (1982: 10).

8   Coleman and Coleman (1982: 10-11).

9   Coleman and Coleman (1982: 11-12).

20   Coleman and Coleman (1982: 12); Leonard (1974: 39).

21   Coleman and Coleman (1982: 13).

22   Leonard (1974: 39-40); Rea 1974: 57-58).

23   Rea (1974: 79); Tebeau (1980: 86-87, 89).

24   Tebeau (1980: 73, 76-77).

25   Arana and Manucy (1977: 54-55).

26   Paige (1980: 41-45).

27   Paige (1980: 47-49); Billington (1960: 193-195).

28   Gannon (1965: 86-89).

29   Rea (1974: 74).

30   Tebeau (1980: 85); Thrapp (1988: II: 531).

31   Tebeau (1980: 85); Thrapp (1988: II: 531).

32   Coleman and Coleman (1982: 15-17).

33   Coleman and Coleman (1982: 23). The story of the capture of Pensacola by Gálvez is told in Parks (1981).

34   Sánchez (1991).

35   Brammer (1988: 245-246); Stokes and Tregle (1978: 432f).

36   Bannon (1970: 204); Clark and Guice (1989: 83-84).

37   Clark and Guice (1989: 86-97).

38   Gannon (1965: 93); Tebeau (1980: 92).

39   Arana and Manucy (1977: 58).

40   Gannon (1965: 89, 93).

41   Arana (1980: 81). Arana's report details this period of the history of Matanzas.

42   Holmes (1974: 91-93).

43   Coleman and Coleman (1982: 29).

44   Bearss (1977: 5-6).

45   Coleman and Coleman (1982: 28).

46   Coleman and Coleman (1982: 25, 28).

47   Coker (1984: 23).

237

48 Billington (1960: 243-244).

49 Bearss (1977: 9).

50 Coleman and Coleman (1982: 29).

51 Coleman and Coleman (1982: 29-30).

52 Coleman and Coleman (1982: 30-31).

53 Chace and Carr (1988); Tebeau (1980: 114). These events are also neatly summarized in Caruso (1963: 365-374). For the line in the west drawn as a result of the Adams-Onís Treaty, see Stephens and Holmes (1989: map 19).

54 Holmes (1974: 106).

55 Wilds (1983: 102-103, 112).

56 Coleman (1987: 51).

57 Din (1988: 13). An earlier Spanish governorship, that of Alexander O'Reilly, is elaborated by Bjork (1932).

58 Din (1988: 15, 18-19).

59 Yakubik (1989: 14-16, 18-19).

60 Smith (1990: 45, 50-51); Wilds (1983: 111).

61 Cowan (1983: 242-243).

62 Coleman (1987: 51).

63 Coleman (1987: 51).

64 Coleman (1987: 52, 55).

65 Coleman (1987: 55-58).

66 Coleman (1987: 59).

67 Coleman (1987: 60).

68 Coleman (1987: 59-67).

69 Coleman (1987: 69).

70 Coleman (1987: 69-72).

71 Billington (1960: 241-243); Coleman (1987: 73-74). The complexity of relationships between Americans and Spaniards in this region is described in Whitaker (1969).

72 Coleman (1987: 74).

73 Billington (1960: 244-245); Coleman (1987: 74).

74 Coleman (1987: 74, 76).

75 Crouch, Garr, and Mundigo (1982: 117-117); Foley (1971: 20-22).

76 Foley (1971: 23-24).

77 Foley (1971: 27-29). Further details are in Nasatir (1932: 239-261).

78 Foley (1971: 30-31).

79 Cook (1973: 435).

80 The story of American-Spanish relations in Louisiana is outlined with supporting documents in Kinnaird (1932).

81 Foley (1971: 42-43).

Foley (1971: 44, 46, 50).

Nasatir (1976). This book, more than any other, provides an overview of the history and strategic and diplomatic significance to Spain of her 1762-1803 "ownership" of Louisiana.

Leutenegger and Perry (1976: 22).

Anonymous (n.d.: 67-68); John (1975: 102, 104, 110-111); Stephens and Holmes (1989: map 12).

John (1975: 187-189, 192).

Stephens and Holmes (1989: map 12).

The best discussion of the identification of the Indians of the San Antonio missions is that by Campbell and Campbell (1985). Also see Schuetz (1976: 3-4).

John (1975: 223); MacMillan (1976: 84-85); Teja (1991: 29). The record of Alarcón's founding of San Antonio de Béxar is in the document of Céliz (1935). Also see Cruz (1988: 52-80).

Anonymous (n.d.: 169-170).

John (1975: 224-225); Leutenegger and Perry (1976: 25-26).

Leutenegger and Perry (1976: 26).

Leutenegger and Perry (1976: 26-27).

Habig (1968: 70).

Habig (1968: 81, 84-85, 103, 111-112, 114).

Habig (1968: 81-82, 88-92).

Bringas y Manzaneda (1977: 13-17).

Habig (1968: 96-98, 102-104, 106).

Habig (1968: 98-99).

10 Quoted in Habig (1968: 101-102).

11 Habig (1968: 102).

12 Habig (1968: 111-112); Stephens and Holmes (1989: map 16); Thrapp (1988: III: 1146).

13 Habig (1968: 119-121); Meyer and Sherman (1987: 296).

14 Almaráz (1989: 29).

15 Almaráz (1989: 4); Casso (1979: 91); Leutenegger and Perry (1976: 27).

16 Leutenegger and Perry (1976: 27).

17 Casso (1979: 99).

18 Casso (1979: 100-101). An excellent and well-illustrated discussion of the still-performed matachines dance is in Champe (1983).

19 Fox (1988).

20 Almaráz (1989: 29); Fox (1988: 5); Stephens and Holmes (1989: map 17).

21 Casso (1979: 88-91); Ferrando Roig (1950: 158). San Juan's Spanish-period history is summarized by Schuetz (1968: 10-58).

22 Leutenegger and Perry (1976: 28).

23 Leutenegger and Perry (1976: 28).

24 Habig (1968: 99, 116).

25 Casso (1979: 91).

239

[116] Almaráz (1989: 47-48); Ivey (1983: 35); Leutenegger and Perry (1976: 28).

[117] Almaráz (1989: 48-49); Leutenegger and Perry (1976: 29).

[118] This history is set forth in Ivey (1983).

[119] León (1979: 29-30).

[120] Almaráz (1979: 8; 1989: 5).

[121] This particular story is told by Weddle (1991). Also see Hackett (1932).

[122] Stephens and Holmes (1989: maps 15 and 19).

[123] See the maps in Jones (1988: xvi-xx).

[124] Weddle (1976: 412). The Rivera inspection is reported in full in Naylor and Polzer (1988). The best discussion of presidios along this frontier, including maps showing their locations at different periods of time, is in Moorehead (1991).

[125] Tyler (1975: 27, 32-34); Weddle (1976: 413).

[126] Weddle (1976: 413).

[127] Tyler (1975: 36-37).

[128] Kinnaird (1958: 1-2).

[129] Tyler (1975: 38-41).

[130] Tyler (1975: 42).

[131] Weddle (1976: 414-415).

[132] Morfi (1935); Tyler (1975: 43-44).

[133] Tyler (1975: 44). Both presidios are thoroughly described in Ivey (1990). For San Carlos, also se Gerald (1968: 37-39).

[134] Tyler (1975: 45).

[135] Tyler (1975: 48-49). Ugalde's 1789-1790 campaign is described in Moorhead (1968: 254-257).

[136] Tyler (1975: 49).

[137] Scurlock and others (1974: 19).

[138] Salinas (1990: 17-20).

[139] O'Connor (1966: 18-19); Scurlock and others (1974: 19).

[140] John (175: 293-297); Scurlock and others (1974: 20).

[141] Brown (1991: 54); Scurlock and others (1974: 20-21).

[142] Scurlock and others (1974: 20-21).

BLOOMING AND DYING IN THE WEST

[1] Beck (1962: 89).

[2] Kessell (1979: 302).

[3] Kessell (1979: 299).

[4] Kessell (1979: 299).

[5] Beck (1962: 92); Kessell (1979: 302).

Kessell (1979: 303-304).

Kessell (1979: 304-307, 309).

Kessell (1979: 309).

Kessell (1979: 288-289, 292).

) Kessell (1979: 229-230, 295).

1 Kessell (1979: 303-304).

2 Kessell (1979: 310-311).

3 Kessell (1979: 312).

4 Kessell (1979: 316).

5 Kessell (1979: 317).

6 Kessell (1979: 320, 359).

7 John (1975).

8 Kessell (1979: 370-371, 386).

9 The story is told in Hötz (1970).

0 Kessell (1979: 387).

1 Kessell (1979: 389, 391). The story of French and New Mexican trade is further elaborated in
Bolton (1964c).

2 Kessell (1979: 12, 364-368).

3 Kessell (1979: 334, 372-373).

4 Kessell (1979: 374-378).

5 Kessell (1979: 380-381).

6 Kessell (1979: 383, 385, 391-397).

7 Two excellent accounts of this journey are those by Briggs (1976) and Chavez and Warner
1976). Mention of the still-unpublished Rivera report is in Baker (1990: 40).

8 Kessell (1979: 397, 399-401); Trimble (1978: 24).

9 Kessell (1979: 349, 401-409).

0 Officer (1987: 68); Palmer (1990: 1); Slater (1961: 23-24).

1 Kessell (1979: 407); Thrapp (1988: III: 1481-1482). The story of Pedro Vial, wilderness
adventurer extraordinaire, is in Loomis and Nasatir (1967).

2 Kessell (1979: 352-353, 355, 410).

3 Kessell (1979: 415).

4 Schaafsma (1980: 328, 330); Thrapp (1988: II: 1041-1042).

5 Mabery (1990: 13).

6 Slater (1961: 15-16).

7 Slater (1961: 17). The role of Protector General of the Indians is described by C. Cutter (1986).

8 Officer (1987: 28).

9 Slater (1961: 18-19, 150 n. 34).

0 Slater (1961: 19-20).

41 Murphy (1989: 11, 13); Slater (1961: 20).

42 Donohue (1969: 105); Slater (1961: 20-21).

43 Slater (1961: 21).

44 Slater (1961: 24).

45 Kessell (1979: 433-434).

46 Kessell (1979: 444-445).

47 Kessell (1970: 29-31).

48 Hammond (1929: 227-236).

49 Kessell (1970: 43-54).

50 Kessell (1970: 54-58).

51 Kessell (1970: 61-62).

52 Donohue (1969: 80).

53 Kessell (1970: 62-74); Officer (1987: 31-32).

54 Donohue (1969: 104-105); Mills (1932: 47-48).

55 Ives (1989: 101, 103); Mills (1932: 49).

56 Compare the accounts in Dunne (1955: 21-23) and Mills (1932: 112-114 and 202-204) with that in Manje (1954: 85-86). Also see Dunne (1955: 46, n. 33).

57 Kessell (1970: 82-85).

58 Ives (1989: 104-105).

59 Sedelmayr (1748). Also see Donohue (1969: 120); Dunne (1955: 55-66); and Mills (1932: 153-164).

60 Dunne (1955: 67-68); Mills (1932: 69).

61 Sedelmayr (1751a).

62 Sedelmayr (1751b).

63 Ives (1989: 104-105); Pfefferkorn (1989: 258-259).

64 Kessell (1970: 79-80).

65 Kessell (1970: 91-92).

66 Kessell (1970: 100).

67 Kessell (1970: 102-105).

68 Kessell (1970: 105-106, 134).

69 Ives (1989: 107-109).

70 Dunne (1955: 9); Kessell (1970: 108, 113-114).

71 Donohue (1969: 131-133); Kessell (1970: 142-143).

72 Kessell (1970: 125).

73 Kessell (1970: 127).

74 Pfefferkorn (1989: 260-261).

75 Pfefferkorn (1989: 34).

76 Kessell (1970: 144).

77 Kessell (1970: 156).

8   Kessell (1970: 161-162, 168).

9   Kessell (1970: 160, 164-165). Father Pfefferkorn survived later service at the Sonoran missions of Oposura and Cucurpe. Before he died in his native Germany in the late eighteenth century, he wrote his classic work, *Sonora: A Description of the Province*.

0   Kessell (1970: 172).

1   Kinnaird (1958: 105-106).

2   Kessell (1970: 173, 176).

3   Kessell (1979: 181-184, 190).

4   Kessell (1976: 19-20).

5   Kessell (1976: 20, 24).

6   Kessell (1976: 24).

7   Kessell (1976: 37-40, 88).

8   Holterman (1973: 75-78).

9   Kessell (1976: 57).

0   Holterman (1973: 93-103); Kessell (1976: 57-60).

1   Holterman (1973: 118-167). A summary of this trip has also been published by Bolton (1917).

2   Kessell (1976: 72-73).

3   Chapman (1946: 207-231).

4   Holterman (1973: 193-196).

5   Bolton (1930: II: 2, 12, 24, 44, 310, 314, 323).

6   Bolton (1930: II: 127-128).

7   Chapman (1946: 254-272).

8   Kessell (1976: 103-110).

9   Bolton (1930: III: 1-2, 206).

100 Bolton (1930: IV: 18-19).

101 Bolton (1930: IV: 34-37).

102 Bolton (1930: IV: 38-41).

103 Coues (1900: II: 386-388).

104 Anonymous (1989); Bolton (1930: IV: 316-422); Chapman (1917: 384).

105 Bolton (1930: IV: 249, 432, 459).

106 Bolton (1930: IV: 482-484); Garcés (1965: 74-75, 85-88, foldout map at rear of book).

107 Bolton (1930: IV: 490-519).

108 Kessell (1976: 142-146).

109 Kessell (1976: 130).

110 Thomas (1932: 207-215).

111 Hartmann (1989: 73); Ives (1968; 1984: 160-168; 1989: 179-211); Sánchez (1990: 58-59, 70, 109-112).

112 Fontana (1971: 73-74); Kessell (1976: 170-171, 207-214).

113 Bringas y Manzaneda (1977: 98-99, 113, 118); Kessell (1976: 183-187).

114 Bleser (n.d.: 20).

115 Bleser (n.d.: 20-21, 24-25); Meyer and Sherman (1987: 296).

116 Chapman (1946: 222-223); Servín (1979: 126).

117 Chapman (1946: 222-224); Servín (1979: 120-121).

118 Servín (1979: 122).

119 Servín (1979: 122-123).

120 Bringas y Manzaneda (1977: 122).

121 None of California's twenty-one Hispanic-period missions or mission asistencias (visitas) is in the National Park System. A convenient guide to them is the book by the Sunset Editors (1979).

122 Bolton (1964b: 276-277).

123 Bolton (1964b: 277-278).

124 Bolton (1964b: 279); Sunset Editors (1979: 83).

125 Chapman (1946: 230-231, 253, 272-273, 288-289); Sunset Editors (1979: 100-137).

126 Langellier and Rosen (1991: 24).

127 Engstrand (1988: 36).

128 Beck and Haase (1974: map 37); Curtis (1959: 15); Engstrand (1988: 36); Robinson (1939: 145); Shumway (1988: 31).

129 Beck and Haase (1974: maps 36, 37); Shumway (1988: 28-29).

130 Engstrand (1988: 36, 39); Greenwood (1989: 452-453).

131 Anonymous (1975); Langellier and Rosen (1991: 27-28); Santa María (1971).

132 Bolton (1930: IV: 333, 336).

133 Langellier and Rosen (1991: 36-37, 40-43); Sunset Editors (1979: 139-141).

134 Langellier and Rosen (1991: 43).

135 Sunset Editors (1979: 141).

136 Langellier and Rosen (1991: 78-83).

137 Langellier and Rosen (1991: 85-86).

138 Langellier and Rosen (1991: 86-88).

139 Langellier and Rosen (1991: 91-97, 131).

140 Chapman (1946: 411-412).

141 Langellier and Rosen (191: 166-167).

142 Chapman (1946: 414-415); Chevigny (1965: 102-108); Langellier and Rosen (1991: 171-172, 176).

143 Chapman (1946: 415-417); Chevigny (1965: 109-110).

144 Langellier and Rosen (1991: 177-178).

145 Langellier and Rosen (1991: 179-180).

146 Hart (1987: 170); Langellier and Rosen (1991: 181-182).

147 Langellier and Rosen (1991: 183, 185-186, 193-199).

148 Geiger (n.d.: 2). The conscripted involvement of Eskimos in the Russian-promoted fur trade is described by Clark (1984: 187).

Geiger (n.d.: 3-12).

Ellison (n.d.: 37, 77, 81-89); Heizer and Elsasser (1973: ii, iv).

Cook (1973: 234-236).

Colston (1982: 61).

Colston (1982: 62, 64-65, 69-70).

Anonymous (1989: 83); Bowman (1951: 59-60); Langellier and Rosen (1991: 187-190).

Chapman (1946: 441-452); Hart (1987: 57); Langellier and Rosen (1991: 202-204).

Langellier and Rosen (1991: 204).

Chapman (1946: 452-453); Langellier and Rosen (1991: 205).

Beck and Haase (1974: map 18); Langellier and Rosen (1991: 209-210).

Bobb (1962: 165).

Archibald, quoted in Fontana (1979: 19). Among the many authors who have written about the ects of the Spanish occupation of California on its Native American population are Cook (1978: -92) and Castillo (1978: 99-104). Also see Hoover (1989).

Cook (1973: 50-51).

Cook (1973: 54-69). For the Nootkans, see Arima and Dewhirst (1990).

Cook (1973: 69-83); Powell (1990: 435).

Cook (1973: 85-88).

Cook (1973: 80, 93-95).

Cook (1973: 97).

Cook (1973: 97).

Cook (1973: 97-99).

Cook (1973: 100-117).

Cook (1973: 119-129).

Cook (1973: 146-199).

Cook (1973: 271-278). For the Catalonian Volunteers in Nootka, see Sánchez (1991: 86-88).

Cook (1973: 247).

Cook (1973: 118-119, 306-307); Cutter (1976: 28-35; 1991: 1-70).

Cutter (1976: 34-40).

Cook (1973: 331-333); Engstrand (1991); Moziño (1970).

Cook (1973: 345-353); Cutter (1990; 1991: 111-135).

Cook (1973: 362-396).

Cook (1973: 409-417).

Cook (1973: 419); Wessen (1990: 414-416).

Cook (1973: 421-423).

Cook (1973: 460-483).

Clark and Guice (1989: 45); Cook (1973: 514-520, 535-536); Stephens and Holmes 989: map 19).

MEXICO

[1] The only book summarizing the brief period of Mexican history for the present states of Texas, New Mexico, Arizona, and California is that by Weber (1982).

[2] Meyer and Sherman (1987: 297).

[3] McDonald (1992: 34-35); Stephens and Holmes (1989: map 22); Teja and Wheat (1991: 3-4).

[4] McDonald (1992: 35-39); Stephens and Holmes (1989: map 22); Teja and Wheat (1991: 23).

[5] Almaráz (1989: 17-19); Habig (1968: 135).

[6] Almaráz (1989: 20); Teja and Wheat (1991: 6).

[7] Almaráz (1989: 14-15, 17).

[8] Almaráz (1989: 20); Langum (1987: 271).

[9] Almaráz (1989: 38).

[10] Almaráz (1989: 37-39).

[11] Almaráz (1989: 39-40, 44, 46).

[12] Almaráz (1989: 50-51).

[13] Almaráz (1989: 57).

[14] Barr (1990: 18); Stephens and Holmes (1989: map 24).

[15] Barr (1990: 17-19, 22).

[16] Barr (1990: 22-26); Stephens and Holmes (1989: map 24).

[17] Stephens and Holmes (1989: map 26).

[18] Teja and Wheat (1991: 24).

[19] Collins (1992: 76-77).

[20] Meyer and Sherman (1987: 315-316).

[21] Kessell (1980: 32 n. 8).

[22] Kessell (1979: 439, 441-442).

[23] Kessell (1979: 445).

[24] Kessell (1979: 445-448).

[25] Nasatir (1976: 86-106); Simmons (1977: 110). A summary of the trail's history in the Mexican period is in Krakow (1991).

[26] Quoted in Kessell (1979: 449-451).

[27] Kessell (1979: 452-455).

[28] Kessell (1979: 458-463, 465).

[29] Slater (1961: 25).

[30] Meyer and Sherman (1987: 346-347).

[31] Beck (1962: 133); Beck and Haase (1969: maps 19, 26); Faulk (1967: 57-86); Walker and Bufkin (1979: map 19). The most complete discussion of the subject is that by Griswold del Castillo (1990).

[32] Kessell (1976: 249-250).

Bleser (n.d.: 26-27).

Bleser (n.d.: 28-31); Kessell (1976: 250).

Kessell (1976: 264, 267-268).

Houk (1987: 16); Kessell (1976: 268); Walker and Bufkin (1979: map 17).

Kessell (1976: 269-271).

Kessell (1976: 277-281, 293).

Kessell (1976: 283).

Fontana (1971: 76-77).

Fontana (1971: 77, 79).

Quoted in Fontana (1971: 77-78).

Fontana (1971: 80).

Kessell (1976: 293).

Kessell (1976: 294).

Kessell (1976: 293, 295-296).

Kessell (1976: 297, 300).

Kessell (1976: 302).

Couts, quoted in Kessell (1976: 305).

Couts, quoted in Kessell (1976: 307).

Ahlborn (1974: 80-81, 103, 111-115); Kessell 1976: 308).

Bleser (n.d.: 35-38); Kessell (1976: 309-310).

Bean and Mason (1962: 13-15).

Bean and Mason (1962: 28, 77); Officer (1987: 102-103).

Wilcox and Shenk (1977: 11-15).

Bartlett (1965: II: 283-284).

Bean and Mason (1962: 88).

Bean and Mason (1962: 90-91).

Quoted in Fontana (1981: 57).

Officer (1987: 153-154).

Hoy (1992).

Officer (1987: 164-166).

Elías (1865: 126-127, 134).

Quoted in Hartmann (1989: 83).

Hartmann (1989: 82).

Hoy (1990: 118-120).

Hart (1987: 21, 483).

Chapman (1946: 455).

Greenwood (1989: 453-454).

70 Langellier and Rosen (1991: 215-216).

71 Langellier and Rosen (1991: 222, 240).

72 Langellier and Rosen (1991: 235-236).

73 Quoted in Langellier and Rosen (1991: 223).

74 Quoted in Langellier and Rosen (1991: 224).

75 Langellier and Rosen (1991: 224); Shumway (1988: 76).

76 Langellier and Rosen (1991: 239).

77 Langellier and Rosen (1991: 250).

78 Weber (1982: 63, 180-181, 206).

79 Weber (1982: 63-64).

80 Weber (1982: 67).

81 Weber (1982: 205).

82 Bogard (1989: 10); Shumway (1988: 21).

83 Hart (1987: 413); Shumway (1988: 40).

84 Buller and Delgado (1984: 40); Shumway (1988: 39).

85 Shumway (1988: 88).

86 Shumway (1988: 114).

87 Burke and others (1991: 6-9); Langellier and Rosen (1991: 298); Shumway (1988: 20).

88 Shumway (1988: 67, 104).

89 Hart (1987: 277-278).

90 Hart (1987: 351).

91 Ellison (n.d.: 40-42).

92 Ellison (n.d.: 43).

93 Weber (1982: 138-139).

94 Quoted in Buller and Delgado (1984: 38-39).

95 Richard Henry Dana, quoted in Buller and Delgado (1984: 41).

96 Buller and Delgado (1984: 40-43).

97 Burke and others (1991: 6-9).

98 This period of California's history is related in detail in Harlow (1982).

99 Weber (1982: 206).

100 Burke and others (1991: 9-12).

101 Burke and others (1991: 6).

Ahlborn, Richard E.

1974 *The Sculpted Saints of a Borderlands Mission: Los Bultos de San Xavier del Bac*. Tucson, Southwestern Mission Research Center.

Almada, Francisco

1983 *Diccionario de Historia, Geografía y Biografía Sonorenses*. Hermosillo, Gobierno del Estado de Sonora.

Almaráz, Félix D., Jr.

1979 *Crossroad of Empire: The Church and State on the Río Grande Frontier of Coahuila and Texas, 1700-1821* [Report on the Archaeology and History of the San Juan Bautista Mission Area, Coahuila and Texas, no. 1]. San Antonio, Center for Archaeological Research, The University of Texas at San Antonio.

1989 *The San Antonio Missions and Their System of Land Tenure*. Austin, University of Texas Press.

Anonymous

n.d. *Texas*. Austin, State Department of Highways and Public Transportation.

1972 *The Spanish Texans*. San Antonio, The University of Texas, Institute of Texan Cultures.

1975 The San Carlos Expedition. *Sea Letter of the San Francisco Maritime Museum*, Summer, pp. [1]-[7]. San Francisco, San Francisco Maritime Museum.

1985 *Monumentos Históricos Nacionales de San Juan/San Juan National Historic Site, Puerto Rico*. Washington, D.C., Government Printing Office.

1989 The Presidio. Another Great Park for San Francisco? *Sunset*, Vol. 183, no. 5 (November), obverse and reverse of front cover and pp. 78-85. Menlo Park, California, Lane Publishing Company.

Arana, Luis

1980 The Second Spanish Period or the Disintegration of Fort Matanzas, 1784-1821. In Fort Matanzas Stabilization Team (1980: 51-81).

1991 Fortifications of Spanish Florida, 1565-1763. *Courier*, special issue, October, pp. 26-30. Washington, D.C., U.S. Department of the Interior, National Park Service.

Arana, Luis, and Albert Manucy

1977 *The Building of Castillo de San Marcos*. N.p., Eastern National Park & Monument Association.

Arima, Eugene, and John Dewhirst

1990 Nootkans of Vancouver Island. In Sturtevant (1990: 391-411).

Arnold, J. Barto, III, and Robert Weddle

1978 *The Nautical Archaeology of Padre Island*. New York, Academic Press.

Austin, Mary

1983 *The Land of Journey's Ending*. Re-edition. Tucson, The University of Arizona Press.

Baker, Steve

1990 Northern Plains and Mountain States. *The Society for Historical Archaeology Newsletter*, Vol. 23, no. 2 (June), pp. 40-41. Pleasant Hill, California, Society for Historical Archaeology.

Bannon, John F.

1970 *The Spanish Borderlands Frontier, 1513-1821*. New York, Holt, Rinehart and Winston.

Bannon, John F., editor

1964 *Bolton and the Spanish Borderlands*. Norman, University of Oklahoma Press.

REFERENCES

249

Barr, Alwyn

1990 *Texas in Revolt: The Battle for San Antonio, 1835.* Austin, University of Texas Press.

Bartlett, John R.

1965 *Personal Narrative of Explorations and Incidents in Texas, New Mexico, California, Sonora and Chihuahua connected with the United States and Mexican Boundary Commission during the Years 1850, '51, '52, and '53.* Two volumes. Reprint edition. Chicago, The Rio Grande Press.

Bartlett, Katharine

1942 Notes Upon the Routes of Espejo and Farfán to the Mines in the Sixteenth Century. *New Mexico Historical Review*, Vol. 17, no. 1 (January), pp. 21-36. Santa Fe and Albuquerque, Historical Society of New Mexico and the University of New Mexico.

Bean, Lowell, and William M. Mason

1962 *Diaries & Accounts of the Romero Expeditions in Arizona and California, 1823-1826.* Palm Springs, Palm Springs Desert Museum.

Bearss, Edwin C.

1977 *Historic Structure Report and Historic Resource Study, Fort Barrancas, Gulf Islands National Seashore, Florida.* N.p., U.S. Department of the Interior, National Park Service.

1989 San Juan Fortifications: Study, Nomination and Inscription on the World Heritage List. *CRM Bulletin*, Vol. 12, special issue, pp. 11-14. Washington, D.C., U.S. Department of the Interior, National Park Service, Cultural Resources.

Beck, Warren A.

1962 *New Mexico: A History of Four Centuries.* Norman, University of Oklahoma Press.

Beck, Warren A., and Ynez D. Haase

1969 *Historical Atlas of New Mexico.* Norman, University of Oklahoma Press.

1974 *Historical Atlas of California.* Norman, University of Oklahoma Press.

Billington, Ray A.

1960 *Westward Expansion: A History of the American Frontier.* Second edition. New York, The Macmillan Company.

Bjork, David K.

1932 Alexander O'Reilly and the Spanish Occupation of Louisiana. In Hackett and others (1932: I: 165-182).

Bleser, Nicholas J.

n.d. *Tumacacori: From Ranchería to National Monument.* Tucson, Southwest Parks and Monuments Association.

Bobb, Bernard E.

1962 *The Viceregency of Antonio María Bucareli in New Spain, 1771-1779.* Austin, University of Texas Press.

Bogard, Travis

1989 *Eugene O'Neill at Tao House.* Tucson, Southwest Parks and Monuments Association.

Bolton, Herbert E.

1917 The Early Explorations of Father Garcés on the Pacific Slope. In Stephens and Bolton (1917: 317-330). Also in Bannon (1964: 255-269).

1936 *Rim of Christendom: A Biography of Eusebio Francisco Kino, Pacific Coast Pioneer.* New York, The Macmillan Company. [Also later re-editions.]

1960 *The Mission as a Frontier Institution in the Spanish-American Colonies*. Reprint edition. El Paso, Academic Reprints, Inc.

1964a *Coronado: Knight of Pueblos and Plains*. Reprint edition. Albuquerque, University of New Mexico Press.

1964b Fray Juan Crespi with the Portolá Expedition. In Bannon (1964: 270-280).

1964c French Intrusions into New Mexico, 1749-1752. In Bannon (1964: 150-171).

Bolton, Herbert E., editor

1925 *Spanish Explorations in the Southwest*. New York, Charles Scribner's Sons.

Bolton, Herbert E., translator and editor

1930 *Anza's California Expeditions*. Volumes 2-4. Berkeley, University of California Press.

Booth, Cathy, and Michael P. Harris

1990 Good Guy or Dirty Word? *Time*, Vol. 136, no. 23 (November 26), p. 79. New York, The Time Inc. Magazine Co.

Bowman, J.N.

1951 Adobe Houses in the San Francisco Bay Region. In *Geologic Guide Book of the San Francisco Bay Counties: History, Landscape, Geology, Fossils, Minerals, Industry, and Routes to Travel* [Bulletin of the Division of Mines, no. 154]. San Francisco, State of California, Department of Natural Resources, Division of Mines.

Bragg, Bea

1989 *The Very First Thanksgiving: Pioneers on the Rio Grande*. Tucson, Harbinger House.

Brain, Jeffrey P.

1985 Introduction: Update of De Soto Studies since the United States De Soto Expedition Commission Report. In John R. Swanton, *Final Report of the United States De Soto Expedition Commission*, reprint edition, pp. xi-xxii. Washington and London, Smithsonian Institution Press.

Brammer, Dana B.

1988 Mississippi. *The Encyclopedia Americana, International Edition*, Vol. 19, pp. 232-247. Danbury, Connecticut, Grolier, Inc.

Briggs, Walter

1976 *Without Noise of Arms: The 1776 Domínguez-Escalante Search for a Route from Santa Fe to Monterey*. Flagstaff, Northland Press.

Bringas de Manzaneda y Encinas, Diego

1977 *Friar Bringas Reports to the King: Methods of Indoctrination on the Frontier of New Spain, 1796-97*. Translated and edited by Daniel S. Matson and Bernard L. Fontana. Tucson, The University of Arizona Press.

Brown, Joseph E.

1991 *Padre Island: The National Seashore*. Tucson, Southwest Parks and Monuments Association.

Brown, Lenard E.

1991 Columbus Landing Site. *Courier*, special issue (October), pp. 31-32. Washington, D.C., U.S. Department of the Interior, National Park Service.

Bullen, Ripley

1978 Tocobaga Indians and the Safety Harbor Culture. In Milanich and Proctor (1978: 50-58).

Buller, David, and James Delgado

1984 Losses of Major Vessels Within the Drakes Bay Survey Area. In Murphy (1984: 35-84).

Burke, Steven M., Diane L. Rhodes, Kevin L. Baumgard, Mark L. Tabor, and Charles R. Svoboda

1991 "Historic Structure Report: Martinez Adobe." Uncorrected draft of an unpublished manuscript John Muir National Historic Site, Martinez, California; United States Department of the Interior National Park Service.

Bushnell, Amy

1983 The Noble and Loyal City. In Waterbury (1983: 27-55).

Campbell, T. N., and T. J. Campbell

1985 *Indian Groups Associated with Spanish Missions of the San Antonio Missions National Historical Park* [Special Report, no. 16]. San Antonio, Center for Archaeological Research, The University of Texas at San Antonio.

Caruso, John A.

1963 *The Southern Frontier*. Indianapolis and New York, Bobbs-Merrill Co.

Casso, M. Carmelita

1979 The Mission Nuestra Señora de la Purísima Concepción from Its Humble Beginnings to Its Zenith. In Ortego y Gasca (1979: 83-107).

Castillo, Carlos, and Otto F. Bond

1977 *The University of Chicago Spanish-English, English-Spanish Dictionary*. Third edition. New York, Pocket Books.

Castillo, Edward D.

1978 The Impact of Euro-American Exploration and Settlement. In Sturtevant (1978: 99-127).

Céliz, Francisco

1935 *Diary of the Alarcón Expedition into Texas, 1718-1719* [Quivira Society Publications, Vol. 5]. Translated by Fritz L. Hoffman. Los Angeles, The Quivira Society.

Chace, James, and Caleb Carr

1988 The odd couple who won Florida and half the West. *Smithsonian*, Vol. 19, no. 1 (September), pp. 134-136, 138, 140, 142, 144-146, 148, 150, 152, 154, 156-158, 160. Washington, D.C., Smithsonian Associates.

Champe, Flavia W.

1983 *The Matachines Dance of the Upper Rio Grande: History, Music, and Choreography*. Lincoln and London, University of Nebraska Press.

Chapman, Charles E.

1917 The Founding of San Francisco. In Stephens and Bolton (1917: 373-386).

1946 *A History of California: The Spanish Period*. New York, The Macmillan Company.

Chavez, Angelico, translator, and Ted J. Warner, editor

1976 *The Domínguez-Escalante Journal: Their Expedition through Colorado, Utah, Arizona, and New Mexico in 1776*. Provo, Brigham Young University Press.

Chevigny, Hector

1965 *Russian America: The Great Alaskan Venture, 1741-1867*. New York, Ballantine Books.

Clark, Donald W.

1984 Pacific Eskimo: Historical Ethnography. In Sturtevant (1984: 185-197).

Clark, Thomas D., and John D. W. Guice

    1989 *Frontiers in Conflict: The Old Southwest, 1795-1830.* Albuquerque, University of New Mexico Press.

Coker, William S.

    1984 The Village on the Red Cliffs. *Pensacola History Illustrated,* Vol. 1, no. 2, pp. 22-26. Pensacola, Pensacola Historical Society.

Coleman, James C., and Irene S. Coleman

    1982 *Guardians on the Gulf: Pensacola Fortifications, 1698-1980.* Pensacola, Pensacola Historical Society.

Coleman, Roger E.

    1987 *The Arkansas Post Story* [Professional Papers no. 12]. Santa Fe, Division of History, Southwest Cultural Resources Center, National Park Service, Department of the Interior.

Collins, Michael L.

    1992 Statehood, 1845-1860. In *The Texas Heritage,* edited by Ben Proctor and Archie P. McDonald, second edition, pp. 75-95. Arlington Heights, Illinois, Harlan Davidson, Inc.

Colston, Stephen A.

    1982 "San Joaquín": A Preliminary Historical Study of the Fortification at San Diego's Punta de Guijarros. In *Fort Guijarros* [Tenth Annual Cabrillo Festival Historic Seminar, Vol. 1, no. 10], pp. 61-83. San Diego, Cabrillo Historical Association.

Cook, Sherburne F.

    1978 Historical Demography. In Sturtevant (1978: 91-98).

Cook, Warren L.

    1973 *Flood Tide of Empire: Spain and the Pacific Northwest, 1543-1819.* New Haven and London, Yale University Press.

Costo, Rupert, and Jeanette H. Costo, editors

    1987 *The Missions of California: A Legacy of Genocide.* San Francisco, Indian Historian Press.

Coues, Elliott, translator and editor

    1900 *On the Trail of a Spanish Pioneer: The Diary and Itinerary of Francisco Garcés (Missionary Priest) in His Travels through Sonora, Arizona, and California, 1775-1776.* Two volumes. New York, Francis P. Harper.

Cowan, Walter G.

    1983 Things To Do and See. In Cowan and others (1983: 242-246).

Cowan, Walter G., and others

    1983 *New Orleans, Yesterday and Today: A Guide to the City.* Baton Rouge and London, Louisiana State University Press.

Crosby, Alfred W., Jr.

    1972 *The Columbian Exchange: Biological and Cultural Consequences of 1492.* Westport, Connecticut, Greenwood Press.

    1990 The Biological Significance of 1992. *Nuevo Mundo,* Vol. 2, no. 2 (June), pp. 7-8. San Diego, Cabrillo Historical Association.

Crouch, Dora P., Daniel J. Garr, and Alex I. Mundigo

1982 *Spanish City Planning in North America*. Cambridge and London, MIT Press.

Cruz, Gilbert R.

1988 *Let There Be Towns: Spanish Municipal Origins in the American Southwest, 1610-1810*. College Station, Texas A&M University Press.

Curtis, Freddie

1959 *Arroyo Sequit* [Papers of the Archaeological Survey Association of Southern California, no. 4]. N.p., Archaeological Survey Association of Southern California.

Cutter, Charles R.

1986 *The Protector de Indios in Colonial New Mexico, 1659-1821*. Albuquerque, University of New Mexico Press.

Cutter, Donald C.

1976 Malaspina's Grand Expedition. *El Palacio*, Vol. 82, no. 4, pp. 28-41. Santa Fe, Museum of New Mexico.

1990 *California in 1792: A Spanish Naval Visit*. Norman and London, University of Oklahoma Press.

1991 *Malaspina & Galiano: Spanish Voyages to the Northwest Coast*, Vancouver/Toronto, Douglas & McIntyre; Seattle, University of Washington Press.

Deagan, Kathleen

1983 *Spanish St. Augustine: The Archaeology of a Colonial Creole Community*. New York, Academic Press.

Din, Gilbert C.

1988 *The Canary Islanders of Louisiana*. Baton Rouge and London, Louisiana State University Press.

Dobyns, Henry F.

1983 *Their Number Become Thinned: Native American Population Dynamics in Eastern North America*. Knoxville, The University of Tennessee Press.

Donohue, John A.

1969 *After Kino: Jesuit Missions in Northwestern New Spain, 1711-1767* [Sources and Studies for the History of the Americas, Vol. 6]. Rome, Italy, and St. Louis, Missouri, Jesuit Historical Institute.

Duncan, David E.

1991 The Black Legend. *The Atlantic*, Vol. 268, no. 2 (August), pp. 30-31. Boston, The Atlantic Monthly Co.

Dunn, William E.

1917 *Spanish and French Rivalry in the Gulf Region of the United States, 1678-1702: The Beginnings of Texas and Pensacola* [University of Texas Bulletin no. 1705]. Austin, University of Texas.

Dunne, Peter M., translator and editor

1955 *Jacobo Sedelmayr: Missionary, Frontiersman, Explorer in Arizona and Sonora. Four Original Manuscript Narratives, 1744-1751*. Tucson, Arizona Pioneers' Historical Society.

Elías, José

1865 Jornadas. Seguidas por Don José Elías para la Alta California, desde la Villa de Guadalupe ó el Altar. *Boletín de la Sociedad Mexicana*, Tomo 11, núm. 2, pp. 126-137. México, Ignacio Cumplido.

Ellison, William H., editor

n.d. *The Life and Adventures of George Nidever [1802-1883]*. Reprint. Santa Barbara, McNally & Loftin; Tucson, Southwest Parks and Monuments Association.

Engstrand, Iris H. W.

1988 An Enduring Legacy: California Ranchos in Historic Perspective. *Journal of the West*, Vol. 27, no. 3 (July), pp. 36-47. Manhattan, Kansas, Dean Coughenour and Robin Higham.

1991 José Mariano Moziño: Pioneer Mexican Naturalist. *Columbia*, Vol. 5, no. 1 (Spring), pp. 16-22. Tacoma, Washington State Historical Society.

Espinosa, J. Manuel, translator and editor

1988 *The Pueblo Indian Revolt of 1696 and the Franciscan Missions in New Mexico: Letters of Missionaries and Related Documents*. Norman and London, University of Oklahoma Press.

Ewen, Charles R.

1990 Soldier of Fortune: Hernando de Soto in the Territory of the Apalachee, 1539-1540. In Thomas (1990: 83-91).

Faulk, Odie

1967 *Too Far North . . . Too Far South*. Los Angeles, Westernlore.

Ferrando Roig, Juan

1950 *Iconografía de los Santos*. Barcelona, Ediciones Omega.

Flowers, Sylvia

1991 Letter to Bernard L. Fontana from the Assistant Chief Ranger, datelined Ocmulgee National Monument, Macon, Georgia. Copy on file with Bernard L. Fontana, Tucson, Arizona.

Foley, William E.

1971 *A History of Missouri. Volume 1, 1673 to 1820*. Columbia, University of Missouri Press.

Fontana, Bernard L.

1971 Calabazas of the Río Rico. *The Smoke Signal*, no. 24 (Fall), pp. 65-88. Tucson, Tucson Corral of the Westerners.

1979 *Tarahumara: Where Night Is the Day of the Moon*. Photographs by John P. Schaefer. Flagstaff, Northland Press.

1981 *Of Earth and Little Rain: The Papago Indians*. Photographs by John P. Schaefer. Flagstaff, Northland Press.

1990 Church and Crown. *Journal of the Southwest*, Vol. 32, no. 4 (Winter), pp. 451-461. Tucson, University of Arizona Press and the Southwest Center.

Fort Matanzas Stabilization Team

1980 *Historic Structure Report for Fort Matanzas National Monument, St. John's County, Florida*. Denver, Denver Service Center, Southeast/Southwest Team, Historic Preservation Branch, National Park Service, U.S. Department of the Interior.

Fox, Anne A.

1988 *Archaeological Investigations at Mission Concepción, Fall of 1986* [Archaeological Survey Report no. 172]. San Antonio, Center for Archaeological Research, The University of Texas at San Antonio.

Gannon, Michael V.

1965 *The Cross in the Sand: The Early Catholic Church in Florida, 1513-1870*. Gainesville, University Presses of Florida.

Garcés, Francisco

1965 *A Record of Travels in Arizona and California, 1775-1776.* Edited by John Galvin. San Francisco, John Howell Books.

Geiger, Maynard

n.d *Juana María: The Lone Woman of San Nicolás Island, 1835-1853.* Santa Barbara, The Serra Shop.

1937 *The Franciscan Conquest of Florida (1573-1618).* Washington, D.C., The Catholic University of America.

1940 *Biographical Dictionary of the Franciscans in Spanish Florida and Cuba (1528-1841).* Paterson, New Jersey, St. Anthony Guild Press.

Gentry, Howard S.

1982 *Agaves of Continental North America.* Tucson, The University of Arizona Press.

Gerald, Rex E.

1968 *Spanish Presidios of the Late Eighteenth Century in Northern New Spain* [Museum of New Mexico Research Papers no. 7]. Santa Fe, Museum of New Mexico Press.

Gibson, Charles

1966 *Spain in America.* New York, Evanston; London, Harper & Row.

Gray, Paul

1991 The trouble with Columbus. *Time,* Vol. 138, no. 14 (October 7), pp. 52-56. New York, The Time Inc. Magazine Co.

Greenwood, Roberta S.

1989 The California Rancho: Fact and Fancy. In Thomas (1989: 451-465).

Griswold del Castillo, Richard

1990 *The Treaty of Guadalupe Hidalgo: A Legacy of Conflict.* Norman and London, University of Oklahoma Press.

Habig, Marion

1968 *San Antonio's Mission San José: State and National Historic Site, 1720-1968.* San Antonio, The Naylor Company.

Hackett, Charles W.

1932 Policy of the Spanish Crown Regarding French Encroachments from Louisiana, 1721-1762. In Hackett and others (1932: I: 107-145).

Hackett, Charles W., and others, editors

1932 *New Spain and the Anglo-American West: Historical Contributions Presented to Herbert Eugene Bolton.* Two volumes. Los Angeles, privately printed.

Hallenbeck, Cleve

1987 *The Journey of Fray Marcos de Niza.* Introduction by David Weber. Dallas, Southern Methodist University Press.

Hammond, George P.

1929 Pimería Alta after Kino's Time. *New Mexico Historical Review,* Vol. 4, no. 3 (July), pp. 220-238. Santa Fe, Historical Society of New Mexico; Albuquerque, University of New Mexico.

256

Hammond, George P., and Agapito Rey

1940 *Narratives of the Coronado Expedition, 1540-1542*. Two volumes. Albuquerque, University of New Mexico Press.

1953 *Oñate: Colonizer of New Mexico*. Two volumes. Albuquerque, The University of New Mexico Press.

Hammond, George P., and Agapito Rey, translators and editors

1927 *The Gallegos Relation of the Rodríguez Expedition to New Mexico* [Historical Society of New Mexico Publications in History, Vol. 4]. Santa Fe, Historical Society of New Mexico.

1929 *Expedition into New Mexico Made by Antonio de Espejo, 1582-1583, as revealed in the journal of Diego Pérez de Luxán, a member of the party* [Quivira Society Publications, Vol. 1]. Los Angeles, The Quivira Society.

1966 *The Rediscovery of New Mexico, 1580-1594*. Albuquerque, The University of New Mexico Press.

Hann, John H.

1990 Summary Guide to Spanish Florida Missions and *Visitas* with Churches in the Sixteenth and Seventeenth Centuries. *The Americas*, Vol. 46, no. 4 (April), pp. 417-514. Berkeley, Academy of American Franciscan History.

Harlow, Neil

1982 *California Conquered: War and Peace on the Pacific, 1846-1850*. Berkeley, Los Angeles, and London, University of California Press.

Hart, James D.

1987 *A Companion to California*. Revised edition. Berkeley, Los Angeles, and London, University of California Press.

Hartmann, William K.

1989 *Desert Heart: Chronicles of the Sonoran Desert*. Tucson, Fisher Books.

Heizer, Robert F., and Albert B. Elsasser

1973 *Original Accounts of the Lone Woman of San Nicolás Island*. Ramona, California, Ballena Press.

Herring, Hubert

1968 *A History of Latin America from Beginnings to the Present*. Third edition. New York, Alfred A. Knopf.

Hötz, Gottfried

1970 *Indian Skin Paintings from the American Southwest*. Norman, University of Oklahoma Press.

Holmes, Jack D. L.

1974 Pensacola: Spanish Dominion, 1781-1821. In McGovern (1974: 90-115).

Holterman, Jack

1973 "God's Vagabond: An Interpretation of Francisco Garcés." Unpublished manuscript; copy on file with Bernard L. Fontana, Tucson.

Hoover, Robert L.

1989 Spanish—Native Interaction and Acculturation in the Alta California Missions. In Thomas (1989: 395-406).

Horvath, Elizabeth A., and George C. Smith

1991 "Conflict, Shipwrecks, and Survivors: The Quest for Florida in 1565." Unpublished manuscript on file in the National Park Service, Southeast Archeological Center, Tallahassee, Florida.

Houk, Rose

1987 *Casa Grande Ruins National Monument*. Tucson, Southwest Parks and Monuments Association.

Hoy, Wilton

1990 Sonoita and Santo Domingo: A Story of Two Sonoran Towns and the River that Ran By *Journal of Arizona History*, Vol. 31, no. 2, pp. 117-140. Tucson, Arizona Historical Society.

1992 "Spanish Afterglow—Mexican Prelude: The Poor Papago, 1821-1850." First draft of an unpublished manuscript. Copy on file with Bernard L. Fontana, Tucson.

Hudson, Charles

1976 *The Southeastern Indians*. Knoxville, The University of Tennessee Press.

Hudson, Charles, Chester B. DePratter, and Marvin T. Smith

1989 Hernando de Soto's Expedition through the Southern United States. In Milanich and Milbrath (1989: 77-98).

Hurt, Wesley R.

1990 *The 1939-1940 Excavation Project at Quarai Pueblo and Mission Building, Salinas Missions National Monument, New Mexico* [Southwest Cultural Resources Center Paper, no. 29]. Santa Fe, Division of History, Division of Anthropology, National Park Service.

Irving, Washington

n.d. *The Life and Voyages of Christopher Columbus*. New York: Belford, Clarke & Company.

Ives, Ronald L.

1984 *José Velásquez: Saga of a Borderland Soldier (Northwestern New Spain in the 18th Century)*. Tucson, Southwestern Mission Research Center.

1989 *Land of Lava, Ash, and Sand: The Pinacate Region of Northwestern Mexico*. Compiled by James W. Byrkit; edited by Karen J. Dahood. Tucson, Arizona Historical Society.

Ives, Ronald L., editor

1968 From Pitic to San Gabriel in 1782: The Journey of Don Pedro Fages. *The Journal of Arizona History*, Vol. 9, no. 4, pp. 222-244, Tucson, Arizona Pioneers' Historical Society.

Ivey, James E.

1983 *Archaeological Testing at Rancho de las Cabras, 41 WN 30, Wilson County, Texas, Second Season* [Archaeological Survey Report no. 12]. San Antonio, Center for Archaeological Research, The University of Texas at San Antonio.

1988 *In the Midst of a Loneliness: The Architectural History of the Salinas Missions* [Southwest Cultural Resources Center Professional Papers no. 15]. Santa Fe, Division of History, Southwest Cultural Resources Center, Southwest Region, National Park Service, Department of the Interior.

1990 *Presidios of the Big Bend Area* [Southwest Cultural Resources Center Professional Papers no. 31]. Santa Fe, Division of History, Southwest Cultural Resources Center, National Park Service, U.S. Department of the Interior.

John, Elizabeth A. H.

1975 *Storms Brewed in Other Men's Worlds: The Confrontation of Indians, Spanish, and French in the Southwest, 1540-1795*. College Station, Texas A&M University Press.

Johnson, James G.

1924 *The International Contest for the Colonial Southeast, 1566-1763.* Berkeley, University of California Press.

Johnson, William T., Jr., Jesse M. Richardson, and Charles G. Summersell

1978 Alabama. *The World Book Encyclopedia,* Vol. 1, pp. 247-266b. Chicago, World Book-Childcraft International, Inc.

Jones, Oakah L., Jr.

1976 *Nueva Vizcaya: Heartland of the Spanish Frontier.* Albuquerque, University of New Mexico Press.

Jones, Paul A.

1929 *Quivira.* Wichita, Kansas, McCormick-Armstrong Co.

Juderías, Julián

1954 *La Leyenda Negra.* Thirteenth edition. Madrid, Editora Nacional.

Judge, Joseph

1988 Exploring Our Forgotten Century. *National Geographic,* Vol. 173, no. 3 (March), pp. 330-363. Washington, D.C., National Geographic Society.

Kelsey, Harry

1985 *Juan Rodríguez Cabrillo.* San Marino, California, Huntington Library.

Kessell, John L.

1970 *Mission of Sorrows: Jesuit Guevavi and the Pimas, 1691-1767.* Tucson, The University of Arizona Press.

1976 *Friars, Soldiers, and Reformers: Hispanic Arizona and the Sonora Mission Frontier, 1767-1856.* Tucson, The University of Arizona Press.

1979 *Kiva, Cross, and Crown: The Pecos Indians and New Mexico, 1540-1840.* Washington, D.C., National Park Service.

1980 *The Missions of New Mexico Since 1776.* Albuquerque, The University of New Mexico Press.

Kessell, John L., editor

1989 *Remote Beyond Compare: Letters of don Diego de Vargas to His Family from New Spain and New Mexico, 1675-1706.* Albuquerque, University of New Mexico Press.

Kinnaird, Lawrence

1932 American Penetration into Spanish Louisiana. In Hackett and others (1932: I: 211-237).

1958 *The Frontiers of New Spain: Nicolás de Lafora's Description* [Quivira Society Publications, Vol. 13]. Berkeley, The Quivira Society.

Kino, Eusebio F.

1966 Relación Diaria. Translated and edited by Fay Jackson Smith. In Smith and others (1966: 8-34).

Krakow, Jere

1991 Hispanic Influence on the Santa Fe Trail. *Courier,* special issue (October), pp. 21-23. Washington, D.C., U.S. Department of the Interior, National Park Service.

Landrum, L. Wayne

1990 *Biscayne: The Story Behind the Scenery.* Las Vegas, KC Publications.

Langellier, John P., and Daniel P. Rosen

1991 "El Presidio de San Francisco: A History under Spain and Mexico, 1776-1846." Uncorrected first draft of an unpublished manuscript. Denver, National Park Service, Denver Service Center.

259

Langum, David J.

1987 *Law and Community on the Mexican California Frontier*. Norman and London, University of Oklahoma Press.

Lanning, John T.

1935 *The Spanish Missions of Georgia*. Chapel Hill, University of North Carolina Press.

Lenihan, Daniel

1984 Drake and Cermeno Expeditions. In Murphy (1984: 25-34).

León, Arnoldo de

1979 The Mixed-Bloods and the Missions: Unsung Heroes in the Spanish Borderlands. In Ortego Gasca (1979: 23-30).

Leonard, Irving A.

1932 Don Andrés de Arriola and the Occupation of Pensacola Bay. In Hackett and others (1932: 81-106).

1974 Pensacola's First Spanish Period (1698-1763): Inception, Founding, and Troubled Existence. In McGovern (1974: 117-145).

Leonard, Irving A., translator and editor

1939 *Spanish Approach to Pensacola, 1689-1693* [Quivira Society Publications, Vol. 9]. Albuquerque The Quivira Society.

Leutenegger, Benedict, and Carmen Perry

1976 The Spanish Missions of San Antonio. Part I. The Establishment of the Missions and the World of the Missionary Fathers. In Schuetz and others (1976: 22-46).

Loomis, Noel M., and Abraham P. Nasatir

1967 *Pedro Vial and the Roads to Santa Fe*. Norman, University of Oklahoma Press.

Lorant, Stephen

1965 *The New World: The First Pictures of America*. Revised edition. New York, Duell, Sloan and Pearce.

Lyon, Eugene

1982 "Forts Caroline and San Mateo: Vulnerable Outposts." Unpublished manuscript, on file at Fort Caroline National Memorial and Timucuan Ecological and Historic Preserve, Jacksonville, Florida.

1990a The Enterprise of Florida. In Thomas (1990: 281-296).

1990b Track of the Manila Galleons. *National Geographic*, Vol. 178, no. 3 (September), pp. 5-37 Washington, D.C., National Geographic Society.

Maberry, Marilyne

1990 *El Malpais National Monument*. Tucson, Southwest Parks and Monuments Association.

MacMillan, Esther

1976 Government and Life in San Antonio, 1731-1784. In Schuetz and others (1976: 84-98).

Manje, Juan M.

1954 *Luz de Tierra Incógnita: Unknown Arizona and Sonora, 1693-1701*. Translated by Harry J. Karns. Tucson, Arizona Silhouettes.

Martín Bernal, Cristóbal

1966 Diary of Lieutenant Cristóbal Martín Bernal. Translated and edited by Fay Jackson Smith. In Smith and others (1966: 35-47).

Mathes, W. Michael

1968 *Vizcaíno and Spanish Expansion in the Pacific Ocean, 1580-1630*. San Francisco, California Historical Society.

McDonald, Archie P.

1992 Anglo-American Arrival in Texas. In *The Texas Heritage*, edited by Ben Procter and Archie P. McDonald, second edition. Arlington Heights, Illinois, Harlan Davidson, Inc.

McGovern, James R., editor

1974 *Colonial Pensacola*. Revised edition. Pensacola, Pensacola—Escambia County Development Commission.

Meyer, Michael C., and William L. Sherman

1987 *The Course of Mexican History*. Third edition. New York and Oxford, Oxford University Press.

Milanich, Jerald, and Susan Milbrath, editors

1989 *First Encounters: Spanish Explorations in the Caribbean and the United States, 1492-1570*. Gainesville, University of Florida Press and the Florida Museum of Natural History.

Milanich, Jerald, and Samuel Proctor, editors

1978 *Tacachale: Essays on the Indians of Florida and Southeastern Georgia during the Historic Period*. Gainesville, The University Presses of Florida.

Mills, Hazel E.

1932 "Jacobo Sedelmayr: A Jesuit in Pimería Alta, 1736-1767." M.A. thesis, University of California, Berkeley.

Moorhead, Max L.

1968 *The Apache Frontier: Jacobo Ugarte and Spanish-Indian Relations in Northern New Spain, 1769-1791*. Norman, University of Oklahoma Press.

1991 *The Presidio: Bastion of the Spanish Borderlands*. First paperback edition. Norman and London, University of Oklahoma Press.

Morfi, Juan A.

1935 *History of Texas, 1673-1779* [Quivira Society Publications, Vol. 6, parts 1 and 2]. Translated by Carlos E. Castañeda. Albuquerque, The Quivira Society.

Moriarty, J. R., and M. Keistman

1968 *A New Translation of the Summary Log of the Cabrillo Voyage in 1542*. La Jolla, California, San Diego Science Foundation.

Morison, Samuel Eliot

1942 *Admiral of the Ocean Sea: A Life of Christopher Columbus*. Two volumes. New York, Little, Brown.

1971 *The European Discovery of America: The Northern Voyages, a.d. 500-1600*. New York, Oxford University Press.

1974 *The European Discovery of America: The Southern Voyages, a.d. 1492-1616*. New York, Oxford University Press.

Morkovksy, Mary C.

1979 The San Antonio Missions: Original and Displaced. In Ortego y Gasca (1979: 117-145).

Moziño, José Mariano

1970 *Noticias de Nutka: An Account of Nootka Sound in 1792*. Translated and edited by Iris H. Wilson. Seattle and London, University of Washington Press.

261

Murphy, Dan

1989 *El Morro National Monument.* Tucson, Southwest Parks and Monuments Association.

Murphy, Larry, editor

1984 *Submerged Cultural Resources Survey. Portions of Point Reyes National Seashore and Point Reyes—Farallon Islands National Marine Sanctuary. Phase I — Reconnaissance. Sessions 1 and 2, 1982* [Southwest Cultural Resources Center Professional Papers no. 1]. Santa Fe, Submerged Cultural Resources Unit, Southwest Cultural Resources Center and Western Regional Office, National Park Service, U.S. Department of the Interior.

Nasatir, Abraham P.

1932 St. Louis During the British Attack of 1780. In Hackett and others (1932: I: 239-261).

1976 *Borderland in Retreat: From Spanish Louisiana to the Far Southwest.* Albuquerque, University of New Mexico Press.

National Park Service, U.S. Department of the Interior

1975 *Fort Matanzas.* Washington, D.C., Government Printing Office.

1988 *Fort Jefferson.* Washington, D.C., Government Printing Office.

National Park, Service, U.S. Department of the Interior, and Division of Historical Resources, Florida Department of State

n.d. *De Soto in La Florida.* N.p.

Naylor, Thomas H., and Charles W. Polzer

1988 *Pedro de Rivera and the Military Regulations for Northern New Spain, 1724-1729: A Documentary History of His Frontier Inspection and the Reglamento de 1719.* Tucson, The University of Arizona Press.

O'Connor, Kathryn S.

1966 *The Presidio La Bahia del Espíritu Santo de Zúñiga, 1721 to 1846.* Austin, Von Boeckmann-Jones Co.

Officer, James E.

1987 *Hispanic Arizona, 1536-1856.* Tucson, The University of Arizona Press.

Olds, Dorris L.

1976 *Texas Legacy from the Gulf, a Report on 16th Century Shipwreck Materials Recovered from the Texas Tidelands.* Austin, Texas Antiquities Committee.

Ortego y Gasca, Felipe de, editor

1979 *Contemporary Perspectives of the Old Spanish Missions of San Antonio.* San Antonio, The Old Spanish Missions and Our Lady of the Lake University of San Antonio.

Palmer, Gabrielle G.

1990 *El Camino Real: Un Sendero Histórico.* Santa Fe, Camino Real Project.

Parks, Virginia, editor

1981 *Siege! Spain and Britain: Battle of Pensacola, March 9-May 8, 1781.* Pensacola, Pensacola Historical Society.

Pérez de Villagrá, Gaspar

1933 *History of New Mexico.* Translated by Gilberto Espinosa; introduction and notes by Frederick Webb Hodge. Los Angeles, The Quivira Society.

Pfefferkorn, Ignaz

1989 *Sonora: A Description of the Province*. Translated by Theodore Treutlein. Re-edition, with an introduction by Bernard L. Fontana. Tucson, The University of Arizona Press.

Polzer, Charles W.

1991 Of Places and Peoples—Reflections on the Quincentenary. *CRM*, Vol. 14, no. 7, pp. 20-23. Washington, D.C., U.S. Department of the Interior, National Park Service, Cultural Resources.

Polzer, Charles W., and Ernest J. Burrus, translators and editors

1971 *Kino's Biography of Francisco Javier Saeta, S. J.* [Sources and Studies for the History of the Americas, Vol. 9]. Rome, Italy, and St. Louis, Missouri, Jesuit Historical Institute.

Powell, James V.

1990 Quileute. In Sturevant (1990:431-437).

Powell, Philip W.

1971 *Tree of Hate*. New York and London: Basic Books, Inc.

Poyo, Gerald E., and Gilberto M. Hinojosa, editors

1991 *Tejano Origins in Eighteenth-Century San Antonio*. Austin, University of Texas Press.

Ramenofsky, Ann F.

1987 *Vectors of Death: The Archaeology of European Contact*. Albuquerque, University of New Mexico Press.

Rea, Robert R.

1974 Pensacola Under the British (1763-1781). In McGovern (1974: 57-82).

Reff, Daniel T.

1991 *Disease, Depopulation, and Culture Change in Northwestern New Spain, 1518-1764*. Salt Lake City, University of Utah Press.

Robinson, W. W.

1939 *Ranchos Become Cities*. Pasadena, San Pascual Press.

Rodack, Madeleine T.

1985 Cibola Revisited. In *Southwestern Culture History: Collected Papers in Honor of Albert H. Schroeder* [The Archaeological Society of New Mexico, 10], edited by Charles H. Lange. Santa Fe, Ancient City Press.

Roncière, Ch. de la

1928 *La Floride Française: Scènes de la Vie Indienne peintes en 1564*. Paris, Les Editions Nationales. [A 1990 English translation by Jean Chastain of the chapter on de Gourges is on file at the Fort Caroline National Memorial and Timucuan Ecological and Historic Preserve, Jacksonville, Florida.]

Sale, Kirkpatrick

1990 *The Conquest of Paradise: Christopher Columbus and the Columbian Legacy*. New York, Alfred Knopf.

Salinas, Martín

1990 *Indians of the Río Grande Delta: Their Role in the History of Southern Texas and Northeastern Mexico*. Austin, University of Texas Press.

Sánchez, Joseph P.

1989 The Spanish Black Legend: Origins of Anti-Hispanic Stereotypes. *Encounters*, no. 1 (Winter), pp. 16-17, 19-21. Albuquerque, Latin American Institute of the University of New Mexico and the

263

Spain '92 Foundation of Washington, D.C.

1990 *Spanish Bluecoats: The Catalonian Volunteers in Northwestern New Spain, 1767-1810.* Albuquerque, University of New Mexico Press.

1991 Free Black Soldiers in the Spanish Empire. *Courier,* special issue (October), pp. 12-13. Washington, D.C., U.S. Department of the Interior, National Park Service.

Santa María, Vicente de

1971 *The First Spanish Entry into San Francisco Bay, 1775.* Edited by John Galvin. San Francisco, John Howell Books.

Sauer, Carl O.

1971 *Sixteenth Century North America.* Berkeley and Los Angeles, University of California Press.

Schaafsma, Polly

1980 *Indian Rock Art of the Southwest.* Santa Fe, School of American Research; Albuquerque, University of New Mexico Press.

Schroeder, Albert H.

1979 Pueblos Abandoned in Historic Times. In Sturtevant (1979: 236-254).

Schroeder, Albert H., and Daniel S. Matson

1965 *A Colony on the Move: Gaspar Castaño de Sosa's Journal, 1590-1591.* Santa Fe, School of American Research.

Schuetz, Mardith K.

1968 *The History and Archeology of Mission San Juan Capistrano, San Antonio, Texas,* Vol. 1 [Report no. 10]. Austin, State Building Commission, Archeological Program.

1976 Indians of the San Antonio Area. In Schuetz and others (1976: 1-21).

Schuetz, Mardith K., and others

1976 *San Antonio in the Eighteenth Century.* San Antonio, San Antonio Bicentennial Heritage.

Sedelmayr, Jacobo

1748 [Letter datelined Mission of San Pedro and San Pablo (of Tubutama) in the Pimería Alta, November 16, 1748.] Photocopy of original and of a translation into English by Daniel S. Matson on file with Bernard L. Fontana, Tucson.

1751*a* [Letter to Father Provincial Juan Antonio Baltasar, datelined Tubutama, January 9, 1751.] Photocopy of original and of a translation into English by Daniel S. Matson on file with Bernard L. Fontana, Tucson.

1751*b* [Letter to Father Provincial Juan Antonio Baltasar, datelined Tubutama, January 13, 1751.] Photocopy of original and of a translation into English by Daniel S. Matson on file with Bernard L. Fontana, Tucson.

Servín, Manuel P.

1979 California's Spanish Heritage: A View into the Spanish Myth. In Weber (1979: 117-133).

Sheridan, Thomas E.

1988 Kino's Unforeseen Legacy: The Material Consequences of Missionization. *The Smoke Signal,* nos. 49 & 50 (Spring & Fall), pp. 151-167. Tucson, Tucson Corral of the Westerners.

Shumway, Burgess McK.

1988 *California Ranchos: Patented Private Land Grants Listed by County* [Stokvis Studies in Historical Chronology and Thought no. 11]. San Bernardino, California, The Borgo Press.

Simmons, Marc

1977 *New Mexico: A Bicentennial History*. New York, W.W. Norton & Co., Inc, and Nashville, American Association for State and Local History.

1991 *The Last Conquistador: Juan de Oñate and the Settling of the Far Southwest*. Norman and London, University of Oklahoma Press.

Skowronek, Russell K.

1984 *Trade Patterns of Eighteenth Century Frontier New Spain: The 1773 Flota and St. Augustine* [Volumes in Historical Archaeology]. Columbia, The South Carolina Institute of Archaeology and Anthropology, The University of South Carolina.

Scurlock, Dan, Warren M. Lynn, and R. Thomas Ray

1974 *An Assessment of the Archeological Resources of Padre Island National Seashore, Texas* [Office of the State Archeologist Special Reports, no. 11], Austin, Texas Historical Commission.

Slater, John M.

1961 *El Morro, Inscription Rock, New Mexico: the rock itself, the inscriptions thereon, and the travelers who made them*. Los Angeles: The Plantin Press. [Reprinted in 1992 in Tucson by Southwest Parks and Monuments Association.]

Smith, Fay J., John L. Kessell, and Francis J. Fox

1966 *Father Kino in Arizona*. Phoenix, Arizona Historical Foundation.

Smith, Griffin, Jr.

1990 The Cajuns: Still Loving Life. *National Geographic*, Vol. 178, no. 4 (October), pp. 40-65. Washington, D.C., National Geographic Society.

Smith, Hale G., and Mark Gottlob

1978 Spanish-Indian Relationships: Synoptic History and Archeological Evidence, 1500-1763. In Milanich and Proctor (1978: 1-18).

South, Stanley

1991 *Archaeology at Santa Elena: Doorway to the Past* [Popular Series, 2]. Columbia, The University of South Carolina, South Carolina Institute of Archaeology and Anthropology.

Spicer, Edward H.

1962 *Cycles of Conquest: The Impact of Spain, Mexico, and the United States on the Indians of the Southwest, 1533-1960*. Tucson, The University of Arizona Press.

Spielmann, Katherine A.

1898 Colonists, Hunters, and Farmers: Plains—Pueblo Interaction in the Seventeenth Century. In Thomas (1989).

Spielmann, Katherine A., editor

1991 *Farmers, Hunters, and Colonists: Interaction between the Southwest and Southern Plains*. Tucson, The University of Arizona Press.

Stapleton, Laurence, editor

1960 *H. D. Thoreau: A Writer's Journal*. New York, Dover Publications, Inc.

Stephens, A. Ray, and William M. Holmes

1989 *Historical Atlas of Texas*. Norman and London, University of Oklahoma Press.

Stephens, H. Morse, and Herbert E. Bolton, editors

1917 *The Pacific Ocean in History*. New York, The Macmillan Company.

Stokes, George A., and Joseph G. Tregle, Jr.

1978 Louisiana. *The World Book Encyclopedia*, Vol. 12, pp. 418-433. Chicago, World Book-Childcraft International. Inc.

Sturtevant, William C., editor

1978 *Handbook of North American Indians*. Vol. 8, *California*, edited by Robert F. Heizer. Washington, Smithsonian Institution.

1979 *Handbook of North American Indians*. Vol. 9, *Southwest*, edited by Alfonso Ortiz. Washington, Smithsonian Institution.

1984 *Handbook of North American Indians*. Vol. 5, *Arctic*, edited by David Damas. Washington, Smithsonian Institution.

1990 *Handbook of North American Indians*. Vol. 7, *Northwest Coast*, edited by Wayne Suttles. Washington, Smithsonian Institution.

Suárez Barnett, Alberto

1991 The Pimería Alta. In *Voices from the Pimería Alta* (Nogales, Arizona, Pimería Alta Historical Society), pp. 172-192.

Sunset Editors

1979 *The California Missions: A Complete Pictorial History and Visitor's Guide*. Menlo Park, California, Lane Publishing Company.

Swanton, John R.

1946 The Indians of the Southeastern United States. *Bulletin of the Bureau of American Ethnology*, no. 137. Washington, D.C., United States Government Printing Office.

Tebeau, Charlton

1980 *A History of Florida*. Revised edition. Coral Gables, University of Miami Press.

Teja, Jesús F. de la

1991 Forgotten Founders: The Military Settlers of Eighteenth-Century San Antonio de Béxar. In Poyo and Hinojosa (1991: 27-38).

Teja, Jesús F. de la, and John Wheat

1991 Béxar: Profile of a Tejano Community. In Poyo and Hinojosa (1991: 1-24).

Thomas, Alfred B.

1932 *Forgotten Frontiers: A Study of the Spanish Indian Policy of Don Juan Bautista de Anza, Governor of New Mexico, 1777-1787*. Norman, University of Oklahoma Press.

Thomas, David H.

1987 *The Archaeology of Mission Santa Catalina de Guale: 1. Search and Discovery* [Anthropological Papers of the American Museum of Natural History, Vol. 63, part 2, pp. 47-161]. New York, American Museum of Natural History.

1988 *St. Catherines: An Island in Time*. Atlanta, Georgia Endowment for the Humanities.

Thomas, David H., editor

1989 *Columbian Consequences. Volume 1. Archaeological and Historical Perspectives on the Spanish Borderlands West*. Washington and London, Smithsonian Institution Press.

1990 *Columbian Consequences. Volume 2. Archaeological and Historical Perspectives on the Spanish Borderlands East*. Washington and London, Smithsonian Institution Press.

Thornton, Russell

 1987 *American Indian Holocaust and Survival*. Norman, University of Oklahoma Press.

Thrapp, Dan L.

 1988 *Encyclopedia of Frontier Biography*. Three volumes. Glendale, California, The Arthur H. Clark Company.

Torres, Louis

 1977 "Historic Resource Study: Cumberland Island National Seashore, Georgia, and Historic Structure Report, Historical Data Section of the Dungeness Area." Unpublished manuscript, Denver Service Center, Historic Preservation Division, National Park Service, United States Department of the Interior, Denver, Colorado.

Toulouse, Joseph H., Jr.

 1949 *The Mission of San Gregorio de Abó: A Report on the Excavation and Repair of a Seventeenth—Century New Mexico Mission* [Monographs of the School of American Research no. 13]. Santa Fe, School of American Research, and Albuquerque, The University of New Mexico Press.

Trimble, Steve

 1978 *Great Sand Dunes*. Second edition, revised. Globe, Arizona, Southwest Parks and Monuments Association.

Tyler, Ronnie C.

 1975 *The Big Bend: A History of the Last Texas Frontier*. Washington, D.C., Office of Publications, National Park Service, U.S. Department of the Interior.

Udall, Stewart L.

 1987 *To the Inland Empire: Coronado and Our Spanish Legacy*. Garden City, New York, Doubleday & Company.

Uslar Pietri, Arturo

 1989 When They Discovered Us. *Encounters*, no. 1 (Winter), pp. 13, 15. Albuquerque, Latin American Institute of the University of New Mexico and the Spain '92 Foundation of Washington, D.C.

Von der Porten, Edward P.

 1972 Drake and Cermeno in California: Sixteenth Century Chinese Ceramics. *Historical Archaeology*, Vol. 6, pp. 1-22. Lansing, Michigan, Society for Historical Archaeology.

Wagner, Henry R.

 1929 *Spanish Voyages to the Northwest Coast of America in the Sixteenth Century*. San Francisco, California Historical Society. [Reprinted in 1966 in Amsterdam by N. Israel.]

Walker, Henry P. and Don Bufkin

 1979 *Historical Atlas of Arizona*. Norman, University of Oklahoma Press.

Waterbury, Jean P., editor

 1983 *The Oldest City: St. Augustine, Saga of Survival*. St. Augustine, St. Augustine Historical Society.

Weber, David J.

 1982 *The Mexican Frontier, 1821-1846: The American Southwest under Mexico*. Albuquerque, University of New Mexico Press.

Weber, David J., editor

 1979 *New Spain's Far Northern Frontier: Essays on Spain in the American West, 1540-1821*. Albuquerque, University of New Mexico Press.

Weddle, Robert S.

1976 The Vanguard. In *La Hacienda*, compiled by the Whitehead Memorial Museum and the Val Verde County Historical Commission, pp. 411-415. Del Rio, Texas, Whitehead Memorial Museum and the Val Verde Historical Commission.

1985 *Spanish Sea: The Gulf of Mexico in North American Discovery, 1500-1685*. College Station, Texas A&M University Press.

1991 *The French Thorn: Rival Explorers in the Spanish Sea, 1682-1762*. College Station, Texas A&M University Press.

Wessen, Gary

1990 Prehistory of the Ocean Coast of Washington. In Sturtevant (1990: 412-421).

Whitaker, Arthur P.

1969 *The Spanish-American Frontier: 1783-1795. The Westward Movement and the Spanish Retreat in the Mississippi Valley*. Re-edition of 1927 edition. Lincoln, The University of Nebraska Press.

Wilcox, David R., and Lynette O. Shenk

1977 *The Architecture of the Casa Grande and Its Interpretation* [Arizona State Museum Archaeological Series no. 115], Tucson, Cultural Resource Management Section, Arizona State Museum, The University of Arizona.

Wilds, John

1983 Eighteenth Century. In Cowan and others (1983: 102-112).

Wilson, John P.

1985 *Quarai: Salinas National Monument*. Tucson, Southwest Parks and Monuments Association.

Winship, George P.

1896 The Coronado Expedition. In *Fourteenth Annual Report of the Bureau of American Ethnology*, Part 1, pp. 329-613. Washington, D.C., Government Printing Office.

Yakubik, Jill-Karen

1989 *Archaeological Investigations of Six Spanish Colonial Sites, Barataria Unit, Jean Lafitte National Historical Park and Preserve, Louisiana* [Southwest Cultural Resources Center Professional Papers no. 22]. Santa Fe, Branch of Cultural Resources Management, Division of Anthropology, National Park Service.

276

284

285

286